Carryin' On in the
Lesbian and Gay South

Carryin' On in the Lesbian and Gay South

EDITED BY

John Howard

New York University Press

NEW YORK AND LONDON

NEW YORK UNIVERSITY PRESS
New York and London

Chapter 2 © Martin Duberman. Originally published in somewhat
different form in *Journal of Homosexuality,* Vol. 6, Nos. 1/2, Fall/Winter
1980–81, pp. 85–102.

Chapter 7 © 1995 Cambridge University Press. Originally appeared in
Radical History Review, Vol. 62 (Spring 1995), pp. 166–187. Reprinted
with the permission of Cambridge University Press.

Chapter 9 © 1996 James T. Sears. "Race, Class, Gender and Sexuality in
Pre-Stonewall Charleston" is an abbreviated version of material that
appears in *Generations: A Cultural and Oral History of Lesbian and Gay
Southern Life.* HarperCollins Publishers.

Library of Congress Cataloging-in-Publication Data
Carryin' on in the lesbian and gay South / edited by John Howard.
p. cm.
Includes bibliographical references and index.
ISBN 0-8147-3513-4 (cloth : acid-free paper). —ISBN
0-8147-3560-6 (paper : acid-free paper)
1. Gays—Southern States—History. 2. Homosexuality—Southern
States—History. I. Howard, John, 1962–
HQ76.3.U52S273 1997
306.76'6'0975—dc21   97-4881
                           CIP

New York University Press books are printed on acid-free paper,
and their binding materials are chosen for strength and durability.

Manufactured in the United States of America

10   9   8   7   6   5   4   3   2   1

For A. A., H. H., & R. R.

Contents

Acknowledgments

Social change happens through consistent, collective action over time. This project dragged on for five years; the people who influenced it are legion. Let's hope we see some small change—in the historical profession, in American culture broadly—as a result.

Of the many whose input improved this book, I'm grateful first to New York University Press editor Niko Pfund, for having faith. He took a chance with me at an early stage in my academic career. Little did he suspect that he subsequently would witness a good portion of it. Though at a New York pace, his was a gentle, reassuring, and encouraging voice.

On my way to sign the contract with Niko, I bumped into Patricia Penn Hilden in Washington Square. Over lunch, Pat warned me of the challenges and hinted at the rewards. She was right on both scores. She also was a constant source of support.

Two mentors have profoundly shaped my thinking yet in no way bear responsibility for my lapses. They know that I often ignore the best counsel. Rose Gladney mixed advising and friendship in such a way that I can no longer view academic work as dispassionate, objective, or lifeless. By example she demonstrated that caring is the key requisite to inspired scholarship. Similarly, Allen Tullos's regard for human particularities and his vision of social and economic justice set a lofty standard toward which I'm still reaching. I respect and attempt to emulate his unassuming morality and his egalitarian sensibility.

Nancy Koppelman is my reading buddy. We swap manuscripts and commentary as we share a deeply satisfying friendship. In Atlanta, I was baby-sitter to her daughter Rosie, and Nancy cooked delicious meals for me in return. Throughout we balanced heady conversation with lots of laughter. Though she's now back home in Olympia, Washington, and I'm in Durham, North Carolina, I still value her keen analytical skills and her fantastic sense of humor.

I've shared the ideas that structure this anthology with many groups and individuals who provided invaluable feedback. They include my former students at DeKalb College and Emory University; audiences at Brown, Columbia, Duke, and Harvard Universities, the University of Georgia, the High Museum in Atlanta, and the Valentine Museum in Richmond; and my former colleagues at The National Faculty, particularly Robert Baird, Steve Blakeslee, Martha Boonin-Vail, Karin Calvert, Jill Corson, Andrea Fowler, Michael Friedland, Michael Lomax, Brinton Ramsey, Marcia Wade, and Geri Stanton, who read the entire manuscript. Of the many talented scholars affiliated with The National Faculty, I owe special thanks to Michael Cowan, Kathi Kern, and Paul Skenazy for their suggestions.

Other friends and scholars who contributed—sometimes unwittingly—through conversations and correspondence, brief and lengthy, include Julie Abraham, Lynne Adrian, Makungu Akinyele, Patrick Allen, David Allyn, Ellen Arnold, Brett Beemyn, Michael Bellesiles, Allida Black, Cynthia Blakeley, Wayne Blankenship, Ralph Bogardus, Martin Bonsangue, Eva Bosch, William Brockwell, David Brody, Rudolph Byrd, David Carrasco, René Castillo Qüehl, Peter Carroll, Dan Carter, Patrick Cather, George Chauncey, Jeff Cheek, Stella Connell, Blanche Cook, Cita Cook, William Cook, Howard Cruse, John D'Emilio, Melissa Delbridge, Peter Dowell, Martin Duberman, Lisa Duggan, Marilyn Frasca, Chris Freeman, John Fritchie, Bryan Garman, Jewelle Gomez, Carol Harvey, Lisa Hazirjian, Chad Heap, Nancy Hewitt, Peter Hocking, Pippa Holloway, Elizabeth Kennedy, Andrew Koppelman, Clifford Kuhn, Hisa Kuriyama, Amy Lang, Ian Lekus, Neal Lester, Rick Lester, Cristine Levenduski, Lori Levy, Brian Liem, James Loewen, Rebecca Mark, Rudy Martin, Don Mauldin, Tripp McKenney, George McMillan, Doug Mitchell, J. C. Mutchler, Alan Nasser, Catherine Nickerson, Mary Odem, Mauricio Ortiz, Tom Payton, José Luis Salazar Mateo, Amy Scott, Ray Shiflett, Avra Sidiropoulou, Joshua Smith, Marcia Smith, Kerry Soper, Rainier Spencer, Kim Springer, Steve Springer, Talmage Stanley, Marc Stein, Corey Stewart, Susan Strasser, Frank Susko, Lisa Swanson, Jake Tapia, Duncan Teague, Susan Tibbits, Urvashi Vaid, John Wai, Dana White, Alan Yang, Susan Yohn, and Lamar York. (Whew.)

Those who contributed essays to this collection—many of whom are close friends—were a pleasure to work with. They demonstrated extraordinary patience and tact during a process fraught with anxiety and delay. Their research and writing greatly inform my own.

Novid Parsi proofed the manuscript, compiled the index, and in countless other ways made this volume possible. At New York University Press, Despina Gimbel shepherded the project through editing and production with skill and grace.

For financial support of various stripes, I'm grateful to the American Studies Program, the Graduate Institute of the Liberal Arts, and the Graduate School at Emory University. I'm also indebted to the Delfina Studio Trust, London, for allowing me both to ponder and to explore lesbian and gay cultures while in residence at Casa Manilva, Manilva, Spain. John D. Howard Sr. is my benefactor in perpetuity.

I'm luckier than most gay Southerners, I think, in that my family of origin is largely supportive of me and my work. My mother, Betty Holmes Howard, and my sister, Lisa Howard Purvis, have shown love as they've attempted to reconcile my identity with their religious understandings. My brother, Lance B. Howard, is cool—no other word will suffice. I will always admire my father for driving over to Tuscaloosa, Alabama, that Saturday afternoon to ask me the most difficult of questions. He listened and responded, then and ever since, with compassion and courage.

The book is dedicated to three men. Each, in turn, has shown me love of another sort. Who could be so stupid and heartless to say that what we had was wrong?

Chapter One

Introduction: Carryin' On in the Lesbian and Gay South

John Howard

Y'all better stop that carryin' on.

When my grandmother said that to us children, we knew we were in trouble. My brother and sister and I and our cousins—seven of us in all, spanning six years—loved and feared Gama, as we called her (rhymes with "drama"). Implicit in her declaration was a threat. We had "better stop," or else. Corporal punishment—or corporeal punishment, inflicted on the body; simply put, a spanking—was not usually administered by my grandmother. Gama could count on our parents for that, if she told them we had "carried on" while under her care.

To say we had been "carryin' on" meant we had misbehaved. In our play we had talked or laughed too loudly—yelled, screamed, hollered. We had disagreed, not gotten along. We had used foul language. We had been *bad*. To use a term currently in vogue among academics, we had *transgressed*.

Growing up in Brandon, Mississippi, in the sixties and seventies, I heard another, seemingly contradictory use of that phrase. In referring to Friday or Saturday night, or to any raucous social occasion, my parents and their friends might say they were "carryin' on and havin' a *good* time." Their carryin' on, like that of their children, might not have been quite right from a moralistic point of view. It might have involved alcohol, in what was then a dry county. But it was fun. Slightly naughty, but fun.

The phrase, I soon realized, held multiple, complicated meanings—all charged with ethical implications.

Not surprisingly, later in life, when I began to interview older lesbian and gay Southerners, when I sought out our past through the stories they told, I heard this phrase over and over. I read it in books of lesbian and gay history. I even caught it on film. Again, it had a variety of referents.

Even when used by just one person, it denoted different things. I met a gay Alabamian, a man I call "Barry Kline," who was born in 1917. His was one of the first oral history narratives I recorded and collected.[1] He told me stories from World War II, episodes of sharing a bed with a fellow officer. In close quarters, away from the watchful eyes of superiors, they "carried on"—that is, they had sexual intercourse. Kline's choice of words indicated the nature of their exchange to me but also allowed him to be both indirect and polite—befitting his proper upbringing. Thus he didn't have to utter seemingly base words such as fuck or even sex. On another occasion, however, he used the phrase to describe a liaison in his hometown of Birmingham, where he "came out" immediately after the war in 1945. "Carryin' on" designated the foreplay leading up to the sex act, the kissing and touching that, in this case, did not result in penetration.

For Barry Kline, carryin' on denoted either "petting," as it was then called, or the next logical step, insertive sex, oral or anal—the kind we would now refer to as ordinary, white-bread sex. "Jeff Barker," in contrast, gave the phrase a more explicit tie to the exotic or extreme. A native of rural Mississippi, he was initially shocked at the sex acts he observed in New York's backroom bars, sex clubs, and bathhouses, where he got his start performing in drag in the late seventies. Now renowned as part of the Wigstock set, he still recalls his sense of bewilderment at the sight of it: "You should have seen what some of those guys were doing to each other. They were carryin' on like mad."[2]

Of course, carryin' on—for folks of all sexual persuasions throughout the English-speaking world—might refer to almost any human exchange: boisterous conversation, laughter, amusements of all kinds. But for lesbians, gays, bisexuals, and transgender persons, it often also marks a crossing, a stepping over some perceived line of propriety. It's having a good time while being bad. Or, to call up another phrase used by Gama and adopted by one of today's most inventive and influential activist groups, it's ACTing UP.

"Jeb Alexander," an Atlanta-born resident of Washington, D.C., described carryin' on in his diary. During the thirties and forties, in his cozy downtown apartment, gay friends would regularly get together. On many occasions, especially Halloween, the young men would don women's clothing; or they would swap jokes and camp it up, effecting outlandish gestures and mannerisms: "The arrival of Dash's camera produced a lot of effeminate carrying on. Isador chattered and screamed, although I tried to discourage him."[3] Such carryin' on, such gender nonconformity, made the reserved and rather stoic Jeb uncomfortable, much in the same way that persistent, internalized homophobia leads today's parade organizers and participants to lament media coverage of the "more stereotypical" members of our communities.

But gender nonconformity pleased "Clark" of South Carolina. And it helped keep him and his army buddies entertained while under the stresses of World War II barracks life. Clark shared his experiences with historian Allan Bérubé and with filmmaker Arthur Dong, who turned Bérubé's groundbreaking study *Coming out under Fire: The History of Gay Men and Women in World War Two* into a remarkable documentary film.[4] Despite the looks of straight comrades, Clark said, gay GIs would carry on while waiting outside the base movie theater. They showed off in anticipation of the show. A patrolman, Clark playfully scolded the "girls," insisting they get back in line.

I was delighted to find any number of my queer forebears using the phrase, shaping and bending it to suit their needs. But was its use limited, like my early interviews, to people like me—white, middle- or upper-middle-class, gay male Southerners? Did lesbian/gay/bisexual/transgender (l/g/b/t) African Americans similarly incorporate into their oral traditions these words of English (and before it, French) etymology? Were white lesbians inclined to use it?

As I talked to more and more Southerners—young and old; male and female; black, white, Asian American, and Latino—I discovered an even greater prevalence of the phrase, a more expansive utility.

"Betty Dudley," a white woman from Madison, Mississippi, came out in the late sixties and early seventies—a time when many, in the South and elsewhere, found release in chemical substances, ease in experimentation. Etched in her memory is an excursion she took with several new lesbian friends. The group piled into cars and headed down to a state park on the Strong River outside D'Lo, Mississippi, population 318. Like many others I interviewed, these women enjoyed getting out of the larger towns and cities. They felt safer in sparse, rural settings—in sharp contrast to the subjects of most American lesbian and gay history, the migrants to New York, San Francisco, and Los Angeles, the ones who historians say developed gay identities and cultures there. Dudley forged her friendships, began to develop lesbian networks, that day in Simpson County. She and the other women were "carryin' on smokin' pot," watching the vivid colors play off the running water, laughing, getting to know each other.[5]

Instead of moving to the big city, or to the not-so-big city of Jackson, many Mississippians drove there when time allowed. In the early eighties, often on weekends, blacks from the Delta carpooled, sharing rides to Bill's Club downtown. As "Anthony Greene" described it to me, a friend would leave Greenville, pick Anthony up in Cleveland, and then proceed to add passengers in towns such as Tchula, Louise, and Yazoo City. The trip down and back was as much a part of the excursion as were the glitz and music of the disco. The friends would catch one another up on the latest local news and, always, spread gossip—"really carry on." Like "dissin' " or "throwin' shade," carryin' on was lively, wild, occasionally mean-spirited, but always fun.[6]

It's tempting, in this first book of Southern lesbian and gay history, to try to point to a certain distinctiveness in queer cultures down South. Southern history broadly—its existence and its focus—is premised on a sectional uniqueness. Whereas the Midwest—the "heartland," as it's called—might be seen as somehow representative of America, the South is set apart, a counterpoint to it.[7] *The* South—a wrongly homogenized, monolithic South—is different, Southern history asserts. (Compared to what? it might be asked.)

But Southern history has not served us well. Largely, it has ignored us. However, as Martin Duberman demonstrates in the pathbreaking second chapter of this volume, the keepers of Southern history, the archivists, have sometimes actively worked to thwart us, to exclude us from the fold.[8] Some Southerners and Southern historians may take pride in eccentricity and difference here in "the perverse section," as C. Vann Woodward called the South.[9] But we queers are just a tad too perverse.

Neither, unfortunately, has American lesbian and gay history accommodated us. That history, like many others, evinces a bicoastal bias—a focus on persons and events from the East and West Coasts. And as Donna Smith shrewdly and insightfully shows in this book's concluding essay, the very theoretical model our field is founded on effectively discounts and marginalizes Southerners. The history of (homo)sexuality, as currently framed, is less about sex or desire than it is about identity, community, and politics. Southerners, rural people especially, don't fit. Industrialization and urbanization don't figure prominently enough in their lives. Many never move to the city and "come out" in the traditional sense. But to say that individuals don't become a part of an urban culture, don't self-identify as lesbian or gay, doesn't preclude the experience of same-sex desire. Nor does it preclude acting on that desire.

Just as queer Southerners don't fit neatly into the master (or meta-) narrative of American lesbian and gay history, neither do all queer Southerners fit neatly together into a cohesive group. (Indeed, many take offense at the very category "queer Southerner.") It's difficult to make generalizations. To parrot postmodernist discourse, it's best to avoid universalizing, totalizing statements—even more so, I would argue, here in the South. We have a dangerous intellectual history, a tradition that forwards selected notions of the past as widely shared values. "Southern heritage" frequently amounts to a mythologized, planter-class world imbued with racism and misogyny. These concepts are rarely identified as conservative, white male, heterosexist constructs. Instead, they are made to speak for all.

That said, I'd still like to offer some threads, as I see them, running through this early swatch of Southern lesbian and gay history. I point to three areas of concern (not necessarily commonalities) that appear in many of these chapters and likely will appear in many works yet to come. They are—as I clumsily referred to them in my first few lectures on Southern lesbian and gay history—the three r's: race, religion, and rurality.

The South holds no monopoly on racism. However, legally sanctioned racism (including the Indian Removal Acts of the 1830s), statutory segregation, and their legacy distinguish the South from other parts of the nation over much of its history. Racial categories inform and structure homosexual interactions in profound ways. Religiosity and religious persecution of sexual nonconformists likewise are apparent all over the United States. But in teasing out the legal, medical, and religious discourses shaping the lives of lesbians and gays, Christianity—particularly Protestant evangelicalism—proves vital in the South. And the continued, insistent religiosity of many lesbian and gay Southerners means religion is anything but a one-way, oppressive force. Finally, for reasons mentioned above, the rural nature of most Southern life over time means our histories must account for space and movement. Any person, all alone, can experience same-sex desire. Acting on that desire requires the meeting of two or more people, the traversing of distances, great or small.

Thus I have applied a rudimentary analysis to the essays collected here in this volume. Simply ordering and grouping these chapters amounts to another level of interpretation, one that may or may not prove useful to you, the reader. So I'll spell out my intentions—the connections as I see them—and then encourage you to dispense with them if need be.

Generally speaking, the chapters are arranged in chronological order. They begin in the early nineteenth century and close in the late twentieth.[10] The first three, spanning several decades just before and after the Civil War, rely on letters as building blocks of history, pointing up their power as devices for uncovering deeply held, often unspoken desires and wishes. Along with diaries, newspaper articles, police and court reports, historians use letters and other "traditional historical documents" to piece together our past. The historical profession at its core then, is discriminatory. By insisting on such written materials, we alienate those who don't read or write.[11] The class and racial biases are readily apparent—in the South especially, where enslaved Africans and African Americans could be executed for learning to read. A bias against us queer folk is also at the foundation of the historical profession. When you're persecuted severely for homosexual desire, you're unlikely to write about that desire in your journal or in your correspondence.

Fortunately, however, some people did, and we do indeed have increasing numbers of letters, diary entries, and even photographs that give evidence of homosexual activity in the past. Still, you can't walk into an archive in the South, look under h for "homo," and expect to find a lot. And if you do find something amid the cobwebs, archivists may do their best to see that those papers remain fodder for rodents. Again, Martin Duberman's experience is instructive; Katy Coyle and Nadiene Van Dyke, meanwhile, demonstrate the residual power of elite classes to fashion (posthumously, even) the stories told about them. The authors further explore new ways of getting at the lived experiences of those who, like Storyville's sex workers, left little written record.

In scrutinizing the correspondence of one nineteenth-century Georgia woman, Elizabeth Knowlton tackles some of the thorniest questions in American, and now Southern, lesbian and gay history. What allows us to label historical figures with the relatively recent categories of "lesbian" and "gay?" Isn't genital contact irrelevant? In rural areas, before the advent of the automobile, how did two people maintain contact, build relationships, across the then formidable distance of a few dozen miles?

Like Duberman's correspondents, who went on to noteworthy careers as public figures, the subjects of the next two chapters, William Alexander Percy and Lillian Smith, were well positioned to make their views known and, with crucial exceptions, have their words saved for history. "Women and Men of Letters: The Jim Crow Era," as I've titled this part, denotes their literary pursuits. Percy was a revered man of letters, to use the gender-exclusive phrase of the era. A woman fighting to be heard, Smith understood the sexism working against her; she wrote about it and about racism in compelling essays and fiction. But the title of this part refers to the two chapters' authors as well, William Armstrong Percy III and Margaret Rose Gladney. Both describe their complex, long-term associations with their subjects, the challenges of writing honestly about them. They thereby expose the impossibility of a history that is detached and objective (as is *ostensibly* the case in the sciences). Indeed, all of this book's first five chapters display the complicated matrix of university life, archival procedures, historical practice, and racial and class privilege, past and present, which ensure that certain parts of our histories are told and others are not.

"Ordinary Men and Would-Be Women: The Cold War Era" utilizes histories of criminality and celebrity to describe white Southern men involved in homosexual activity and cross-dressing, as well as the case of one male-to-female transsexual—Gordon Langley Hall/Dawn Langley Simmons. Indeed, these chapters show that while we're often silenced and excluded, we appear throughout police and court records. We have an age-old relationship with the legal establishment. We've been outlaws ever since the founding of this nation.

James Schnur's study of oppressive state activity in Florida confirms this antagonistic relationship but minimizes the role of the church. By virtue of a Freedom of Information Act query, Schnur opened the sealed files of the Johns Committee—so named not for its surveillance of men's public lavatories, which it indeed carried out, but for its cantankerous chair, State Senator Charley Johns. Officially known as the Florida Legislative Investigative Committee, the body persecuted homosexuals in public service, particularly in the state university system, from 1956 through 1965. Schnur sees the purges as a microcosm of the larger, national movement by U.S. Senator Joseph McCarthy and his emulators to rid the government of dangerous subversives. My own work on white gay male cultures in Atlanta during the 1950s reaches a different conclusion. While

politicians and policemen surely were instrumental in the scandalous
Atlanta Public Library Perversion Case of 1953—in which twenty men
were arrested for committing sodomy in the library's basement restroom—and in the highly touted crackdowns in Piedmont Park, known as
a stronghold for nighttime gay cruising, religious authorities spearheaded
the campaigns. In Atlanta, public policy makers and clergy were often
one and the same, and law enforcers and administrators regularly cited
biblical injunctions as justification for their actions.

If we've been outlaws through the years, demonized for our criminal
behavior, we've also been curiosities held up as consumerist spectacle.
James Sears shows that the public appetite for deviant sexuality and
gender nonconformity was considerable, when viewed from a safe distance through filtered media representations. In Charleston, South Carolina, elite classes could tolerate eccentricity, homosexuality, even gender
reassignment, Sears suggests; but race was the ultimate taboo. Unlike
William Armstrong Percy, who describes black-white male intercourse as
an accepted class prerogative for wealthy whites, Sears sees interracial,
cross-class relationships as unforgivable for most Charlestonians.

"Lesbians, Communities: The Mid- to Late Twentieth Century" charts
the development of lesbian identities and cultures in three cities, three
distinctive *regions* of the *section* known as the South. In the Mid-South
city of Memphis, Tennessee, the trade capital of the agriculturally rich
Mississippi River Valley, a lesbian community formed around sport and
recreation, a limited, circumspect network of closets and performances, as
Daneel Buring describes it. Kathie Williams focuses on a major urban
center of the Upper or Peripheral South, Louisville, Kentucky. She shows
the import of feminist thought in helping lesbians craft institutions of
their own—in particular, a Lesbian Feminist Union free of the sexism of a
gay male–dominated liberation movement and the homophobia of the
women's movement. Saralyn Chesnut and Amanda Gable take an on-the-
ground look at feminist thought, focusing on a lesbian-feminist bookstore
and the community that sprang up with it. Located in Atlanta's Little Five
Points neighborhood, Charis Books and More was just that—more than a
bookstore, more than a public space or community center. It was a multifaceted locus of families and friends, texts and images, thoughts and
ideas, reflecting a community and a city in flux. 'Becca Cragin builds
on this work as she elaborates today's biased media representations of
post-lesbian-feminism. Cragin interviews three Atlanta Lesbian Feminist
Alliance members and offers a critique not only of pat definitions of

lesbian-feminism but also of the early historiographical biases evident in American lesbian history monographs and surveys, such as Lillian Faderman's *Odd Girls and Twilight Lovers*.[12]

"AIDS and Beyond" presents what I see as two of the most theoretically sophisticated works of Southern lesbian and gay history. Meredith Raimondo and Donna Smith offer scathing indictments of business as usual in both the popular and academic discourses around lesbian and gay life. Raimondo examines AIDS reporting in the 1980s and finds that a nationalized narrative was fashioned, so that regional differences were effaced and individuals' experiences of AIDS were consequently erased. To the extent that such reports often influence policy makers, the struggles aren't merely over representations, Raimondo tells us, but over lives. Raimondo's call for a new vocabulary to depict more accurately the sociopolitical experience of AIDS in Atlanta parallels Smith's call for a more precise, regionalist methodology in the writing of lesbian and gay history.

Our critical toolchest, outfitted with the precepts of race, class, and gender among other things, should further include the suppositions of place. The valuable conceptual frames of multicultural pluralism, historical materialism, and feminism can be enhanced and supplemented by recent work in cultural geography. The object of our revisionist history, which seeks to give credence to the lived experience of traditionally *silenced* peoples (Michel Foucault notwithstanding), thus is not only to deconstruct the artificial and often marginalizing labels of race and gender and to understand the imperatives of class position but also to denaturalize and to specify the spaces within which these modes of power are exercised.[13]

Now that this book, five years in the making, is complete, now that I have provided an outline of the three r's—race, religion, rurality—and mentioned a host of other analytical tropes, I would add a fourth "r" to the mix. As I have spoken to many, many people about queer Southerners across time and place, they have helped me see the incredible *resilience* of our friends and forebears. To carry on means, perhaps most profoundly, to persevere, to get through, to resist, to endure. If, as many surveys attest (but at least one contributor to this volume discounts), it's more difficult to be queer in the South than almost anywhere else,[14] then our resilience (or what Gerald Vizenor has referred to in the Native American context as "survivance")[15] is all the more impressive. Despite the odds, we have carried on.

This book will disturb, even enrage some people—and not just our traditional enemies. Many within our own, varied lesbian, gay, bisexual, and transgender communities will find faults. So be it. But at a minimum, I hope this book will engage you, the reader, in a discussion with this collection of writers; and if not discussion, then dispute. Challenge us, take offense, write us, write for others, react. Or scrap our work, and we'll start all over, if you choose. We've got much ground yet to cover. It's a task that none of us can do single-handedly. So, to draw on yet another phrase Gama liked to use, "Let's us do it together."

NOTES

Portions of this essay were presented to the American Studies Association Conference, Nashville, TN, 28 October 1994.

1. John Howard, "Place and Movement in Gay American History: A Case from the Post–World War II South," in *Creating a Place for Ourselves: Lesbian, Gay, and Bisexual Community Histories*, ed. Brett Beemyn (New York: Routledge, 1997). Audiotape recordings and partial transcriptions of the interviews with "Barry Kline," conducted 5 September 1992 and 12 January 1993, are on deposit at W. S. Hoole Special Collections, Scientific Collections Building, University of Alabama, Tuscaloosa, AL. Names in quotations indicate the use of pseudonyms.

2. Interview with "Jeff Barker," New York, NY, 8 June 1996.

3. Ina Russell, ed., *Jeb and Dash: A Diary of Gay Life, 1918–1945* (Boston: Faber & Faber, 1993), 155.

4. Allan Bérubé, *Coming out under Fire: The History of Gay Men and Women in World War Two* (New York: Free Press, 1990). The Arthur Dong film version, *Coming out under Fire*, appeared in 1994.

5. Interview with "Betty Dudley," Madison, MS, 16 June 1994.

6. Interview with "Anthony Greene," Atlanta, GA, 15 February 1996.

7. John Michael Vlach, "The National Grid and American National Character: Space, Place and Ideology" (paper presented to The National Faculty Delta Teachers Academy Summer Institute, Oxford, MS, 18 June 1996).

8. Notable exceptions include Elizabeth Knowlton and her colleagues at the Georgia Department of Archives and History. I have received enthusiastic assistance from staff members at the Mississippi Department of Archives and History and at the Archives and Special Collections, University of Mississippi.

9. C. Vann Woodward, *The Origins of the New South* (Baton Rouge: Louisiana State University Press, 1951), ix.

10. Among the omissions and deficiencies—too numerous to count—there is no discussion of so-called third-sex peoples of Native American tribes. There is

more on whites than on blacks, and nothing on Asians and Latinas (unless the latter, especially, can be presumed to be among Storyville's creoles, described in Coyle and Van Dyke's chapter). A look at the ever-growing scholarship on two-spirit people, or those the colonizers labeled *berdache*, might begin with Walter L. Williams, *The Spirit and the Flesh: Sexual Diversity in American Indian Culture* (Boston: Beacon Press, 1986). See also Harriett Whitehead, "The Bow and the Burden Strap: A New Look at Institutionalized Homosexuality in Native North America," in *The Lesbian and Gay Studies Reader*, ed. Henry Abelove, Michèle Aina Barale, and David M. Halperin (New York: Routledge, 1993), 498–527.

For complex reasons, African American historians often have better access to materials, oral and written, on African American historical subjects. With that in mind, I set out to find persons of any race researching and writing on black lesbians and gays in the South. In addition to the broad calls I posted in professional settings, I targeted scholars at HBCUs (historically black colleges and universities), the great majority of which are located in the South. An announcement sent to history departments at every HBCU; to a national conference of lesbian, gay, bisexual, and transgender African Americans; and to the Shango Project—the National Archives for Black Lesbians and Gay Men in Bloomington, IN—yielded only one response but no essay. Discrimination in academe against persons of color is exacerbated when those individuals are lesbian or gay or when they pursue "gay" topics. For lack of evidence, I resist assertions about African American communities as somehow more homophobic than European American communities. See bell hooks, "Homophobia in Black Communities," in *Talking Back: Thinking Feminist, Thinking Black* (Boston: South End Press, 1989), 120–26. Increasingly, my own work examines both black and white Southerners, but I understand that levels of access and disclosure, subtleties of language and customs, and innumerable other factors will be inscribed and affected by enduring racial categories.

11. Lawrence Levine's eloquent explanation of this problem, written at the advent of the new social history, bears repeating: "The abundance of those sources United States historians have considered accessible and important has produced a poverty of understanding of those groups which have not left behind them traditional written remains or have not been in the mainstream of American society and politics. The result has been that we know infinitely more about the clergy than about their parishioners; more about political spokesmen than about their constituents; more about union leaders than workers; more about troop movements during America's various wars than about the migrations that transformed the face of the United States from generation to generation; more about the aspirations and life styles of large entrepreneurs than about those of small shopkeepers, merchants, or artisans; more about social workers than about the poor to whom they administered; more about men than women; more about Protestants and whites than about members of other religious and racial groups" (*Black Culture,*

Black Consciousness: Afro-American Folk Thought from Slavery to Freedom [New York: Oxford University Press, 1977], x). To that list, of course, we could add our own variously defined sexual and gender outgroups.

12. Lillian Faderman, *Odd Girls and Twilight Lovers: A History of Lesbian Life in Twentieth-Century America* (New York: Columbia University Press, 1991).

13. Michel Foucault's debunking of what he calls the repressive hypothesis, particularly his assertion of a "discursive explosion" around issues of sexuality, strikes me as—forgive the pun—overblown. (*A History of Sexuality*, Vol. 1: *An Introduction*, trans. Robert Hurley [New York: Random House, 1978], 17). Although his is a useful way of complicating the notion of an absolute (or progressively eased) repression marked by silencing, he glosses over the realities of lived experience. My interviews with lesbian, gay, bisexual, transgender, straight, and sexually unidentified Southerners indicate that silence often was not only an effective strategy of resistance but also an imperative for physical and psychic survival. An effective elaboration of the tensions between discourse and silence would account for differences across particular places and historical moments.

14. David Greenberg summarizes survey research from the early 1980s which showed that in America, "Respondents from the South, from small towns, and from rural areas, who [we]re older, poorer, and less well-educated, [we]re more likely to think homosexuality morally wrong and to oppose gay rights" (*The Construction of Homosexuality* [Chicago: University of Chicago Press, 1988], 468). The University of Michigan's Survey Research Center (Center for Political Studies) presidential election–year surveys from 1972 to 1984 indicate that white Southerners' ill feelings toward lesbians and gays were exceeded only by their distaste for radical students, black militants, and marijuana users. For black Southerners, negative reactions toward lesbians and gays exceeded those for all other categories. Cited in Earl Black and Merle Black, *Politics and Society in the South* (Cambridge, MA: Harvard University Press, 1987), 62, 69.

15. Gerald Vizenor, *Crossbloods: Bone Courts, Bingo, and Other Reports* (Minneapolis: University of Minnesota Press, 1990), viii.

Men and Women of Letters
The Antebellum and Postbellum Periods

Chapter Two

"Writhing Bedfellows" in Antebellum South Carolina

Historical Interpretation and the Politics of Evidence

Martin Duberman

The two manuscript letters that form this article's centerpiece have been concealed from public view for 150 years. No portion of them has been previously published, nor even obliquely paraphrased. Yet as will be seen at a glance, the content of the letters is startling, and opens up suggestive new avenues for historical exploration. The importance of the letters requires that they be introduced on several levels.

To start with the simplest, we need to identify the sender ("Jeff") and the recipient ("Jim"). In 1826, when the letters were written, Jeff and Jim were inconsequential young men—yet both destined for distinguished careers, Jim (James H. Hammond) eventually achieving national renown. Jeff (Thomas Jefferson Withers) was also to cut a considerable, if lesser swath—as journalist, lawyer, "nullifier," and judge of the South Carolina Court of Appeals.

In 1826, twenty-two-year-old Jeff Withers was studying law at South Carolina College—discontentedly. "An useful man," he wrote Jim Hammond, "must, at last, be self-educated." In Jeff's view, it was "behind the state of society" to concentrate on the "dead languages" of Greek and Latin; it was time "murdered," preparing a student poorly for "the duties of life." By 1826 Jeff Withers had reached some basic decisions about his future. Henceforth, he wrote Jim, he would "sacrifice" his previous "Northern mania" and devote himself to what he now realized was his "appropriate sphere of action"—the southern states. Though in general he did not have "strenuous opinions upon political matters," he did feel strongly about the intensifying controversy between "strict" and "broad" constructionists—over the kind and amount of power the Constitution had given to the federal government. Withers stood with the strict constructionists. South Carolina Senator William Smith, probably the country's fiercest defender in the early 1820s of the sovereign and "inviolable" rights of the individual states against the threatening encroachments of national power, had become his hero.[1]

To activate his newfound convictions, Jeff Withers in 1828 became editor of the *Columbia Telescope*, an organ of the powerful nullification movement that had arisen in South Carolina to protest and defy the recent federal tariff. For several years thereafter he gave full energies to the struggle, delaying the completion of his law studies until 1833 (the same year he married Elizabeth Boykin, whose niece, Mary Boykin Chestnut, later won enduring fame for her Civil War journals, published as *Diary from Dixie*). Elected a common-law judge soon after, Withers later moved up to the state Court of Appeals, where he served until his death in 1866. His moment of greatest public prominence came in 1861, when he was chosen to be one of fifty delegates sent by the seven seceded states of the lower South to meet in Montgomery, Alabama, there to draw up a provisional government for the pending new Confederacy.[2] Except for a few additional details, little more is known about Withers' public career.

Still less is known about his private life. He seems to have been generally viewed as an "irritable" man, quick-tempered and sarcastic, though we have the testimony of at least one close friend that Withers was "a very kind-hearted gentleman and most indulgent and affectionate in all relations of life."[3] It's tempting—given the contents of the letters printed below—to read innuendos into that description; but since such phraseology was then commonplace, the temptation is better resisted.

We know a great deal more about "Jim." James H. Hammond became one of the antebellum South's "great men," his career ranging from politics to agricultural reform to pro-slavery polemics. At various times he was governor, congressman, and senator from South Carolina, a leading exponent of southern economic diversification, and a highly influential "moralist" whose theories in defense of slavery became cornerstones of the South's "Pro-Slavery Argument." Hammond's name may not be well known today, but in the antebellum period he was likened in importance to John C. Calhoun—and considered his likely heir.[4]

For the limited purpose of elucidating two letters from 1826, a detailed description of Hammond's subsequent public career would be gratuitous—especially since it has been ably recounted many times.[5] Still, certain aspects of Hammond's public life, plus what little is known of his private life, are indeed vital to our attempt at interpreting young Jim's erotic activities, as described in the 1826 letters—and for tracing continuities in Hammond's behavior and temperament over time.

We need to begin by getting acquainted with young Jim himself—the lusty roisterer revealed for the first time in these 1826 letters.

The Documents

The following letter was written by Withers to Hammond, May 15, 1826, Columbia, South Carolina.[6]

Dear Jim:

I got your Letter this morning about 8 o'clock, from the hands of the Bearer . . . I was sick as the Devil, when the Gentleman entered the Room, and have been so during most of the day. About 1 o'clock I swallowed a huge mass of Epsom Salts—and it will not be hard to imagine that I have been at dirty work since. I feel partially relieved—enough to write a hasty dull letter.

I feel some inclination to learn whether you yet sleep in your Shirt-tail, and whether you yet have the extravagant delight of poking and punching a writhing Bedfellow with your long fleshen pole—the exquisite touches of which I have often had the honor of feeling? Let me say unto thee that unless thou changest former habits in this particular, thou wilt be represented by every future Chum as a nuisance. And, I pronounce it, with good reason too. Sir, you roughen the downy Slumbers of your Bedfellow—by such hostile—furious lunges as you are in the habit of making at him—when he is least prepared for defence against the crushing force of a Battering Ram. Without reformation my imagination depicts some awful results for which you will be held accountable—and therefore it is, that I earnestly recommend it. Indeed it is encouraging an assault and battery propensity, which needs correction—& uncorrected threatens devastation, horror & bloodshed, etc. . . .

The remaining two pages of the letter deal with unrelated matters of no special interest. But the way the letter signs off is:

> With great respect I am the old
> Stud,
> Jeff.

Withers' second letter to Hammond is dated September 24, 1826:

My dear Friend,

... Your excellent Letter of 13 June arrived ... a few weeks since.[7] ... Here, where anything like a systematic course of thought, or of reading, is quite out of the question—such system leaves no vacant, idle moments of painful vacuity, which invites a whole Kennel of treacherous passions to prey upon one's vitals ... the renovation of spirit which follows the appearance of a *friend's* Letter—the diagram of his soul—is like a grateful shower from the cooling fountains of Heaven to reanimate drooping Nature. Whilst your letters are Transcripts of real—existing feeling, and are on that account peculiarly welcome—they at the same time betray too much *honesty* of purpose not to strike an harmonious chord in my mind. I have only to regret that, honesty of intention and even assiduity in excition [execution?] are far from being the uniform agents of our destiney [sic] here—However it must, at best, be only an a priori argument for us to settle the condemnation of the world, before we come in actual contact with it. This task is peculiarly appropriate to the acrimony of old age—and perhaps we had as well defer it, under the hope that we may reach a point, when 'twill be all that we can do—

I fancy, Jim, that your *elongated protuberance*—your fleshen pole—your [two Latin words; indecipherable]—has captured complete mastery over you—and I really believe, that you are charging over the pine barrens of your locality, braying, like an ass, at every she-male you can discover. I am afraid that you are thus prostituting the "image of God" and suggest that if you thus blasphemously essay to put on the form of a Jack—in this stead of that noble image—you will share the fate of Nebuchadnazzer of old, I should lament to hear of you feeding upon the dross of the pasture and alarming the country with your vociferations. The day of miracles may not be past, and the flaming excess of your lustful appetite may drag down the vengeance of supernal power.—And you'll "be damn-d if you don't marry"?—and felt a disposition to set down and gravely detail me the reasons of early marriage. But two favourable ones strike me now—the first is, that Time may grasp love so furiously as totally[?] to disfigure his Phiz. The second is, that, like George McDuffie,[8] he may have the hap-hazzard of a broken backbone befall him, which will relieve him from the performance of affectual family-duty—& throw over the brow of his wife, should he chance to get one, a most foreboding gloom—As to the first, you will find many a modest good girl subject to the same inconvenience—and as to the second, it will only superinduce such domestic whirlwinds, as will call into frequent exercise rhetorical displays of impassioned Eloquence, accompanied by appropriate and perfect specimens of those gestures which Nature and feeling suggest. To get children, it is true, fulfills a department of social & natural duty—but to let them starve, or subject them to the alarming hazard of it, violates another of a most important character. This is the dilemma to which I reduce you—choose this day which you will do.

Commentary

The portrait of young Hammond that emerges from these 1826 letters is in startling contrast with the standard view of the adult Hammond. Nineteen-year-old Jim's "flaming excess" and "lustful appetite" bear no resemblance to James H. Hammond of the history books—conservative moralist, staid traditionalist pillar of the traditional Old South. In an effort to reconcile this gross disparity in Hammond's image, some additional biographical details are needed.

By birth, Hammond was a "commoner"—his father a native New Englander who had gone south to teach school, his mother a native South Carolinian of undistinguished ancestry. Through his own talent and drive (Hammond graduated near the top of his college class) and then through what is called a "fortunate" marriage, Hammond entered the ranks of the southern planter aristocracy. His wedding to the Charleston heiress Catherine Fitzsimmons was critically important: Overnight Hammond became owner of Silver Bluff, a 10,000-acre plantation on the Savannah River worked by 220 slaves—thereby instantly rising into the ranks of the ruling elite.[9]

He used his opportunities well. Always the apt pupil, Hammond quickly acquired the cultivated externals—manners, rituals, and social preoccupations—of the master class. Just as quickly, he internalized its values. By the mid-1830s, Hammond had already won high regard as a "brilliant" advocate of "states' rights," a zealous defender of slavery, and a "superb" manager of his landed estates. (He had also acquired a reputation for willingness to use the lash and to send his slaves to cut fodder in malaria-infested swamps.)[10] A number of Hammond's contemporaries thought his temperament more enigmatic than his social values, often describing him as mercurial and impetuous, as well as aloof, vain, willful, and proud as well, though to be described as having such traits was not for that region, class, and time necessarily to be derided.

That Hammond the adult was sometimes considered "impetuous" does suggest that the tumultuous young Jim of 1826 had never been wholly superceded in later life by the Statesman and Seer. We have few details about the nature of his adult "impetuousness," but of those we do, none suggests it ever took the form it had in his youth—of "furious lunges" at male bed partners, lusty "charges over the pine barrens" to seek out "she-males." If those youthful penchants and impulses did continue to exert some hold over him in adulthood (given how pronounced they had been in his youth, it's hard to believe they totally disappeared), if homoerotic images did maintain some subterranean sway on his fantasies, there is no scintilla of evidence he acted them out.

But there is considerable evidence that Hammond's lusty appetite in general—however much its loci may have shifted—continued to be strong throughout his life, his public image notwithstanding. As an adult, Hammond had the reputation for stern rectitude, and was at pains to reinforce it. For example, he haughtily denounced as "grossly and atrociosly exaggerated" the abolitionists' charge that racial mixing was common on southern plantations; the actual incidence of miscegenation, he insisted, was "infinitely small" in contrast to the "illicit sexual intercourse" known to be widespread among the factory populations of England and the North. As a plantation owner, he sternly enforced puritanical sexual mores among his slaves. He allowed the slaves on his plantation to marry but not to divorce unless a slave couple could manage to convince him that "sufficient cause" existed; even then he subjected both members of the couple to a hundred lashes and forbid both the right to remarry for three years.[11]

Hammond's entrenched reputation as the guardian and exemplar of traditional morality got a sudden, nasty jolt in 1846. In that year, George McDuffie resigned his seat in the U.S. Senate, and the state legislature seemed on the verge of choosing Hammond to succeed him. Hammond's brother-in-law, Wade Hampton, thwarted that result. He warned Hammond that he would publicly reveal an incident that took place three years earlier unless Hammond immediately removed his name from contention for the Senate seat. The nature of that incident was finally revealed twenty years ago, when the historian Clement Eaton discovered and published excerpts from Hammond's secret diary. That diary reveals that Hammond had attempted to seduce Wade Hampton's teenage daughters.[12]

Hardly a peccadillo, one might think. Yet Hammond himself apparently viewed it as no more than that. He agreed to withdraw his candidacy for the Senate; rumors of the sexual scandal had already circulated and Hammond could hardly afford to let Hampton confirm them. Hammond also gave up his family mansion in Columbia and retired to manage his estates—a retirement which lasted fourteen years. But he did none of this in a spirit marked by contrition or chagrin. The dominant tone he adopted (in diary entries and in letters to friends) was aggrieved petulance—*he* was the wounded party! Merely for "a little dalliance with the other sex," for an incident marked by "impulse, not design," he wrote, he had been forced into political retirement, whereas numerous other public figures, past and present, had indulged "amorous & conjugal infidelity" without incurring censure or retribution of any kind.[13]

Hammond's unapologetic tone, astonishing in itself, reveals much about his actual (as opposed to his rhetorical) sexual morality. The casual view he took of "dalliance" suggests that he had far more personal experience with it than we can currently document (indeed, aside from the 1846 run-in with Hampton we have no documentation). But his attitude toward "dalliance" is the least of it. His truculent defense of seducing teenage girls—relatives through marriage, no less—as an event of neither great import nor cause for remorse makes it hard to imagine what if any erotic expression he considered beyond the pale.

The "two" Hammonds—the youthful sexual adventurer of 1826 and the staid eminence of 1846—no longer seem unrelated. Hammond's range of sexual tastes as an older man may have narrowed (*may*; that impression could be due to the paucity of extant evidence), but his sex drive apparently remained strong, impulsive, self-justifying, defiant of the conventional mores of the day. The external circumstances of Hammond's life changed radically from youth to middle age, but his inner life apparently underwent less of a sea change.

As both a young and a middle-aged man, his lust—whether aroused by male college friends or by teenage female relatives—continued strong, arrogantly assertive, ungoverned. Hammond never seems to have struggled very hard to control it. Certainly not as a young man. Nothing in the 1826 letters suggests that Jim Hammond expended much energy or saw any reason to restrain his impulses and curtail his pleasures. He may have made more of an effort as an older man, if only to maintain his public image for rectitude and to safeguard his privileges. Even that is conjecture; conjecture based, moreover, on our assumptions about what constitutes "logical" behavior for a man of Hammond's position. Judging from his actual behavior in the 1840s, and his indignant reaction to discovery and threatened exposure, our logic and values don't seem to coincide at all closely with Hammond's own.

Which deepens the enigma. How might we understand this uncategorizable man? Looked at from the angle of 1826, Hammond seems (by my mores) admirably playful, exploratory and freewheeling, uninhibited and attractively unapologetic. Looked at from the angle of 1846, he seems merely repulsive: grossly insensitive and irresponsible, perhaps pathologically willful. But possibly the change in perspective is at bottom a function of a shift in *our* angle of vision (and the moral assumptions which underlie it), not in Hammond himself; the shift in context between the 1826 and 1846 episodes encouraging us to adopt radically different judgments of what were in fact unwavering traits in his personality.

The discomforting fact is that we understand very little—whether about Hammond the man, or the alien social climate which made possible the 1826 Withers letters. Having exhausted the scanty historical data available for trying to construct a plausible context in which to read the erotic meaning of those letters, we can only fall back on conjecture. The tone of Withers' letters—consistently ironic and playful—strongly suggests that his erotic involvement with Hammond carried no "romantic" overtones. Not that we can be sure. Irony, as we know, is a common device for concealing emotion. Besides, an occasional phrase in the letter—such as Withers' reference to the "exquisite touch" of Hammond's "long fleshen pole"—could be read as more than "playful." Unfortunately, no other correspondence from the period of remotely comparable content exists to which we might turn in an attempt to draw parallels, clarify attitudes, consolidate or amplify tentative "conclusions."

Given our impoverished results in trying to pin down what the two letters mean, it might be thought foolish to move beyond the Withers/ Hammond relationship itself and try posing broader questions still: "foolish," because to do so invites additional futility and frustration. Yet broader questions are implicit in the material—they seem to suggest themselves—and posing them may alone be of value, though answers prove elusive.

The critical question, historically, is whether the same-gender erotic experiences suggested in the two letters should be regarded as "anomalous" or "representative." Was Withers's and Hammond's behavior unique or does it reveal and illustrate a wide pattern of male-male relationships—till now unsuspected and undocumented, yet in some sense "typical" of their time, region, race, and class? The question, on its face, is an enigma wrapped in a mystery. At best, we can approach, not resolve it. Let the reader be forewarned: What follows is hypothesis nearly pure, to be taken with generous grains of salt.

The best clues are provided by the internal evidence of the letters themselves, and especially their tone. It has a consistent ring: offhanded, flip. Jeff's bantering call to repentance is transparently mocking, his "warnings of retribution" uniformly irreverent—"campy," in the modern vernacular. The letters are *so* devoid of any serious moral entreaty or fervor, of any genuine attempt to inspire shame or reformation, as to take on negative significance. The values and vocabulary of evangelical piety had not yet, in the 1820s, come to permeate American consciousness and discourse. Even when those values carried most influence—roughly 1830–1870—they seem to have held sway in the South to a lesser extent.[14]

So the geographical locale and time period in which Jeff and Jim grew up may be important factors in explaining their freewheeling attitudes. The American South of the latter part of the eighteenth and early part of the nineteenth century was (for privileged, young, white males) one of those rare "liberal interregnums" in our history when the body could be treated as a natural source of pleasure and "wanton" sexuality viewed as the natural prerogative—the exemplification even—of "manliness."

In this sense, Jeff and Jim's relaxed attitude toward sex in general, far from being anomalous, may have been close to mainstream mores. Whether that also holds for their high-spirited, unself-conscious attitude about same-gender sexuality is more problematic. At the least, Jeff's light-hearted comedic descriptions of male bedfellows "poking and punching" each other with their "fleshen poles" seem so devoid of furtiveness or shame that it is possible to believe male-male sexual contact was nowhere nearly stigmatized to the degree long assumed. Withers and Hammond, after all, were ambitious aspirants to positions of leadership and power. Could Hammond have indulged so freely (and Withers described so casually) behavior widely deemed disgraceful and abhorrent, outside the range of "permissible" experience? If homoeroticism had been utterly taboo, wouldn't one expect Withers's tone to betray some evidence of guilt and unease? Instead, it is breezy and nonchalant, raising the possibility that sexual contact between males (of a certain class, region, time and place), if not commonplace, was not wholly proscribed either. Should that surmise be even marginally correct, our standard view of the history of male homosexuality in this country as an unrelieved tale of concealment and woe needs revision.[15]

The surmise, of course, is shaky, lacking any corroborating evidence, any additional documentation from the period recounting attitudes and experiences comparable to those of Jeff and Jim. That much is undeniable, but perhaps not in itself sufficient proof that same-gender sexuality never (or rarely) happened. Other corroborating records may still survive, and are only waiting to be retrieved. After all, to date we have accumulated only a tiny collection of historical materials that record the existence of *heterosexual* behavior in the past. Yet no one claims that that minuscule amount of evidence is an accurate measure of the actual amount of heterosexual activity which took place.

Just so with Jeff and Jim. What now appears unique and anomalous behavior may one day come to be seen as unexceptional—casually tolerated, if not actively encouraged or institutionalized. This will only happen if the new generation of scholars continues to press for access to previously suppressed materials and if the new generation of archivists continues to cultivate its sympathy toward such scholarship, declassifying "sensitive" data at an accelerated pace. I myself believe that additional source material, possibly a great deal of it, relating to the history of homosexuality has survived and awaits recovery from well-guarded vaults. I base this belief on my own research experiences over the past decade. The two Withers/Hammond letters presented here are a case in point. Until they turned up, few if any scholars (myself included) would have credited the notion that "carefree" male-male eroticism ever existed in this country (let alone in the 1820s)—or that offhanded, unemphatic descriptions of it could ever be found.

In that vein, it may be worth providing some additional details about how the Withers/Hammond letters were discovered. The tale might encourage other scholars to persevere in the search for long-suppressed material; might suggest tactics for extracting it; might alert them to some of the obstacles and ploys custodial guardians will use to deflect the search—and might suggest how these can be neutralized or counteracted.

Recovering the Withers/Hammond Letters

In offering this cautionary tale, the chief purpose is not to establish the villainy of archivists. As a group, they are no more the enemy of innovative scholarship or the defenders of traditional morality than are historians as a group—most of whom scornfully dismiss the study of sexual ideology and behavior as a nonsubject. During my research travels to manuscript libraries, several individual archivists have been enormously supportive: people like Stephen T. Riley of the Massachusetts Historical Society, Sandra Taylor of the Lilly Library in Indiana, and Richard J. Wolfe of the Countway Library of Medicine in Boston. Such people (I could name others) acted from the conviction that research into the "history of intimacy" was overdue and held great potential importance for better understanding our national experience and character.

Their attitude is still a minority one within the archival profession as a whole (in the historical profession, too). Many of those who stand guard over the nation's major manuscript collections see their function as protective and preservative—of traditional moral values in general and of a given family's "good name" in particular. They tend to equate—as is true everywhere in academia, and perhaps to a greater degree than in the population at large—the libidinous with the salacious, and to be profoundly distrustful of both. Given this discomfort, some archivists invent obstacles to put in the researcher's path or claim to be hamstrung (and, in truth, even sympathetic curators sometimes *are*) by certain access restrictions which the donor of a given manuscript collection originally appended to the deed of gift.

The six-month tangle I had over the Withers/Hammond letters illustrates all this. The trail began (confining myself to the main outlines) with Catherine Clinton, then a doctoral student in history at Princeton. She first brought the letters to my attention, and although she has modestly asked that her efforts not be detailed, I did at least want to acknowledge her pivotal role.[16] Once having seen the letters and realized their importance, I started in motion the standard procedures for acquiring permission to publish manuscript materials. On March 6, 1979, I sent a formal request to that effect to the South Caroliniana Library (henceforth, SCL), where the original letters are housed.

That move, according to one of the several legal experts I later consulted, was my first, and worst, mistake. By formally requesting permission, I was (to quote the expert) being "super-dutiful" and, in the process, making life infinitely more difficult for *all* parties concerned. Technically, I had done the "correct" thing—I had gone through proper channels, adhered to the terms most manuscript libraries require regarding permission to publish manuscript material. But in real life, my chiding expert added, what is technically correct can prove functionally awkward. In practice, it seems (and after twenty years of archival research, this came as a surprise to me), some scholars publish manuscript material without making any formal request to do so. And libraries, it seems, prefer it that way. A formal request, after all, requires a formal reply. The given library is pressured to make a clear-cut decision, one that can place it (sometimes unwillingly and unfairly) in a no-win situation: Should the library grant permission, it risks the wrath of a donor or family descendant, charges of dereliction, possible loss of future acquisitions; should the library deny permission, it risks accusations of censorship from an outraged scholar.

Let others take note: Though archivists will not or cannot say so openly, they may well prefer to be handed a *fait accompli,* and will feel silently grateful to researchers who adopt what might be called the Macbeth ploy: "Do what ye need to do, but tell me not of it till after 'tis done" (roughly paraphrased).

Lacking such wisdom at the time, I instead sent off a formal letter requesting permission to publish. This left SCL with two choices: to act on my request (which, given the contents of the 1826 letters, almost certainly assured a negative response), or to do nothing. They opted for the latter, letting my letter go unanswered. If SCL had thereby meant to signal me to proceed (quietly) without insisting on their formal acquiescence, I misread the signal. Instead of quietly retreating, I noisily persisted. On April 15 I sent them a second letter, a near duplicate of the first. That, too, went unacknowledged. I got angry (blame it on the Zodiac: Leos can't stand being ignored). In early June, after thirteen weeks without a response, I sent—no, shot off by certified mail—a third letter, this one longer and decidedly more testy than its predecessors. SCL's obdurate silence, I wrote, could be interpreted either as "silence giving consent" or as a subtly calculated attempt at censorship. Should I opt for the first interpretation (my letter went on), I would simply publish the letters without further ado—and on the assumption I had tacit approval. Should I instead opt for the second interpretation—their disapproval—I would then feel an obligation to other scholars to report the incident to the prestigious Joint Committee of Historians and Archivists, a group empowered to deal with matters of censorship. While deciding between the two courses of action, my letter concluded, "I would be glad to receive any information which might have a bearing on my pending decision." (Leos get snotty when pushed.)

Within the week, I got a reply—proving once more, I suppose, that threats may not bring out the best in people, but they do bring out something. The reply came from SCL's director (Dr. Archer, I'll call him). He began by expressing regret that I had "found it necessary to write such a sharp letter"—although he acknowledged that the delayed response to my previous letters might have contributed to my ill temper. Nonetheless, he went on, I could surely understand that he had had to put my letters aside while "awaiting a convenient opportunity" to seek advice "on the status of the restrictions" attached to the Hammond Papers. Such an opportunity had finally presented itself; he was now able to report that the original donor of the Hammond Papers had "asked" (the choice of the word, subsequently pointed out by several of my legal consultants, is significant, implying as it does a request from the donor, not a binding stipulation) that none of the manuscripts be used in a way that might "result in embarrassment to descendants." The donor was dead, but Dr. Archer considered the "restriction" to be "still in force." He was also of the view that the two Withers letters were unquestionably "embarrassing." Therefore, he had decided to deny my request to publish them.

In a curious concluding paragraph, Archer suggested he might reconsider my request if I could provide "full assurances" that the letters would be published in such a way as to disguise their provenance and prevent their identification with Hammond or Withers—if I would agree, in short, to strip the letters of all historical context, a context integral to their meaning and importance, and treat them as floating objects unanchored in time or space. That suggestion struck me as comparable to insisting a Haydn string quartet be performed solely with tambourines and vibraharp. I declined the suggestion.

I embarked instead on a double course: drafting a reply to Dr. Archer and starting up a round of consultations with various scholars, friends, and legal experts about what to include in my reply. My advisers diverged on this or that particular, but concurred on the main one: Legally and morally, I was justified in proceeding straightaway to publication. In support of that conclusion, they cited several arguments but put special stress on the legal doctrine of "fair usage"; an author's right to quote (without permission) an appropriate amount of copyrighted material. The body of law defining what does or does not constitute a "fair" amount of unauthorized quotation has shifted over time, but in recent years (most significantly in *Nizer v. Rosenberg*) the courts have leaned consistently toward a permissive view.*

One of the experts I consulted in copyright law felt "absolutely confident" that I was entitled to publish the two Withers letters *in full*, if I wished—though I ultimately decided to use only the erotic portions as relevant to my purpose. In that expert's opinion, SCL "had already fatally weakened its copyright claim to the Hammond Papers, however unintentionally." The library's long-standing practice of allowing scholars access to the papers (instead of sealing them off) was tantamount to admitting that the original deed of gift had not been encumbered by any substantive,

---

*In the years since the publication of this article, the courts have dramatically curtailed "fair *usage*."

detailed restrictions—and that aside from some vague admonitory advice, the donor had apparently left final discretionary power to the library itself. The fact that SCL had, in addition, cataloged the two Withers letters and provided photocopies of them on request had further weakened their position in the view of the copyright lawyers—indeed, had made my legal right to publish "unassailable." All this I dutifully incorporated in the ongoing draft of my letter to Dr. Archer. In the upshot, I never sent it. My Council of Experts finally persuaded me that I had nothing further to gain and might needlessly stir quiet waters. As one consultant put it, "If you formally notify SCL of your intention to publish, the library might feel obligated to bring suit, though they'd much prefer not to, given their shaky legal case and the additional publicity any litigation would give to the contents of the letters. Do yourself and them a favor: Say and write nothing further; simply proceed to publication."

Which is what I did. Not, I should add, without misgivings. I felt a direct challenge to SCL, though it would likely have involved time-consuming, expensive litigation, might have yielded an important precedent useful to future scholars. I also regretted that Dr. Archer had never gotten the chance to read my unmailed final letter, especially the part in which I had asked him to spell out his specific reasons for deciding that publication of the Withers manuscripts would prove an "embarrassment." "For two men like Hammond and Withers," I had written Archer (hot tongue in hard cheek), "who have gone down in history as among the country's staunchest defenders of human slavery, I should think their reputations could only be enhanced by the playful, raucous—the hu-manizing—revelations contained in the two letters." Yes, I was being patently disingenuous; and yes, it was unlikely I could force from Dr. Archer an explicit avowal of homophobia. Still, it would have done my soul good to try (it's doing it some good just quoting the unsent letter here).

Certain ethical considerations implicit in my decision to publish the Withers letters without authorization leave me the most uncomfortable: that familiar array of moral conundrums (in however diminutive a form) long associated with acts of "civil disobedience." To explain why I proceeded nonetheless, I have to step back a bit and approach the matter indirectly through some general observations.

There is a long-standing and long-sanctified notion that academia consists of a "community of scholars"—in the ideal sense of a disinterested collectivity of truth-seekers. This is an exalted, but to me, illusory conceit.

In practice, as I see it, the notion has served as a useful device for codifying professional behavior and a convenient rationale for denying credentials to those who might challenge the academy's entrenched values—women, gays, ethnic minorities. The conceit of a community of scholars, in short, has characteristically been a blind for parochialism and discrimination.

Yet the *ideal* of such a community remains attractive (as does the related notion that a genuinely unharnessed scholarship could provide needed data for challenging the status quo and nurturing alternative visions of the good society). In my view, a scholar's prime allegiance and responsibility should be to the ideal itself, not to those academic guilds which claim to represent it (even as they enforce standards for membership and employ definitions of "legitimate" inquiry that straitjacket and subvert it). Most of the scholarship emanating from universities functions primarily, if "unintentionally," to rationalize existing arrangements of power; and the academic guilds, in excluding or ostracizing mavericks, play an important role in perpetuating such arrangements.

What may seem obvious on an abstract level becomes less so when reduced to a personal one; then the whole question of "responsibility" becomes much stickier. As someone who chose to join the academic community and to remain in it (with attendant profit, such as a secure salary), it could be argued that I and others like me are obligated either to abide by academe's conventions or—if convinced we cannot—to resign. In response to that argument, I would say that a scholar owes *primary* allegiance to what academe might be—to its promise, not its practice— and would add the specific observation that academe's own official standards about what constitutes "acceptable" professorial behavior and proper scholarly inquiry are muddled and slippery. To give one example, there is no agreement among university-affiliated historians about what constitute "correct" (or even preferred) research procedures, modes of analysis, or styles of presentation: Cliometricians battle impressionists, generalists disparage specialists, literary stylists war with statistical analysts.

Adding to the confusion is academe's contradictory record in its treatment of dissenters. It is not a record of monolithic repression. Many principled and innovative academicians have indeed suffered grievously for their political, personal, and professional nonconformity (as well as for belonging to a particular sex, class, and race). But it is also true that academe has sometimes honored its eccentrics and insurgents, if often belatedly; the political radical William Appleman Williams was elected president of the Organization of American Historians. While the academy is assuredly not the free-swinging arena of open inquiry its champions claim, neither is it as tightly sealed against novelty or as unvaryingly hostile to fractious upstarts, as its detractors insist.

Academe's ambiguous traditions help persuade many intellectuals who by temperament, conviction, or lifestyle are "deviant"—i.e., outside mainstream orthodoxy—to establish and maintain university affiliations. Some of these intellectuals would claim ("lull themselves into believing," left-wing skeptics might say) that academe is one of the few arenas in which innovative inquiry remains possible, and that the "long march through the institutions" at present seems the only promising tactic available for creating substantive social change. But others among the group of "deviant" intellectuals do worry that by retaining their ties to academic disciplines and educational institutions which function essentially as "conservators"—preservers and transmitters of conventional knowledge and norms—they are putting their own values at risk. The danger of co-optation is always present; unorthodoxy and personal integrity can be gradually, sometimes undiscernibly, sapped. The best one can do to guard against that prospect is to try to stay vigilant—in touch with the different drummer within, resistant to the efforts to muffle it. But vows of vigilance, as we know, are more easily made than kept.

Anyway, that's about as close as I can come to delineating (and possibly idealizing) the relationship I've tried to maintain within the academic world, and also to conveying, however circuitous the route, some of the ingredients that went into my inner debate about publishing the Withers/Hammond letters. By finally deciding to publish them against the wishes of their official custodian, my own personal discomfort played a considerable role—discomfort at the prospect of yielding to the prevailing (and to my mind dangerously narrow) view of what is acceptable historical inquiry and, by implication, "permissible" norms of behavior. I also concluded, on more general grounds, that the public *does* have the "right to know"—and in regard to the Withers letters specifically, the gay public has a desperate *need* to know.

That last consideration proved decisive. I felt it was essential to challenge the tradition of suppressing information which might prove useful to gay people in better understanding the historical dimensions of our experience, the shifting strategies we have adopted over time to cope with oppression, and the varied styles we have developed to express our special sensibilities. If the "lawless" tactics I've resorted to seem extreme to some, well, so is our need; more orthodox tactics (like polite letters of inquiry) have done little to meet it. The heterosexist world has long held a monopoly on defining legal and ethical propriety, has long imposed its definitions on the rest of us, using them as weapons for keeping us in line by denying us access to knowledge of our own antecedents. Let heterosexism take the blame then if, having finally despaired of gaining that knowledge by humble petition through proper channels, we now turn, by default and in anger at the continuing impasse, to "improper" tactics. It seems better to stand accused of impropriety than to go on accepting someone else's right to control access to *our* heritage.

Power has created that "right" in the past. In the future, other claims to right must be pressed—like the right of a people to a knowledge of its own history (to *memory*), an indispensable prerequisite for establishing collective identity and for enjoying the solace of knowing that we too have "come through," are bearers of a diverse, rich, unique heritage. To press those claims, it may be necessary to defy entrenched conventions and to risk the attendant consequences, professional and legal, of doing so, which is not the sort of thing one welcomes. Yet the alternative is still less palatable: to continue to accept and abide by anachronistic definitions of what constitutes "sensitive material" and "acceptable" areas of histori-cal inquiry. To go that route is to collaborate in sustaining "things as they are"—to be complicitous, in sum, in our own oppression.

NOTES

1. Thomas J. Withers to James H. Hammond, September 24, 1826, Hammond Papers, South Caroliniana Library, Columbia, S.C. The preceding quotations and paraphrases are from portions of his two letters not printed in this article.

2. Most of what is known about Withers can be found in two studies: William H. Freehling, *Prelude to Civil War: The Nullification Controversy in South Carolina, 1816–1836* (New York: Harper & Row, 1965); and Charles Robert Lee, Jr., *The Confederate Constitutions* (Chapel Hill: University of North Carolina Press, 1963).

3. Lee, *Confederate Constitutions*, pp. 28, 71, 75, 135.

4. See, for example, Clement Eaton, *The Mind of the Old South* (Louisiana State University Press, 1964), p. 21.

5. For those interested, the following studies (along with those by Freehling and Eaton, already cited) are the most authoritative. For Hammond's political career: Charles S. Sydnor, *The Development of Southern Sectionalism* (Louisiana State

University Press, 1948); Allan Nevins, *The Ordeal of the Union* and *The Emergence of Lincoln* (Scribners, 1947; 1950); Avery Craven, *The Growth of Southern Nationalism* (Louisiana State University Press, 1953); Holman Hamilton, *Prologue to Conflict* (University Press of Kentucky, 1964); and Steven A. Channing, *Crisis of Fear* (Simon & Schuster, 1970). For Hammond's economic views: David Bertelson, *The Lazy South* (Oxford, 1967); Robert S. Starobin, *Industrial Slavery in the Old South* (Oxford, 1970); Richard C. Wade, *Slavery in the Cities* (Oxford, 1964); R. R. Russel, *Economic Aspects of Southern Sectionalism* (University of Illinois Press, 1924); and Eugene Genovese, *The Political Economy of Slavery* (Pantheon, 1965). For Hammond's theories on slavery (and his treatment of his own slaves): William S. Jenkins, *Pro-Slavery Thought in the Old South* (University of North Carolina Press, 1935); William Stanton, *The Leopard's Spots* (University of Chicago Press, 1960); Eugene Genovese, *The World the Slaveholders Made* and *Roll, Jordan, Roll* (Pantheon, 1969; 1974); Kenneth Stampp, *The Peculiar Institution* (Knopf, 1956); William Taylor, *Cavalier and Yankee* (Braziller, 1957); John Hope Franklin, *The Militant South* (Belknap, 1956); and Herbert G. Gutman, *The Black Family in Slavery and Freedom* (Pantheon, 1976).

6. For reasons explained in the article, I've excerpted and published here only the erotic portions of the two letters. The remaining material is at any rate of little historical interest, dealing as it does with various mundane matters—news of friends, complaints about the Boredom of Life, youthful pontifications on public events.

7. If Hammond's letter is extant, its whereabouts are unknown.

8. A leading figure in politics in the antebellum period.

9. Freehling contains the best description of South Carolina in this period and the lifestyle of its ruling elite (see *Prelude*, especially pp. 11–24). Eaton is most helpful for biographical detail on Hammond himself. I've relied heavily on both books for the factual material in this section.

10. For additional details on Hammond's severity as a slaveowner, see Gutman, *Black Family*, pp. 221–2; Freehling, *Prelude*, pp. 68–71; and Genovese, *Roll*, p. 455, 561. For more on Hammond's skills as a planter, see Nevins, *Ordeal*, pp. 482–3.

11. Wade, *Slavery*, p. 122; Gutman, *Black Family*, pp. 62, 572.

12. Eaton's account (*Mind*, pp. 30 ff.), or perhaps the secret diary itself, is blurred on the central question of whether (and in what manner) Hammond's seduction proceeded. In a book published after the appearance of this essay, Drew Faust has argued that the seduction consisted of Hammond repeatedly fondling his four teenage nieces in their "most secret and sacred regions" over a two-year period, until one of his nieces finally told her father, Wade Hampton, about it (Drew Faust, *James Henry Hammond and the Old South: A Design for Mastery* [Baton Rouge: 1982]).

13. Eaton, *Mind*, pp. 31–32.

14. The importance of regional variations in sexual mores is marginally con-

firmed in the linkage Walt Whitman made (in a letter to John Addington Symonds, August 19, 1890): "My life, young manhood, mid-age, *times South* [italics mine], etc., have been jolly bodily. . . ."

15. Orlando Paterson (in his review of Bertram Wyatt-Brown, *Southern Honor: Ethics and Behavior in the Old South*, in *Reviews in American History* [March 1984]), makes this provocative comment: "There is not a single reference to homosexuality in the work. I draw attention to this not out of intellectual fashion, but simply because anyone acquainted with the comparative ethnohistory of honorific cultures will be immediately struck by it. Homosexuality is pronounced in such systems, both ancient and modern. Southern domestic life most closely resembles that of the Mediterranean in precisely those areas which are most highly conducive to homosexuality. Does the author's silence imply its absence in the pronounced male bonding of the Old South?"

16. This seems the appropriate point to thank several other people whose advice or expertise proved of critical importance: Jesse Lemisch, Joan Warnow, Jonathan Weiss, Eric Foner, Martin Garbus, and Ann Morgan Campbell. To prevent any one of them being held accountable for actions and decisions for which I alone am ultimately responsible, I deliberately refrain from specifying which individual gave what advice or recommended which line of strategy.

Chapter Three

"Only a Woman Like Yourself"
—Rebecca Alice Baldy
Dutiful Daughter, Stalwart Sister, and
Lesbian Lover of Nineteenth-Century Georgia

Elizabeth W. Knowlton

Women in general have been missing from the annals of American history. In particular, the stories of Southern women who fall into some culturally defined outgroup—the working class; blacks, Jews, and Native Americans; and homosexuals—have been obscured beyond recognition. Documentary sources that would enable us to "uncover and collect our history denied to us previously by patriarchal historians in the interests of the culture that they serve"[1] remain both rare and unacknowledged. Therefore, I introduce to you Alice Baldy, a nineteenth-century white Georgia lesbian who was neither famous nor notable in the usual sense, and whose life is known only from various sources discovered at the Georgia Department of Archives and History.

I first heard of Alice Baldy (b. 1835) about twenty years ago when Sandy Bayer, then involved in a research project at the Department of Natural Resources, brought some of Alice's letters, dating from 1870–1871, to my attention. These were addressed to Narcissa Josephine Varner—"Miss Joe" to the world and "Josie" to her close friends, the proprietress of the Indian Springs Hotel at what is now the Indian Springs Historic Site, just off U.S. Route 23, once a main thoroughfare from Atlanta to Macon, Georgia. Ms. Bayer immediately recognized the documents as love letters and transcribed most of them, her main interest being Miss Joe, a dynamic and striking woman who never married but who held the respect and admiration of both men and women until her death in 1929 at the age of ninety-one.

The Varner Family Papers were later loaned to the Georgia Archives to be microfilmed, together with other Varner family material in Atlanta, before being returned to their depository at the Georgia Historical Society in Savannah. On the microfilm inventory, Folder 19 (containing the Alice Baldy letters to Miss Joe) was described as containing only "personal matters" and "news of mutual friends." I decided to investigate Alice Baldy further when I worked on the Morcock/Baldy/Smith/Williams Family Papers at the Georgia Archives and discovered that they coincidentally contained many letters by my unknown lesbian to her family, including seventy-five to her youngest brother, Edwin, covering forty years. Research led me to the federal census, family histories, estate records, other private papers, and even the Georgia Lunatic Asylum records.

I set out then to search for a sister, an Amazon—a woman who successfully defied the Victorian roles for woman as wife, mother, housekeeper, and servant of men; a woman who triumphed and found her happiness despite the constraints of sexism, religious dogma, racism, and economic handicaps. I did not find a goddess or even, sadly, a woman very much outside her time, class, or race. I did find one woman who loved another, and I wish to share with you her extraordinary, ordinary nineteenth-century life.

After reviewing several scholars' definitions and ideas of lesbian attraction, sexuality, culture, and community, I explore Alice Baldy's life as portrayed in her letters, paying particular attention to education, work, illness, roles, and religion. Next, I examine the category of *lesbianism* in relation to Alice's love for Miss Joe Varner in light of similar relationships, female and male, within and without her region and time period.

Alice Baldy appears in no history. Unlike some other female educators, such as M. Carey Thomas and Constance Maynard in the nineteenth century and Jeanette Marks and Mary Wooley of the early twentieth, she earned no college degrees, founded no schools, and lacked the financial security to create a safe, permanent home for herself and her beloved. Lesbian historians Martha Vicinus[2] and Leila Rupp[3] describe these women as participating in same-sex relationships, both as part of romantic couples and as teachers who inspired and educated by serving as role models to the young who had crushes on them. By the twentieth century, white, middle-class, privileged women formed community and couple relationships with other women, becoming well known to mainstream professionals, becoming the mainstream themselves, without ever having to identify themselves as a sexual group. But unlike some of these better-known lifelong companions, Alice Baldy left a concrete record of her love that offers a rare opportunity to examine the nineteenth-century lesbian experience.

I define Alice Baldy as a lesbian based on Blanche Wiesen Cook's definition: a woman who wishes "to nurture and support" her female beloved "and create a living environment in which to work creatively and independently."[4] It is these desires, in addition to the romantic effusions common to many nineteenth-century women's correspondence, that distinguish the homoeroticism of Alice's letters from those of her contemporaries who also loved women but expected and planned for marriage, children, and economic dependence on men.

Unlike the young women cited by Carroll Smith-Rosenberg in "The Female World of Love and Ritual," Miss Baldy was a mature, thirty-five-year-old schoolteacher, sole support of a once-affluent family, with no time to waste on adolescent crushes. In letters to others, she presented an entirely different face from that in letters to Miss Joe, although it was common at that time to write sentimentally and romantically to sisters and mothers as well as to friends. In *Surpassing the Love of Men,* Lillian Faderman's 1981 study of women's romantic friendships from the sixteenth to the twentieth century, the author seems to think that most of these women were not sexual; however, if women are ignorant of sex and unable to forge separate lives for themselves, it is useless to measure the importance of their relationships with other women by how frequently they went off together and had orgasms.[5]

Leila J. Rupp, in " 'Imagine My Surprise,' " states that "we are faced with a choice between labelling women lesbians who might have violently rejected the notion or glossing over the significance of women's relationships by considering them asexual."[6] I question whether we should routinely consider asexual relationships as less significant than sexual ones. I also wonder why we worry about calling women *lesbians,* especially dead women. Is there something negative about being a lesbian? Many people are mistaken for heterosexuals in the course of a day, and I have never heard of any particularly active movement to rectify this publicly.

Rather, I notice how infrequently we consider sexuality, sex, class, and race together. Working-class women, unprotected by niceties, might see and hear much sexual activity that is, however, never written down. In earlier, less-documented times, dykey women could pass as men, have other women live with them as wives, and no record would be left. These same women might experience many forms of sex without choice or realization that choice was possible: sex with men, especially as sex workers; unwanted pregnancies; and so forth. At the other extreme, upper-class women might have little sexual experience at all, discouraged by families, society, and science from thinking about their bodies and "protected" by respectability from heterosexual sex, lesbian sex, masturbation, and orgasms alike.

Rupp suggests four questions to identify a lesbian: "Did a woman feel attachment to another woman or women? Did she act on this feeling in some positive way? Did she recognize the existence of other women with the same commitment? Did she express solidarity with those women?"[7] The first two are certainly true of Alice Baldy. The weakest area of "proof" is probably that of sources, since we do not have the letters of Miss Joe. However, that she asked Alice to destroy them[8] is certainly suggestive. And even if Alice's passion was entirely one-sided, it was still a passion. It is aggravating and humiliating to have to require genital proofs between lesbians when such are not required in "heterosexual" couples, as Cook points out in "The Historical Denial of Lesbianism."[9] Nobody is arguing that Alice Baldy was a homosexual rights activist, a concept outside her place and time; only that she was a lesbian.

There is little consensus about the definition of lesbian self or community. Lesbian culture, as we identify it, probably did not begin until the late nineteenth century in cities such as Paris. Obviously, a larger group of women were committed to women in everyday life, whether or not we can prove they had genital sex. This is the difference between identity and sexual behavior.

Ann Ferguson, in *Lesbian Philosophies and Cultures*, suggests that there are continuous, discontinuous, and deconstructionist approaches to lesbian culture.[10] Some say that a "culture" requires the sharing of symbols, a language, artifacts, abstract ideas.[11] Those in the culture must have a common interest in opposing their oppressions. And even given this, other group identities (such as race or class) may be stronger.[12] Patriarchy prevented a separate women's culture by insisting that women must be tied to men in some way, even if only through a woman's belief that a man's friendship with her is more important than women's in general. A "culture of resistance" such as lesbianism challenges the status quo.[13] In our "need for historical *continuity:* we seek to identify with foresisters who also deviated from the strictures of compulsory heterosexuality in their age and society."[14] Continuity approaches include (1) the fact of early women-loving women; (2) the idea that all women are on a lesbian continuum (Adrienne Rich); and (3) the suggestion that lesbians and gays have important roles in the general culture (Judy Grahn).[15]

But Ferguson states that we must accept *discontinuity* also, the fact that there was no lesbian liberation movement before the 1970s. The discontinuity approach means that lesbian community worked when it could. Capitalism led to the "separation of kinship and economic organization"[16] and allowed women more independence as they earned money and lived separately from blood families. In other words, an identity developed separately from actual sexual practices. The *deconstructive* approach focuses on "gender rebellious women, . . . any woman who violates the assumptions of gender dualism." The "mere possibility of lesbianism challenges the naturalness of the category 'woman.'"[17] The problem with this line of thought is that these women are the visible ones and seen only in negative terms—as whores, too sexual, or mannish.

I was interested to see which of these concepts applied to Alice Baldy: Was she a woman-loving woman? Did she convey cross-gender information? Was she gender-rebellious? Did her economic independence lead her to independence from her kinfolk?

Nine letters or fragments, totaling over seventy pages, survive of what Alice wrote to Josie. The majority of these fall between January 1870 and January 1871, nearly twenty years after they probably first met at La-Grange College in LaGrange, Georgia, which they attended together with Miss Joe's only sister, Amanda, who was Alice's age. The Varners had moved to Indian Springs Resort in 1850 from Putnam and Jasper Counties, where they had operated a store and a plantation, and the sisters and their mother continued running the family hotel after the death of brothers in the Civil War and the insanity and subsequent death of Mr. Varner in the state asylum in 1869.

Their difficult times pale, however, before the life of Alice Baldy, whose father, William H. Baldy, a wealthy plantation owner in the Burke County, Georgia, area, had died in 1856 when Alice was twenty-one. His estate papers survive in the collection of Dr. Baldwin B. Miller (also in the Georgia Archives), his executor, and give evidence of declining fortunes as well as mismanagement at a time when Alice would have had little financial experience or authority.[18]

The history of lesbianism and women in general cannot be separated. Like other white and, sadly, many black women in the post–Civil War South, Alice suffered for the rest of her life from the political and economic changes necessary to end slavery and preserve the Union. By the 1860s, the Baldy family was living in Griffin, Georgia, just west of Indian Springs, in a house forever in need of repairs, which would serve as their home into the twentieth century. Of the four original brothers, two were dead; one proved a ne'er-do-well, with a growing family of his own; and the fourth was still a boy. Alice's mother became a sickly widow in her fifties; the older sister, Mary Jane, was slowly going blind; and the younger sisters were either married, dead, or still children. In other words, we have a family reared to expect a comfortable existence (especially the oldest girls, Mary Jane and Alice) who increasingly had to struggle through every day of their adult lives.

Alice and Mary Jane's spinsterhood may be viewed in several ways. Some Southern female friends from country families have shared with me an early twentieth-century philosophy that marriage for a woman could be seen as "luck" (not necessarily good or bad) that might or might not come to a woman. In some eras, such as Alice Baldy's, a dearth of men made marriage unlikely (although note that Alice was about twenty-five when the Civil War began, an old maid for her day). The single life was a hard life but also a good one, respected and with its own rewards.[19] Probably the hardest thing about it was that one had no children to show for a life's work and also to provide care in old age.

Alice's main source of income was teaching, perhaps as early as 1864 in Athens. By 1869 she operated a small school by herself in Indian Springs, a natural place to go because of her friends Amanda and Joe Varner. In a letter to young brother Eddie late that year (December 11, 1869), she wrote, "Sometimes I think I am in the road that leads to rest at last, and that I see some little indications of God's love and care for me in a *special* way."[20] She was thirty-four years old. This letter was written only a month before the letters to Miss Joe began, and Alice uses similar language to that used in female friendships as described by Martha Vicinus in "Distance and Desire: English Boarding School Friendships, 1870–1920."[21]

Apparently, the academic year of 1868–1869 was her last or only year to teach in Indian Springs. On January 31, 1870, Alice wrote Josie from her new teaching position in a Dr. Ellis's household outside Griffin:

I ripped a binding off a dress I wore last winter, this aftn—and took out much sand & gravel that I took up going to your house—other places too I suppose—but I passed your house every time—Dear Josie I am pining for a sight of you.

Will the time ever come when your voice, so low & sweet & musical, yet so clear & distinct, will be the last sound I hear every night, & your face the first object I see every morning? I hope so, if it is best for you. If not, of course I do not wish it. I would be happy all the time I know.[22]

This plan to live together Alice envisioned as a school to be run by Josephine and herself with the help of their sisters. A year later she wrote:

—I want so much to get our school underway—yours and Mary J's & mine— Amanda and Mary J would keep domestic affairs straight—and I think you & I could manage quite a number of children. I look forward to that as the happiness in store for me.[23]

Alice's isolated dream was a classic for her time. Martha Vicinus suggests that "women's homoerotic friendships require specific preconditions,"[24] in which women are free of family and kinship responsibilities. Economic dependence (as in many so-called Third World countries today) prevented women from living together in the United States and Europe much before 1870. Exceptions were often well-off eccentrics like the Ladies of Llangollen.[25] More common were lifelong friendships between women without their ever sharing a home, as in Alice Baldy's case. Note that it was in 1870–1871 that she was dreaming of living with Joe Varner, using a school they would found as the means and the excuse. Although their sisters Mary Jane and Amanda would live with them, it was Miss Joe whom Alice would see first thing each morning.

Alice took her position as a breadwinner and an educator seriously and never seemed to question that she should battle the world herself, despite her sensitivity and discomfort at having to live continually among people for whom she worked but had nothing in common:

So I love you and *want* to take care of you—I would do it if I could, & save you every contact with anything rough, or harsh. I don't like it myself, but I can stand it better than you, I think. I can stand anything but being looked on as a machine by people who have not soul enough to understand or appreciate what worth I have, and being compelled to live with them—that kills me Josie—I pine & waste away. Give me plenty of love though, & everything is easy to be endured.[26]

Although Alice attended annual teachers' meetings and wished for more schooling ("O what would I not give, if I had it for a *thorough* and *liberal* education," she wrote Eddie when she was fifty),[27] her teaching duties grew more difficult each year. From the position outside Griffin in 1870/71, where she was at least able to get home for parts of weekends, she moved to Effingham County, her mother's birthplace down in the Savannah River Basin, where her physical health as well as her spirit suffered considerably.

Nearly ten years later, on May 29, 1879, Alice (aged forty-four) wrote Eddie that she had left her "place at Capt. Stallings' last Fall, as his mill-pond was so sickly—they had this hemorrhage from the kidneys every fall nearby, & chill and fever too, nearly all the year. . . . Taught the fall-term in Effingham at Mr. Chris Foy's. There I was ten miles from the Savannah River swamp, but I found I was only 3 miles from the Ogeechee swamp, & in as bad a chill & fever spot." [28] And at the end of another decade of teaching, now fifty-four, she again wrote Eddie (May 2, 1889): "The school had grown very monotonous. I felt myself *chained to it* and I would not have gone on, I know, without a little rest." [29] The word *chained* was not used loosely here. Teachers in private homes were expected to baby-sit and do housekeeping. In a contract for October 1883–July 1884 in Greenville, Florida, where she was paid $40 and board per month, Alice had to specify how many children she would teach, what subjects would be covered, and the exact times she would have free for her own pursuits. [30]

Despite these safeguards, by 1887 nonboarding contracts were providing only $20 to $35 a month. Alice took a position in Lorane, Georgia, near Griffin, where economics forced her to share a room and bed with a stranger, the widow Sarah Johnston, who at least, she commented in a letter to her mother (October 1, 1887), did not mix up their pillows. [31] Or was this a case of her hiding warmer feelings? We could wish it.

This, then, was the adulthood of Alice Baldy—a narrowing of possibilities, an endless number of poorly paid, isolated, and unhealthy situations. Yet what other choices were open to her? She and Eddie discussed becoming typists, a new occupation; but she felt she was too old to learn quickly and could not afford to stop her present work and take lessons. Most of the money she earned she sent home to pay the bills of her dependents, to make repairs on the crumbling old house at 812 West Poplar Street. When she was at home, she grew much of their food in a garden. While she was away, she wrote Mary Jane and Eddie detailed instructions on how to deal with grocery, repair, and dental bills. [32]

Alice Baldy was not able, therefore, to create an independent and fulfilling life for herself through paid employment and geographical distance from home. Rather, like women today who must work outside the home against their wishes and return each night to child care and house-work, Alice had the worst of all worlds: no opportunity to study, travel, work, or live with friends and no secure place in a family home, supported by a father, brother, or husband. Her "friendship" and daydreams of a future with Joe Varner enabled Alice better to carry out her duties to others. Ann Ferguson insists that women's spiritual friendships did not challenge patriarchy, rather accentuated the idea of women's purity and sexlessness. Alice Baldy's life illustrates this. Women's friendships could be seen as a way to occupy women temporarily or permanently without men.[33]

The early social constructionists (those who view our behavior as constructed by the societies we live in) did not think that pre-twentieth-century gays had an identity as such because people of those times saw homosexual activity as a sin of which anyone was capable, like general fornication. It was the unregulated sex (outside of marriage) that those societies commented on, not the identity of the people who did it. Much worldwide disapproval of homosexuality is less of the act, which many engage in at least at some time during their lives, than of the "shirking of vital family duties,"[34] that is, procreation and child rearing, known as "the family." Homosexual sex sometimes, in fact, makes up part of a society's training for heterosexuality, as a form of birth control or as a coping mechanism in sexually segregated work systems. Alice Baldy continued to support a "normal" family of the old, single, and disabled, thereby freeing at least two other siblings to marry and procreate. Any love nest she might have created with Miss Joe would, of course, have been shared with their blood sisters and mothers.

Alice had already assumed the duties of supporting a family by 1870, when she confided in Josie:

My idea is to sell two building lots at the back, & the present house, then build a little cottage on the remaining lot for ourselves. . . . Please consider these plans of mine quite private—I only tell you because you are my *other self*—& I tell you anything.[35]

Alice Baldy's responsibilities for her mother and sister were heavy enough when, in the 1870s, her youngest brother and sister, Eddie and Marianna Josephine, became so severely mentally ill that they intermittently had to be hospitalized in the Milledgeville Asylum. Eddie's condition developed after he had meningitis at the age of nineteen, and Marianna's appeared with puberty, although the State Medical Records give her age at the onset of her condition as twenty-two. None of the Baldys seemed happy with the idea of confining their relatives. However, both

Eddie and Marianna were paranoid and violent—certainly more than old Mrs. Baldy or disabled Mary Jane could handle. Marianna pounded on the piano for hours[36] and believed Eddie wanted to kill her. Eddie was arrested at least once and, when suffering his delusions, thought all women were his enemies. Since Mr. Varner had been insane also, Joe Varner would have seemed an obvious confidant for Alice. A typical letter in 1870 from Alice to Joe tells of a visit home: "I found Mama better than I expected, but Josie [Marianna] had feverish symptoms—had missed one period again & had a singular sore mouth. Her stomach is very much disordered."[37] Miss Joe did offer some advice and money after Eddie's arrest, but there is no evidence that she assisted the family otherwise.

Marianna was hospitalized at least three times between 1878 and 1889 for a total of about five years, and Eddie was in and out of Milledgeville also. When the two were at large, the family attempted different living situations for them: Eddie helping his widowed sister Maggie run a boardinghouse in Atlanta until it failed, Marianna accompanying Alice on a teaching assignment to Florida around 1884. When they were hospitalized, Alice was called on to handle their problems and sew wardrobes for Marianna, who refused to wear institutional clothing. Once when feeble Mrs. Baldy and Marianna traveled to the Milledgeville Asylum by train, Alice secretly accompanied them in a separate car because Marianna often could not abide the sight of her sister.

As Alice grew older, her usual sore throats, headaches, and eye problems grew more frequent. A comment such as the following to Miss Joe was common: "I have a cold again—not much sore throat, but soreness lower down in my chest & lungs & a bad cough. I have been prudent I think—don't know how I took it."[38] With daily life among so many small children, the source is obvious. By middle age Alice suffered also from kidney trouble and muscular rheumatism, and from 1882 to 1883, as she confided to Maggie in an unusually frank and detailed letter for that time, she went through menopause:

Dear Maggie, I might as well be plain and candid or you and Eddie will not believe half I say. I am now, and have been since April [1882] passing through a critical period called "change of life." In April I had a spell that I thought would be my last. . . . I was too sick to be in school for several weeks, but I hung on until I had to give up. I was prostrated—stomach, bowels, and every internal organ except my kidneys and bladder seemed to be upset. I passed ulcers from the stomach and bowels—sometimes it [was] like the contents of a small boil, and it was only after being long at the stool and with great pain that it would come. My stomach refused everything but the weakest gruel and tea—sage tea did me good—and I of course was nearly starved. The inability to eat was long before I went to bed utterly prostrated. I was further weakened by the other drain which, each month, amounted to almost a hemorrhage. It was a long time after I got up before I was strong.[39]

These letters about bodily functions (Marianna's period, Alice's own illnesses and menopause) show Alice's willingness to record everything in her life, not just vague spiritual effusions. Although illness sometimes became the life of the nineteenth-century lady, Alice truly never had the time to become a professional invalid.

As the decades passed, Alice's viewpoint predictably narrowed and became even more parochial than it had been. In early letters to Josie, she had sometimes talked of books and literary magazines; later, even these references largely disappeared, and there was no mention at all of politics or current events except crackpot rumors about investments and inflation. Like other middle-class, white women, she never discussed race or blacks in general, although occasionally she mentioned a particular black person in letters to Eddie.[40]

Conspicuous, however, were her twin concerns with woman's role and religion. In an undated letter to her mother,[41] Alice reminded her that she (Alice) had "no husband to help her along" and so must be independent. The theme repeats itself in letters to Josie: "It is right hard to be man & woman at the same time—to have the cares of a family, know that they look to you to provide for them, and be obliged to be away from them all the time."[42] Another interesting angle is Alice's perception of Josephine Varner, who tended to play the man in her own family at Indian Springs. Alice saw that one could fit into more than one role and wrote flirtatiously to Josie:

I wish I could see you in your long collar. I know it becomes you, shows the pretty contour of your throat and neck—you look like Cleopatra don't you? or someone prettier and better than she was. You look like—well, like Josephine Varner I suppose—a woman, intensely womanly, soft, tender, sweet, pliant, yielding, passive, loving, and *so sweet*—so *very* soft that one would almost fear to touch her roughly lest it should crush her—or cause her to vanish like a soft morning.[43]

And again, to and about Miss Joe:

She is entirely too sweet for everyday and commonplace affairs—too sweet for anything but just *what she is*—somebody to be loved & petted and kissed & cared for, & taken care of—a soft, gentle, *sweet, womanly* woman— [44]

And in a letter dated April 29, 1870:

I am only a woman like yourself, yet you never had, & never can have a more devoted, sincere & constant lover than you have in me; and mine, my dear, is a love that will never tire.[45]

. . . I want you to be a *wide-awake, energetic,* business woman & do wonders; only when I am with you must you be the soft, passive, charming embodiment of sweetness & loveliness that I love with a passionate tenderness & intensity that I cannot describe.[46]

Alice, like other lesbians, "replicated heterosexual love" in her communications,[47] using what she had at hand to "show" her love. Much of the confusion concerning butch roles comes from outsiders not understanding that lesbians not only are duplicating men's surface gestures but are also creating ingenious signals for others that we exist. More important to me here is Alice's clear perception of them both as women.

Alice's focus on religion runs all the way through her correspondence; yet she blends dogma with her own beliefs. To Josephine Varner:

Dear Josie, what is it makes me love you so? You must love me very much or you would not give me so much happiness. I am sure it is no harm, and I think God is not displeased—that He orders it all Himself—therefore I do not fear I will commit sin, for I keep it in subordination—at least I think God keeps it in subordination to the greater duty & devotion & love I owe Him for I hope I would not risk his displeasure to please *any one*.[48]

Nowhere in Alice's letters does she mention any acts of love more physical than kissing and petting (possibly head or arm stroking). I interpret the above admonition to herself as Alice's awareness that to put any human being ahead of God in one's affections was very wrong. She excuses her great love for Josie as created by God and therefore entirely harmless as long as it is kept in subordination to the "duty & devotion & love I owe Him." In fact, she goes further in the letter quoted below and implies that God has sanctified their love:

Let us promise each other to be as much together as we possibly can as long as we both live, & let us both "strive to enter in at the straight gate"—and pray to God to lead us both by the True and Living Way to eternal rest and peace when our work here is ended that we may never more be separated. I wish I had known you long ago as well as I do now—I have lost much, & it might have been better for you too but God knows best. Now that I know you so well, your trust, your worth, your sweetness of disposition, your greatness of soul, your contempt for all that is mean & little and dishonorable, the warmth and constancy of your love, it gives me the greatest happiness that earth can bestow, to be with you. Nor does earth bestow it—God who made the earth, is the Author and Giver of all happiness. Dear friend, you have no idea how it makes me feel to have you put your arms around me and give me one of your earnest affectionate kisses with that smile on your lip, that light in your eye, that look on your face, that I know so well, & love so dearly. I would cling to you forever to be loved that way—it is so pure & sweet a love.[49]

Many of Alice's letters contain the religious vocabulary noted by Martha Vicinus, in both her article[50] and her book, as often used between women in their relationships. I have never seen a historical study of the effects of religion on Southern homosexuals. However, despite evangelical Christianity's fire-and-brimstone language, some of my Southern lesbian friends managed to develop a logical religious explanation for their feelings: God is love; all love is OK and divine; my feelings for this woman (or all women) are love; therefore, my feelings can't be wrong.[51] For many of us, hearing nothing about lesbians before 1970 left us free to develop our own rationales. I myself decided as a teenager that because heterosexual sex was so dangerous and immoral, relations with girls must be better and purer.

Historians stress the negative effects of religion on gay people, yet many nineteenth-century American women gained support from religion, much in the way we now do from psychology. Alice's focus on religion runs all the way through her correspondence; yet she blends dogma with her own beliefs. The religious environment allowed women to socialize together in the church and outside in meaningful and intense ways. And it gave them a language of approved desire and comfort.

Martin Duberman's hypothesis in " 'Writhing Bedfellows' in Antebellum South Carolina: Historical Interpretation and the Politics of Evidence"[52] that there was less "evangelical piety" in the South, even at its height in 1830–1870, is, I think, both right and wrong. Religion was and is a very powerful and pervasive force in the South; witness Lillian Smith's analysis, in *Killers of the Dream*, of how it intertwined with sex and racism to form every twentieth-century Southern child.[53] However, the individuality of Southern churches, the lack of a central governing body in most of them (as compared with Roman Catholicism and Episcopalianism), meant that there was more room for interpretation of doctrine and works among the Baptists and even the Methodists. The region prides itself on not taking up "Yankee" ways and mores, on avoiding what may be standard practice elsewhere in the United States. Based on my observation that waves of thought, both secular and religious, come to the South later (because of geography and poverty) than to some other regions may give this one quite different dates for its evangelical peak. Dancing was not abolished among some communities until around the 1880s, while camp meetings and revivals continued to be major events well into the twentieth century.

However, what we really want to know is what happened between Alice Baldy and Joe Varner. What happened within their relationship? What brought it to a close?

On October 13, 1872, we find Alice writing to her mother,[54] requesting that she have Alice's bed moved to an upstairs room in preparation for Miss Joe's visit with her in Griffin. The next year, Alice wrote to Eddie that she had visited Indian Springs "out of season."[55] There was no comment about Miss Joe, however. Indeed, no more letters from Alice to Josephine exist, nor do any from Alice to anyone survive for the period immediately following, 1874–1877.

We can assume that Alice was attracted to Miss Joe for many, many years before the letters we have—perhaps as far back as their days at LaGrange College. The raves or crushes of nineteenth-century boarding schools flourished both on a discussion of feelings and in the hiding of them.[56] As a middle-aged Southern woman, Alice would be careful to disguise many strong feelings from others; however, she attempted to create her relationship with Miss Joe on paper through long and frequent letters. Years after the letters to Miss Joe ceased, Alice wrote to Eddie, "When I was young I used to write things I would not like seen, but I am more prudent and careful now."[57] And in the same letter, analyzing her personality and how she faced difficulties: "I have afterwards found that it was not worth the feeling I wasted on it, and I would have crushed out the trouble and conquered my adversary by silence as to words and even ignoring it by my manner."[58]

Fortunately for us, she was not more prudent earlier. However, Miss Varner was. In March 1870, Alice wrote, "But I have not finished the task of looking over your letters—not a task to read them darling, but you imposed upon me the task of looking over them for the purpose of burning all that *others* must not see. It was a hard thing to do, but rest easy; now sweet, there is nothing in those to compromise you in any way."[59] In the same letter Alice describes Josephine as "genuine gold, *tried & true.*" I am afraid I do not share that opinion, because it was Miss

Joe, so careful of her own reputation, who left Alice's letters for all of us to read:

O Josephine my darling, I am glad you love me. I could not be happy—I could not enjoy *anything* now without your affection. I could not endure "the heat & burden of the day" without this light to cheer me.[60]

Dear Josie, best loved of all my friends, my blessing, my greatest comfort and sweetest solace on earth, my precious gift from God—write just as you feel—let your letters be long or short, grave or gay—just so they tell me you are living, and I can read *your heart* and *just that you care for me.* It makes me happy to love you, but happier still to know that you love me as well, and I am happiest when I am with you, & *feel* & *know* that you love me. . . . You must not ever say that "I must not *tax myself* to write to you"—You must feel sure that nothing I do to please you is a tax to me. If it were, I should not do it. Even should I write to you twice a day, & then get up in the middle of the night to write again, you must never think it a "tax," you must feel sure it has a pleasure to me or I would not do it. You are laughing now at me for such a far-fetched supposition. Of course I do not expect to do that, but *if I should* it would be no "tax" because I would like it. So Miss Josie, never a word more about *"tax"* or I'll tax *you* with forty thousand kisses and collect them too—you know that would be dreadful—might make you a bankrupt—so take care.[61]

Do you know that if you only touch me, or speak to me there is not a nerve or fibre in my body that does not respond with a thrill of delight? . . . You remember the morning you came in the parlor where I was with Amanda, and, taking my head in your arms, you bent down with *such* a smile & *such* a look! and gave me the sweetest kiss any body could imagine. I don't suppose you do remember, but *I do*—the action, and the *manner* of it were so unexpected & so sweet I was quite happy—[62]

Although I thought there would be little in common between the men of Martin Duberman's " 'Writhing Bedfellows' " and my spinster Alice— they were younger than she and obviously genitally active, while she may not have been—I recognize a similarity of tone in several passages. Duberman acknowledges that the men's relationship is conjecture, as is Alice and Miss Joe's. He calls it "ironic and playful"[63] and therefore thinks it cannot be romantic but admits that it might be all these things, the tone serving to keep the romance hidden. Alice Baldy's little riff about rising numerous times in the night to write to Miss Joe, repeating how it is "no tax" so many times, threatening with "forty thousand kisses," is unexpected and delightful, certainly as ironic and playful as is the Carolina gentleman's.

Alice's letters are rollicking and realistic, down-to-earth and spiritual, business-like and romantic. Martha Vicinus tells us that nineteenth-century school guides hinted at the tensions in boarding school life caused by the juxtaposition of desirable friendship and duty to one's family. She quotes Elizabeth Sewell, author of one of these guides, as saying, "When romantic friendship puts itself forward as having a claim above those ties which God has formed by nature, it becomes a source of untold misery."[64] As larger schools developed in the 1850s, the previous "emphasis on private duty and renunciation" slowly developed into the public "ethic of service and discipline." The larger public domain that developed under industrial capitalism made the desire "for a special cherished friend"[65] even stronger, but the goal of friendship remained unattainable (because of age, position, marriage, and economics), existing only to inspire sacrifice and work.

Alice Baldy saw herself as having to live as both a man and a woman because of economic necessity. But I would not call her gender-rebellious. Over the years, she grew more and more bound to her family, never escaping their demands. Rather, she sacrificed all desire to discipline and service to others. To Miss Joe she wrote:

I am very precious of myself now for your sake. I am afraid if I were to die or get killed that nobody else would fill my place to you. I don't believe there is any one else who loves you as dearly & as unvaryingly the same as I do. I do not see how it is possible—yet I know that others have eyes, & hearts, & ears, to see & hear & love you, as well as I. They may not make so good use of them however, as I do.[66]

I have never told you that Mrs. Dempsy spoke to Mama about having one of us go with her as a Governess in her family, and also for companionship during her stay in Europe. Of course I would not think of going. Even if I did not know that M.J. was so anxious to go abroad, & had been pining for a sea voyage for a long time, I would not leave you. I could not think of it—once the prospect would have pleased me if M.J. & I could both make the trip, but now I could not put the ocean between you and me for any earthly consideration.[67]

I can see your face any time I want to, no matter what is before my eyes. I see the trees, the sky, anything I happen to look at, but between those objects & my vision floats another distinct & clearly defined image of a sweet face with eyes like two magnets that draw my very soul to them.[68]

Dear Josie, if you were faultless you would not be enough like me to be my friend—I would have to stand *afar off* and *admire*. As it is, I can come closer to you, lay your cheek on mine, kiss your lips, and call you mine own sweet friend without fear of repulse as an inferior. But I have wandered far from my original design, which was to warn you against too much light reading.[69]

Dear Josie, if I could only see you to kiss you myself—I have so much to say to you—Perhaps it would not amount to much, but it would be you hearing me— you answering & talking—your eyes looking at me—your voice in my ears— your lips to kiss—your dear hand to hold in mine—The time seems long that I must wait to see you—[70]

Why didn't Josephine Varner arrange for Alice and her family to come live at Indian Springs? They could have operated the hotel and a school and several other businesses, given the location and their talents. If the Varner Collection and my own instincts serve me right, I think the answer is simply that Miss Joe did not love Alice Baldy the way Alice loved her. She merely accepted Alice's attentions, compliments, and petting—just as she accepted the attentions of other women whose letters she also saved.[71] She enjoyed the social life of the springs, the Georgia gentlemen and ladies of note who came to take the waters. Although she had taught school when she was young, she now had more entertaining ways to make her living, without the stresses of mad siblings and an invalid mother.

Still, the letters to her stand as a monument to the fact that Alice Baldy "chose and loved"[72] another woman. Endearing, erotic, playful, and spir- ited, Alice's hopes and visions inspire all of us who choose the same and search for our foremothers through the uncertainties of history.

. . . I will "please to say" that I can never love [a] human being more than I do you—that I want you every day, to sew, & read, & talk with me—that every night I want you with me that you may take me in your arms & and let me kiss you to sleep—that every morning I want you with me that I may wake you with a kiss— that I wish I could always make you happy & that you would always love me. Will you love me always Josie, even when I am old? Will you promise to be with me as much as you can so long as I live?[73]

You must not think from anything I have written that I am unhappy—it is a fact that I always wish for you and would be very happy if I were always where I could see you & talk to you daily, and that I look forward to such a time not exactly with hope but with desire—as to some great good—almost too much for me to even think of—[74]

NOTES

1. Statement, *Lesbian Herstory Archives News,* no. 8 (winter 1984).

2. Martha Vicinus, *Independent Women: Work and Community for Single Women, 1850–1920* (Chicago: University of Chicago Press, 1985) and "Distance and Desire: English Boarding School Friendships, 1870–1920," in Martin Duberman, Martha Vicinus, and George Chauncey Jr., eds., *Hidden from History: Reclaiming the Gay and Lesbian Past* (New York: Meridian Books, 1990), pp. 212–29 (hereafter *HFH*).

3. Leila Rupp, " 'Imagine My Surprise': Women's Relationships in Mid-Twentieth Century America," in *HFH,* pp. 395–410.

4. Blanche Wiesen Cook, " 'Women Alone Stir My Imagination': Lesbianism and the Cultural Tradition," *Signs* 4, 4 (summer 1979): 738.

5. Carroll Smith-Rosenberg, "The Female World of Love and Ritual: Relations between Women in Nineteenth-Century America," *Signs* 1, 1 (autumn 1975): 1–29; and Lillian Faderman, *Surpassing the Love of Men: Romantic Friendship and Love between Women from the Renaissance to the Present* (New York: William Morrow & Co., 1981).

6. Rupp, " 'Imagine My Surprise,' " p. 398.

7. Ibid., p. 409.

8. Alice Baldy letter, 3/23/1870, p. 1, in Folder 19, Letters of Alice Baldy to Miss Joe, 1870[sic]–1871 and n.d., in the Varner Collection of Family Papers (also known as the Varner-Roundtree Papers and hereafter cited as the Varner Papers), ac77–391 microfilm, Georgia Department of Archives and History (hereafter cited as GAr), Atlanta. Originals at the Georgia Historical Society, Savannah, GA.

9. Blanche Wiesen Cook, "The Historical Denial of Lesbianism," *Radical History Review* 20 (1979): 64.

10. Ann Ferguson, "Is There a Lesbian Culture?" in Jeffner Allen, ed., *Lesbian Philosophies and Cultures* (Albany: SUNY Press, 1990), p. 63.

11. Ibid., p. 65.

12. Ibid., p. 67.

13. Ibid., p. 69.

14. Ibid., p. 70.

15. Adrienne Rich, "Compulsory Heterosexuality and Lesbian Existence," in *Blood, Bread, and Poetry* (New York: W. W. Norton & Co., 1986), pp. 22–75; Judy Grahn, *Another Mother Tongue: Gay Words, Gay Worlds* (Boston: Beacon Press, 1984).

16. Ferguson, "Lesbian Culture," p. 74.

17. Ibid., p. 73.

18. Baldwin Buckner Miller, M.D. (1798–1873), Papers, ac75–451 photocopies, GAr, Atlanta. Baldy's estate was valued at over $30,000, including thirty-two slaves who sold for $22,000 and a plantation that went for $5,000. After debts were paid, $15,000 remained to be divided among eight heirs.

19. I thank my writers' group, especially Southerners Charlene Ball and Jill Spisak, for their comments on the role of spinsters in their extended families.

20. Alice Baldy letter, 12/11/1869, p. 4, Series Two, in Folder 7, Letters of Alice Baldy to Edwin H. Baldy, 1864–1903 and n.d., in the Morcock/Baldy/Smith/Williams Papers (hereafter cited as the Morcock Papers), ac37–102, GAr.

21. Vicinus, "Distance," p. 215.

22. Alice Baldy letter, 1/31/1870, Varner Papers, p. 8.

23. Ibid., 1/31/1871, pp. 3–4.

24. Vicinus, "Distance," p. 213. See also Faderman, *Surpassing Love of Men,* pp. 85–102; Smith-Rosenberg, "Female World," pp. 19–27; and also Jean Friedman, *The Enchanted Garden: Women and Community in the Evangelical South, 1830–1900* (Chapel Hill: University of North Carolina Press, 1985), pp. xii and chap. 4 and 5.

25. Vicinus, "Distance," p. 214.

26. Alice Baldy letter, 1/31/70, Varner Papers, p. 6.

27. Alice Baldy letter, 1/14/1885, Morcock Papers, p. 2.

28. Ibid., 5/29/1879, p. 4. Alice is referring to the sicknesses, such as malaria, rampant at that time in low-lying areas of stagnant water infested with mosquitoes.

29. Ibid., 5/2/1889, p. 2.

30. Ibid., Series Two, in Folder 13, Alice Baldy Miscellaneous Business Papers, 1876–1915, Morcock Papers.

31. Ibid., 10/1/1887, Series Two, in Folder 6, Alice Baldy letters to Eliza Jane Polhill Baldy, 1860–1895, Morcock Papers.

32. Ibid., Series Two, in Folder 7 and Folder 9, Alice Baldy letters to Mary Jane Baldy, 1872–1885.

33. Ferguson, "Lesbian Culture," p. 71.

34. "Introduction," *HFH,* p. 11.

35. Alice Baldy letter, 4/29/1870, Varner Papers, p. 2.

36. Alice Baldy letter, 8/4/1879, Series Two, in Folder 7, Morcock Papers, p. 4.

37. Alice Baldy letter, 4/29/1870, Varner Papers, p. 1.

38. Ibid., p. 8.

39. Alice Baldy letter to Eddie and Maggie (E. Margaret Baldy Harris), 9/29/1883, Series Two, in Folder 7, Morcock Papers, pp. 2–3.

40. Ibid., 8/4/1879, p. 1; 7/23/1883, crosswise p. 1; and 12/23/1888, p. 2.

41. Ibid., n.d., Series Two, in Folder 6, p. 1.

42. Alice Baldy letter, 4/20/1870, Varner Papers, p. 1.

43. Ibid., 8/23/1867, p. 5.

44. Ibid., 1/31/1870, p. 6.

45. Ibid., 1/29/1870, p. 5.

46. Ibid., p. 8.

47. Vicinus, "Distance," p. 213.

48. Alice Baldy letter, 2/7/1870, Varner Papers, p. 4.

49. Ibid., 4/29/1870, pp. 8–9.

50. Vicinus, "Distance," p. 213.

51. Thanks again to conversations in my writers' group.

52. Martin Duberman, " 'Writhing Bedfellows' in Antebellum South Carolina: Historical Interpretation and the Politics of Evidence," in *HFH*, p. 160; see also Chapter 2 in this book.

53. Lillian Smith, *Killers of the Dream*, rev. and enlarged ed. (New York: W. W. Norton & Co., 1978).

54. Alice Baldy letter, 10/13/1872, Series Two, in Folder 6, Morcock Papers, p. 2.

55. Ibid., 9/26/1873, Series Two, in Folder 7, Morcock Papers, p. 2.

56. Vicinus, "Distance," p. 217.

57. Alice Baldy letter, 5/2/1889, Series Two, in Folder 7, Morcock Papers, p. 2.

58. Ibid., p. 3.

59. Alice Baldy letter, 3/23/1870, Varner Papers, p. 1.

60. Ibid., 8/23/1867, p. 5.

61. Ibid., 1/31/1870, pp. 1–2.

62. Ibid., 2/7/1870, pp. 3–4.

63. Duberman, " 'Writhing Bedfellows,' " in *HFH*, p. 160; see also Chapter 2.

64. Vicinus, "Distance," p. 214.

65. Ibid., p. 215.

66. Alice Baldy letter, 2/13/1870, Varner Papers, p. 2.

67. Ibid., pp. 3–4.

68. Ibid., 4/29/1870, p. 3.

69. Ibid., p. 4.

70. Ibid., 1/31/1871, crosswise pp. 1–2.

71. Folders 16–18 and 20–21 in Varner Papers.

72. Cook, " 'Women Alone,' " p. 738.

73. Alice Baldy letter, 4/29/1870, Varner Papers, p. 8.

74. Ibid., 2/2/1870, p. 8.

Chapter Four

Sex, Smashing, and Storyville in Turn-of-the-Century New Orleans
Reexamining the Continuum of Lesbian Sexuality

Katy Coyle and Nadiene Van Dyke

In October 1893, the *New Orleans Mascot*, a weekly newspaper that covered activities in the tenderloin district, ran a cover picture depicting two prostitutes lounging together on a couch—one leaning back provocatively, the other on her knees leaning into her consort's breast. The caption proclaimed, "Good God! The Crimes of Sodom and Gomorrah Discounted."[1] Although the sensational headline teased at the subject, it did not record any information about the lives of the several lesbians who lived and worked in the brothels of New Orleans's infamous Storyville between the last years of the nineteenth century and the end of World War I.

During this same period, just a few blocks uptown from the red-light district, the first coordinate college in the country, H. Sophie Newcomb College of Tulane University, opened its doors to "white girls and young women."[2] Isolated from the Tulane campus, the college in its earliest years provided an ideal setting for typical Victorian-era female "smashes."[3] Newcomb women, like their Northern counterparts, developed intense homosocial relationships with their classmates, held women-only dances, and wooed their upperclass crushes. As Figure 4.2 illustrates, they also snuggled in their beds, "big enough for two but made for one," until the early morning hours.[4]

At first glance these two worlds, less than a mile apart, seem antithetical. On the one hand, as archetypal genteel, middle-class white, Victorian women, Newcomb students represented all the innocence and chastity

4.1. Intended to titillate, this drawing warned of "crimes" against natural laws by suggesting that sexual liaisons between women occurred in Storyville, New Orleans's tenderloin district. (Cover of *New Orleans Mascot*, October 21, 1893. Al Rose Collection, Rare Books and Manuscripts, Tulane University, New Orleans, LA.)

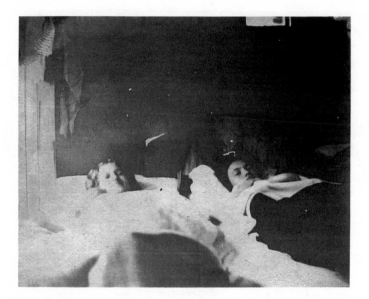

4.2. This photo, presumably taken by a classmate, depicted two
Newcomb women cuddling together in their homemade double
bed. These students obviously preferred this arrangement since additional scrapbook photos and a school brochure illustrate spacious
dorm accommodations. (From Julia Frotscher Koch scrapbook, Newcomb College Archives, New Orleans, LA.)

historians attribute to Southern ladies and "romantic friends." The madams and "working girls," on the other hand, provided a mirror image—
fallen women, notoriously lewd, predatory and dangerous to both women
and men. These women lived on opposite sides of the public/private
split, both physically and symbolically. A streetcar ride geographically
separated the Downtown red-light district below Canal Street from the
respectable Uptown Garden District. This physical separation made concrete the fictional dichotomy between the virgin and the whore, arche-
types defined in the South in terms of race and class. For both turn-of-the-
century New Orleans society and modern historians, the two worlds were
locked in a dialectic dance.

This chapter suggests that race and class shaped perceptions of lesbian
sexuality and sexual activity in turn-of-the-century New Orleans. Moreover, race and class affected the way women represented that sexual
activity to the public. We assert that both Newcomb students and Sto-

ryville prostitutes practiced a fluid range of public and private lesbian sexual behaviors. For both groups of women, however, the privileges and restrictions concomitant with their social stations influenced how they expressed their sexuality and how others perceived their sexuality. Further, an examination of these two groups illuminates a multiplicity of lesbian histories.

In New Orleans, economic affluence alone did not assure class standing. Rather, a complex mosaic of family and racial backgrounds along with financial influence provided entrée to power and status. In fact, New Orleans's red-light market may problematize traditional markers of class construction and maintenance. Successful madams could acquire wealth but could never attain the respectability related to middle-class status. It could also be argued that these madams and prostitutes had intimate access to avenues of power closed to virtuous women, even while they were excluded from the formal institutions of that power. To problematize their status further, some of these Storyville women made no secret of the fact that they engaged in private sexual relationships with other women.

Within the framework of romantic friendship, white middle-class Newcomb women could never be seen as lesbians, either by their contemporaries or by modern scholars. By virtue of their privilege, they could express their passions publicly through rituals and writings, as well as some degree of physical intimacy, without threatening their social standing. At the same time, to remain protected by the privileges of Southern, white, middle-class womanhood, they had to maintain the public perception of asexuality.

By definition, the historiographical construction of romantic friends has delimited the boundaries of "Victorian" women's relationships.[5] Exceptional evidence of sexual activity is required to overturn persistent assumptions of celibacy intrinsic to romantic friendship. Precisely because questions addressing Newcomb women's sexuality appear to invade their private lives, and because they saw their own sexual activities as private and therefore protected, evidence of explicit lesbian sex is anecdotal.

In contrast, the working-class prostitutes of Storyville, primarily ethnic and racial minorities, could never be viewed as romantic friends.[6] Excluded from the boundaries of Victorian womanhood, they could be seen only in sexual terms. In general, both lesbian historians and women's historians, looking to recover historical identities, have been reluctant to claim prostitutes.[7] Nonetheless, prostitutes provided the historical counteridentity for romantic friendship, and their inclusion expands the historiographical scope of the lesbian continuum. In counterpoint to Newcomb students, Storyville prostitutes not only publicly practiced a wide range of sexual behaviors, they openly acknowledged these behaviors. Because their sexual activity was public, it is accessible to historians. However, prostitutes' personal, affectional relationships remain as hidden from history as romantic friends' sexual activities.[8]

At the intersection of these two worlds stood the prosperous, influential, and highly respectable white men who founded, controlled, and patronized Storyville. Contemporary accounts indicate that the elaborate mansions of the tenderloin district drew the majority of their clients from elite white New Orleans society, many of whom had significant financial interests in the district. In fact, according to jazz great Bunk Johnson, the expensive sporting houses employed "light colored women, . . . strictly for white" clientele. Jelly Roll Morton concurred, stating, "No poor men could even get in these mansions."[9]

In addition, the district's newspapers frequently noted the city fathers' financial and social liaisons with the red-light district. Numerous articles in Storyville papers, such as the *Sunday Sun* and the *Mascot,* as well as in mainstream dailies such as the *New Orleans Item,* connect wealthy, influential men to Storyville. For example, one *Mascot* cartoon, published in the early years of the district, depicts "prostitutes' progress" aided by "the high-toned owners returning from church." Likewise, a 1914 photograph documents an engagement dinner honoring Anna Deubler, niece of Storyville madam Josie Arlington; also in attendance were Gertrude Dix, madam of the brothel at 209–11 Basin Street, Mayor Martin Behrman, former mayor Paul Capdeiville, Judge Otero, and State Senator Tom Anderson. Anderson, who owned significant property in the tenderloin, was often referred to as the Mayor of Storyville.[10]

These same men had daughters, wives, and sisters who defined Southern womanhood for the post–Civil War era. Indeed, many of these women comprised the first generation of Newcomb students.[11] The same men who assumed Victorian asexuality for the women of their own class participated in the entire range of sexual activities offered within the red-light district. Studying the intersection of these two worlds provides a lens with which to view the interaction of race, class, gender, and sexuality.[12]

Historians of women have recently examined the interlocking aspects of class, race, and gender, but few have included sexuality in their analysis.[13] In contrast, lesbian history for the Progressive era has focused on the definitional and perceptual shift from romantic friendship to sexual inversion.[14] Because white middle-class romantic friends were the first subjects of study, issues of race and class remain largely unexamined in lesbian history.

Certainly, "smashing" is a much-studied form of female friendship, best documented in women's colleges in the Northeast. Helen Lefkowitz Horowitz found evidence of female crushes at the Seven Sisters colleges just before the turn of the century, although she took no stand about the sexual nature of those relationships. More recently, Lillian Faderman examined college "smashes," "crushes," and "spoons." She maintains they continued through the turn of the century, with "romantic all-women dances" commonly held at Smith and Vassar. While she clearly includes these women within the "lesbian continuum," she minimizes the importance or existence of sexual activity.[15] Only Nancy Sahli has closely studied American women's collegiate romances in "Smashing: Women's Relationships before the Fall."[16] As her title suggests, this model theorized a romantic "golden age" in lesbian history, during which same-sex relationships between women, sexual or not, enjoyed freedom from condemnation. The reluctance to label such relationships as "sexual," as well as use of the standard of "genital contact" to establish the sexual nature of a relationship, imply the desire to maintain the fallacy of women's lack of sexual drive. Such a construction perpetuates phallocentric interpretations of sexuality, assuming sex to be a single vector of analysis.

Like the students of the Northeastern women's colleges, young women at Newcomb College engaged in elaborate courting rituals. Letters, poems, and sentimental cards, intricately decorated, cut into hearts, or pressed with flowers, expressed a student's devotion to her "Lady of Dreams."[17] These flowery, romantic sentiments appeared frequently both throughout the early years of the students' literary magazine, the *Newcomb Arcade*, and in the numerous student and Alumnae Association scrapbooks.[18] Students cherished mementos of these relationships by placing them in scrapbooks, which they saved for years, eventually donating them to the college archives.[19] In doing so, graduates demonstrated the importance of smashing as part of their college experience.

Poetry was one of the most frequent expressions of student crushes, often passionate and sexually suggestive. Poems in verse and rhyme, odes to the graces and beauties of lovers, adorned the pages of both personal correspondence and institutional publications. The 1912 poem "My Lady of Dreams" exemplifies the romantic language and unabashed sentiment of this phenomenon:

> Like the blue of the sea are My Lady's eyes,
> Like a benediction, her face;
> And the sunbeams that touch her hair with light
> But reveal all her gentle grace.
>
> And the song that is on My Lady's lips,
> That she sings in her voice of gold,
> Doth pass to my soul with its message of hope,
> With its meaning manifold.[20]

Drawing on the imagery of the Romantic poets, Newcomb students sanctified their lovers' physical attributes with spiritual meaning and natural perfection. "Fairest of all," this lady's love possessed a "voice of gold," hair touched by "sunbeams," and a face "like a benediction." As yet unrequited, the author's love held promise for the future with a "message of hope, . . . its meaning manifold." Students gave voice to such romantic desires publicly, unselfconsciously confessing their affections in college publications. Such flowery language may well have contributed to the view that smashing was "girlish" and therefore not reflective of sexual desire.

In addition to original works, students claimed suggestive writings from other sources, both ancient and contemporary, as their own. In 1916, for example, Alice Perrin Norton won the student-awarded Arcade translation prize for her version of Catullus's poem "Kisses," in which one woman confesses her love to another:

> My Lesbie, let us live, Lesbia,
>   and love.
> A penny has value far,
>   far above
> The censure of old men
>   in senile decay . . . .
> So kiss me, my Lesbia,
>   a thousand, and then
> A hundred, a thousand, a
>   hundred more, when
> A thousand should follow, a
>   hundred more, dear

> Then so many thousands it will
> be quite clear
> The reckoning's lost—e'en we
> the count lose.
> No one upon us, our love
> to confuse
> Can an evil eye cast, when
> he shall know
> There were just so many
> kisses in love's glow.[21]

Although it is doubtful that this student understood the term *lesbia* in the modern sense, the translation obviously describes same-sex sexual activity. The poem describes two women so lost in passion that "e'en we the count lose." Further, no observer to their passion would mistake or condemn the true nature of their love; in fact, the lovers disdain the threatened "censure of old men in senile decay." That this student chose to translate a work that contained explicit lesbian references suggests both a personal interest in the topic and its acceptance in the Newcomb community, indicated by its commendation and publication.

It is clear that students shared the sentiments expressed in this classical poem, because their private writings reveal the explicit nature of their own crushes. The following student-authored scene depicts two women caught in the throes of newly requited passion:

> Scene—on the pier in the moonlight
> *Cate:* How pretty the moon is!
> *Adaline:* Yes it makes me think of you
> *Cate:* Oh why—Adaline
> *Adaline:* Yes, Cate—darling—I've wanted to tell you for so long. I—I—I—
> *Cate* (falling off pier): You need not tell me—I know, I know just how you
> feel. I felt that way for a year.
> *Adaline:* Oh, Kate *[sic]*
> Curtain, as Adaline swoons in Cate's arms to the tune of a loud smack.[22]

This scene, scribbled on the back of a 1919 newspaper and later preserved in a personal scrapbook, was not intended for public consumption. In it Katherine Wilson revealed her private fantasy. In the scene, she presumably saw herself as "Cate," experiencing the fulfillment of her romantic desires.

"The Lad-woman," authored by a "Barnard Bear" and reprinted in the *Newcomb Arcade*, suggests not only a consciousness of sexual roles but the students' awareness of their own ambiguities regarding these roles.

From her eyes peeps a mischievous lad,
With a heart that is fearless and glad,
Her's the wild throbbing joy of an innocent boy,
    But her mouth is tender and — sad,
    Womanly tender — and sad.

Oh! tell me, dear heart, tell me true:
Do your eyes or your lips reveal you?
And she laughed and she sighed, and she said, neither lied:
    I'm a lad and a woman, too,
    Lad and woman, too.[23]

The author, clearly in love with the "lad-woman," sees the attributes of both the boy and the woman in the object of her affection. The lad-woman's "womanly tender" lips reveal her female nature, while her "mischievous" eyes disclose "the wild throbbing joy of an innocent boy." She readily embraces the duality of her own identity.

During this period, such young women often donned the trappings of the opposite sex, in settings where such behavior was socially sanctioned. For instance, Newcomb women frequently dressed and acted as men at dances and in student plays. Throughout the Progressive era, students held several women-only dances a year at which women in "drag" accompanied their dates in dresses. As late as 1918, the city newspaper printed a picture of an all-women dance held at Newcomb. Half of the young women, attired in formal dress, attended the dance with their "dates," dressed as soldiers.[24]

In fact, pictures offer rare insight into these women's relationships. Two photographs from the early years of the twentieth century document the physical intimacy that some students shared. The first, from Lydia Frotscher's scrapbook, depicts her spacious dormitory room with canopied twin beds pushed together in the middle of the room. The size of the room and the fact that the camera captured the entire space, along with a classmate's recollection that the beds were "big enough for two but made for one," certainly suggests that students slept together.[25] The second photograph (Figure 4.2, above) provides conclusive evidence that some young women unabashedly cuddled together in bed.[26]

As demonstrated above, students expressed a range of social behavior that included courting, dating, kissing, cuddling, and sleeping together. As numerous historians have concluded, these public demonstrations of affection strongly suggest parallel private sexual activity. However, the realities of late nineteenth- and early twentieth-century mores, as well as the historiographical construction of romantic friendships, have obscured these women's sexuality from view, both then and now. By virtue of their class and racial status, Newcomb students could—in fact, had to—protect any sexual activity within the cloak of privacy.

Constructions of race and class afforded social protection to those Newcomb students who did have sex; privilege placed these women's private sexual lives beyond question. Innocent girls would not engage in sexual activity, and Newcomb students were, by definition, innocent. This tautological reasoning that protected Newcomb students' position of privilege provides the context for viewing the photograph in Figure 4.2 in asexual terms. At the same time, the *Mascot* illustration refers to prostitutes who lacked the protections of race and class privilege. Invoking the horrors of Sodom and Gomorrah, the caption appeals to fears of lesbianism; prostitutes' sexuality and deviance are unquestioned. However, juxtaposed with the 1893 *Mascot* cover, the assertion of sexual activity for some Newcomb middle- and upper-class white women becomes not only thinkable but logical. Placed side by side, but without the benefit of contextual clues, the photo of the two Newcomb women in bed certainly is more suggestive. Storyville prostitutes, by virtue of their working-class, ethnic, and racial minority backgrounds, legitimized genteel womanhood.

In New Orleans, the repeated references to "Octoroons," "Coloreds," "Creoles," "Jews," and "women of all nations" among the Blue Book advertisements highlight the nexus of working-class status and the inherent sexualization of women of color.[27] Cast as the archetypal reflection of the innocence of Southern ladies, prostitutes lacked the protections of privilege, opening even their private sexuality to public scrutiny. Their visibility, however, freed them to acknowledge their sexuality, making their sexual histories more accessible to historians. The spectrum of lesbian activity among prostitutes can be documented through their own words, through decoding Storyville advertisements, and through recollections of Storyville customers. With these sources, we can begin to re-create a range of lesbian sexual activity among Storyville prostitutes: lesbian acts performed for male customers, private lesbian sex, and primary identification with female sexual partners.[28]

Well publicized among the brothels in Storyville, "French houses" advertised a specialty in oral sex and voyeurism. Women pantomimed fellatio in the windows of these houses in order to draw business in from male passersby or from passengers on the Basin Street train. In addition, these establishments, most notably Emma Johnson's French House, provided "erotic circuses" for the viewing pleasure of large audiences.

Advertisements for these houses in the famous "Blue Books," guides to the tenderloin district, used the term *French* with reference to women to suggest sexual exoticism and lesbianism. For example, the advertisement for Diana and Norma's, in a pre-1912 edition of the Blue Book, queried:

> Why visit the play houses to see the famous parisian model portrayed,
> when one can see the French damsels, Norma and Diana?
> Their names have become known on both continents, because
> everything goes as it will, and those that can not be satisfied there
> must surely be of a queer nature.
> Don't fail to see these French models in their many poses.[29]

This advertisement identifies Norma and Diana as "French damsels," whose establishment provided men with the opportunity to purchase oral sex. Further, the admonition that "those that can not be satisfied there must surely be of a queer nature" suggests a connection to homosexual activities. By the second decade of the twentieth century, homosexual men used the term *queer* as a self-descriptor that indicated their homosexual interest.[30] More than one possible interpretation of the above admonition is possible. Perhaps we can assume that, as the only advertisement in the Blue Books that uses the term *queer,* it was a coded message to those interested in watching or participating in lesbian sex. In contrast, it may be taken literally, as a claim that only gay men would not find satisfaction there.

Regardless, the term *French* described only those houses that provided this specialty or women who engaged in it. All of these houses were run by madams known as "notorious" lesbians.[31] According to contemporary accounts, neither Diana nor Norma concealed their lesbianism. In addition, observers of Storyville culture agreed that both Lulu White and Emma Johnson readily acknowledged their preference for women as sexual partners.[32] In her early days, Emma Johnson gained the title "French Emma." The 1906 *Sunday Sun* described her as the "originator of the French studio," claiming that Ms. Johnson had "established a line of business envied by most of the French women ... The French Studio is crowded with girls of all nations and to those who are looking for a genuine circus [this] is the place [sic]." As the first edition of the Blue Book announced, "Everything goes here."[33]

Emma Johnson's "mammoth sex carnival" was well known for its depravity. The leading exhibitionist show in the tenderloin, the circus included ponies, dogs, and women who "specialized in public display of explicit sexual acts." Notably, the circus employed only one man throughout more than a dozen years of operation.[34] One young female performer recounted her act in the circus:

> I was twelve and Edna had been sendin' me over there nights to be in the circus. . . . There was another kid my age. . . . By this time we were getting a little figure and looked pretty good . . . and neither one of us was afraid to do them things the johns liked. . . . We came on with everything we could think of, includin' the dyke act. . . . We did a dance we had worked out where we jerked ourselves and each other off.[35]

This quote graphically illustrates that there was a significant market for lesbian exhibitions, which French houses recognized and satisfied.

Early jazz musicians such as Jelly Roll Morton performed background music in many of the Storyville bordellos and have provided firsthand accounts of such activities. Jelly Roll, pianist at Emma Johnson's French Studio, reported that "they did a lot of things there that probably couldn't be mentioned, and the irony part of it is that they always picked the youngest and most beautiful girls to do them right before the eyes of everybody."[36] According to these accounts, the "dyke act" was a staple of the nightly circus shows.

In the process of working out the dyke act to perform it for the pleasure of men, prostitutes sometimes incorporated lesbianism into their private sexual lives. "We got to like it so much," the young prostitute quoted above disclosed, "we'd lots of times do it when we was by ourselves."[37] With this admission, she described lesbian activity as part of her personal sexual repertoire. However, this revelation cannot necessarily be taken as evidence that she considered herself either lesbian or bisexual. Although this woman practiced lesbian sex while a prostitute, after the district closed, she married one of her customers and gave birth to four children. According to her recollections, her early lesbian experiences played no significant role in the formation of her identity, sexual or otherwise. In fact, she framed her memory of private lesbian activity within the story of the loss of her virginity, not in reference to her own sexual awakening. Her youth at the time of her Storyville experiences notwithstanding, she provides evidence not only of the range of sexual activity but that sexual activity alone does not necessarily influence the formation of identity.

The dyke act became so popular in Storyville that in addition to Emma Johnson's French Studio and Diana and Norma's French house, "Sapho" House began welcoming clients in 1912.[38] The house's name obviously referred to the Greek poet Sappho, synonymous with lesbianism. Tellingly, unlike most Storyville bordellos, Sapho House did not announce its madam's name in the Blue Book. However, the advertisement used virtually identical wording to the advertisement for Diana and Norma's, suggesting that the two women either ran both houses or were involved in the founding of Sapho House. "Why visit the play houses to see the famous parisian model portrayed, when one can see the French damsel at the Cosmopolitan?" the ad inquired. "Don't fail to see these French models in their many poses."[39]

Presumably, Sapho House catered to clients interested in voyeurism or in a ménage à trois. The presence of Sapho House, dedicated specifically to lesbian sex, unmistakably documents both a social awareness of lesbianism and the market for it among the Storyville clientele. The clients of Sapho House, like those of the other fancy houses, came from the upper echelons of white New Orleans society.[40]

Although men moved easily between the sporting world and polite society in New Orleans without sacrificing their status or reputation, women did not enjoy the same freedom. A woman's class and racial status depended greatly on context. Countless generations of miscegenation and the social upheaval caused by the economic devastation of the Civil War necessitated complex signifiers of status. In fact, city fathers created Storyville as a distinct geographical entity simultaneously to protect respectable women from notoriety and to identify lewd and lascivious women.[41] Josephine Louise Newcomb, the donor of Newcomb College, even expressed explicit concern that the initial site of the college in the Garden District exposed "white girls and young women . . . [to] common boarding houses, filled with baser class [sic] of humanity, thus subjecting the girls and young women, to scenes and sights of immoral influences."[42] Once the city had cordoned off the district, administrative fears that a bordello might open next door to the college evaporated.

One example that illustrates that the distinction between respectable women and "notorious" women relied on context took place along the geographical dividing line between Uptown and Downtown. On Sunday afternoons, when they had the afternoon off, prostitutes shopped along fashionable Canal Street. In doing so, they ostentatiously breached the barrier between the sporting world of Storyville and respectable society. Presumably in response to this well-known practice, between 1911 and 1917 Newcomb's "Rules for Student Residence" specifically prohibited the students, even those escorted by chaperons, from "walking on Canal Street on Sunday." In 1918, the year after Storyville was dismantled, Newcomb lifted the restriction.[43]

In a city with fluid racial classifications, where prosperous prostitutes—both heterosexual and lesbian—obtained the accoutrements of the middle class, only context and their enforced separation protected "respectable" women from depravity. In contrast, these same conventions and regulations excluded marginalized women from protection: neither store-bought attire nor "walking Canal Street" provided entrée into respectable society.

This examination suggests that gay and lesbian historians must contextualize sexuality by including analyses of race and class, in order to uncover the range of lesbian activities and identities. In turn-of-the-century New Orleans, race and class significantly shaped the way women represented their sexual activity to the public and provided the context through which the public viewed their sexuality. The above evidence demonstrates that both Newcomb students and Storyville prostitutes practiced a fluid range of lesbian sexual behaviors, from romantic courting rituals to graphic lesbian exhibitions.

The lack of evidence of both sexual activity among romantic friends and of romantic friendship among prostitutes reflects not merely the historical absence of these relationships but the problems inherent in the definition of the terms. The tautological reasoning inherent in the historical and historiographical construction of romantic friendship precludes the broadening either of the range of women included within its boundaries or of the sexual behaviors associated with it. On the one hand, middle-class Victorian white womanhood required the public perception of asexuality. Hence, overturning this stereotype requires explicit evidence of genital contact, resulting in a skeptical reading of the extant sexual evidence. On the other hand, the public perception of prostitutes as fundamentally sexual beings proscribed them from the paradigm of romantic friendship. These same assumptions obscure prostitutes' interior lives, including the affectionate commitment intrinsic to romantic friendships.

In this chapter, we have argued for an expansion of the range of women and activities defined as lesbian. Not only do those women who fall within the rubric of romantic friendship contribute to our understanding of lesbian histories, but so do those women who are excluded from that rubric. Newcomb romantic friends and Storyville prostitutes are historically and historiographically entwined—each illuminates the other.

NOTES

This work has been a joint effort throughout the research, conceptualization, and writing process. The alphabetical listing of our names in no way indicates any hierarchy of authorship. We would like to acknowledge the assistance of both Diana Rose, Tulane University Jazz Archives, and Genevieve Bell, whose insightful and provocative comments improved this chapter.

1. *Mascot*, October 21, 1893, no. 609, p. 1 (New Orleans Public Library, City Archives, microfilmed newspapers). Since the *Mascot* covered only activities in the red-light district, the inference is clearly that these women, pictured in the gaudy decor of a high-class brothel, were prostitutes.

2. For Newcomb College, the initial construction of the "coordinate" plan included a completely independent campus; separate degree, faculty, and administration; but an executive board and treasury in common with Tulane University of Louisiana (Josephine Louise Newcomb, donation letter to Tulane Educational Board, quoted from Brandt V. B. Dixon, *A Brief History of H. Sophie Newcomb Memorial College, 1887–1919: A Personal Reminiscence* [New Orleans: Hauser Publishing Co., 1928], pp. 9–10).

3. "Smashing," "spooning," and "crushes" refer to the historical phenomenon of same-sex romantic courting and dating behaviors.

4. "Homosocial relationships" in Carroll Smith-Rosenberg, "The Female World of Love and Ritual: Relations between Women in Nineteenth-Century America," *Signs* 1 (1975): 1–29. See the *Newcomb Arcade*, 1909–1914 (Newcomb College Archives, hereafter NCA; all volumes of the *Newcomb Arcade* are located in the Newcomb Archives); Julia Frotscher Koch scrapbook, Beatrix M. Fortune scrapbook (NCA). In the process of preparing this article, a reader warned us that in using this photograph to illustrate the possibility of lesbianism among Newcomb students, we opened ourselves to the threat of a civil action. Ironically, this concern was expressed only with reference to the Newcomb students, not the Storyville prostitutes, exemplifying our contention that race and class privilege provide social protection, even after one's lifetime. We agree with Martin Duberman's assessment of such situations. Recovering these histories is vital: "The public *does* have the 'right to know' ... the gay public has a desperate *need* to know" (" 'Writhing Bedfellows' in Antebellum South Carolina: Historical Interpretation and the Politics of Evidence," in *Hidden from History: Reclaiming the Gay and Lesbian Past*, ed.

Martin Duberman, Martha Vicinus, and George Chauncey Jr. [New York: Meridian Books, 1990], p. 167; see also Chapter 2 in this book).

5. The construction of Victorian womanhood continues to be influential, despite evidence to the contrary. See Blanche Wiesen Cook, *Eleanor Roosevelt*, vol. 1: *1884–1933* (New York: Viking Penguin, 1992), who points out that the fiction of Victorian asexuality has persisted well beyond Queen Victoria's reign; Katherine B. Davis's evidence of significant lesbian sexual activity in *Factors in the Sex Life of Twenty-Two Hundred Women* (New York: Harper, 1929); and Karen Lystra, *Searching the Heart: Women, Men and Romantic Love in Nineteenth-Century America* (New York: Oxford University Press, 1989).

6. For demographic information about prostitutes in New Orleans we have used the "Blue Books." Two major collections of these advertisements of brothels exist. The largest is in the New Orleans City Archives, New Orleans Public Library; the other is part of the Al Rose Manuscript Collection, Manuscripts and Rare Books Division, Howard Tilton Library, Tulane University, New Orleans.

7. As Carolyn Steedman asserts in "Bimbos from Hell," *Social History* 19 (January 1994): 66, scholars "use history as a source of identity, and in order to provide accounts of their own selfhood, their own interior depths, their own subjection." See also Judith Walkowitz, *Prostitution and Victorian Society: Women, Class, and the State* (New York: Cambridge University Press, 1980).

8. As John D'Emilio and Estelle Freedman point out in *Intimate Matters: A History of Sexuality in America* (New York: Harper & Row, 1988), prostitutes' sexual activity was public not just because it was commercial but because "within working-class neighborhoods, sex retained its public presence." The underworld provided the setting in which "middle-class men purchased the services of working-class women" (pp. 130, 131).

9. Bunk Johnson quoted in Alan Lomax and Jelly Roll Morton, *Mister Jelly Roll* (New York: Hawthorn Books, 1973), pp. 104–5; Jelly Roll Morton quoted in Al Rose, *Storyville: Being an Authentic, Illustrated Account of the Notorious Red Light District* (Tuscaloosa: University of Alabama Press, 1974), p. 90. While class and race divisions were complicated within the African American community of New Orleans, only white women could claim the protection of Southern womanhood. This chapter does not address prostitution within the "cribs," shabby individual rooms opening onto the street and rented by the half day to solitary prostitutes. Rather, we consider the large "fancy houses" run by madams, which employed many prostitutes at a time and catered primarily to upper-class white men. This decision was entirely pragmatic. We recognize that including the poorest prostitutes would add another layer of complexity to our analysis, but the women who worked in these large houses left a larger and more accessible body of documentation, including interviews and advertisements.

10. Although the *Mascot* folded before the legal establishment of Storyville, the district had long been a red-light area. Photograph from the Al Rose Manuscript

Collection. *Mascot*, October 21, 1893, no. 609, p. 1. For Tom Anderson as "Mayor of Storyville," see Rose, *Storyville*, pp. 43–44.

11. See Newcomb Registers for the years 1887 to 1918, for evidence that Newcomb students came overwhelmingly from New Orleans's white middle and upper classes (NCA).

12. This analytical methodology relies on Michel Foucault and the queer theorists who furthered his work, who legitimized sexuality and sexual analysis as crucial vector of analysis.

13. Kathy Peiss, *Cheap Amusements: Working Women and Leisure in Turn-of-the-Century New York* (Philadelphia: Temple University Press, 1986); Walkowitz, *Prostitution and Victorian Society*; Deborah Gray White, *Ar'n't I a Woman? Female Slaves in the Plantation South* (New York: W. W. Norton & Co., 1985); and Christine Stansell, *City of Women: Sex and Class in New York, 1789–1860* (New York: Alfred A. Knopf, 1986), have examined sexual stereotypes for working-class, immigrant, and African American women. This work has not yet been done for United States lesbian history. Specifically, the construction of romantic friendship has left a historiographical gap with respect to race and class.

14. This debate began in 1975, when Smith-Rosenberg published "The Female World of Love and Ritual." See also Carroll Smith-Rosenberg, "The New Woman as Androgyne: Social Disorder and the Gender Crisis, 1870–1936," in Carroll Smith-Rosenberg, ed., *Disorderly Conduct: Visions of Gender in Victorian America* (New York: Alfred A. Knopf, 1985). Lillian Faderman, in *Surpassing the Love of Men: Romantic Friendship and Love between Women from the Renaissance to the Present* (New York: William Morrow & Co., 1981) and later in *Odd Girls and Twilight Lovers: A History of Lesbian Life in Twentieth-Century America* (New York: Penguin Books, 1991), sparked significant debate on both the sexual nature of romantic friendships and the effect of the sexologists on the development of lesbian identity. Adrienne Rich argued for the historical existence of a lesbian continuum in "Compulsory Heterosexuality and Lesbian Existence," *Signs* 5 (1980): 631–60. Martha Vicinus's article "Distance and Desire: English Boarding School Friendships, 1870–1920," *Signs* 9 (1984): 600–622, and Nancy Sahli in "Smashing: Women's Relationships before the Fall," *Chrysalis* 8 (1979): 17–27, specifically examined the existence of "smashes" at women's schools. Leila Rupp examines the contours of these threads in " 'Imagine My Surprise': Women's Relationships in Mid-Twentieth Century America," in Duberman, Vicinus, and Chauncey, eds., *Hidden from History*, pp. 395–410. This smashing/romantic friendship paradigm has recently been adopted by women's historians whose work is primarily outside gay and lesbian history: Helen Lefkowitz Horowitz, *The Power and Passion of M. Carey Thomas* (New York: Alfred A. Knopf, 1994).

15. Helen Lefkowitz Horowitz, *Alma Mater: Design and Experience in the Women's Colleges from their Nineteenth Century Beginnings to the 1930s* (New York: Alfred A. Knopf, 1984), pp. 65–68; and Faderman, *Odd Girls and Twilight Lovers*, p. 20.

16. Sahli, "Smashing," 17–27.

17. Anonymous, "My Lady of Dreams," *Newcomb Arcade* 4 (January 1912): 18.

18. The *Newcomb Arcade* ran from 1909 through the 1930s. Notably, evidence in the scrapbooks and in the student publications indicates that smashing continued throughout this period, well into the 1920s. This suggests that smashing was more persistent than Sahli proposes.

19. Rather than donate their scrapbooks to the Tulane University Archives, women kept them in their possession until the Newcomb Archives opened in 1989.

20. Anonymous, "My Lady of Dreams," p. 18.

21. Alice Perrin Norton, "Kisses," *Newcomb Arcade* 8 (June 1916): 14.

22. Katherine Lucinda Wilson Elder's scrapbook (NCA), circa 1917–1919. Dated June 2, 1919.

23. Barnard Bear, "The Lad-woman," *Newcomb Arcade* 5 (June 1913): 59.

24. In the Elder scrapbook, "New Year's Dance," no page numbers given.

25. Lydia Frotscher scrapbook (NCA); Fortune scrapbook.

26. Koch scrapbook.

27. Blue Books, Al Rose Manuscript Collection and New Orleans City Archives.

28. An examination of arrest and committal records for this period yielded no information regarding lesbian activity among prostitutes. In general, even though sodomy laws remained on the books, police arrested Storyville prostitutes only for violent acts or for plying their trade in integrated settings.

29. Unknown edition Blue Book, pre–1912–1915, Al Rose Collection.

30. George Chauncey Jr., *Gay New York: Gender, Urban Culture, and the Making of the Gay Male World, 1890–1940* (New York: Basic Books, 1994), pp. 14–16.

31. Rose, *Storyville*, pp. 77, 50. According to Rose, Emma Johnson was "early drawn to lesbianism" and "had a strange power over many of her sex."

32. For Diana and Norma, Rose, *Storyville*, p. 77; for Emma Johnson, ibid., p. 50; for Lulu White, see Al Rose, *Miss Lulu White de Basin Street, Nouvelle Orleans* (Paris: Gaston Lachurie, 1991). This information was confirmed in interviews with Diana Rose, archivist, Jazz Archives, Tulane University. See also Russell Levy, "Of Bards and Bawds: New Orleans Sporting Life before and during the Storyville Era, 1897–1917" (M.A. thesis, Tulane University, July 1967), pp. 46, 137–41.

33. *Sunday Sun*, February 25, 1906, p. 6, col. 1, in New Orleans City Archives; Rose, *Storyville*, p. 145.

34. Rose, *Storyville*, pp. 100, 29, 59.

35. Unnamed prostitute, quoted in ibid., pp. 149–50.

36. Lomax and Morton, *Mister Jelly Roll*, p. 127.

37. Unnamed prostitute, interviewed in Rose, *Storyville*, p. 150.

38. Blue Book, 5th ed., New Orleans City Archives.

39. Ibid.

40. See note 6, above.

41. Ordinance No. 13,032, Council Series, January 29, 1897, read "Be it or-

dained, . . . that from the first of October, 1897, it shall be unlawful for any public prostitute or woman notoriously abandoned to lewdness to occupy, inhabit, live or sleep in any house, room or closet situated without the following limits: Southside of Customhouse street from Basin to Robertson street, eastside of Robertson street from Customhouse to St. Louis street, from Robertson to Basin street." By Storyville's very definition, any prostitute had to live inside the district; any woman outside the district was therefore, *de facto,* not lewd.

42. Josephine Louise Newcomb to William Preston Johnson, January 14, 1887, *Brief on behalf of Respondent Brandt V. B. Dixon,* New York Supreme Court, vol. 1, 2,707–13, vol. 4, 5,694ff., in Dixon Papers, Protest Records 3, 244, NCA.

43. Josephine Louise, "Rules for Student Residence," House regulations, 1918; see Elder scrapbook, 1918.

Women and Men of Letters
The Jim Crow Era

Chapter Five

William Alexander Percy (1885–1942)
His Homosexuality and Why It Matters

William Armstrong Percy III

William Alexander Percy devoted a significant portion of his life to poetry. Yale University Press published the first three of his four volumes of verse—*Sappho in Levkas* (1915), *In April Once* (1920), *Enzio's Kingdom* (1924), and *Selected Poems* (1930)—and made him editor of the Yale Series of Younger Poets in 1923, 1925, and from 1927 to 1931. When Allen Tate, John Crowe Ransom, and others founded the *Fugitive*, Percy was among the "three or four poets in the South" asked to contribute to their December 1922 "visitors number."[1] Although Percy eventually abandoned writing verse, this evident homage from a group of poets destined to transform Southern letters testifies to Percy's literary reputation in the decades following World War I. The year before his death, Percy published his autobiography and family history, *Lanterns on the Levee* (1941), which in 1983 a critic called "one of the South's favorite books."[2]

Percy (known in my family as Uncle Will) was born into a prosperous Southern clan that traced its roots back to one Charles Percy, who in 1775 or 1776 sailed from the West Indies with a boatload of slaves to Louisiana. The territory was then called West Florida and held by the English. The Peace of Paris (1783) transferred it to Spanish control. In recognition of his growing prominence in the colony, the Spanish governor made Charles Percy an *alcalde*, that is, a local officer with both administrative and judicial powers. Over time, "Don Carlos's" descendants continued to play a significant role in the life of the Deep South. LeRoy Percy, Will's father, was U.S. senator from Mississippi; Walker Percy, grandson of one of Will's uncles, became a distinguished novelist in our own day.

A rapid study of the Percy family could convey, and often has conveyed, the impression that it embodied the ways and mores of the old planter aristocracy, replete with its prominence, hard drinking, public service, and eccentricities. The venerable Charles Percy (1740–1794), known to suffer from melancholia, one day tied a kettle to his neck and drowned himself in a creek.[3] Suicide ended the lives also of Charles's grandson Leroy Pope Percy (1825–1882) and great-grandson Walker (1864–1917) and of Walker's son LeRoy Pratt Percy (1889–1929). Prior to their deaths, depression plagued these descendants of the *alcalde*, as it haunted Uncle Will. His novelist cousin once wrote of Uncle Will: "When I try to remember [his eyes], I cannot see them otherwise than as shadowed by sadness."[4]

In some family members the depression led to mental breakdowns rather than death. Sarah Percy Ellis Ware (1781–1836), eldest daughter of Charles Percy, had to be treated at the Pennsylvania Hospital. Lady Percy McKinney entered the Phipps Psychiatric Clinic in Baltimore soon after her brother Walker killed himself in 1917. Uncle Will's cousin Ellen, too, suffered from severe mental illness, and Walker Percy (1916–1990) was known to experience "moods." When a medical student in New York, he spent considerable time with the psychiatrist Janet Rioch. According to his biographer, Rioch's approach "helped him to see that there were aspects of [his Southern] heritage that could be quite lethal, including its obsession with honor" (*PR*, 140), a burden that weighed no less heavily or depressingly on Uncle Will. Even individuals who married into the clan sometimes exhibited its extraordinary temperament. Uncle Will's greataunt Fanny was a morphine addict. LeRoy Pratt's wife died when her car plunged into a bayou, giving rise to persistent talk that she had killed herself. Little wonder, perhaps, that the prose of both Will and Walker Percy speaks more than once of family decline (*PR*, 59). Indeed, Will's autobiography has, virtually without exception, been said to relate Will's melancholy yet clear-eyed reflections on the passing away of the position and values of the planter class.[5]

It is my conviction that this reading of *Lanterns*, even as recast by Philip Castille to include reflections on the extinction of the Southern planter class as "part of a larger destruction of Old World Culture" ("EH," 101), is an incomplete assessment of Uncle Will, although he was indeed strongly attracted to the Old World culture that Castille mentions. Interestingly, studies of Will often use words like "conflict," "loneliness," and "ambiguity,"[6] yet none has sought an explanation for these traits outside Will's

5.1. William Alexander Percy. Courtesy of
Mississippi Department of Archives and
History.

sadness over lost traditions. To my knowledge, only two critics have ever
raised the possibility that Will was gay. The first to do so was Richard
King, whose insightful article goes so far as to report that "near the end of
[Lanterns on the Levee] Percy casts back over his past to recall several
fleeting and apparently unfulfilled homoerotic encounters" ("MM," 262).
He is referring to such lines as Will's "I hear voices unbelievably soft . . .
that murmur: Don't go, don't leave me, I love you."[7] As we shall see, the
absence of any indication of the sex of the speaker characterizes much
that Will wrote in this vein, but King was not fooled. Why at this point
the critic decides that these encounters were "apparently unfulfilled" I do
not grasp. Can it have been words and glances alone that brought the
speaker in Will's poem to pronounce, "I love you"? Moreover, King insists
on withholding the conclusion to which he would seem to lead us. Despite this recognition of "homoerotic encounters," the study ends on a
note of eternal mystery: "Percy knew that something was wrong, but he

could never quite put his finger on exactly what it was and who was responsible" ("MM," 263). I shall not step back from the inescapable conclusion, and so I maintain here that Uncle Will was gay.

The second critic to speak about Uncle Will and homosexuality is Bertram Wyatt-Brown, Richard J. Milbauer Professor of History at the University of Florida, whose brilliantly researched *The House of Percy: Honor, Melancholy, and Imagination in a Southern Family*[8] investigates the behavioral patterns of the many generations of my family. This perceptive book focuses in particular on the interplay of those features enumerated in its subtitle. They involve a desire to act in conformity with a code elaborated over time by family and caste and imaginatively translated into illustrative legends. Complicating that desire is the memory (and presence) of the persistent depression and suicides that I mentioned above. Wyatt-Brown shows that in certain cases such depression gave rise to a literary expression that sought to find order amid the tensions.[9]

Uncle Will figures prominently among the literary Percys.[10] Wyatt-Brown's discussion of his life offers us an intriguing mosaic of diverse and divergent elements. The homosexuality of many of Will's friends is squarely faced, as when Wyatt-Brown writes about the eldest of the poet's three wards: "When he was growing up, Walker felt at ease with his guardian's friends whose sexual orientation differed greatly from Walker's inclinations" (*HP*, 300). Wyatt-Brown records Will's lack of any sexual interest in women; alludes to his yearnings "for male sexual companionship" when in Paris, after his graduation from the University of the South at Sewanee; and, like King, refers to unmistakable homoerotic passages in *Lanterns on the Levee* (*HP*, 192, 203, 282). Yet his portrait of Will remains that of a "sexually sequestered," "puritanical" entity who enjoyed the company of gays and even shared their desires but never brought himself to know their carnal pleasures.[11] For the reasons given below, I am hard pressed to accept this conclusion. Uncle Will, I am convinced, knew both the difficulties and the physical joys of homosexuality.

My thesis cannot explain everything about William Alexander Percy, and it is not offered as a refutation of much good work that has gone before on Will's prose and poetry. Rather, in the spirit of the most useful advances effected by gay studies, I should like to show that by snatching Will back from all efforts to ignore or deny his homosexuality,[12] we shine light into many dark corners and learn in the bargain something about gay life for Delta planters in the early twentieth century.

The Evidence

Had Will's published writings spoken openly about his homosexuality, there would be no need for this discussion. If the public had access to his unpublished papers, there might be no need for this discussion. However, according to a reputable source, when a researcher was once shown sealed files containing papers of William Alexander Percy, Will's heirs (the novelist Walker Percy and his two brothers whom Will adopted after their parents' deaths) declared that he could not examine them. Furthermore, they threatened legal action if the scholar wrote explicitly about Will's homosexuality. Deprived of access to those same papers, I am obliged to rely on the hearsay of others and the hints supplied by Will's own pages. Neither provides conclusive proof, but such is the inevitable predicament of those who seek to prove what the famous seek to conceal.

My choice of the word *conceal* is perhaps inaccurate. True, Will never spoke directly of loving other males, but we may not overlook the many features of his writing that raise such a possibility. Chapter 26 of *Lanterns on the Levee* contains the references to those "homoerotic encounters" mentioned by King. It unfolds as Will recounts treasured memories. Not a single woman is featured there. Rather, we meet a shepherd boy, a "young man, white and naked," who sings as he swims; the crew of a ship sailing to Rio, "the moonlight turning their bodies slender, . . . daubing . . . the arch of their chests or their buttocks with pallor" (*LOL,* 340–41).

Similar passages appear in Will's poetry, but (perhaps because they were published when he was still a young man) with no clear indication that a man is admiring another male. The third poem in his "Four Capri Impromptus" is a case in point.[13] It tells of an Italian boy whom the speaker imagines in the act of making love: "The sweat beads pearling still the curve of his shoulders / And his breast still heaving." The speaker is not identified in any way. For all the depth of feeling expressed in "At Parting" (*CP,* 74), the text gives no hint whatsoever as to the sex of the beloved, although Will's description of their bond ("We lingered long! / . . . You for the flattery, / I for your beauty strong") sketches the most typical of man-boy relationships: the older adores the physical perfection of the younger; the younger drinks in the adulation of his admirer.

"Sappho in Levkas" (*CP,* 12–28), one of the earliest of Will's major poems and the poem that gives the title to his first volume of verse, is equally suggestive. In it Sappho announces to Zeus her decision to commit suicide. Born "unto perfection," she has discovered the sin of passion in the arms of the shepherd Phaon. Sappho is, of course, the famous Greek poetess who, like Uncle Will, frequently left unspecified the gender of the individuals in her poems. Although the modern world associates her almost exclusively with lesbian love, the ancients often linked her with heterosexual affairs.[14] More than once the poem invites an autobiographical reading. The speaker is a poet, is obliged to "feign simplicity" in order to speak the language of the humble Phaon. (No one has accused Uncle Will of writing in the common idiom!) Sappho relates that her companions were "heroes and kings, sea-wanderers, poets, priests"—not an inappropriate boast of a member of the Percy family and a decorated officer in World War I. More to the point still is the fact that the speaker in Will's poem is a woman who underscores her "nobility," now undone by sexual feelings for "a slim brown shepherd boy with windy eyes / And spring upon his mouth!" The words *shame* and *sin* are pronounced, and the poem closes with Sappho throwing herself into the "cleansing of the sea," not just because she has been "sickened" by her passionate encounter but also because, asking the gods to see Phaon once more, she realizes that her desire is ineradicable as long as she lives. After so pointed a presentation of guilt over sexual desire for an unacceptable object, I reiterate my surprise that King could consider Will unsure about what "was wrong."

In the preceding I have quoted and speculated aloud. To many who lived in Greenville, Mississippi, there was no speculation. One such person is still alive and lives near me in Boston. She had many times gone out of her way to speak with me, and I finally discovered why. Knowing my family name, she was curious to learn whether I might be related to Uncle Will. When I got to know her better, I discovered that Mrs. Millie Commodore had come north from Greenville, where she was born on May 17, 1915. She went to school and lived in Greenville until her marriage in 1938 to Augustus ("Buster") Commodore. Shortly thereafter she and her husband moved to Boston.

In the course of my recorded interviews with her in June 1990 and July 1992, we discussed her recollections of William Alexander Percy. They were vivid. In particular, she spoke easily about Will's black boyfriends. According to Millie, "At that time down there it was very prevalent with the richer class of people. They had their boys working for them. Treated them royal. They, most of them, had cars at that time, which fifty years ago was a rarity unless you was rich to have those kinds of things." Millie had herself known two of Will's boyfriends: a chauffeur she remembered only as Ernest and Ford Atkins, a classmate and close friend of her husband:

> [Ford] might have been fifteen or sixteen when [Mr. Percy] took up with him. A young boy. He was very fond of Ford. Medium build, very nice looking young fellow, mulatto skin. The family of Ford, a mother, worked as a maid in the house.[15] Ford was the one who seemed to have the upper hand with Mr. Percy. He worked for him over a period of years and then he decided, being what he was, he wanted to see him get an education, so he sent him to Detroit. He specialized in mechanics. After he finished, he came back to Greenville. But after he had got a taste of city life, I don't know if things didn't click too well.

Millie's reflections on Ford Atkins are especially interesting since Will devoted an entire chapter of *Lanterns on the Levee* to this man. Millie recalled the collapse of their relationship in these terms:

> And I understand he was giving fresh talk back and Mr. Percy finally came to the conclusion that the fellow just didn't like him any more. He realized he had lost Ford's like for him or love, and he had to let him go. He wasn't gone too long. Say about three years. But I think he was making trips back and your uncle was going to see him, too.

Will's own account is characteristically less explicit. Seen in the shower by Ford, Percy hears his "retainer" (Percy's word) declare, "You ain't nothing but a little old fat man." As a consequence, they "parted" (*LOL*, 287).

This passage has not gone unnoticed by critics, but viewed, like *Lanterns on the Levee*, from the perspective of Old South history, it becomes symbolic of further erosion of the dominance of the planter class: "But could Percy accept the existential validity of Ford's image of his bare humanity, stripped of the caste signifier, bereft of all the accoutrements of his social dignity?"[16] Clearly lines between the men had been crossed, but I find Millie's reading the more credible, especially in light of Will's portrait of Ford in the autobiography. Long before the episode in the shower, Ford had seen and commented on Will's "bare humanity." "That I have any dignity and self-respect is not because of but in spite of Ford," Will confesses (*LOL*, 288). By the same token, long thereafter Will's love and concern for Ford linger (*LOL*, 297, 326, 330).

To understand why Millie Commodore is a reliable witness here, an individual with no desire to malign William Alexander Percy, I must say something about her distinctive background. Both of her grandfathers were white and from well-to-do families in Greenville. Her father was intelligent and educated beyond most blacks in the Mississippi of that day. Moreover, as often happened with men of mixed race who were considered "Negro," he served as a leader of the black community.

Not surprisingly, Millie's family had threats from the Ku Klux Klan (KKK); they were never injured by it, however. Uncle Will's stand against the Klan, Millie intimated, was part of the reason for her family's immunity and a large source of their admiration for him. In *Lanterns on the Levee*, Will does indeed describe how he and his friends armed themselves to protect the Percy house from the KKK. His father LeRoy confronted the organization even more directly. When, in 1922, a Klansman attempted to convince the citizens of Greenville that the Catholics were determined to take over the nation's government, LeRoy Percy denounced the speaker's lies with terrifying ridicule and stout courage: "Any Southern man standing out and proclaiming himself as a champion of Southern womanhood and white supremacy should do it in the broad light of day, in the noonday sun, thanking his God that he can stand on his feet and battle for the right. You don't need a masked face for that kind of declaration. . . . I do not care anything about this war on Catholics and war on Jews. . . . They can take care of themselves, but I know the terror this organization embodies for our negro population and I am here to plead against it." "The crowd rocked and cheered," noted Will (*LOL*, 233).

Respect and gratitude explain one side of Millie's offhand reflections on her Greenville past, but another facet of that past explains why such gay relationships between blacks and whites as she described produced tacit acceptance in her community. "Aristocratic people, you didn't hear scandal about them," she said.

> This Ford business, Ford was a worker like so many young boys. It was a way to get ahead. It was hard to refuse [men like Mr. Percy] if they picked you out because, at least, it was a living and education or something. It put you in another category of life. So it was accepted by quite a few of the younger ones, you know. I wouldn't say they took advantage of them. It gave them an opportunity!

The Effects

Millie Commodore's almost casual observations about the homosexual relations between blacks and whites in her hometown stand in heavy contrast to the anguish we read in Will's poetry, and in that regard,

"Sappho in Levkas" may serve both as evidence for Will's awareness of his sexual feelings and as testimony to the dire effects of that awareness. Although we should not wonder that this man, by his own words "gourd-green, fearful" (*LOL*, 111), might choose to speak of homosexual desire with less than unrestrained directness, it still amazes me how many aspects of Uncle Will's personality have intrigued critics without their proposing the explanation I am advancing here.

Of Will's much-noted isolation King has written, "Will Percy felt homeless where he should have felt most secure" ("MM," 258). Indeed! Of all the worlds Percy had known in his lifetime (on which more later), the Delta was easily the most hostile to any open expression of homosexual love.[17] A novel by fellow Greenvillian Charles Bell portrays Will as an "overly precious, sissified aesthete" (*PR*, 87). Even Walker Percy, whose affection for his adoptive father cannot be questioned, introduced Will into his fiction as a woman: Aunt Emily of *The Moviegoer* (*HP*, 321).

King writes also of Will's relationship with his father, reminding us—quite correctly—that Will "felt small and physically unprepossessing beside his virile father and grandfather" ("MM," 257). The critic goes on to cite a passage from *Lanterns* in which, upon returning home from Harvard Law School, Will admits he was in effect "a sissy" and no doubt a disappointment to his father: "His heart must often have called piteously for the little brother I had lost, *all boy*" (*LOL*, 126; my emphasis). Whatever the complex feelings between Will and LeRoy Percy encompassed, this passage is about something quite specific: the inability to be the kind of male his "virile" father was.

In her study of metaphors in *Lanterns*, Carolyn Holdsworth interprets the levees of the title to signify tradition: "As a staunch Southern aristocrat, Percy firmly believed in the erection and maintenance of tradition to keep in control not just general nature but also human nature."[18] I concur and would point out how the new Sewanee graduate, barely beyond his teens and sent to Paris to recover from overstudying, describes his encounter in the Louvre with a Greek statue of a hermaphrodite: He examined it "with horror and fascination." Subsequent discussion of his effort to understand the mind that produced the statue leads to this *aperçu:* "It is a grievous and a long way you travel to reach serenity and the acceptance of facts without hurt or shock" (*LOL*, 111). Again (to return to my response to King's analysis of Will), the issue formulated by Percy is not one of understanding but of acceptance, the acceptance of *fact*.

Lewis Baker's intelligent study of the Percy family insists that Will did

5.2. William Alexander Percy in his garden in Greenville, MS, 1938. Courtesy of Mississippi Department of Archives and History.

not marry because he "was never able to find a woman who reconciled purity and sensuality."[19] Appended in support of the statement is a piece Will wrote comparing Samoan and Southern attitudes toward love. There the South is seen as making "all women either whores or heroines" (*PM*, 197). If Will felt tainted by this Southern perspective—and there is some evidence that he did—the fact remains that in "Sappho in Levkas" a rather different problem presents itself. As Baker himself has said, Sappho commits suicide "rather than remain prey to physical lust" (*PM*, 67). Fear and the inability to accept the fact of lust might be engendered by the opposite sex, but how much more understandable is such a response when seen as the reaction of a homosexual to a lust he feels and yet knows is universally decried!

Accommodation

To a man so aware of male beauty yet beset by fear, life is hard; but it must have been particularly hard in Greenville, Mississippi. Ernest and Ford Atkins provided one form of accommodation. My own aunt Lady (Percy), herself a lesbian, spoke often of Will's gay life in Mississippi. My father, who had once spent a year in Greenville with Will and his family (Will's father had become my father's guardian), often spoke disapprovingly of his "effeminate" cousin. Mother, using the oblique language common to parents, made mention of Will's "boyfriend" Tommy Shields, whom she had met on more than one occasion. Baker reports in moving detail Tommy's death: "During his last days Shields cried out for Will in his lucid moments" (*PM*, 172). Will saw to it that Tommy—a white man— was buried in the Percy plot.

Will also arranged to be surrounded by attractive men and boys whose names are well known to students of the Percy family. Bob Horton, once a football player at the University of Tennessee, frequently stayed with Uncle Will when not on the road selling chicken feed. Will approached Shelby Foote at the local country club swimming pool and invited Foote to his home. Foote, then an adolescent, was about the same age as Will's three adopted cousins, and Will was seeking to provide them with suitable company in an unfamiliar town. To David Scott, a black teenager who worked at a Greenville pharmacy, Will promised a position should Scott ever need one. Scott eventually left the pharmacy, became Will's chauffeur, and took flying lessons at Will's expense (*PR*, 89, 83, 146, 130).

Will's life and writings signal another quite different accommodation:

travel. I call it an accommodation because the places Will visited, the people he came to know, and the contacts he established point more than once to the world of male homosexuality. For example, his verse cites both Capri and Taormina, each a well-known gay colony in his day. The popularity of Taormina can be attributed to the Baron Wilhelm von Gloeden, who was and still is renowned for his photographs of young boys. Von Gloeden resided in Taormina from 1876 until 1931, and it is difficult to imagine that Will, who first traveled there in 1909, could have sojourned in the area without encountering this celebrity. At Capri, the equivalent colony was lorded over by the British writer Norman Douglas. Will not only knew this openly homosexual expatriate but also composed a short foreword to Douglas's *Birds and Beasts of the Greek Anthology*, which appeared in New York in 1929. It is a chatty piece that *en passant* makes reference to Douglas's love affairs and quotes a suggestion made by Douglas that Percy should visit the Etruscan artifacts at Volterra, where, he adds, "the charming boys . . . are all lightly powdered with alabaster dust, even their eyelids."[20]

Wyatt-Brown assures us that Will did not take Douglas's advice and, moreover, that Will "undoubtedly" belonged among those acquaintances from whom Douglas chose to conceal "his seamier side" (*HP*, 219–20). Yet the content of Will's own foreword argues against such a conclusion. The foreword makes no effort to hide Douglas's homosexuality or his naughty enjoyment in linking the study of ancient art to the pursuit of exotic youths. Missing, admittedly, is any statement by Uncle Will that he shared Douglas's appreciation of those "charming boys," but such is the nature of all his published works. What the foreword does present is a Norman Douglas who speaks in unambiguous terms to Uncle Will, who then happily records those terms under his own name for all to read. The words and atmosphere may appear somewhat precious today, but camp need not denote inhibitions. It is a way of speaking about what one does and feels, not an indication that one disapproves of any particular act or feeling. I readily concede that Will most probably experienced great inner conflict over his homosexuality, but the biographical facts of his life show him again and again in the company of homosexuals and traveling to places where homosexuality flourished. As the frankness of his foreword illustrates, this is not a man who ran forever from his deepest desires.

An even more remarkable intersecting of Will and homosexual culture occurred only a few years before Douglas's translations from the *Greek Anthology* appeared. The 1924 anthology of pederastic poems titled *Men and Boys* contains one work by Will. It bears the title "A Page's Song" and is signed A. W. Percy. The work is almost identical to a poem from *Sappho in Levkas* (1915) called "A Page's Road Song." Some words have been changed. In the original poem, the page asks Jesus to "fringe [his] bridle path, both sides, / With tulips, red and free." In *Men and Boys* the request reads "my boyhood's path / With lads-love fine and free." Only the pun on "lads-love" (an alternate name for wormwood) qualifies the poem for a place in a pederastic collection; yet its presence does imply ties between Will and the gay world of his day. A number of the poems included in *Men and Boys* are by the English Uranian poets (as a circle of boy-lovers in the early decades of the twentieth century often called themselves), and Timothy d'Arch Smith's summary of Uranian themes and attitudes in his study of those poets affords distinct parallels with Will's verse.[21] Such links, like Will's appearance in *Men and Boys*, accentuate anew a distinct awareness of and even contact with an international gay community.

In his own country, Will had three prominent gay friends: the art historian Gerstle Mack, who popularized Picasso in America; Harry Stack Sullivan, a prominent psychiatrist; and Huger Jervey, professor of international law at Columbia. Indeed, with Jervey, Will bought Brinkwood, a summer house in Mount Eagle, Tennessee, near Sewanee.

Why It Matters

Although I have attempted to show how Will Percy's homosexuality informs many of his pages, it is not to that role that I was alluding in my chapter's title. Will's homosexuality matters because it was a stimulus to his creative imagination and a source of distinct elation. Whatever has been said about Will's "conflicts" must, in all fairness to our subject, be set against the moments of joy, recorded in both prose and poetry, when Will beheld the beauty of the male form.

Will's homosexuality matters also because it contributed to his willingness to foster change and kindness in a society whose repression he himself must have felt. Baker has perhaps summarized it best:

> Will decided that the local newspaper was too reticent in pointing out violations of the public trust, and he encouraged Hodding Carter to establish his Delta *Star* in Greenville. . . . David Cohn lived in the Percy home for a year while he prepared his study of delta blacks, *God Shakes Creation*. When Hortense Powdermaker arrived in nearby Indianola to begin her own study of delta race relations, she received a cool welcome from local whites until

Will, who had never met her before, told the mayor of Indianola that she was an old friend of his family. After that, Powdermaker was able to rent the only room in town with a private bath. Will even opened his own plantation to the scrutiny of Raymond McClinton, a graduate student at North Carolina. Will believed that a little sunshine was good for everyone. (*PM*, 161)

To be sure, Will was not the public figure cut by his father. Will fought for his causes in his own way. Millie Commodore observed how he once solved a painful dilemma. It was the custom for gentlemen to take off their hats to white ladies but not to black women or girls. To avoid the problem, Will quit wearing hats altogether. In a similar vein, Will went against the ways of Greenville by persistently receiving into his home individuals who, by their color, sexual persuasion, sophistication, or dedication to the arts, defied the local definition of "proper folk." Wyatt-Brown records how, for example, Dorothy Parker, Stephen Vincent Benét, and Vachel Lindsay (surely a remarkable house guest in Greenville in that day) all enjoyed Will's hospitality (*HP*, 277).

Will's homosexuality matters because to claim him for the gay community continues the long process of "Queering the Canon"[22] and of rewriting the history of American letters to reflect the true contribution of gay and lesbian authors to that history.

Will's homosexuality matters because of what his life can teach us about gays of his generation. The existence and extent of interracial sex among heterosexual Southerners have long been recognized. But the earliest evidence of homosexual activity in the same population documented by the participants themselves bears the date 1826 and involves two white men: James H. Hammond and Thomas Jefferson Withers. (We know of their relationship through two letters they exchanged. See Martin Duberman's " 'Writhing Bedfellows,' " Chapter 2 in this collection.) And what of interracial homosexual relations? Former U.S. representative Jon Hinson of Mississippi reported to me during a telephone conversation in early 1994 that as a boy he overheard adults discussing the story of a white youth who had been fucked by a black adolescent. The white boy came from the planter class and was promptly sent to a boarding school in Jackson, even though it was said that "he had been ruined for life." When I asked if that phrase referred to the boy's reputation, Hinson replied that he thought the speaker meant rather that the white boy's sexual appetite for black men had been aroused and was not likely to go away.[23] Later, as an undergraduate at the University of Mississippi, Hinson was told by a faculty member that it had been the practice among planter families to provide their young sons with a black companion of the same age, much as the patrician class at Rome secured slave boys for their sons—and with the same tacit understanding of the possibility of sexual relations. Certainly, many similar stories have been passed on; Millie Commodore's words, however, provide us with our earliest first-hand account of that facet of Southern life, perhaps as old as its heterosexual counterpart yet unsung and unrecorded until this remarkable black woman shared with me her recollections of William Alexander Percy.[24]

At the same time, I regret that we know so little about Will's friendship with Tommy Shields. It is especially remarkable that Will could speak at length about Ford in his autobiography and say nothing comparable there about Tommy, whom, according to my mother, Will brought with him into society. Must we assume that just as Millie's world understood the "opportunity" prosperous whites afforded young blacks, so Will believed his world would accept a portrait of an irreverent black "retainer" more readily than one depicting a white "companion"? If so, again we see how deeply Southern ways conditioned Will's actions.

Of their effect on Will's soul, it is more difficult to speak. Bertram Wyatt-Brown's book stresses the frequent occurrence of depression and melancholia in the Percy family. Although knowing only too well the presence of these traits among the Percys, I am disinclined to attempt to distinguish neatly between the effects of the family and the effects of the Deep South on Will. If, as Wyatt-Brown hypothesizes, Will chose to live in Greenville with his parents because he "feared their censure, their confirmation of how inadequate he felt himself to be" (*HP*, 205), other considerations kept him wedded to that spot for the twenty years that elapsed between their death and his. Southerners can, I suspect, understand those considerations better than most, just as they will grasp why Will could write extensively of Ford Atkins in *Lanterns on the Levee* yet say nothing of Tommy Shields.

Uncle Will presents us with the story of a sad and secretive life characteristic not only of certain Percys but also of so many homosexuals who have chosen to live in rural America. "I will carry terrible things to the grave with me: / So much must never be told" ("Safe Secrets," *CP*, 217). These lines open the poem Percy offered to the *Fugitive*. While they explain no more than do other passages that could be read as intimations of Will's homosexual secret, the use of such words as *terrible* and *never* translates the momentous interdiction Will had internalized against whatever revelations he was in a position to make. The sources of that interdiction were certainly multiple. They were also powerful, whence, I have suggested, arose Will's love of travel and, indeed, his need of travel. Whether Will Percy would have felt more comfortable as a gay man in this post-Stonewall era is debatable. The triumph of "dishonor and corruption" that so saddened him has not gone away; and yet, had he felt freer to love the beauty he could so brilliantly describe, perhaps that triumph would have mattered just a little less.

NOTES

This discussion owes a special debt to three individuals: Millie Commodore, who so graciously welcomed the author into her home; Arthur Warner, who wisely grasped the import of Millie's testimony; and Donald Stone, who provided invaluable editorial assistance.

1. Jo Gulledge, "William Alexander Percy and the Fugitives: A Literary Correspondence, 1921–1923," *Southern Review* 21 (1985): 421.

2. Philip Castille, "East toward Home: Will Percy's Old World Vision," in *Southern Literature in Transition: Heritage and Promise*, ed. Philip Castille and William Osborne (Memphis: Memphis State University Press, 1983), p. 101; hereafter cited as "EH."

3. For this detail and much invaluable information about the Percy family, see Jay Tolson's *Pilgrim in the Ruins: A Life of Walker Percy* (New York: Simon & Schuster, 1992), hereafter cited as *PR*.

4. Walker Percy, *Signposts in a Strange Land* (New York: Farrar, Straus & Giroux, 1991), p. 54.

5. See, for example, Edward J. Dupuy, "The Dispossessed Garden of William Alexander Percy," *Southern Quarterly* 29 (1991): 31–41; and James M. Cox, "Trial for a Southern Life," *Sewanee Review* 97 (1989): 238–52.

6. See, respectively, Richard H. King, "Mourning and Melancholia: Will Percy and the Southern Tradition," *Virginia Quarterly Review* 53 (1977): 249, 251 (hereafter "MM"); Dupuy, "Dispossessed Garden," p. 31; and Jan Nordby Gretlund, "Southern Stoicism and Christianity: From William Alexander Percy to Walker Percy," in *The United States South: Regionalism and Identity*, ed. Valeria Gennaro Lerda and Tjebbe Westendorp (Rome: Bulzoni, 1991), p. 148.

7. William Alexander Percy, *Lanterns on the Levee* (Baton Rouge and London: Louisiana State University Press, 1993), p. 337; hereafter cited as *LOL*.

8. Bertram Wyatt-Brown, *The House of Percy: Honor, Melancholy, and Imagination in a Southern Family* (New York: Oxford University Press, 1994), hereafter cited as *HP*.

9. Given the subject of this chapter, I must point out that Wyatt-Brown espies a further tendency in the family, to wit, the formation of strong bonds between men. It surfaces first with the friendship between Thomas G. Percy (1786–1841) and John Williams Walker, about which Wyatt-Brown notes, "Their experience of brotherly affection established a pattern in the family's culture" (*HP,* 65). (See also note 12, for Jay Tolson's observation about repetition of this pattern in the life of the novelist Walker Percy.) Although it is not possible to produce documentation of any homosexual activity in these relationships, I am reminded of a remark by my Aunt Lady to the effect that, according to Will, Thomas G. Percy's bachelor son John Walker, named for the father's best friend, and one of Thomas's daughters were gay. The remark cannot be verified, of course; yet of my aunt's lesbianism and my own gayness there can be no debate. As a result, I am convinced that to understand the behavior of several members of the Percy clan, such pronounced male bonding and, indeed, homosexuality deserve a place beside the issues of honor and melancholia so prominently featured by Wyatt-Brown in his study.

10. For a fascinating discussion of four Percy (or Percy-related) women writers of the nineteenth century, see Bertram Wyatt-Brown, *The Literary Percys: Family History, Gender, and the Southern Imagination* (Athens: University of Georgia Press, 1994). Among them, Eleanor Percy Ware Lee, Catherine Ann Ware Warfield, Sarah Anne Ellis Dorsey, and Kate Ferguson produced eighteen books, including novels and works of poetry and biography.

11. See in particular *HP,* pp. 205 and 219. Elsewhere, Will is described as a "bachelor with severe inhibitions," and of his poem "A Page's Song," which would appear in an anthology of pederastic verse (see below), Wyatt-Brown writes that it "was meant to be ethereal and delicate—much yearning, no touching" (*HP,* 222).

12. Shortly before he died, Walker Percy wrote me to insist that although he lived with Will for a number of years, he never heard a single word that would have indicated that Will was gay; and as recently as January 1996, a distant cousin of mine who knew and corresponded with Will from the early 1920s until his death told me in a letter that there was no truth to Will's "having intimate relations" with any black men. During a telephone conversation with Shelby Foote in April 1993, Foote assured me that Uncle Will would not have wanted to be outed. Such action, Foote believed, went against everything that Percy stood for. I understand Foote's reaction. Uncle Will belonged to a world that frequently left much unsaid. Walker's point of view, however, may stem more from his own feelings about homosexuality than from the reality he experienced in Greenville. Jay Tolson's intriguing biography gives every indication that Walker may have been far more conflicted than even Uncle Will. Tolson cites various comments made by Walker indicative of a hostile attitude toward "artsy," "fey" behavior (cf. *PR,* 114, 207) yet espies in *The Last Gentleman* "the attraction of the homophile alternative to the life of married desperation" (*PR,* 333). Tolson believes that the attraction was not sexual in nature. By the same token, "distant models can be

found in Percy's own relationships with male mentors, Will Percy, Willie von Glahn, and even Huger Jervey" (*PR*, 333).

13. See *The Collected Poems of William Alexander Percy* (New York: Alfred A. Knopf, 1943), pp. 259–60; hereafter cited as *CP*.

14. The most famous work depicting Sappho's love for Phaon is Ovid's *Heroides* 15, where, however, Phaon is not a shepherd but rather a ferryman.

15. Mrs. Louisa Atkins was, in fact, Uncle Will's cook (see *HP*, 266).

16. William L. Andrews, "In Search of a Common Identity: The Self and the South in Four Mississippi Autobiographies," *Southern Review* 24 (1988): 54.

17. For an extensive analysis of the Delta mentality, see James C. Cobb, *The Most Southern Place on Earth: The Mississippi Delta and the Roots of Regional Identity* (New York: Oxford University Press, 1992).

18. Carolyn Holdsworth, "The Gorgon's Head and the Mirror: Fact versus Metaphor in *Lanterns on the Levee*," *Sewanee Literary Journal* 14 (1981): 38.

19. Lewis Baker, *The Percys of Mississippi: Politics and Literature in the New South* (Baton Rouge and London: Louisiana State University Press, 1983), p. 197; hereafter cited as *PM*.

20. William Alexander Percy, foreword in Norman Douglas, *Birds and Beasts of the Greek Anthology* (New York: J. Cape and H. Smith, 1929), xi, xii. On Douglas' homosexuality and the content of Will's foreword Baker is noticeably silent (153). To his credit, Wyatt-Brown presents a far more frank account of Douglas' life and behavior (*HP*, 219).

21. The summary is given on p. 163–201 of Timothy d'Arch Smith's *Love in Earnest: Some Notes on the Lives and Writings of English 'Uranian' Poets from 1889 to 1930* (London: Routledge & Kegan Paul, 1970). Will's use of classical material to relate personal situations and emotions, as well as the expression of guilt and religious feeling, he shares with the Uranian poets.

22. This was the title of a series of lectures I gave in October 1994 in Alabama, Mississippi, and Louisiana, to expand upon the importance of gay Southern writers.

23. Such thinking has, interestingly enough, been supported by Alfred Kinsey's research: "The data which we have already published on social levels show that by fourteen years of age perhaps as many as eighty-five percent of all boys have acquired the patterns of sexual behavior which will characterize them as adults, and something like nine out of ten of them do not materially modify their basic patterns after sixteen years of age" ("Concepts of Normality and Abnormality in Sexual Behavior," in *Psychosexual Development in Health and Disease*, ed. Paul H. Hock and Joseph Zubin [New York: Grune & Stratton, 1949], p. 21).

24. I was able to speak by telephone with Millie's brother, John K. McMiller, who now lives in New York City. He was less informed about Will's homosexuality but confirmed that homosexual relations between blacks and whites definitely existed at the time.

Chapter Six

Personalizing the Political, Politicizing the Personal

Reflections on Editing the Letters of Lillian Smith

Margaret Rose Gladney

The publication of *How Am I to Be Heard? Letters of Lillian Smith* in the fall of 1993 marked the culmination of fifteen years of research and writing about a woman whose life and work had influenced mine for over twenty years.[1] Beyond that personal relationship of a scholar with her subject, however, my work on Lillian Smith embodied and reflected the movements for social change that have defined and made real our highest ideals of social justice and human liberation in a democratic society: the African American liberation and civil rights movements, which inspired both the women's liberation and the lesbian, gay, bisexual, and transgendered liberation movements. Because of the work of those movements I, a southern white woman, could earn a Ph.D.; be employed in a Deep South state university; find redress in the courts when I was initially denied tenure at that university; subsequently secure institutional support from that university to write a book about Lillian Smith, a woman whose life and work challenged her culture's fundamental ideas about race and sex; and have that book published by a southern university press, with a feminist editor and in a series devoted to works on gender and culture.

Reflecting on that history, I remember the collective and interconnecting work of many who have gone before, and many who continue to challenge the prescribed limits of social and political categories. Remembering that history, I consider Lillian Smith's letter to the Student Nonviolent Coordinating Committee (SNCC) in the early 1960s especially helpful in assessing the sometimes bitter debate about the place of lesbigay issues in contemporary American life.

Organized in April 1960 to coordinate the activities of the student-initiated sit-ins that protested segregated public facilities throughout the South, SNCC quickly became the most radical arm of the civil rights movement. From the first sit-in in Greensboro, North Carolina, Lillian Smith supported, and encouraged her friends in older civil rights organizations to support, the bold activism of those black and white students. She was invited to speak at the first SNCC conference in Atlanta, and a number of the SNCC leaders visited Smith in her mountain home near Clayton, Georgia. By December 1962 or January 1963, when she wrote the letter excerpted here, violent resistance to the sit-ins, marches, and demonstrations was increasing throughout the South, and the young activists were, understandably, discouraged:

Dear All of You at SNCC:
I read your Newsletter with a sinking heart. It sounds so terribly bad. But things are breaking and thawing: we must hold on to that. A frozen river is a quiet thing; in thaw it is a roaring monster. We are in thaw in the South: there is bound to be much noise, much individual cruelty, much collective madness. But underneath, change is taking place—not only in streets and places but in human hearts. And this we must every one remember. I remember when I first began writing my magazine *South Today* things were so frozen that people actually thought I was mad. (And not only the Ralph McGills—but truly wise and good people thought so). I remember the stunned faces in Raleigh N.C. at a meeting of the Southern Churchmen (their faces were all right—the audience's collective face is what I remember) when I quietly said segregation is morally wrong, psychologically wrong, culturally wrong: all of us, white and Negro are harmed by it. The whites' souls are harmed, the Negroes' bodies and minds. That gasp from the audience. This was in 1943. I kept on writing, speaking out, and more important, thinking, thinking, letting this dilemma, this sickness relate, as it must, to all the other sicknesses of our soul and confusions of our mind. And people thought I was half out of my mind! Of course. That was the frozen period. If you think this thaw is bad, I wish you could have experienced the hard frozen sterile quality of those times. I say this not to minimize the horror of today but to give perspective, to help us see that sometimes noise and blood and screams and blows are not a sign of things worsening but of things getting better.[2]

Two of Smith's observations seem particularly appropriate in light of the increasingly heightened resistance to any effort to act openly or inclusively in support of lesbian, gay, bisexual, and transgendered peoples.

First, it is important to remember that we, too, are in "a time of thaw" — Smith's perspective that evidence of increased resistance to civil rights activism was itself a sign of what happens naturally, inevitably, in the course of working for social change. Second, it is significant how she addressed the most pressing social dilemma of her time, her society's response to racial differences: by "letting this dilemma, this sickness relate, as it must, to all the other sicknesses of our soul and confusions of our mind." Not only is Lillian Smith remembered today because she spoke against racial segregation in a time when few other whites of her class and region were doing so; her work remains significant because she insisted that issues of race cannot be understood in isolation, apart from every other aspect of human mind and heart—or, to phrase it in contemporary language, from any of our other social constructions of class, gender, or sexuality.

I did not begin to write about Lillian Smith with the idea of writing lesbian history or biography. When I began my research in the summer of 1978, I did so as a southern white feminist, especially interested in how Smith had stretched and challenged the limits imposed by the traditional construction of southern white ladyhood.

Long before the publication of her magazine *South Today* and of her best-selling novel *Strange Fruit* established Lillian Smith as the South's most liberal white writer, she was known to hundreds of young white women and their families throughout the South as "Miss Lil," director of Laurel Falls Camp, a highly popular, educationally innovative summer camp for girls in the mountains of northern Georgia. It was through her work with the camp that Smith first began systematically to examine and then to confront her society's concepts of race and gender. Hence I began my study of Smith as an oral history project in which I interviewed more than fifty women who had been Laurel Falls campers or counselors, including Paula Snelling, assistant camp director and coeditor of the magazine, whom I knew first as Smith's "life-long friend and companion."

Invariably, when I presented my first papers about Smith and Laurel Falls Camp at regional and national women's studies meetings, the question came from the audience: What was the nature of the relationship between Lillian Smith and Paula Snelling? Always my answer was: How can we know? Smith didn't identify herself as lesbian. Of course, the obvious way to "settle the question" was to ask Paula Snelling. She was still alive, though by then in a nursing home, paralyzed on her left side

6.1. Paula Snelling and Lillian Smith, Laurel Falls Camp, fall 1945. Courtesy of Jean Friedlander, former Laurel Falls camper, Milwaukee, Wisconsin.

from a stroke. I had interviewed her on several occasions about Laurel
Falls Camp but had never asked her about the "nature" of her relationship
with Lillian Smith.

What did I think she would say? Why hadn't I asked her? Here was
the tricky part, and a prime example of why questions of sexual identity
or sexual expression cannot be fully examined in isolation. Ironically, the
very characteristics that had initially led me to identify so closely with
Smith and her worldview—our both being born female into small-town,
upper-class, white southern families—now served to inhibit and blind
my research. How could I ask Paula Snelling about her sexual relationship
with Lillian Smith? That was her private business, wasn't it? What difference did it make? That was the question I asked myself. That was the
question my closeted lesbian friends and lovers asked me. And I could
not give an answer. I was blinded by my own class and gender socializa-
tion and by my closeted lesbian sexuality. As long as we hold the illusion
of sexuality and sexual expression as purely private matters, it is too easy
to dismiss the questions about same-sex relationships in historical research as mere speculation or gossip or as the insidious desire of those
queer others to project their own queerness onto historically recognized
figures. I knew I wanted to believe that Lillian Smith and Paula Snelling
were lovers, but I feared it was only because I so admired Smith and her
stand as a southern white woman for racial justice that I wanted her to
affirm the lesbian love I was afraid to acknowledge. Still blind to the
power of compulsory heterosexuality to distort and inhibit personal as
well as cultural and systemic analyses, I stood firm publicly on scholarly
objectivity and said of Smith's sexual identity, "We simply cannot know."
At the 1981 Berkshire Conference on Women's History, when a representative from the Lesbian Herstory Archives left her card on the podium
requesting a copy of my paper on Smith and Laurel Falls Camp for the
archives, I never responded. Trying so hard to be "professional"—that
is, "safe," especially when dealing with socially taboo areas of sexual
expression—I allowed my own unexamined fears to become my most
effective censors.

A year later, in the summer of 1982, I spent two weeks in Lillian
Smith's home near Clayton, Georgia, at the request of Lillian's sister and
brother, Esther and Frank Smith, sorting and collecting the papers that
had not been previously donated to the major Smith collections at the
University of Georgia and University of Florida. Larry Gulley, archivist
for the University of Georgia special collections, drove up from Athens to

help me. We examined thoroughly every file drawer, closet, cabinet, and chest in the remodeled camp cabins occupied by Lillian Smith, before she died in 1966, and Paula Snelling, until her stroke in 1978. We even recorded the titles of several hundred books in the camp library. After four days of sorting and packing, Larry left with his pickup truck filled with archival boxes, and I went back to what had been Paula Snelling's house to lock the door before returning to Alabama. As I made one last safety check to be sure nothing was left open, I found a small leather case, stuck back in a cabinet. How had we missed it before? It is one of the intriguing mysteries of which many biographers and historians tell. It was not locked. I opened it. There, among old photographs, picture postcards from Snelling to her brother and parents when she was at Columbia University, and a brown paper bag containing Paula Snelling's parents' courtship letters, lay a small packet marked "private." In it were a handful of letters, dated in the 1940s and 1950s, from Lillian Smith to Paula Snelling, and a few from Snelling to Smith.

There I read what I had found nowhere else in Smith's correspondence: unmistakably clear expressions of their physical as well as intellectual intimacy. Writing to Paula from Brooklyn, New York, where she lived in February 1946 while working on the Broadway production of *Strange Fruit*, Smith closed with these words: "I'd love to feel your lips on mine . . . and I can imagine other feelings too. Better guard these letters." [3] The letter that stood out for me, however, was one in which Smith confessed ambivalence about her sexuality. In June 1952, again from her apartment in Brooklyn, Smith wrote Snelling:

Paula—
What a nice letter you write me! It did you good to go through the old letters, didn't it. The picture of you swung me back through the years. You were so darned cute and attractive. You are "sweeter," "finer" now but you had something then that was so *young* and—nice, that bi-sexual charm which no one dares admit is seductive—except in real life.

I am sorry my letters are burned, that is my ambivalence. My shame about something different and completely good. It has been that shame that has destroyed the keen edge of a pattern of love that was creative and good. Blurring it, dulling it.[4]

The letters had been guarded, and I continued to guard them. I knew I had to show them to Paula Snelling, but it took me several months to arrange the time and work up my courage to see her. Happily surprised to see the contents of the case, she told me she thought all her personal papers had been destroyed. "I don't know why I saved these," she said, "except perhaps to read in my very old age!" Snelling asked that her parents' letters be deposited at Emory University with the Snelling family papers because, she said, the subjects—her parents—were long since dead; and besides, she added, "their relationship was normal." When I told her I thought her relationship with Lillian Smith was also "normal," she smiled and said, "I know you do, but . . . ''

When I asked Paula specifically about the nature of her relationship with Lillian Smith, she replied, "We shared everything; we loved each other very much, and sometimes we expressed that love physically." But she did not agree with those who said Lillian Smith was a lesbian. No, she insisted, Paula was the lesbian in the relationship, because she never desired a relationship with a man. Lil, by contrast, could have been happily married, had the right man come along.

That evening I left the letters with Paula Snelling. When I returned the next morning, Paula asked me to do something I had never expected. She asked me to read some of the letters aloud to her. It was a rare moment of intimacy I shall never forget.

What emerged as the most important lesson from that experience was not that I had, by some fluke, found the "evidence" to confirm the sexual nature of a relationship between two women. Rather, it seems now far more significant that the presence of those letters opened an opportunity, created a new space, for communication based on trust between Paula Snelling and me. After I read those letters to her, Paula said to me, "I have talked more intimately with you than I have with anyone except Lil." As I read and asked questions, Paula added comments, clarifying some part of a letter from her perspective and at times saying, "Lil was just wrong about that." She talked openly about her own life, as well as about Lillian Smith's, in ways she had not done before, telling about her childhood and her relationship with her family as compared to Lillian Smith's family life.

I did not uncover a consciousness on Snelling's part of having lived what we would call today a lesbian lifestyle. In *Odd Girls and Twilight Lovers*, Lillian Faderman described middle-class, especially professional, lesbians in the 1930s and 1940s as being totally closeted, even to other lesbian friends.[5] When I asked Snelling specifically if she and Smith had ever discussed their relationship with other women friends, even those I thought seemed to have lived as lesbian couples themselves, Snelling said no, their friendships with the other women were based on other shared interests and activities. Most important, in the course of that conversation I gained a much fuller sense of Paula's personality and attitudes—and indirectly, of Lillian Smith's as well—thereby confirming for me one of the reasons it is so important to acknowledge sexual expression in historical research. Something very liberating can happen when part of a person that has been previously hidden, denied, or demeaned is finally affirmed.

Snelling clearly accepted her lesbian sexuality, defining it as an abnormality of her genes but not as a sin and as nothing to feel ashamed about. She said she felt Smith hid their relationship, not to deny it but to protect it. Sadly, though not surprisingly, her lifetime sense of the necessity of "protecting" and "guarding" was not easily changed. Paula told me more than once how much she appreciated my bringing those letters to her, but in the end, she also said I must destroy them. "You want me to destroy these?" I asked incredulously. Then came my reprieve, my escape valve: "When you are finished with them," she replied. That last clause was all I needed; after consulting with Larry Gulley, I deposited the letters at the University of Georgia with the rest of Smith's papers.

Even though the letters were saved, the question remained: How could I use them in writing about Lillian Smith? Could they even be included in a volume of her collected letters? They were, after all, still guarded, still restricted material. Historian Blanche Wiesen Cook observed in the introduction to her biography of Eleanor Roosevelt that the restrictions on Eleanor Roosevelt's papers reflect the restrictions on women's lives and, therefore, our knowledge of women's history. She further noted that Eleanor Roosevelt herself and her friends exercised control over those letters and over the construction of their public lives, and that it was very important to them to maintain that control.[6]

Like Eleanor Roosevelt, Lillian Smith was quite conscious of herself as a historically significant figure. She wanted her life to be remembered. With the exception of the correspondence between her and Snelling, which I discovered in the hidden leather case and which Snelling herself had intended destroyed, it is no accident that Smith's letters were available for publication. At least for the last decade of her life, she kept carbons of her correspondence and arranged for her papers to be preserved. Yet the voice preserved in Smith's letters is often a public voice, for most of her personal papers were destroyed. A fire in 1955 destroyed Smith's home and with it many of her unpublished manuscripts, as well as her personal correspondence with her family. Even before 1955, however, it seems evident that Smith and Snelling intentionally destroyed most of their correspondence with each other, at least in part because they feared the disclosure of the intimate sexual nature of their relationship. Like Eleanor Roosevelt, and like most people I know, Lillian Smith and Paula Snelling had sought to exercise and maintain control over the construction of their public and private lives.

The problem, or question, for me as biographer was: Must I honor their desire to remain closeted? Was it possible, in effect, to write with integrity while trying to perpetuate the illusion that the supposedly offending expressions of sexuality could be effectively separated from all other aspects of their lives? Or would it be more helpful to address the question of why it was so important to Smith and Snelling to keep the full nature of their relationship hidden? What was the source of Smith's ambivalence and shame about her sexual attraction and love for Snelling? Was she ambivalent because she was attracted to men as well as to women? Or, as Smith so effectively demonstrated through her novels, *Strange Fruit* and *One Hour*, perhaps her ambivalence stemmed from her acute perception of the inadequacy of language, the inevitable failure of all labels, to convey the depth and complexity of human relationships. As Paula Snelling once remarked to me, "There's no word for what we do with words! As soon as we open our mouths to speak, we limit communication."

Yet, having finally acknowledged and begun to accept my own lesbian sexuality, I knew I could ignore neither the nature of Smith's relationship with Snelling nor the fact that her struggle with the ambivalence in her own heart greatly influenced not only her choices of self-definition but also the structure and content of her work. After months of indecision and avoidance, I began to see how the power behind the heterosexual/homosexual dichotomy that kept Smith closeted was likewise inhibiting my ability to write about her. Determined to confront my own demons, I began writing an essay on Smith's treatment of homosexuality. In the process, I realized that even while acknowledging the arbitrary and limiting nature of categories or labels, it was critical to redefine and push the limits of those categories, thereby claiming the power to create a new and more inclusive view of Smith, her life and her work.

Then, just as I decided I must return to Paula Snelling and ask her permission to use the letters she had told me to destroy, she died, in February 1985. In March, I presented the paper at the Southeastern Women's Studies Association Conference in Tuscaloosa, Alabama, but before I could determine how to gain permission from the Smiths to publish the quoted passages from some of the private letters, I received a letter from

Frank Smith, Lillian's brother, saying an unnamed source had told him about my recent paper, which he called "a little coup." He threatened to sue me if I published anything referring to Lillian Smith as lesbian. Shocked, I called to discuss the letter with Frank and reminded him that Paula had discussed their relationship with me. His response was that Paula was sick and had no right to say what she did. I called another member of the Smith family, a niece, whom I felt might reason with Frank. She asked to see a copy of the paper, which I sent. I then received a letter from Lillian Smith's sister Esther, saying, "You have killed my sister." I realized that my naming Lil as a closeted lesbian had, in fact, killed Esther Smith's image of her sister. The first time I met Esther, she had greeted me with these words: "I adored my sister." Clearly, she could not—at least, at that moment—adore a sister who was lesbian.

It was a scholar's nightmare. Without the Smiths' permission, I could not submit that essay for publication. For the next four years I felt effectively silenced, blocked in my writing, and I often wondered if Lillian Smith would ever be heard in her own full voice.

Still, I continued to search for and collect Smith's letters and tried to keep open the door of communication with the Smith family; but our formerly warm and supportive relationship was deeply strained. I felt Esther and Frank Smith believed I had betrayed their trust. I was plagued, at times, not only by a strong sense of rejection but also by grave doubts about my own perceptions, my own reading of Smith's life and work.

Finally, however, I realized I would complete the project of editing Smith's letters only if, once again, I faced my own fears, listened to my own voice, and wrote about her life as I saw it. As feminists and African American historians had done before with issues of gender and race, I moved the question of Smith's sexuality from the margin to the center, honoring her closeted relationship with Snelling as a source of power and inspiration, as well as ambivalence and shame, in Smith's life. Then, and only then, did the pieces of her life—her work as camp director, journalist, novelist, social activist; her personal and public friendships—begin to fall into place and assume the clarity I had not seen before.

I am not saying that writing the book was then easy. I labored for three more years to complete the manuscript, never knowing if, at the end, the Smith family would grant permission to publish the letters. As it turned out, my editor at the University of North Carolina Press was correct in believing that the value and power of the whole portrait would persuade the family not to censor what, taken in isolation, they had so vehemently condemned and denied. After reading the manuscript in its entirety, Esther Smith gave not only her permission to publish but also her praise.

Our expressions of sexuality, like our expressions of gender, race, and class, do not exist in isolation but emerge in relationship with one another. All are necessary in any effort to create a full portrait, whether of an individual or of a people, in any time or place. Lillian Smith was fond of saying that racial segregation was both symptom and symbol of the fragmented age in which she lived. Something similar may be said of the dichotomized structuring of sexual expression, which leads us to honor only what we call heterosexual or any one definition of lesbian or gay. While we cannot address sexuality in isolation, neither can we create the new, more nearly complete portrait of a subject until we can move what has been marginalized to a place of honor and respect. We have to step through the internalized as well as externally imposed boundaries of heterosexism. We have to step out of that seemingly safe spot called "normality" to make a new space from which to view the multifaceted subjects of our research, the complexity of ourselves and of our world.

NOTES

1. This chapter is a revised version of a talk given as part of "The Importance of Gay and Lesbian Library History" session, sponsored by the American Library Association's Library History Roundtable and Social Responsibilities Roundtable in honor of the twenty-fifth anniversary of the Gay, Lesbian, and Bisexual Task Force, Chicago, June 24, 1995.

2. Margaret Rose Gladney, ed., *How Am I to Be Heard? Letters of Lillian Smith* (Chapel Hill: University of North Carolina Press, 1993), p. 302.

3. Lillian Smith Collection #2337, Hargrett Rare Books and Manuscript Library, University of Georgia Libraries, Athens, GA.

4. Gladney, ed., *How Am I to Be Heard?* p. 136.

5. See Lillian Faderman, "Wastelands and Oases: The 1930s," in *Odd Girls and Twilight Lovers: A History of Lesbian Life in Twentieth-Century America* (New York: Columbia University Press, 1991).

6. Blanche Wiesen Cook, *Eleanor Roosevelt* (New York: Viking Penguin, 1992).

Ordinary Men and Would-Be Women
The Cold War Era

Chapter Seven

The Library, the Park, and the Pervert
Public Space and Homosexual Encounter in Post–World War II Atlanta

John Howard

Public restrooms are chosen by those who want homoerotic activity . . . for a number of reasons. They are accessible, easily recognized by the initiate, and provide little
public visibility. Tearooms thus offer the advantages of
both public and private settings.

—Laud Humphreys (1970)[1]

As children draw on toward maturity, they need, no less
than their parents, inviolate apartments in which their
hot discussions, their high confidences, their first essays
in courtship, may take place. For lack of such space in
America, a whole generation of girls and boys has grown
up, cramped in the vulgar promiscuities of the automobile, from which they are too often graduated proudly
into the no less shabby intimacies of the roadhouse or the
overnight cabin: carrying into their erotic life the taint of
something that is harried, esthetically embarrassing and
emotionally disintegrating. The home, the garden, and
the park, must be planned for lovers and for love-mak-
ing: that is an essential aspect of an environment designed for human growth.

—Lewis Mumford (1938)[2]

Any struggle to reconstitute power relations is a struggle
to reorganize their spatial bases.

—David Harvey (1990)[3]

Why were the 1950s an especially oppressive period for homosexual men in America? What unique forms, if any, did oppressive activity take in the American South? Historians of sexuality have offered various answers to the former question; they have overlooked the latter. Primarily a story of identity and culture formation in the cities, American lesbian and gay history has often ignored the experiences of women and men of the South—a section that more slowly evolved from a rural, agrarian economy to an urban, industrial one. By examining events in Atlanta, Georgia, during the height of the Cold War era, I will argue that a distinctive constellation of forces was at work in the lives of white, gay, male Southerners.

Specifically, I will show that the tenets of Protestant Christianity suffused institutional responses to a growing homosexual threat in postwar Atlanta, even as the targets of such surveillance—gay men caught in the act, in public spaces—likewise shared deep personal ties to an evangelical tradition. Elected officials, concerned with the state's expanding role in policing sexual morality, relied on religious precepts as guides to constructing public policy. Law enforcers and judicial interpreters enlisted religious leaders in their campaigns to eradicate deviant sexualities. Consequently, homosexual men were forced to negotiate the conflicting realms of individual spiritual life vis-á-vis an increasingly hostile, religiously based political climate. The nature of these linkages—between religious conviction and social tolerance, between spirituality and polity—suggests a cultural configuration unique to the Bible Belt South.[4]

Atlanta at mid-century was the Deep South's most populous metropolitan area. The lives of white Atlantans, therefore, cannot be made to speak for all Southerners, a vast number of whom still lived in rural areas. Black Southerners, working within and along the boundaries of a rigidly segregated society, confronted pervasive restrictions on economic and social mobility. The conclusions reached in this essay thus may have little or no applicability to the African American gay experience in the Jim Crow South, because the public places discussed were open only to whites. This article, in calling for a regionalist methodology in American lesbian and gay history, suggests the need for localized studies throughout the South *as elsewhere* and speculates that, in addition to its particular religious structures, the Southern lesbian and gay past will be characterized by its enduring racial categories.

The discourse generated in Atlanta over the use of public spaces for sexual activity, while pointing to peculiar religio-political formations, also offers new explanations for the increased surveillance and persecution of male homosexuals across the United States following World War II. More than an effort to resolidify gender norms tested by the trials of war, 1950s-era condemnation of homosexuality resulted from a heightened awareness of nonconforming sexualities made possible by the increasing movement of middle-class, heterosexual courtship into public spaces, the very spaces long occupied by marginal groups. Seemingly incompatible sexualities collided on the city's public terrain, forcing a binarized hetero-sexual/homosexual culture clash. Gay men became the scapegoats, as appropriate and inappropriate public sexualities were articulated. Thus, though they faced regionally specific forms of oppression, homosexual men implicated in the Atlanta Public Library Perversion Case and the Piedmont Park cleanup of the 1950s provide useful insights into the origins of the public outcry against homosexuality in towns and cities throughout the nation.

The Atlanta Public Library Perversion Case of 1953

On 4 September 1953, Pittman Davis, a twenty-eight-year-old male of ruddy complexion and medium build, entered the men's restroom of the Atlanta Public Library *not* for the purpose of using the toilet. An Atlanta resident, Davis knew, as did the blond-haired, blue-eyed, twenty-seven-year-old Robert Billings, that casual sexual encounters with other men could be had there. Neither Davis nor Billings was aware, however, that the Atlanta Police Department had staked out the facility at the request of library officials. Vice squad detectives witnessed the activity in the rest-room that day via a two-way mirror. They arrested the two men for sodomy, a felony under Georgia law, after Pittman Davis, as the charge read, "did have carnal knowledge of and connection with Robert Billings, against the order of nature . . . by taking and inserting the male organ of the said Billings into his . . . mouth." Davis and Billings were escorted to the city jail and booked. So were nine other pairs of men during eight days of arrests at the library. On 15 September solicitor general Paul Webb, a former Methodist preacher turned attorney, presented evidence to the Fulton County Grand Jury, which subsequently indicted all twenty men involved. Under the state statute, the accused faced extensive fines and maximum sentences of up to ten years in prison.[5]

The Atlanta Public Library Perversion Case, as it was dubbed by the daily *Atlanta Constitution*, resulted from distinct sexual practices that were not unique to the region or the era. Public space and homosexual encounter had long been linked, and to this day, men continue to find opportunities for homosexual intercourse in so-called public places, especially restrooms or "tearooms," as they are known in gay circles.[6] Yet the twenty men arrested in September 1953 belonged to a specific historical moment. They were subject to precise social and political forces, many of which were particular to the time and place. An examination of these men's experiences helps outline the contours of homosexual existence in post–World War II Atlanta and illuminates the practice of casual homosexual intercourse outside the private sphere. Furthermore, it suggests an understanding of public space and homosexual encounter that must go beyond issues of male sexual "promiscuity" and social, legal, and religious oppression to consider the spatial terms of the conflict. As the case shows, in an increasingly urbanized environment, subject to ever-expanding demands on common areas of access, a burgeoning gay male culture, limited in its alternatives, visibly and assertively made its stake along with other often competing interests on the city's publicly contested terrain.

Under questioning that Labor Day weekend in 1953, Pittman Davis told police that he was born in the small town of LaGrange, Georgia, near the state line of Alabama, where his mother still lived. College-educated, he had found a job as a personnel technician with the state government in Georgia's capital city of Atlanta. Similarly, Robert Billings had parlayed a college education along with seminary training into a ticket out of the rural South. Born in McComb, Mississippi, he had relocated to Atlanta and completed a divinity degree at Emory University. Three out of four defendants in the Atlanta Public Library Perversion Case were migrants to Atlanta. They came from the rural areas, communities, towns, and smaller cities of Alabama, Florida, Georgia, Mississippi, North and South Carolina, and Tennessee.[7] These men represented one small part of the process of urbanization that historically has been of vital importance to the development of lesbian and gay cultures in American cities.

While some of these men may have been sexual migrants, consciously opting for a freer arena of sexual expression over the constraints of family life, many were also drawn by the economic opportunities available to white men in segregated Atlanta during the 1950s. Most of the men, like Davis and Billings, enjoyed the benefits of higher education. Thus, these able-bodied, well-schooled young adults, the majority of whom were in their late twenties or early thirties, landed positions in a variety of occupations, ranging from working class to—more commonly—middle and upper-middle class. Many were clerks. Some were laborers, while others were among Atlanta's burgeoning professional class. Two were students; another a teacher. Yet, after news of the library arrests appeared several times in both the morning *Atlanta Constitution* and the evening *Atlanta Journal*—including the names and addresses of the accused—all of the men lost their jobs (with the exception of Jesse Hatcher, a butcher at an A & P supermarket).[8] The state of Georgia presumably fired Pittman Davis for his conduct. Under pressure, Robert Billings resigned the appointment he had received just months prior as Director of Youth Work for the Methodist Church's South Georgia Conference.[9]

Many of the library arrestees had little left to lose by the time they appeared in Fulton County Superior Court in December 1953. Yet they could not have expected leniency. Cold War America was in the throes of a moral panic previously unparalleled in twentieth-century experience.[10] Medical authorities and psychiatrists were disseminating jeremiads against sexual perverts and psychopaths in both the professional and popular media, while elected officials such as Senator Joseph McCarthy decried the homosexual menace threatening the nation's domestic front and its international security.[11] Locally, the Atlanta press reinforced these efforts, provoking public fears through a series of editorials and feature stories that often equated adult male homosexuals with child molesters.[12] At the dawn of the 1950s, according to the *Atlanta Constitution*, "Atlanta police view[ed] increasing sex crimes as the number one social problem of the day,"[13] and local politicians were demanding strict sentencing of sex offenders.[14]

Facing seemingly irrefutable evidence and hoping for mercy, Pittman Davis, Robert Billings, and all eighteen other defendants pled guilty to the charges of sodomy.[15] Their pleas were entered before Judge Virlyn B. Moore, who, at roughly eighty years of age, was nonetheless known for his sexual license. Defense attorneys had requested that their case be heard before Moore because he was, as Billings's lawyer James Mackay recalls, "a wonderful man. He had been through a number of marriages, and whatever libido is, he had more of it than all the rest of us put together. We figured that that would be a good guy to go for . . . a powerful heterosexual." As a result, however, the defendants were subjected to a great deal of ridicule and tactless courthouse humor, not only from the bench but also from their own attorneys (many of whom were reported to have overcharged their stigmatized clients, unlikely as they were to protest). Judge Moore asked one defendant if he had ever had intercourse with a woman, and when told "no," the judge admonished, "Now that's where you made your first mistake." The defense team viewed James Mackay, a former Georgia legislator and later U.S. congressman, as the best orator and most appropriate spokesperson for the group and elected him "mouthpiece" for the accused.[16]

In his decision, Judge Moore accepted the guilty pleas, imposed fines of up to two hundred dollars, and sentenced Davis and Billings and all but one of the others to two- to three-year terms. All sentences were either probated or suspended.[17] The ruling appeared "humane" to counsel, but the defendants could not have been pleased.[18]

While the media coverage and exploitation of the trial of the twenty men assured their loss of employment and their consequent economic marginality, the terms of probation enforced a geographic marginality, a reassertion of state control over public space. All men were instructed never again to "visit the Atlanta Public Library on any occasion for any purpose." Additionally, most were required to leave the area and, in the words of one probation order, "re-locate in some suitable community other than Atlanta." Furthermore, the legal system reaffirmed the societal dominion of the nuclear family and Protestant Christianity. In addition to being sent to "live at home in LaGrange, Georgia," with his mother, Pittman Davis was told to have all his probation reports countersigned by Presbyterian minister John Wilson of LaGrange. Though Robert Billings was not forced to return to his father in McComb, Mississippi, Judge Moore sent him to Memphis, where his brother resided, and put him under the supervision of Methodist pastor Charles Grant. Baptist preachers were also enlisted in service to the state, as at least five of the other felons were told to report to clergymen.[19]

Of the six men who were married at the time of the arrests, all but one were allowed to remain in Atlanta. As one of the reasons for granting probation to Jesse Hatcher, Judge Moore noted that Mary Hatcher, the defendant's wife, was expecting a child. Judge Moore gave the more desirable suspended sentences to Stanley T. Martin, a husband and father, and to Raymond Redmond, who had redeemed himself by signing on with the U.S. Army, despite its ten-year-old directive against homosexual enlistees.[20] Those who stayed in Atlanta, though able to secure new jobs, suffered from chronic underemployment. Martin, who worked as a branch manager for the Internal Revenue Service at the time of the arrests, became a salesman for Vulcan Paper. William Jones had his own business as a building contractor in 1953. By 1955, he was working as a tile setter with another company.[21]

Those accused in the Atlanta Public Library Perversion Case shouldered the burden of an institutionalized homophobia that permeated the city's legal, political, commercial, religious, and media structures. With the sole exception of Judge Moore's seemingly lenient sentencing, decisions made by those in positions of power assured that the twenty men bore the severest consequences for their actions. Most damaging was the local media's repeated printing of the arrestees' names and addresses before they were even tried. While not uncommon in contemporary press reporting—indeed, most anyone jailed or hospitalized during the era might be named in the Atlanta papers—editors indicated an added sense of responsibility in this so-called morals case. A need to shame defendants and thereby discourage others was evident in the frequency of the practice: editors of the jointly owned *Journal* and *Constitution* listed names and addresses in this case on at least six different occasions.

Remembered by some Georgians as "the most famous case of the decade,"[22] the Atlanta Public Library Perversion Case of 1953 represented just one of innumerable police crackdowns on homosexual activity in localities throughout the nation during the 1950s. Triggered by federal government purges begun in March of 1950, these actions reflected the social unease that lay beneath the veneer of domestic tranquillity and prosperity in the Atomic Age.[23] The oppression suffered by men caught in or suspected of homosexual acts indicated the severity with which social and sexual nonconformity could be treated. Legal sanctions, medical interdiction, media persecution, economic marginalization, and—perhaps more so in the Bible Belt South than elsewhere—religious indoctrination adhered to those who stepped out of line.

Tearooms and other public domains such as Atlanta's Piedmont Park constituted more than places of last resort for gay individuals who had few institutions with which to build a culture. The public sphere, for gay male urbanites in particular, was (and is) an institution in and of itself—dynamic, vibrant, evolving, and profoundly impacted in its evolution during and after World War II, as gay male cultures emerged. The homosocial environments that resulted from the massive mobilization of troops and workforces during the early 1940s, as well as the discursive explosion in which millions of recruits were asked about homosexual tendencies, fostered awareness and community among lesbians and gays at unprecedented levels.[24] As another vital gay institution, the bar, became embedded in the Southern urban landscape after the war, the tearoom and other public spaces increasingly became the haven for more closeted or covert members of the culture. During the 1940s and 1950s, however, prior to the widespread establishment of gay bars in Atlanta, the local tearooms and the parks apparently harbored many self-identified gay persons.[25]

Meanwhile, the heightened visibility of the gay male culture combined with the housing shortages and congestion of the postwar years forced a renegotiation of urban geography. A sexual turf war ensued. Legal, medical, media, commercial, and religious figures mediated existing public territorial boundaries, all the while revealing the fluidity of public and private realms. While white gay males continued to advance their claim on public places, authorities employed the most draconian methods of surveillance and retribution to probe and punish their intimate encounters, with troubling implications for society as a whole.

Piedmont Park and the Illumination of the Illicit

Legal-political scrutiny of sexuality was applied as well to Atlanta's heterosexual denizens, though with considerably more candor and jocularity, as a case from the same period illustrates. Between the time of the arrests and the sentencing of the defendants in the Atlanta Public Library Perversion Case, the plight of young heterosexual lovers in Atlanta attracted national and international press attention. Touched off by police concerns over public decency in city parks, a three-year intermittent debate over government policy ensued. In the process, participants helped to define and redefine local mores regarding sexuality, attempted to reestablish parameters for public and private domains, and outlined acceptable and unacceptable behaviors, heterosexual and homosexual, in both arenas.

In his attempt to prohibit the parking of automobiles in the city's parks from sundown to sunup, Police Chief Herbert Jenkins threatened what *Newsweek* magazine called "an Atlanta institution, dating back almost to the invention of the gasoline motor—the practice of parking bumper-to-bumper in Piedmont Park to smooch or pet or neck or whatever. . . ."[26] Jenkins called it "spooning" when he acknowledged to the Police Committee of the Atlanta City Council on 28 October 1953 that the vaguely defined practice was not, in and of itself, illegal.[27] However, as a result of the increasing numbers of nighttime parkers and complaints to his office,

Jenkins wanted the authority to make arrests when deemed necessary by his officers. As Jenkins explained his dilemma:

> We're supposed to enforce certain laws governing public decency. The curfew idea came up because of the difficulty in defining public decency. Except in extreme cases, it's a matter of opinion. Some people think kissing in a public place is indecent. Others think necking must go a lot farther than that before it can be called disorderly conduct and merit a court fine. The curfew was suggested as a means of either eliminating the question or getting the City Council to approve parking as long as no city or state morals law is violated.[28]

Approve it the City Council did.[29] Reform-minded Councilman John White led the overwhelming outcry for restoration of parking, conceding that "I used to park in Piedmont Park. . . . If I wasn't a married man and was younger," he added, 'I'd be out there myself."[30] According to an *Atlanta Journal* editorial, arguments for relegalization focused on issues of practicality and safety.

> A crowded city offers little of that privacy so necessary in the development of romance. Jammed housing, picture windows and the abolition of the porch combine to detract from the sentimental side of being young. Given the strange chemistry of youth and the goldfish-bowl nature of modern living, some adjustment in the national mores is inevitable. If youngsters feel bound to stop their cars to further the associations so dear to them, they will do so. Surely it is better for them to pause in city parks than on lonely roads. In a lighted park, police can keep a benign eye on the lovers, protecting them from the bandits who prey on parked couples in more out-of-the-way places.[31]

The Council's vote for parking on 2 November 1953 was unanimous.[32] Over national radio, Arthur Godfrey lauded the decision; Councilman White was a guest on Herb Shriner's TV quiz show *Two for the Money*; and the *Atlanta Journal and Constitution Magazine* proudly proclaimed in the headline of its lighthearted feature story "Love Is Legal in Piedmont Park."[33]

Members of the Atlanta Association of Baptist Churches took the matter much more seriously, however. Within a year, the group of clergy and laymen from one hundred twenty-eight area congregations debated the city statute at its annual meeting. Referring to the law as "an ordinance legalizing petting in Piedmont Park," a report of the social service committee lambasted the City Council and detailed in titillating language alleged wrongdoing in the park. As read by the Reverend Ralph T. Kyle, the document stated that "older men are seen with young girls, young men with older women, and evidences of drinking and sex indulgence are found behind the hedges. Policemen drive through the park and are aware of the evils transpiring," the Baptists lamented, "but are helpless to make arrests."[34]

Councilman John White, himself a deacon of the Second Ponce de Leon Baptist Church, defended the law he authored, noting the international acclaim that accompanied its passage. Moreover, he announced, "many cities and college campuses have followed our practice."[35] Nonetheless, the full body of the Atlanta Association of Baptist Churches approved an amended committee report on 20 October 1954 officially expressing its alarm over the city ordinance and vowing to investigate the situation further.[36]

Perhaps most troubling to the assembly and to some readers of the *Atlanta Constitution* and *Atlanta Journal* who followed the story, beyond the allegations of intergenerational heterosexual intercourse, was the specter of homosexual encounters in the park. Well known in gay circles as a nighttime gathering place and rendezvous for casual sex, Piedmont Park in midtown Atlanta served the intimate needs not only of the city's heterosexual community in the postwar period. The Baptists may have been the first to reveal this fact, however, to the larger populace. As their report stated and as was printed in the *Constitution*, the park, under the White ordinance, was also open to "fifteen hundred sex perverts" who could "legally pursue their devilish designs."[37]

The less-than-reliable figure of fifteen hundred clearly was drawn from a sensational story that the *Constitution* had printed "with some reluctance," given its "ugly subject," just nine days prior. Entitled "1,500 Sex Deviates Roam Streets Here," the article, which filled the entire second page of the 11 October 1954 issue, disclosed that "bulging files of secret police information . . . include names of more than 1,500 known perverts . . . big names and little names, from laborers to executives and professional men."[38] Though the story purported to document activities of a specific class of pervert, the child molester, the text reflected the common tendency among the media of the day to conflate man-man consensual sex with man-boy or man-girl child molestation.[39] Convoluted images of homosexual men and potentially homosexual adolescents surface:

A great majority of the deviates are homosexual, usually not violently dangerous, but—as [an Atlanta vice] investigator pointed out—potentially dangerous if in fear of being caught. Experts here say that evidence indicates that otherwise normal children sometimes come under the influence of molesters and are actually converted to a life of sex perversion. In his more innocuous form, the pervert too often is regarded as merely a "queer" person who hurts no one but himself. The public loses sight of the fact that these sex degenerates are inveterate seducers of the young of both sexes.[40]

As early as 1949, the *Constitution* editor, the venerated civil rights advocate Ralph McGill, called for tougher sex crimes legislation as well as psychiatric treatment for offenders, a more progressive stance.[41] In another editorial that year, the *Constitution* noted a case before the Fulton County Grand Jury involving a young boy and a fifty-year-old man, whose "alleged offense had its beginning in Piedmont Park." "Within the past two years," it was added, the newspaper had "received complaints from parents in that neighborhood of their children being molested."[42] Indeed, Piedmont Park was the site of several cases of alleged child molestation in the 1940s and 1950s. In assessing the perceived explosion in the number of such cases throughout the nation, Police Chief Herbert Jenkins was careful to stress, however, that in Atlanta, at least, "police records show[ed] increases in sex crimes only in proportion to population increases."[43]

Throughout 1955, Baptists and other civic/religious groups, informed by media accounts of sexual misconduct, continued to pressure the City Council for modifications to parking regulations in Piedmont Park. In February, the Atlanta PTA Council, a group of representatives from the Parent-Teacher Associations of the city's eighty-seven white schools, passed a resolution urging the installation of more lights in Piedmont Park, as well as an increase in the frequency and scope of police patrols there.[44] Backed by the Atlanta Association of Baptist Churches and the Atlanta Methodist Ministerial Association, the PTA proposal obscured the underlying threat of homosexual activity and only cryptically implied its continued prevalence, mentioning that "dangerous, immoral practices" in the park were engaged in not only by teenagers in automobiles, but also by adults on foot. They recommended that policemen and park supervisors "be authorized and directed to investigate apparent irregularities of occupants in cars or on park premises."[45]

Councilman John White responded two days later, promising to step up patrols, to illuminate unlighted portions of Piedmont Park, and to modernize existing lighting as needed. Additionally, new fines were mandated for the vandalization of lighting systems. Plagued by incidents of lights being shot out and wires cut—eighteen lights installed a few months later in "one of the favorite spots for spooners" shone for only two hours—the Council instituted a penalty of $200 for destruction of property and granted rewards of $25 to those who reported vandals.[46] By spring of 1956, the city had spent $30,000 to illuminate the park and vowed to spend $35,000 the following year in Grant Park in south Atlanta.[47] On 31 March 1956, when Mayor William B. Hartsfield threw the switch in the lighting ceremony at Piedmont Park, he was able to declare that, for the safety of Atlanta's citizens, the new systems would provide nighttime visitors and police patrolmen with "almost daylight" conditions.[48]

Illumination meant revelation of the gay culture which already occupied Piedmont Park. In seeking first and foremost to shed light, and thus a measure of safety, on heterosexual couples parking on the grounds, city fathers uncovered the homosexual activity that had long been a trademark of this and other public spaces. As heterosexual courtship assumed a new visibility and legitimacy in the public sphere, homosexual men shared in that visibility, but became all the more illegitimate. Thus, lighting served the dual purpose of, first, keeping heterosexual romance within acceptable, preferably nonsexual bounds and, second, exposing and thereby eliminating, it was hoped, the previously unmentionable homosexual presence in the park. But as John D'Emilio avers, using classic Foucaultian logic, such visibility, while facilitating police crackdowns and mustering public sentiments against homosexuality in the short run, permitted a discourse and awareness that helped forge gay identity and aided the development of lesbian and gay cultures over the long run.[49] While pastors, politicians, policemen, and physicians felt compelled, though "with some reluctance," to address the "ugly subject" of homosexuality, the very act of doing so promoted the culture they hoped to squelch. Visibility fostered identity, and with identity came community.[50]

Policing Sexuality and Gender in Atlanta, 1945–1959

Though initially reluctant to serve as enforcers of sexual conduct in Piedmont Park, preferring to close the park in the evenings rather than monitor nighttime strollers and parkers, the Atlanta Police Department by the late 1950s had assumed the central role in maintaining sexual order in the city. Their jurisdiction spilled over from public spaces such as streets and parks into commercial spaces such as newsstands, theaters, and hotel rooms. From World War II through the dawn of the 1960s, law enforcement officers, prodded by religious authorities, increasingly insinuated themselves into a sexual milieu that crossed the boundaries of public and private spheres.

The spread of syphilis and gonorrhea during World War II touched off fears of an epidemic in Atlanta as elsewhere.[51] An important wartime production center and hub for nearby military installations, the city witnessed police raids on hotel rooms and arrests for prostitution that peaked at the war's end.[52] Also, in the late 1940s, undercover policewomen staked out downtown moviehouses to catch "wolves"—men making unwanted advances on female patrons.[53]

Again area Baptists were instrumental in spurring legal action against the sexually marginal when, in 1957, officials raided a downtown newsstand. Acting on a complaint filed by the Georgia Literature Commission, headed by Reverend James Wesberry of Morningside Baptist Church, solicitor general Paul Webb, who had successfully prosecuted the Atlanta Public Library Perversion Case twenty, took out a warrant to search the News Shop. As a result, the Fulton County Grand Jury indicted three men for selling a magazine seemingly aimed at the homosexual consumer. According to the indictment the newsstand operators were charged with "unlawfully" possessing and offering for sale "a certain indecent, immoral and obscene magazine known as and entitled *Adam*."[54]

The policing of sexual proclivities led quite naturally to the enforcement of gender norms, as officers stepped up efforts in the late 1950s to combat cross-dressing. Thomas Elliott, age twenty-four, an Emory University employee, was arrested at the Atlanta airport on 21 August 1957 on a charge of disorderly conduct–disturbance. Wearing sunglasses, sandals, a skirt, and a scarf over his head, Elliott was given the choice of a $50 fine or fifty days in jail. The municipal court further levied a fine of $200 or sixty days for violating a Klan-era city code that prohibited "wearing a mask, device or hood whereby the face is so hidden or covered as to conceal the identity of the wearer."[55] In March of 1959, Ralph Ferguson, a twenty-six-year-old schoolteacher from Illinois, was passing through Atlanta on his way to Florida for spring break. Spotted by a woman in the ladies' restroom of a downtown theater, Ferguson was arrested for wearing a green jacket, a plaid skirt, a bandanna around his head, and a conspicuously undersized pair of shoes. Ferguson's "big feet," according to police detectives, were "his undoing."[56]

Given this history of public regulation and police surveillance of sexuality in Atlanta, it was only fitting that detectives would use a two-way mirror to stop sodomy violations at the library and that the City Council would approve massive lighting expenditures to allow patrolmen to more closely monitor sexual activity in Piedmont Park. The Atlanta police, Fulton County grand jurors, local residents, and their social, political, and religious leaders grew to expect an aggressive, interventionist, and predominant role for lawmakers and law enforcement officers in the regulation of sexuality in postwar Atlanta. This shift in authority from family to polity signaled a similar transformation taking place in the geographical dynamics of sexual relations. Changes in the powers exerting influence over sexual activity reflected changes in the spaces being utilized for sexual encounters.

Heterosexual-Homosexual Collision in the Public Sphere

Why were the 1950s an especially oppressive period for homosexual men in America? Events in Atlanta suggest a new explanation to be considered along with various other contributing factors. In addition to Cold War–era concerns over the communist threat, family stability, gender roles, and sexual, social, and moral conformity, the public hysteria over homosexuality and the resulting police crackdowns on male homosexual activity in postwar America must be understood in light of the steady movement of heterosexual, primarily middle-class, courtship rituals from a circumscribed private sphere to a broader public realm. The need for ever-wider areas of public access for heterosexual dating prescribed the ways in which the legal-political establishment in Atlanta and elsewhere brokered public lands and demarcated acceptable activities therein.

John D'Emilio explains the "intensification of the penalties directed at lesbians and gay men" in the 1950s in terms of shifting gender and familial arrangements begun two decades prior.[57] The uncertainties of the Atomic Age fostered attempts to stabilize and solidify gender norms and family patterns that were disrupted by the Great Depression and World War II.[58] In so doing, Americans clearly opted for one-half of what Martin Duberman calls

> the schizophrenic split that has always marked our national character: the
> split between our rhetorical defense of "individualism" and the strong con-

tradictory pressure to conform. Now and then, conformist pressure sweeps all before it; a righteous conviction takes hold that there is only one way to be "a good American."[59]

Good Americans got married, raised children, went to church, and moved to the suburbs. In contrast, physicians and psychiatrists, enjoying the continued ascendency of medical authority over matters of sex, love, and homelife, commented on the perversions committed in the dark recesses of the city. As they promulgated a disease model of homosexuality that tied same-sex affections to mental illness, the Kinsey reports reminded Americans just how common such sexual practices could be.[60]

Meanwhile, changes in postwar modes of living did enable the development of viable lesbian and gay communities in the nation's cities. The backlash resulted from real increases in lesbian and gay visibility.[61] Yet the homosexual presence would not have been so keenly felt and the homosexual threat not so deeply feared in the 1950s had not young heterosexual couples extended their romantic forays into the public realm.

In her 1988 monograph, Beth Bailey shows that heterosexual courtship took a peculiarly twentieth-century shape when couples abandoned the tradition of "calling" in the private home and began dating in the public sphere. The automobile enabled the system that predominated from the 1920s onward, as young lovers moved, in the words of Bailey's title, "from front porch to back seat."[62] Postwar prosperity spurred automobile purchases and entertainment consumption; young couples drove to the movies, dances, and ballgames, to soda fountains, restaurants, and community centers, and ultimately to quieter, more intimate settings for romance.[63] Parking and a distinctive petting culture reached their zenith. No longer content to court and spark in their parents' living rooms, teens and young adults used the automobile interior as a surrogate parlor. Large car models featured two roomy bench seats and an expansive flat-top dashboard analogous to the sofas and coffee table of a standard middle-class den. Automobile advertising highlighted such luxuries, showing that mobile Americans could nonetheless enjoy all the comforts of home.[64]

Though initially hesitant, Atlantans ultimately adopted the automobile with vigor. In 1921, a grand jury investigated the connections between cars and moral degeneration in Atlanta, much to the satisfaction of a local judge who declared "that a large percentage of cases are the direct result of too much automobile and too little parental control."[65] Yet by 1930, more motor vehicles were registered in Atlanta than in any other city in the South, and by 1980, more motor vehicles were registered per capita in the South than in any other section of the United States.[66]

As young Atlantans drove into the night, escaping parental authority exercised at home, their final destination was often a secluded lovers' lane. Realizing their loss of control, Atlanta's mothers and fathers deferred to politicians and police officers in monitoring sexual behavior. If young women and men were to take to the public byways for dating, public officials would be held accountable for their actions. Thus, parking was assigned to areas such as Piedmont Park, where under the watchful eye of less-than-benign patrolmen, young heterosexual couples might find romance and love.[67] What they also found and exposed, seemingly for the first time in the 1950s, was a thriving, lively homosexual underground that had previously existed outside the purview of most Atlanta residents.

Religious-Political Power Structures in the South

If changes in heterosexual courtship brought heterosexual and homosexual worlds into conflict over public space—if a sexual turf war indeed was waged—and if the increased visibility of homosexuals prompted an oppressive backlash throughout the United States, the question remains: What unique forms, if any, did oppressive activity take in the American South? The events and players in the sexual controversies of postwar Atlanta suggest that the distinctive religious life of the South influenced the ways in which the public regulation of sexuality proceeded. Responsibility for sexual behavior in the city shifted not only from the family to the legal establishment but from the family to the multifaceted but cohesive religious hierarchy in Atlanta. White Protestant Christianity of an evangelical variety dominated social and political life and thereby began to dominate the ways in which public institutions addressed sexuality.[68]

"The distinctive course of southern religious history," Samuel Hill writes, is to be found in the relationship of religion to politics. "The South's religious-political understanding . . . is [its] singular tradition."

> It derives more from revivalistic Protestantism, its theology and methods, than from any rationalized interpretation of the proper relationship between church and state. In certain respects, it reflects its descent from Calvinism, notably in its conviction that religion and politics (church and state) are partners in creating and maintaining a godly society. . . . The mood is not "the less government the better" nor is it "remove government from public

affairs so that the private sector can do its work. ...." Southern political concern has not sought to lessen the role of government, rather to place the right quality of people in office.[69]

Thus it was that the solicitor general, Paul Webb, who prosecuted the twenty sodomites and the peddlers of homoerotica, was a former Methodist minister. James Wesberry, the head of the Georgia Literature Commission who forced the confiscation of the magazine *Adam*, was a Baptist preacher. The men who denounced sexual libertinism in Piedmont Park and shaped public policy at mid-decade were Baptist and Methodist clergy and laymen. The councilman who defended the city's decision to allow parking was a Baptist deacon. And many of the men who served as parole supervisors for the Atlanta Public Library convicts were Baptist, Methodist, or Presbyterian ministers. (That one of the men convicted, Robert Billings, was in the process of becoming an ordained Methodist pastor points to possible variations in Biblical interpretation, at least at the level of the individual.)

While Clarence Stone's landmark portrayal of Atlanta's nonmachine, coalition politics—"the informal partnership between city hall and the downtown business elite"—glaringly omits references to church leaders,[70] it is inconceivable that the discursive explosion accompanying the reconfiguration of sexual boundaries in 1950s Atlanta could have proceeded without the voices of the city's religious doctrinaires. They customarily directed public policy in a variety of matters, and their insights were particularly valued and solicited regarding issues of sexual morality. But the political structure in Atlanta not only evinced a willingness by politicians to consult clerics. Holders of public office and leaders of religious organizations were often one and the same. The political structure was religious to the core, just as church hierarchies were patently politicized.

Moreover, religious sentiment effected broader public attitudes toward homosexuality in the South.[71] Orthodox Biblical-literalists within the South's Baptist-Methodist hegemony helped make the section one of the most intolerant to issues of sexuality. During one of the most oppressive eras—the 1950s—male homosexuality suffered under the strain of this force that, though incapable of crushing the culture, indelibly molded and shaped its development.

In September 1947, shortly after Herbert Jenkins became Atlanta's Chief of Police, a position he would hold for a quarter of a century, the members of the International Association of Chiefs of Police met in Duluth, Minnesota. There they heard their criminologist, Dr. Carleton Simon, give a disturbing account of rising sex crimes. Opening with a reference to the Biblical cities of Sodom and Gomorrah, Simon recited FBI statistics "verifying" the upsurge in sex offenses in the United States, and he detailed the harrowing practices and "perverse sex instincts" of "homosexualists" [sic].[72] Simon's remarks set the tone for police responses to homosexuality in the United States throughout the postwar period.

Making only cursory mention of sex between females and the "unspeakable perversion" of "bulldyking" in women's prisons, Simon painted a lurid picture of male homosexuals as "venal prostitutes," suicidal "blackmailers," and marijuana addicts—"being female in everything but their sex organs." Within this litany of stereotype and falsehood, Simon pinpointed two notably accurate features of gay male cultures in postwar America. First, homosexuals were attracted to large cities, "where the selective field is more expanded and where, if necessary, they can cover up their predilections." Second, "their herding instinct being very pronounced," homosexuals were prone to "gathering in definite places" within the urban landscape, "public latrines [being] their favorite hunting grounds."[73]

As Chief Jenkins soon could attest, men from throughout the rural South migrated to the section's principal urban center, Atlanta, after World War II, strengthening the gay dominion over their traditional spatial bases. In restrooms, parks, and other facilities, men desiring homosexual encounters congregated and intermingled, appropriating public space as legitimate ground for activities deemed illegal. These maneuvers coincided with the dismantling of a heterosexual porch-and-parlor system originating in the Victorian era, in which "courtship [was] an intensely private affair."[74] As middle-class heterosexuals—like working-class Americans of that and previous generations[75]—turned to the streets and parks as sites for romance, homosexual and heterosexual worlds collided.

This contestation over public space and public policy occurred within the context of an ongoing and expanding national discourse over the problems of youth and sex, petting, and going steady; the varieties of sexual practice, as reflected in the Kinsey reports; child molestation and other forms of sexual deviancy; and Cold War–era family structures and gender norms. Americans were paying more attention to sex, increasing the visibility of, but fostering a strident backlash against, gay white males. Sociologists, medical experts, and political figures, with the aid of elec-

tronic and print media, stirred public opinion, and in the South particularly, evangelical Protestantism framed discussions of sexuality and the
state. If the regulation of sexuality was shifting between family and polity,
the transformations would be carefully dictated by church leaders, perpetuating a heightened awareness and monitoring of sexual behaviors
and meanings. For homosexual men in Atlanta, monitoring led to persecution, and the nascent gay culture suffered setback after setback as an
already public sexuality clashed with an increasingly public policing of
sexuality.

NOTES

This essay first appeared in *Radical History Review* 62 (spring 1995): 166–87. Portions
were presented to the Southern American Studies Association Conference in New
Orleans, 28 February 1993, and to the Joint Conference of the California and
Rocky Mountain American Studies Associations in Reno, 1 May 1993. The essay
is dedicated to the memory of Charles Albert Sligh, 1961–1993. For invaluable
commentary, I am grateful to Nancy Koppelman and to Julie Abraham, Lynne
Adrian, Patricia Penn Hilden, Andrew Koppelman, Cliff Kuhn, Catherine Nickerson, Roy Rosenzweig, Allen Tullos, and Dana White.

1. Laud Humphreys, *Tearoom Trade: Impersonal Sex in Public Places*, enl. ed. (New
York: Aldine de Gruyter, 1975; 1970), 2–3.

2. Lewis Mumford, *The Culture of Cities* (New York: Harcourt Brace Jovanovich,
1970; 1938), 432–33.

3. David Harvey, *The Condition of Postmodernity* (Cambridge, MA: Blackwell,
1990), 238.

4. On the usefulness and difficulty of locating and defining a "Bible Belt," a
phrase seemingly coined by H. L. Mencken, see Edwin S. Gaustad, "Religious
Demography of the South," in *Religion and the Solid South,* ed. Samuel S. Hill Jr.
(Nashville: Abingdon Press, 1972).

5. *Atlanta Constitution* (15–16 September 1953). *Atlanta Journal* (5, 9–11, 16
September 1953; 18 November 1953). Fulton County Courthouse, Records of the
Fulton County Grand Jury, Criminal Bench Docket 40, Indictments 69816–69835,
1953.

6. Joan Nestle cautions against assumptions that casual sex in public places
was limited to gay men alone. Though it is "tempting for some Lesbians to see
themselves as the clean sex deviant, to disassociate themselves from public sexual
activity, multiple partners, and intergenerational sex," she says, "public bathrooms
have been social bedrooms for young Lesbians through the years who had no safe
home to take their lovers back to." *A Restricted Country* (Ithaca, NY: Firebrand

Books, 1987). Nonetheless, there are comparatively few accounts of lesbian activity in public spaces as compared to male homosexuality. In the period under question, for example, there are no newspaper accounts of lesbianism in Atlanta.

Regarding sex between men, Julie Abraham writes: "Even if that extensive history of religious and legal attention was punitive, it still offers a wise and complex range of sources for contemporary study. It hardly needs to be said that this history also testifies to a public concern with male behavior. . . . Not only is there no comparably extensive history of reference to lesbian sexuality," she adds, "but assertions of lesbian sexuality are still not easily marked as transgressive," explaining in part the relatively lackluster pursuit of lesbian sex crimes. "I Know What Boys Like: Tales from the Dyke Side," *Voice Literary Supplement* 106 (June 1992): 20.

7. Atlanta Police Department, Bureau of Identification, Numbers 94695–8, 94714–5, 94717, 94721, 94726–7, 94731–2, 94740–1, 94773, 94783–6, September 1953.

8. *Atlanta City Directory,* 1950–51, 1953, 1955, 1956. *Atlanta Suburban Directory,* 1954.

9. *Official Journal and Year Book of South Georgia Annual Conference of the Methodist Church, Eighty-eighth Session* (Albany, 1953), 16, 31. *Official Journal and Year Book of South Georgia Annual Conference of the Methodist Church, Eighty-ninth Session* (St. Simon's Island, 1954), 28, 45.

10. Adopting the term "moral panic" from Jeffrey Weeks, Gayle Rubin compares this period of recodification of sexual relations with 1880s England and late-1970s America. "Thinking Sex: Notes for a Radical Theory of the Politics of Sexuality," in *Pleasure and Danger: Exploring Female Sexuality,* ed. Carole S. Vance (Boston: Routledge & Kegan Paul, 1988), 267–319.

11. Estelle Freedman, " 'Uncontrolled Desires': The Response to the Sexual Psychopath, 1920–1960," in *Passion and Power: Sexuality in History,* ed. Kathy Peiss and Christina Simmons (Philadelphia: Temple University Press, 1989), 199–225. John D'Emilio, "The Homosexual Menace: The Politics of Sexuality in Cold War America," in *Making Trouble: Essays on Gay History, Politics, and the University* (New York: Routledge, 1992), 57–73.

12. *Atlanta Constitution* (13 April 1949; 7–8 December 1949; 27 July 1951; 11, 13 October 1954). *Atlanta Journal* (31 May 1951; 25 June 1959).

13. *Atlanta Constitution* (8 December 1949).

14. *Atlanta Constitution* (14, 17 April 1949).

15. *Atlanta Constitution* (2 December 1953). *Atlanta Journal* (1, 10, 22 December 1953).

16. James A. Mackay, telephone conversation with author, 23 February 1993. Mackay's father was a Methodist minister. As an indication of the friendly rivalry between Baptists and Methodists, Mackay remembers joking that, since he was defending a Methodist seminarian, he was glad there were Baptists among the accused as well.

17. Fulton County Grand Jury. Despite Moore's acquiescence, not all men avoided prison. John Wobbe, who was forced out of his job as a clerk at Rich's department store, relocated to Miami where he secured employment with another department store. Roughly a year and a half later, he was picked up by Miami police for petty larceny on the job. Wobbe's probation was revoked in Atlanta, and he was forced to return to Georgia and serve jail time for the remainder of his sentence on the sodomy conviction. Incarcerated in May of 1955, he was released 17 July 1956. *Atlanta Journal* (20 May 1955). Fulton County Grand Jury, Revoked Order of Probation, Number 69835.

18. Telephone conversation with Mackay.

19. Fulton County Grand Jury Indictments 69816–69835.

20. Ibid.

21. *Atlanta City Directory, 1953, 1955.*

22. Telephone conversation with Mackay.

23. D'Emilio, "Homosexual Menace."

24. Allan Bérubé, *Coming Out under Fire: The History of Gay Men and Women in World War Two* (New York: Plume, 1991; Free Press, 1990). John D'Emilio, *Sexual Politics, Sexual Communities: The Making of a Homosexual Minority in the United States, 1940–1970* (Chicago: University of Chicago Press, 1983).

25. Atlanta's earliest official acknowledgment of gay bars—"night spots where known perverts congregate"—appears to have been a 1955 grand jury present-ment urging greater police surveillance. *Atlanta Journal* (29 April 1955). Only six of the twenty arrestees in the Atlanta Public Library Perversion Case were married (and presumably closeted), whereas a study of one hundred tearoom participants in St. Louis from 1968, a decade and a half later, found that "the majority . . . were married . . . and nearly all of them quite secretive about their deviant activity." Humphreys, *Tearoom Trade*, 41.

26. "Love in Atlanta," *Newsweek* (16 November 1953), 32–33.

27. *Atlanta Journal* (29 October 1953).

28. Olive Ann Burns, "Love Is Legal in Piedmont Park," *Atlanta Journal and Constitution Magazine* (27 December 1953), 8–10.

29. *Atlanta Journal* (3 November 1953).

30. "Love in Atlanta," 33.

31. *Atlanta Journal* (3 November 1953).

32. Ibid.

33. Burns, "Love is Legal," 10.

34. *Atlanta Constitution* (20 October 1954).

35. *Atlanta Journal* (20 October 1954).

36. *Atlanta Journal* (21 October 1954). Some disagreement among the Baptists is evident in their amending of the document, primarily to tone down hyperbolic language. An implied conflict of "personalities" suggested in the newspaper cover-age might refer to White and an equally charismatic figure, James Wesberry,

mentioned later in this essay. As pastor of the eight-hundred-member Morningside Baptist Church, Wesberry also had national television experience (delivering sermons) and had for a short time served as Acting Chaplain of the U.S. House of Representatives. Both Morningside and Second Ponce de Leon were large, affluent churches, in which such leaders could rise to considerable stature and power. As Baptists engaged local political issues and positioned themselves within associational hierarchies, the voices of clergy and laity from smaller, lower-middle- and working-class churches may have been lost in the din of publicity. Wesberry went on to serve as the president of the Georgia Baptist Convention in both 1957 and 1958. The Piedmont Park spooning ordinance is not mentioned in his biography: James C. Bryant, *The Morningside Man: A Biography of James Picket Wesberry* (Atlanta: Morningside Baptist Church, 1975). *The History of the Georgia Baptist Convention, 1822–1972* (Atlanta: Executive Committee, Baptist Convention of the State of Georgia, 1972) is a denominationally funded, positivist tract that elides conflict.

37. *Atlanta Constitution* (20 October 1954).

38. *Atlanta Constitution* (11 October 1954).

39. Indeed, the *Constitution*'s first article on the Atlanta Public Library Perversion Case (15 September 1953) included a "related" story on Jack Calvin Macaulay, a twenty-four-year-old Boy Scout official who was sentenced in adjacent DeKalb County, Georgia, to ten years in prison for sodomizing underage scouts.

40. *Atlanta Constitution* (11 October 1954). A letter from J. Edgar Hoover to editors throughout the country prompted this exposé and hundreds of others like it in the late 1940s and 1950s. For similar accounts in nationally distributed, popular magazines, including a story penned by the FBI Director himself, see J. Edgar Hoover, "How Safe Is Your Daughter?" *American Magazine* (July 1947), 32–33, 102–4; Ralph H. Major Jr., "New Moral Menace to Our Youth," *Coronet* (September 1950), 101–8; "Let's Be Honest about Homosexuals," *Our World* (August 1954), 48–49. In these accounts, homosexuality was seen not only as a recent phenomenon but also as a treacherously escalating one. Homosexual men were invariably portrayed as sick, deranged, and inclined to prey on youths.

41. *Atlanta Constitution* (7–8 December 1949). On the mid-century ascendency of the psychiatric model, see Bérubé, *Coming Out under Fire*, 146–74, 258–60.

42. *Atlanta Constitution* (13 April 1949).

43. *Atlanta Constitution* (8 December 1949).

44. *Atlanta Journal* (4 February 1955).

45. Ibid.

46. *Atlanta Journal and Constitution* (6 February 1955). *Atlanta Journal* (4 June 1955).

47. *Atlanta Journal* (7 February 1955; 6 August 1955). *Atlanta Journal and Constitution* (12 June 1955).

48. *Atlanta Journal* (20 March 1956).

49. D'Emilio, *Sexual Politics*.

50. Documents collected and oral history interviews conducted by a present-day community group known as the Atlanta Lesbian and Gay History Thing are just now being made available to researchers through the Atlanta History Center Archives. These materials tentatively suggest that while distinct commercial spaces frequented by lesbians and gay men were scarce during the 1950s, self-identified gay men congregated not only in public spaces but also at private parties in homes. Circumspect but self-conscious networks of friends and acquaintances attest to at least some level of community development.

51. Allan M. Brandt, *No Magic Bullet: A Social History of Venereal Disease in the United States since 1880*, exp. ed. (New York: Oxford University Press, 1987; 1985), 161–74.

52. For numbers of prostitution arrests as well as tests for venereal diseases, which were disproportionately administered to black female arrestees, see *Atlanta Police Department Annual Report*, 1946–1947, 1949–1951, 1953–1959. For Police Chief Jenkins' justification of the arrests, see Clifford M. Kuhn, Harlon E. Joyce, and E. Bernard West, *Living Atlanta: An Oral History of the City, 1914–1948* (Athens: University of Georgia Press, 1990), 358–60.

53. On "Jenkins' Masher Commandos," police officers Emily Hart and Ruby Barrett, and the theater arrests, see *Atlanta Journal* (31 March 1947).

54. *Atlanta Journal* (31 August 1957). For additional pornography arrests during the period, see *Atlanta Journal* (17 June 1948; 30 January 1952; 16 February 1952). Also see Bryant, *The Morningside Man*, 135–49, for more on Wesberry's twenty-year tenure with the censorious Georgia Literature Commission, organized by Governor Herman Talmadge in 1953.

55. *Atlanta Journal* (29 August 1957).

56. *Atlanta Journal* (30 March 1959).

57. D'Emilio, "Homosexual Menace," 65.

58. See Elaine Tyler May, *Homeward Bound: American Families in the Cold War Era* (New York: Basic, 1988).

59. Martin Duberman, *About Time: Exploring the Gay Past*, rev. exp. ed. (New York: Meridian, 1991; 1986), 180.

60. In "The Scientist as Sex Crusader: Alfred C. Kinsey and American Culture," *American Quarterly* 29 (winter 1977): 563–89, Regina Markell Morantz asserts that the American people, "accepting the legitimacy of [Kinsey's] research with the respect they afforded all science . . . rapidly made his work part of the conventional wisdom." Interestingly, though, both scientists and popularizers tended to ignore Kinsey's non-bipolar model in an attempt to rigidly differentiate heterosexuals and homosexuals.

61. In the case of New York, George Chauncey shows that a complex gay world was "forced into hiding in the 1930s, '40s, and '50s" due to its "very growth and visibility . . . during the Prohibition years of the 1920s and early 1930s . . ." —a time in that city when homosexuality was much more widely tolerated. George

Chauncey, *Gay New York: Gender, Urban Culture, and the Making of the Gay Male World, 1890–1940* (New York: Basic, 1994), 8.

62. Beth L. Bailey, *From Front Porch to Back Seat: Courtship in Twentieth Century America* (Baltimore: Johns Hopkins University Press, 1988).

63. On women's agency in what has long seemed a male-dominated sphere, see Virginia Scharff, *Taking the Wheel: Women and the Coming of the Motor Age* (New York: Free Press, 1991).

64. I am indebted to Catherine Nickerson for insightfully pointing up this analogy. See advertisements from any popular magazine or newspaper from the 1950s.

65. David R. Goldfield and Blaine A. Brownell, "The Automobile and the City in the American South," in *The Economic and Social Effects of the Spread of Motor Vehicles*, ed. Theo Barker (London: Macmillan, 1987), 121.

66. Ibid.

67. See also David L. Lewis, "Sex and the Automobile: From Rumble Seats to Rockin' Vans," in *The Automobile and American Culture*, ed. David L. Lewis and Laurence Goldstein (Ann Arbor: University of Michigan Press, 1983), 123–33.

68. The extent and relative uniformity of religious life in Georgia (and the South more broadly) is impressive. Between 1906 and 1971, Georgian membership in Christian denominations rose from 42 to 60 percent of the populace. Baptists in both Southern Baptist Convention–affiliated and independent congregations accounted for well over half those numbers. When combined with doctrinally similar Methodists, they accounted for 92 and 83 percent of all Georgia church members in 1906 and 1971 respectively. Wayne Mixon, "Georgia," in *Encyclopedia of Religion in the South*, ed. Samuel S. Hill (Macon, GA: Mercer University Press, 1984), 289–304.

69. Samuel S. Hill, "Religion and Politics in the South," in *Religion in the South*, ed. Charles Reagan Wilson (Jackson: University Press of Mississippi, 1985), 147–48.

70. Clarence N. Stone, *Regime Politics: Governing Atlanta, 1946–1988* (Lawrence: University Press of Kansas, 1989), 3.

71. As summarized by David F. Greenberg, *The Construction of Homosexuality* (Chicago: University of Chicago Press, 1988), 468, survey research shows that "religion is a more powerful predictor than any other individual trait" in assessing tolerance of sexual difference, and "evangelical Protestants are the most likely to think homosexuality immoral." Furthermore, he notes, "respondents from the South, from small towns, and from rural areas, who are older, poorer, and less well-educated, are more likely to think homosexuality morally wrong and to oppose gay rights." While these surveys were conducted in the early 1980s, their relationship to values and attitudes in the 1950s is worth considering. That Southern Baptist Convention publications didn't even address the issue of homosexuality until the late 1960s suggests a consensus of opinion that such behavior was sinful, unspeakable even. Certainly, Baptist and Methodist proclamations from the

early 1970s left little room for interpretation: Homosexuality was incompatible with Christian teaching. See Thomas Furman Hewitt, "The American Church's Reaction to the Homophile Movement, 1948–1978" (Ph.D. diss., Duke University, 1983).

72. Carleton Simon, "Homosexualists and Sex Crimes" (paper delivered at the meeting of the International Association of Chiefs of Police, Duluth, MN, 21–25 September 1947), 1.

73. Ibid., 2–4.

74. John D'Emilio and Estelle B. Freedman, *Intimate Matters: A History of Sexuality in America* (New York: Harper and Row, 1988), 75.

75. On working-class formulations of homosexuality and the public sphere in New York, see Chauncey, *Gay New York*. Working-class heterosexuality in the streets and parks of New York is examined in Christine Stansell, *City of Women: Sex and Class in New York, 1789–1860* (Urbana: University of Illinois Press, 1987).

Chapter Eight

Closet Crusaders

The Johns Committee and Homophobia, 1956–1965

James A. Schnur

Sigismond Diettrich received the telephone call on 19 January 1959.[1] The polite caller convinced Diettrich, an eminent scholar and chair of the University of Florida's geography department, to meet with agents of a state investigative body that evening. The dubious inquisitors grilled the professor for nearly ninety minutes. They confronted him with allegations of homosexuality from an informant who conceded that he had never actually witnessed Diettrich in a sexual act. While Diettrich staunchly denied these unsubstantiated accounts, under duress he did acknowledge other brief encounters with consenting adult males.

Diettrich knew that his career at the Gainesville campus had ended when President J. Wayne Reitz and the dean of the College of Arts and Sciences called him into an office on 16 March 1959 and dismissed him from the faculty. After leaving this meeting, Diettrich ingested eighty-five aspirin and contemplated suicide by planning to jump from the upper floor of a classroom building. Though he never carried out his plan, Diettrich left the campus a week later, considering himself a traitor to his family, his colleagues, and the university. The Johns Committee had claimed another victim.[2]

From 1956 to 1965, the Johns Committee sought to curtail civil liberties in the Sunshine State. Officially known as the Florida Legislative Investigation Committee (FLIC), this state agency trivialized civil rights, compromised academic freedom, and threatened the constitutional protections supposedly afforded to all Floridians. As U.S. Senator Joseph McCarthy's national influence waned, the landmark 1954 *Brown v. Board of Education of Topeka* decision and the nascent civil rights movement persuaded Southern politicians to investigate any person or organization that violated customs and traditions preserving racial segregation. Hence the FLIC sanctified the dogma of its namesake member, Senator Charley E. Johns of Starke, Florida, and forwarded the interests of "porkchoppers," the county-seat elites who preserved romantic notions of the past and who blamed a monolithic enemy for any perceived threats to their way of life. When McCarthyite tactics failed to destroy the National Association for the Advancement of Colored People (NAACP) and similar groups, the committee launched a relentless crusade against a contrived "homosexual menace"—a crusade that eventually embarrassed legislators and later compelled them to seal the FLIC's records until 31 December 2028.[3]

Demands to bolster Florida's otherwise liberal public records act reinvigorated interest in the Johns Committee. Lawmakers opened their closet of secrecy after Floridians resoundingly approved a November 1992 constitutional amendment, thereby guaranteeing access to nearly all public documents as of 1 July 1993. While the unveiling of the FLIC's records confirmed the agency's distrust of educational institutions and dislike of integrationists, scrutiny of these manuscripts also revealed a story heretofore untold: The committee's archives recount both the systematic persecution of actual and suspected homosexuals throughout Florida and the FLIC's desire to work with similar bodies to establish regional and national bureaus that would remove legal protections from anyone arbitrarily deemed a "sex pervert." Similar to national studies that have documented the lesbian and gay experience prior to the 1969 Stonewall riots, the historiography of homosexuality in Florida must transcend Anita Bryant's acerbic 1977 campaign to repeal Dade County's gay rights ordinance by evaluating the activities of the Johns Committee in the emerging cold war climate.[4]

As noted, the legislature originally authorized the Johns Committee as a means of decimating the civil rights movement. As acting governor of Florida from 1953 to 1955, Charley Johns had promised to dismiss any educator who supported the NAACP. When Johns returned to the state senate in 1955, he modified his earlier proposal for a body to study criminal activities when he included an anti-integration proviso in the Florida Legislative Investigation Committee Act. He envisaged this legislation as a way to circumvent the *Brown* decision, quell the Tallahassee bus boycott, and halt demands for civil rights reform. After lawmakers empowered the FLIC during the 1956 special session, committee members established operating procedures and initiated investigations. The Johns

Committee conducted many meetings in executive session, allowed the chair to issue public statements only with the approval of fellow members, and refused to share any information before completing its inquiry. Although the state attorney general's office found no provision that permitted the FLIC to cite uncooperative witnesses for contempt, the committee stipulated that "refusal to answer a proper question will subject a witness to contempt proceedings." The FLIC hoped to dismantle Florida NAACP chapters when it denied deponents the right either to consult with counsel during testimony or to place prepared statements in the record without the committee's approval. As the FLIC purged integrationists from university campuses and attempted to seize NAACP membership records, however, Johns faced the specter of informing his senate colleagues that his committee had failed to demonstrate communist complicity by either the NAACP or the academic community. He decided to shock lawmakers into extending his interim committee by searching for a more vulnerable enemy: homosexuals in the state of Florida.[5]

Johns quietly dispatched an investigator to search for homosexuals at the University of Florida (UF) during the summer of 1958. Rumors and innuendo offered the FLIC a long-awaited opportunity to create a conspiracy that linked homosexuality, subversion, and integration. Jerome Johns, the senator's son and a UF student, told his father that effeminate instructors had perverted the curriculum. Soon thereafter, FLIC investigator Remus J. Strickland met a black man who claimed that he had engaged in lascivious acts with male faculty members at the all-white university. Johns enjoined Strickland to conduct his inquiry with the utmost secrecy because the 1957 enabling act did not permit the FLIC to search for homosexuals. Strickland also operated covertly for practical reasons: He hoped to maintain an element of surprise and avoid attracting negative publicity that might threaten the FLIC. Thus Johns sent assignments to Strickland through the committee's chief counsel, Mark Hawes.[6]

Ironically, Johns had shunned a similar opportunity to search for homosexuals during his tenure as acting governor (September 1953–January 1955). When administrators at Florida State University (FSU) forced associate professor Robert L. Leathers to resign, Leathers claimed that FSU president Doak S. Campbell condoned homosexual behavior on campus. Although Johns did schedule a public hearing on Leathers's behalf in December 1954, he later promised FSU administrators that he would not "stick his nose" into the inquiry. While Johns refused to intervene in the earlier controversy at FSU, he knew the UF probe satisfied the expedient political motives of the committee.[7]

Earlier homosexual witch-hunts provided a foundation for the tactics used in the University of Florida probe. During the spring of 1957, committee members and officers from the state Sheriff's Bureau interrogated staff at the Southwest Florida Tuberculosis Hospital in Tampa. While Johns and the sheriff's chief investigator issued a directive ordering state employees to offer full cooperation, they also secretly sent information to the Federal Bureau of Investigation (FBI) for background checks. The committee warned one staff member that if he refused to implicate the hospital's medical director, the FLIC would have him sentenced to prison for twenty years. After the interviewee informed the director of the state Tuberculosis Board of this harrowing session, the Johns Committee sent for the distraught subject, connected him to the polygraph machine, and forced him to submit to further questioning. Testimony gathered from him and from other hospital employees gave the committee the impression that homosexual teachers in Hillsborough County had obtained their positions with the clandestine assistance of subversive university faculty.[8]

To fortify this perceived conspiracy among gays on college campuses, the Johns Committee contacted two UF students who had conducted their own inquiry. In the fall of 1955—prior to the FLIC's creation—two undergraduates undertook a monthlong investigation for the school's newspaper, *The Alligator*. They invited "known deviates" to visit their dormitory and secretly recorded conversations from an adjoining room. When *The Alligator* refused to publish their article, the disgruntled junior detectives gave campus administrators the names of students and faculty mentioned on the tapes. The shallowness of this probe became evident to Hawes and Strickland when they questioned the two students. One of the students acknowledged that he "never knew about these people actively recruiting anyone, except those who wanted to join." When agents pressed the students to divulge names, they claimed they had created the list "without any proof at all." Even though the students admitted that gays posed no menace to the campus community, in his October 1958 progress report, Strickland boasted that he had uncovered "a considerable homosexual operation" that merited further investigation.[9]

The committee looked for homosexual activity in a variety of locations. Hawes and Strickland discovered that gays often congregated at the Burger House bar near campus, as well as at the "chicken farm," a private home in rural Alachua County, five miles outside of Gainesville. They also heard of "purple passion parties," gatherings where young men drank and fraternized in dimly lit rooms. Concerned that faculty members engaged in homosexual acts away from the university, investigators surveyed the Cross Creek residence where Marjorie Kinnan Rawlings—author of *The Yearling* and *South Moon Under*—had once lived. Many prominent faculty, including College of Law professor Phillip Keyes Yonge, went on retreats to the Cross Creek home after Rawlings's death in 1953.[10]

The men's lavatory at the Alachua County Courthouse served as the focal point for much of the UF investigation. The county sheriff, who had once served as chief of the university's police department, agreed to give the Johns Committee full authority to monitor the building's public restrooms. In this corrupt bargain, the sheriff even supported Strickland's plan to keep the facilities open during the evening to attract traffic. Strickland persuaded UF police chief Audie Shuler to reassign a few campus officers from their regular duties so that they could serve as decoys in and provide surveillance of the courthouse restrooms. After police arrested individuals for committing lewd acts, committee members used coercive interrogation tactics to try to link restroom activities with members of the university community. Mark Hawes referred one man arrested at the courthouse to the campus police department so that officers could arrange for him to observe faculty members covertly in their classrooms. Hawes then expected the subject to name every instructor he had witnessed in or near the courthouse. For his part, Strickland preferred guilt by association. For example, he asked one man caught in the restroom if "some of these people were dressed in such a way and their mannerisms were of such nature that they were or could have been connected to the University of Florida."[11]

The committee intimidated the faculty members it interrogated. Strickland hired student informants with FLIC funds, used highway patrolmen to remove professors from the classroom, and telephoned some instructors late at night, demanding that they provide testimony in Strickland's motel room at his convenience. He also prohibited the accused from confronting their complainants, seldom informed subjects of their legal or constitutional rights, and rarely offered them sufficient time to secure an attorney or to prepare their defense. Like the authors of the unpublished *Alligator* article, most informants provided hearsay evidence at best. Often the committee settled for less, even securing the deposition of one student who deemed professors "queer" by "observation of them in class . . . the way they act . . . nothing specific" and another who named an instructor because he wore Bermuda shorts on campus. Although state policy required that teachers charged with moral turpitude receive a formal hearing before the Florida Board of Education, Strickland circumvented the law by acting as both prosecutor and jury. Hawes cautioned one unyielding educator "to testify fully and truthfully before this Committee, or you are going to fail to do so at your own peril." Many interviewees cowered under such pressure and gave the FLIC the names of suspected homosexuals.[12]

Students, too, faced the committee's wrath. While faculty and staff suffered immediate dismissal if accused of homosexuality, gay students could remain on campus only if they visited the infirmary and submitted to psychiatric treatments throughout their academic career. As committee members scrutinized the patient records of the University of Florida's clinic, the threat of expulsion continued to haunt those students under orders to receive counseling. The FLIC compelled personnel at the UF health center to disclose information found in patient records and demanded that medical professionals identify the basic "disturbance" or "illness" that fostered homosexual desires in each of the students obtaining psychiatric care. The committee also reserved the right to seize clinical records, as it did when investigators confiscated paperwork on thirty-five female students who had given birth out of wedlock at the UF facility.[13]

UF president Reitz cooperated with the Johns Committee because his superiors failed to intervene on the University of Florida's behalf. Although Governor LeRoy Collins alienated lawmakers with his moderate stand on racial integration and his campaign for equitable legislative reapportionment, he permitted previous FLIC enabling acts to become law without his signature because he realized that any mediation in the UF probe would jeopardize his programs for the 1959 biennial legislative session. The governing body for Florida's universities, the Board of Control, ceded its authority to the committee by sanctioning abuses in the FLIC's investigations. On 27 September 1958, three Board of Control members met with the committee and soon thereafter directed Reitz to cooperate with Strickland. In February 1959, Reitz and the board each received a report of approximately nineteen hundred pages, documenting the committee's inquiry. A substantial portion of the testimony included the provocative title "Crimes against Nature at the University of Florida."[14]

Two months later the committee shared its findings from the University of Florida investigation with lawmakers in Tallahassee. On 13 April 1959, the FLIC reassured legislators that "in conducting this investigation, it has been and still is the prime concern of this Committee that nothing be done to injure the good name of the university and the vast majority of its faculty and students." Based on the questionable testimony collected by the committee, Johns surmised that an untold number of homosexual teachers allegedly used coercion and manipulation to recruit youngsters for sexual encounters. To reinforce the pervasive anti-intellectual sentiments found in the legislature, the FLIC report insinuated that homosexual behavior tended to increase with educational attainment. Johns encouraged his colleagues to enact provisions requiring a centralized file of personnel records, the fingerprinting of present and potential government employees, and the forfeiting of state retirement benefits for educators dismissed due to moral misconduct. Hawes and Strickland summarized their investigation at a locked-door senate session on 30 April 1959. Although they spoke in general terms and gave few specific details, they persuaded the legislature to extend the committee's life for two more years so it could "investigate any agitator who may appear in Florida." Even the dismissal of more than fifty students and the termination of more than twenty employees did not satisfy Johns, as the university continued to suffer from probes into the 1960s.[15]

Similar homophobic witch-hunts besieged Florida State University. When the school's newspaper, *The Flambeau*, criticized Senator Dewey M. Johnson for attempting to oust an FSU professor, the *Sarasota News* defended Johnson, a former vice chair of the FLIC. Since the Johns Committee had performed so well in Gainesville, the *News* argued that it should relocate to FSU. Although the committee had previously monitored civil rights activities on the Tallahassee campus, it did not launch a thorough probe of homosexuals at FSU until the state hired William Tanner, a former FBI officer, to assist its investigations. Charley Johns may have ignored Leathers's pleas to interfere at FSU in the early 1950s, but he had since discovered that hearsay and innuendo could easily destroy others. The committee worked with FSU campus security officers to entrap students, faculty, and staff. In addition to the informants who frequented parks and other public facilities, the state hired an agent who invited male students to congregate at a house in suburban Tallahassee. The agent gained the confidence of the young men by hosting parties and other social events. When the intended victims gained the trust of their host, they went with him into a bedroom and gossiped about others at the party. The agent secretly taped these conversations and sent them to Tanner, who summoned participants to his office, questioned them about their involvement, and had them expelled.[16]

School officers encouraged the removal of homosexuals from Florida State University. Although Strickland later claimed that FSU's close connections to the committee spared the university from probes similar to those in Gainesville, investigators performed more than a few raids. Indeed, the Tallahassee campaign resembled the earlier purges in both ferocity and disregard for the constitutional protections of the accused. In tactics similar to those used at the Alachua County Courthouse, committee agents and local deputies served as decoys at the Greyhound and Trailways bus station restrooms. Strickland and Burl Peacock from the city's police department planted a tape machine in their vehicle, thereby allowing them secretly to record conversations with suspects before placing them under oath in a formal interrogation session. When university administrators implored the committee to interview their students and faculty on campus, Senator Johns rebuffed this proposal by holding hearings in the capitol and by refusing to allow the chair of FSU's disciplinary committee to attend. (Johns did invite Tanner, however.) The FLIC also hired student informants at FSU, including one woman who first provided Tanner with the names of suspected lesbians and later agreed to lure women into a bugged motel room. Even though this woman fabricated her "evidence," Strickland detained many women on her list and seriously considered her suggestion that the committee hire student informants from each dormitory to "act" gay.[17]

The Committee also visited the nearby Florida Agricultural and Mechanical University (FAMU). The state's university for African Americans, FAMU had endured a Jim Crow system that offered the school only a paucity of financial appropriations and instructional support. Porkchoppers had refused to elevate the college to university status until late 1953, when a growing body of case law necessitated the illusion of separate yet equal facilities. In late 1956 the FLIC launched a covert investigation of FAMU students and faculty who supported the Tallahassee bus boycott and the integrationist Inter-Civic Council. During the course of his inquiry, Strickland located some FAMU students who, under intense interrogation, claimed that at least one-quarter of the university's faculty practiced homosexual acts. Agents frequently asked gay African Americans if they had ever engaged in acts with whites of the same sex. Based on the uncorroborated statements of a few questionable witnesses, the committee proclaimed that a subversive network of homosexuals compromised the university's governance structure. For example, after agents discovered a gay employee in FAMU's purchasing office, they seized requisition forms and attempted to oversee the daily operations of the department.[18]

Investigators derived a perverse pleasure from discrediting African Americans. Just as Southern whites had perpetuated the myth that black males possessed an immoderate virility that endangered white womanhood, the committee hoped its probes would debase black homosexuals by portraying them as less than human. For example, the committee ordered one FAMU student to "name me another person. Do you know a . . . light skinned nigger that lives down there on Macomb Street? . . . Where is this boy now?" And while some agents monitored events at the FAMU campus, Strickland visited the Clearwater offices of the Pinellas County school board. He interrogated many educators at this location, including Thomas F. Pinson and William J. Neal, faculty members at Gibbs Junior College, a black educational institution. St. Petersburg police officers had detained Pinson when they saw him driving in a white neighborhood. After holding him on a charge of night prowling, detectives compelled Pinson to confess to sexual liaisons. Strickland grilled Neal, an instructor in music, for nearly eight hours. When Neal refused to submit to Strickland's tactics, the temperamental investigator warned Neal that he would never teach anywhere in America. Referring to the teacher as an "educated nigra," Strickland constantly reminded Neal that he had taken an oath, asked if he knew the statutory penalties for perjury, and wondered if he had committed crimes "up North." Shortly after this session, Strickland had authorities revoke Neal's certification. Devastated by the FLIC's witch-hunt, Neal relocated to Maryland and filed a lawsuit to restore his teaching license.[19]

As inquiries led Strickland and his agents from Pensacola to Miami, they used their resources to embarrass blacks who supported the civil rights movement. In a manner similar to the detailed lists they had maintained on the NAACP and other integrationist organizations, committee operatives painstakingly recorded hearsay to destroy African American educators, as when they created a file on school administrators who allegedly "derive[d] sex satisfaction through the rectum."[20]

Regardless of their race, gay and lesbian public schoolteachers had much to fear from the Johns Committee's inquisition. Homosexual educators whom the FLIC exposed faced immediate personal humiliation and professional alienation, as one teacher quickly learned when Strickland asked, in McCarthyite fashion, "Do you know now, or have you known in the past any teacher in the public school system of this state who is a homosexual?" Investigators generally concentrated their probes on urbanized counties. Concerned that homosexual teachers might depart before he could interrogate them, Strickland told Hawes to urge county superintendents not to accept resignations unless the instructors willingly forfeited their certificates or consented to exit interviews. In early 1961, Strickland joined forces with highway troopers and officers from the Metro Dade Public Safety Department. During the spring, detectives spent their evenings visiting "gay addresses" and arresting uncooperative residents throughout Dade County, most of them teachers or other public servants. The committee welcomed the services of veteran investigator James D. Barker, a man who shared Strickland's disdain for civil liberties and due process.[21]

While Barker and Strickland entrapped private citizens, Hawes and other committee members prepared reports and potential legislation for the 1961 biennial session. The committee told lawmakers that despite "its limited staff, funds, and time," it had located homosexuals "in shocking and appalling numbers" that surpassed estimates given in the 1959 report. Substituting homosexuality for pedophilia, the FLIC argued that the gay teachers who "permeated even the public school system . . . invariably turn[ed] to the recruitment of young people as sex partners." Committee members cited statistics: Since 1959, they had persuaded the state Board of Education to revoke thirty-nine teaching certificates—with fourteen additional cases pending—and had testimony supposedly incriminating seventy-five additional teachers and seven university professors. The committee also hoped to disquiet legislators by reporting that agents had confiscated nearly eight thousand pieces of "pornographic paraphernalia." This strategy gave the Johns Committee the mandate it desired. The 1961 enabling legislation sanctioned probes documenting the "infiltration of agencies supported by state funds by practicing homosexuals and the policies of state agencies in dealing therewith."[22]

The legislative decree strengthened the committee's resolve. In November 1961, Charley Johns dispatched a generic letter to administrative officers throughout the state bureaucracy, indicating that the FLIC planned to conduct public hearings and to examine departmental policies concerning the employment of homosexuals. He insisted that "it will not be the purpose of the Committee to receive any evidence in regard to the extent of this problem in our various state institutions. Neither will it be the purpose of this Committee to identify or single out any homosexual." According to Johns, the FLIC intended only to perform its legislative mandate by examining the personnel policies of various agencies. Although Johns promised to conduct this inquiry with "a very high level of dignity without injuriously affecting any state department or administrative officer," his belief that lax regulations had permitted homosexuals to endanger the government by moving from one agency to another impelled him to predict a "serious and substantial problem" that would portend numerous terminations.[23]

Authorities tendered prompt responses to Johns's letter. When the senator read these replies, he wrote comments on the letters such as "no real policy," "make further inquiry," or "bull—get facts[;] what about their records?" Johns placed the last annotation on a reply sent by the director of the state Tuberculosis Board. Remembering the FLIC's 1957 purge of the Tampa hospital, Johns ordered Strickland to have the director provide copies of his agency's personnel records to the committee. Johns also put university presidents on the defensive: While Reitz pledged the continued support of UF's police detectives, FSU president Gordon W. Blackwell assured Johns that his school maintained files on dismissed students and staff. John S. Allen, president of the newly opened University of South Florida (USF), believed that "by exchange of information we can be helpful to each other." Strickland visited FAMU president George W. Gore after Johns had ordered the investigator to "get facts." Despite the moderate tone of Johns's November letter, Gore divulged names because he feared the committee's wrath. Many of the school and college authorities who offered to assist Johns in future probes soon had an opportunity to share their ideas with the committee.[24]

The FLIC invited many administrators to testify at its April 1962 hearings. Committee members believed the combination of a centralized employment-records clearinghouse and the fingerprinting of all state workers would "keep homosexuals from infiltrating public jobs." Most educators agreed with the committee's program, although a few of them thought the FLIC's proposal to withhold the retirement benefits of terminated homosexual employees went too far. Some authorities who thought the committee should do even more to punish homosexuals also proffered their suggestions. For example, the personnel director from Polk County's school district believed any suspected homosexual "should not be in a classroom, regardless of whether or not he has been proved guilty" of any crime. A Broward County colleague confessed that he felt uncertain about hiring bachelors or teachers who had resigned during the middle of the school year. One junior college administrator requested an increase in his travel budget so he could journey to the present residences of prospective employees. These witnesses espoused the sentiments of Thomas D. Bailey, Florida's superintendent of public instruction. Bailey praised the cooperative relationship existing between his Board of Education and the committee, a political marriage that gave Strickland unrestricted access to the superintendent's records. FLIC members expressed a sense of pride that their homophobic campaigns had garnered the support of the Florida Education Association (FEA). Bailey's office and Strickland's agents often shared personnel information with FEA leaders. The FEA warned teachers appearing before the committee to yield their Fifth Amendment protections and advocated that the state disqualify from classroom teaching anyone who had ever experienced any type or degree of homosexual contact.[25]

Assistance also came from the executive branch of the state government. In January 1962, Governor C. Farris Bryant welcomed more than sixty patrolmen to an academy he had established in conjunction with the Sheriff's Bureau. Bryant assembled a circuit judge, a prison official, a parole commissioner, and numerous attorneys, all of whom served as the "faculty" that would teach law enforcement officers a variety of ways to expose homosexuals. Worried that the press might reveal their strategy, officials banned journalists from attending these workshops. Meanwhile, Bryant also asked the Florida Children's Commission to forge a cooperative relationship with the FLIC and police departments. While the governor privately envisioned this alliance as a means of expurgating gay employees from the state payroll, he publicly stated that "this problem is serious, but not sensational. . . . We are seeking to approach it with maturity and with understanding." Johns and Strickland, now serving as *de facto* members of the Children's Commission, exploited this additional mandate to their committee's advantage. Strickland boasted that he had collected the names of several thousand homosexuals. Yet, when pressed to provide a more specific estimate, he conceded that "I don't have any idea. . . . There's a lot of them. . . . We have a lot of education work *[sic]* to do." Although the chief investigator continued to cultivate a closeted conspiracy, the acting director of the Children's Commission praised him for his efforts to curb "this social and moral problem."[26]

While legislators on the Johns Committee concluded their hearings in Tallahassee, Hawes and Strickland accepted a new assignment in Tampa. Porkchoppers viewed the University of South Florida as anathema. When he had assembled faculty for the state's first metropolitan university, President John Allen had angered reactionaries by proclaiming that "there are no fences, no boundaries holding us and limiting our search for knowledge or our methods of teaching knowledge." A sense of idealism and missionary zeal thrived on campus after classes began in the fall of 1960. However, by early 1962 a group of concerned Floridians secretly contacted the committee and implored Johns to cleanse USF of supposedly "unpatriotic" individuals. In April 1962, Mark Hawes and Remus Strickland began a stealth probe of homosexual activities, subversive influences, and teaching methods at USF, from a Tampa motel room that was often frequented by prostitutes. Thomas Wenner, a USF instructor sympathetic to the committee's goals, invited approximately forty students to his home for a social gathering and dinner. Although the FLIC later disavowed any connection with Wenner, both Hawes and Strickland attended this function. The chaperons questioned their student guests about conditions at the university, following Johns's edict to quietly collect evidence and to select student informants with the utmost care. After a brief investigation at the Florida School for Boys in Marianna, Hawes and Strickland returned to Tampa and devoted their energies to the USF investigation.[27]

Committee members hoped to cloak their activities in secrecy. As in the UF investigation, police officers removed students from their classes for interrogation. Agents obtained information from vindictive and unreliable sources. One interviewee regarded USF's head librarian as "effeminate . . . possibly a homosexual [and] possibly the weakest link among the faculty." Other professors aroused suspicion because they ate lunch together or had a "butch" haircut. A student accused a dean of homosexual tendencies after he "stirred up a big stink last year with the idea of not wearing shorts on campus." This student later implicated an instructor in English, basing his information entirely on "things kids have said about him in class. I have never had a class with him, but I have seen him. He's very bashful, shy person [sic]." In similar fashion, a few other students made contradictory remarks about a graphics coordinator. Committee members sought to discredit USF president Allen by branding him as a subversive with the "characteristics of a homo." [28]

By May 1962, Wenner viewed himself as USF's expert on political and moral depravity and criticized Hawes for moving too slowly in the investigation. He decided to expedite matters by informing the press of the committee's presence. His plan backfired. After reading Wenner's disclosure in the 18 May 1962 *St. Petersburg Times*, Strickland called the instructor and said he worried "about the possibility of it coming out." While Allen promptly suspended Wenner and Governor Bryant independently sought the insubordinate lecturer's dismissal, the FLIC attempted to distance itself from Wenner by claiming it had come to Tampa to defend the infant university from outside attacks. Allen warned Hawes and Strickland that if they planned to take further testimony, they should do so on campus, in the presence of university authorities. Between 23 May 1962 and 7 June 1962, the FLIC questioned those who chose to appear and gathered nearly twenty-five hundred pages of sworn testimony. Hawes and Strickland concluded their official investigation after only two weeks on campus. Not surprisingly, they continued to conduct interviews in their Tampa motel room. On 6 June 1962, Johns asserted that the FLIC did not find "too much wrong with this beautiful university" yet hinted that he would probably recommend disciplinary action. Although Johns originally promised to transmit the committee's report to board members and campus authorities before releasing information to the public, he allowed a Tampa newspaper to publish a selectively edited, fifty-three page summary on 25 August 1962, at a time when most university officials—including President Allen—spent their vacations outside of Florida.[29]

Johns wanted this report to discredit administrators and faculty at USF. Committee members lambasted Allen for promoting a climate that supposedly allowed "subversive" professors to persuade "naive" students, through salacious reading materials and indoctrination, to question orthodox religious, moral, and sexual practices. However, excerpts released by the newspaper refuted the committee's outrageous suppositions. Admitting in their report that they had devoted scant time or effort to searching for homosexuals, FLIC investigators "believe[d] this problem not to be of great magnitude at the University of South Florida at this time." The testimony also failed to reveal any Communists or fellow travelers at USF. Realizing that gay students and faculty had never posed any threat to the university, the FLIC tried to craft this report to emphasize teaching methods and classroom assignments rather than private behaviors. Thus the FLIC scorned Professor Henry Winthrop for discussing sexuality in his course on human behavior and criticized numerous other faculty members for introducing their students to the "intellectual garbage" written by Margaret Mead, Aldous Huxley, and J. D. Salinger, among others.[30]

Three signal events placed the committee on the defensive before it met with legislators at the 1963 biennial session. During the fall of 1962, Sheldon Grebstein—a recently hired English instructor at USF—assigned a Norman Podhoretz essay critical of beatnik authors to his advanced writing class. The Board of Control and the Johns Committee immediately summoned President Allen to a secret Gainesville meeting and demanded Grebstein's dismissal for exposing students to this *Partisan Review* article. In light of the board's refusal to disclose any of the accusers, clarify the charges, or allow the professor to defend himself, Florida's scholarly community protested this blatant violation of academic freedom. Although Grebstein soon left USF and moved to New York to assume a position in an area with "more freedom in the intellectual atmosphere [and] a more enlightened citizenry," his ordeal prompted public outrage and galvanized the mass media's opposition to the committee.[31]

The second event developed because Strickland so detested members of the press. Robert Delaney—a reporter stationed at the *Orlando Sentinel*'s Tallahassee bureau and frequent critic of the committee—met a woman at a bowling alley who called herself Janet Lee. Two nights later, on 10 February 1963, Delaney met Lee at a motel in Tallahassee. While Strickland peered through a window, Burl Peacock and other police officers watched from an adjoining room. After hearing a signal, agents rushed into the room, took compromising pictures of Delaney, and arrested the reporter for committing an unnatural sex act. But after Delaney's subsequent removal from the *Sentinel* and the capitol press corps, the committee suffered further embarrassment when the public learned that not only had *Strickland* booked the room, he had also permitted Lee to register with an alias and allowed her to disappear before the trial. Soon thereafter the Tallahassee police chief acknowledged that his officers regularly cooperated with Strickland by establishing traps in motel rooms.[32]

A decision by Florida's supreme court constrained the FLIC's investigative powers and represented the third event that placed the committee on the defensive. On 27 February 1963, justices refused to rehear an October 1962 pronouncement in *William Neal v. Farris Bryant, et al.* In this case, the court restored the teaching certificates of three Pinellas County educators, including former Gibbs Junior College instructor William Neal, by asserting that the 1959 FLIC enabling act prohibited the Johns Committee from probing allegations of moral turpitude. When rendering its verdict, the state's supreme court built on its earlier stipulation that the committee could not exceed its duly constituted authority under the guise of uncovering so-called subversive activities in civil rights organizations. According to the justices, the state Board of Education failed to follow departmental policy when it revoked the petitioners' certificates in 1961. The board erred when it permitted R. J. Strickland to conduct hearings on its behalf—knowing that he lacked the statutory mandate to determine probable cause—and used the contents of his dubious testimony as the sole reason for nullifying the teachers' licenses. The court further proclaimed that the committee's enabling legislation during the 1959 biennium never gave Strickland the authority to search for homosexuals, invoke subpoena power against gays, or threaten to call public hearings, regardless of any tacit agreement he had fashioned with Superintendent Thomas Bailey.[33]

The 1963 legislative session marked a turning point for the Johns Committee. Reeling from recent events, the committee tried to justify Delaney's arrest and the USF investigations. Counsel Mark Hawes denied that the FLIC had entrapped Delaney, instead arguing that Strickland had hired the mysterious Janet Lee and other secret informants to capture lesbians. Disavowing any plan to ensnare the committee's critics, Hawes added that agents would never interfere in "any man-woman relationship, regardless of how unnatural it is or how strange." He failed to tell lawmakers, however, that Lee had received generous informant fees to engage in carnal acts at the very time the criminal court in Pensacola had placed her under its supervision because she had killed a former husband. (The Escambia County Court and Strickland had negotiated a secret agreement that made Lee, *de facto*, an employee of the state who earned her salary by seeking sexual favors and thereby violating her probation.) Still, because some legislators had begun to fear the committee's prowess at uncovering liaisons, they offered their support with the hope that agents would refrain from opening any closets in the capitol. On 18 April 1963, Hawes delivered a verbal assault against the University of South Florida, contending that the school's faculty and curriculum brazenly defied taxpayers by endangering the state's welfare. Although USF president Allen received moral support for his subsequent defense of the university and academic freedom, the FLIC persuaded legislators to extend the committee's mandate until 1965 and more than doubled its fiscal appropriation.[34]

The committee sought to distance itself from past blunders. Hawes and Strickland left the FLIC in August 1963, after Representative Richard O. Mitchell assumed the chair from Senator Johns. Although Johns remained a member of the committee, he mourned the changes wrought by this reorganization, exclaiming that even "if Sergeant Strickland never does another thing . . . he's earned every dime this Committee has paid him." In actuality, Strickland continued to conduct secret inquiries, never hesitating to misrepresent himself as a member of the committee or as an operative for a fictitious Governor's Committee on Pornography. While Strickland egregiously violated the law by acting as an unlicensed detective, the committee hired C. Lawrence Rice as chief investigator and John E. Evans as staff director. Evans, former chair of Governor Bryant's Center for Cold War Education, wanted to distance the Johns Committee from its earlier incarnations by avoiding the meddlesome violations of due process practiced by predecessor committees. But the crusade against homosexuals continued. In September 1963, FLIC members met with leaders of private organizations, federal officials, and congressional committees in Chicago and Washington, D.C., who reinforced the committee's suspicion that Communists planned to subvert the American way of life by controlling academic institutions and by corrupting the nation's moral fiber. Believing that constituents demanded action rather than apathy, Mitchell cloaked investigations in the guise of a research project, with the hope that lawmakers might enact comprehensive legislation to control sexual behaviors. By the end of 1963, the committee was seeking to shock Floridians into accepting its program by distributing a summary of its findings on gays and lesbians.[35]

In January 1964, the committee released a booklet titled *Homosexuality and Citizenship in Florida*. Dubbed the Purple Pamphlet because of its conspicuous cover, this work purported to "be of value to all citizens" by revealing homosexuality as "a skeleton in the closet of society." While the Johns Committee admitted that it possessed "no corner on understanding the history or prognosis of homosexuality"—and even selected the biblical description of "abomination" as a suitable definition—it nevertheless concluded that acts between members of the same sex promoted "neuroticism and mental imbalance, a predilection opening pathways to crime and conduct far beyond the veil of rationality." Fearing the proliferation of muscle magazines and Polaroid camera shots, the committee decried the "torrent" of homophile "propaganda" that portrayed gays as "a maladjusted, misunderstood, and mistreated minority, composed of productive people seeking their proper place in the sun." The report instead viewed homosexuals as the carriers of a degenerative disease that posed a greater menace to society than child molesters. The authors of the booklet argued that the heterosexual pedophile "seldom kills or physically cripples his victim. The outlook for the victim of molestation is generally good for recovery from the mental and physical shocks involved and for the enjoyment of a normal life." Homosexual acts represented a far greater threat, according to committee members, because younger "victims" engaging in such acts, would inevitably become first accomplices and later perpetrators as they succumbed to erotic desires. (Despite the committee's proclivity to extract names from witnesses, most of the "expert" authorities quoted in this booklet remained anonymous.) The report contained suggestive photographs, a glossary, and a bibliography. The committee sold copies of the Purple Pamphlet for a quarter and offered a special discount for bulk purchases of over one hundred copies.[36]

The pamphlet's release sparked a maelstrom of controversy. A resounding chorus of constituents voiced their anger at state officials. Weary from fielding a deluge of complaints, Governor Farris Bryant had distanced himself from the Johns Committee by March 1964. Although Bryant admitted to reporters that he had never read the booklet—and said that he doubted if he ever would examine it—he nevertheless seemed reluctant to criticize the committee. Rather than expressing an interest in the civil rights of gay Floridians, Bryant used the uproar as an excuse to chastise the media, saying that "if the press had not been given a copy of the booklet they would have demanded it. . . . They got a copy and they complain." While Bryant merely remarked that the FLIC should consider limiting the circulation of the pamphlet, a Dade County judicial officer threatened to file legal action against the committee. State Attorney Richard E. Gerstein warned the FLIC to cease distribution of this "obscene and pornographic material" to anyone willing to give them a quarter. Ironically, even though the Florida Civil Liberties Union blasted Gerstein for censoring *Homosexuality and Citizenship*, the committee refused to give this organization an extra copy of its booklet, claiming it intended to allocate the remaining issues to "responsible agencies . . . whose conclusions on

the report and this Committee are more open-minded." Evans and Mitchell, who had once thought their pamphlet would become a best-seller,
found themselves responding to countless letters, some addressed simply
to "Sex, Tallahassee." [37]

Committee members defended this publication as part of a broader
program to prohibit homosexual behavior. The Purple Pamphlet marked
only the first salvo in the committee's newest offensive against Florida's
gay population. To preserve heterosexuals' "private liberties ... at all
costs," FLIC counsel Leo Foster promised to confine homosexuals and
subject them to secret hearings whenever their activities threatened "national security." C. W. "Bill" Young, state senator and Committee member,
warned that Floridians could not "stick [their] heads in the sand. The
legislature has responsibilities to the public to expose these people who
have been preying on young people." According to Young, the glossary
allowed police officers "to recognize a homosexual from some words he
used." Evans echoed these sentiments when he explained that in
"exposing the rapid spread and insidious aspects of homosexuality the
Committee is neither crying wolf nor palming off a pipe dream." He
offered to marshal the agency's resources to cleanse Dade County—which
he considered "a major playground for deviates"—and the rest of the
state. Warning that "all the fruit the Sunshine State raises is not confined
to the grove," one supporter praised the FLIC for exposing the state's
schools as "homo factories with desks." (Although the Johns Committee
refused to sell *Homosexuality and Citizenship* to numerous Floridians, it
freely disseminated complimentary copies to sympathetic parties
throughout the United States. Away from the limelight, Evans quietly sent
fifty copies of the pamphlet to the Orlando Police Department and received in return photographs from a lesbian "wedding.")[38]

Public dissatisfaction jeopardized the work of the committee's Homosexual Practices Control Advisory Panel. In early 1964, Chairman Mitchell
recruited twelve Floridians from a variety of professions to suggest legislation for the 1965 biennial session. Unlike the witnesses previously sub-
poenaed by the committee, panelists received per diems, first-class travel
arrangements, and comfortable accommodations. A few spouses also attended at the state's expense. Panel members divided into two distinct
camps as they debated drafts for a proposed Sexual Behavior Act. Judges
and law enforcement officers on the panel sought to take the FLIC's plan
for a centralized records repository a step further and maintain files on all
suspected homosexuals in Florida, not just state employees. These officials

also wanted to retain the state's 1868 sodomy statute, which ambiguously proclaimed, "Whoever commits the abominable and detestable crime against nature, either with mankind or with beast, shall be punished by imprisonment in the state prison not exceeding twenty years." Psychologists and psychiatrists emphasized a therapeutic approach. They called for legislation to define sodomy with precision, to differentiate between homosexuality and pedophilia, and to sanction Britain's 1957 Wolfenden Report, which permitted private homosexual acts between consenting adults. Although panelists ultimately fashioned a compromise draft, their efforts vanished in the smoke of the heated controversy ignited by the committee's booklet.[39]

The Purple Pamphlet alienated porkchoppers and destroyed the committee. Floridians who had ardently supported the committee's prior assaults on civil liberties withheld their adoration after encountering the booklet. Homophile organizations also exacted damage. In June 1964 a gay book club began to sell reprints of the pamphlet for two dollars apiece from its Washington, D.C., office. While Senator Bill Young criticized this activity as "an obvious attempt to belittle the work of the Committee," the president of the homophile Mattachine Society scorned the committee for publishing the report in the first place. Harold "Hal" Call and other members of the Mattachine Society had observed the FLIC's probes from afar for many years. In an open letter to the Johns Committee, Call condemned the agency's pathetic research and repugnant sensationalism. The committee expected readers to select a theory conforming to its own views, and the pamphlet portrayed gays as sex fiends who spent every free moment searching for anonymous partners, recruiting youth, or transmitting venereal diseases. The appendices thoroughly misrepresented homosexuality. The section describing statutory sex offenses listed bestiality as well as heterosexual acts such as adultery and "carnal intercourse with an unmarried female idiot." The glossary gave homosexual connotations to a variety of terms, including *cute, married, dream boat, gerontophilia, kleptomania,* and *masturbation.* With less than one-sixth of its citations serving as valuable sources for the study of homosexuality, the supposedly "complete and responsible" bibliography lacked as many important works as it contained superfluous ones. In response to the committee's continued harassment of gays and lesbians throughout the state, the Mattachine Society started its first Florida chapter in Miami.[40]

On the verge of losing its mandate from the legislature, the Florida Legislative Investigation Committee destroyed some of its records and locked the rest of them away in a closet. Even by 1964, agents had burned photographs and other materials that might ultimately discredit members of the committee. In October of that year Senators Charley Johns and Robert Williams joined Investigator Rice and Staff Director Evans in resigning from the committee. Although a handful of supporters demanded that the 1965 legislature reinvigorate the FLIC as a permanent—rather than an interim—investigative body, Johns saw the futility in such an endeavor. He asked fellow lawmakers to "close the office, lock up the records and save the taxpayers of Florida the remainder of the $155,000 appropriation." Lawmakers disbanded the committee when its enabling legislation expired on 1 July 1965. Claiming that the FLIC operated exclusively under the "executive session" provision of the 1885 constitution, the legislature sealed all public records of this agency from inspection until 31 December 2028.[41]

Although the Johns Committee officially dissolved in 1965, most of its activities remained a mystery until lawmakers opened the records twenty-eight years later. A few themes have emerged from the FLIC's gay and lesbian investigations, including the various definitions of "homosexuality" employed by the committee, its investigative tactics, and its perceived role of maintaining social institutions in the climate of the cold war.

The committee arbitrarily modified its definitions of homosexuality to suit its immediate investigative needs. Agents often equated homosexuality with the "crimes against nature" statute. State employees who admitted to heterosexual oral-genital contact faced possible dismissal for committing sodomy, because the committee defined homosexuality as "the sexual relation between two people of the same sex usually, although it can be practiced by two people of the opposite sex." Strickland would often take this terminology to the absurd extreme, as when he asked one gay man, "Have you ever thought of having homosexual relations with a woman just to find out what it's all about?" While such a broad classification would encompass many Floridians, it would also exempt certain acts between members of the same sex. Hence, Strickland told a different subject that "a homosexual act is a sexual act between two people of the same sex . . . regardless of what the degree of the act itself might be[,] whether it's a petting act or a fondling act or goes beyond that degree." The committee frequently confused homosexuality and pedophilia. After one school system cleared a teacher of fabricated fondling charges, the committee ordered the state Board of Education to reopen the case without offering any evidence. When the educator protested this blatant double jeopardy, an investigator retorted that "when this Committee tried to protect the children of this county . . . then you have the audacity to say this is a witch hunt." Similar perversions of due process appeared in the hundreds of cases and thousands of pages maintained by the committee.[42]

Agents coupled inconsistent terminology with subjective and unreliable testimony. Whereas Janet Lee and others offered their bodies or spread rumors in exchange for lucrative informant fees, many of the committee's accomplices who provided gossip or served as decoys did so in order to stay out of jail or avoid public exposure by the committee. Investigators coached their "expert" witnesses and often visited them in their homes. Comments such as "You told me earlier off the record that . . ." and "If you are following my hand, I'm trying to give you one" pepper the transcripts. One deponent, who volunteered to incriminate a fellow teacher, provided scant evidence and forgot critical events yet received the following praise from an investigator: "You've done wonderful. You've got a phenomenal memory." Agents referred to friendly witnesses as "Mr. X" (or a similar pseudonym) as long as they offered damning innuendo about the committee's adversaries. After gathering information from sympathetic sources, Strickland and his associates kept a file of statements. The following caveat accompanied each of these "investigative leads": This confidential material "does not purport to be either an evaluation or a complete record, but is a listing of information available. It is furnished on a confidential basis and is not to be disseminated or published." Many of these sources provided the foundations for the committee's unscrupulous investigations.[43]

Confidential informants did, however, face the prospect of public humiliation and even threats of incarceration if the committee found their testimony to be deficient. Committee members expected witnesses to disclose names. But they enforced this edict in an arbitrary manner: While the FLIC permitted leaders of the Ku Klux Klan and the White Citizens Council to withhold their membership lists, it threatened homosexuals and civil rights advocates with long prison sentences if they failed to identify their associates. After warning one witness that the committee had no desire to engage in a "fishing expedition," agents told a pastor that "it's rather odd that you can't remember no names [sic]. You are the first person that we have had here out of some 400 that just sit there and don't intend to give any names [sic]." As the inquisitors read the riot act in the form of Florida's perjury statute, many subjects capitulated under pressure, revealed the names of innocent people, and examined mug-shot books to appease the committee. The FLIC also garnered names from the personal possessions of witnesses. For example, after detaining a Pensacola man, Strickland copied the contents of his address book and planned to contact the people listed therein for interrogation sessions. Guilt by association—the hallmark of McCarthyism—found a new home in the Sunshine State.[44]

The committee humbled adversarial witnesses. One case exemplifies the experiences of many Floridians brought before the FLIC. Officers removed a public schoolteacher from his vehicle, placed him in handcuffs, and sent him to the Naples Police Department. While in a locked room awaiting interrogation, the teacher discovered a concealed tape recorder. R. J. Strickland entered the room, falsely identified himself as a lawyer employed by the state Board of Education, and refused to state any charges or reasons for conducting this hearing. When the subject asked to contact his attorney, Strickland denied his request and instead began a three-and-a-half-hour interrogation session, stopping at various times to warn the teacher of the penalties for committing perjury. Strickland produced a stack of papers and claimed he could prove the teacher had associated with others guilty of moral turpitude, yet the teacher could not even tell if the papers Strickland possessed were bona fide affidavits. In other instances, committee members took testimony "off the record," either during the changing of the tapes or at other pivotal moments. Agent James Barker informed one witness that "we're going to cut the machine off from time to time so we can talk for a minute," while Strickland occasionally sent witnesses to a nearby lie detector between audiotape reels and began new tapes by asking, "Is there anything about that record you've made previously that you'd like to change?" Investigators even added comments to the end of testimony given by uncooperative witnesses: For example, when a music teacher denied the committee's allegations of homosexuality, an agent mentioned after the instructor's departure that "the field that he's chosen . . . and a white male . . . waiting for him in [a] Cadillac" proved the teacher's malfeasance.[45]

Prurient questions punctuated interview sessions. Rather than engaging in a pursuit of evidence, agents chose to intimidate their subjects by forcing them to reveal private matters of no investigative value. While interrogating one man, Charley Johns flippantly asked, "Now, when you suck another man's penis, do you get the same sensation out of it as when you have yours sucked?" This question seems tame when compared with the verbal groping commonly practiced by the committee. While interviewing one lesbian, an investigator said, "I want you to tell me exactly what happened, go into details, everything that you did, stripped your clothes, you were in the nude, lay down in bed, what position you got into and what she did." A few children faced inquisitions that no parent would knowingly tolerate without their presence. When agents discovered a teenager who had innocently kissed and held hands with another girl, they wanted her to give them the details. They also lectured her: "Have you ever seen what [homosexuality] can really do to a person? . . . It can completely destroy you. . . . You haven't turned against the male sex then have you?" Even when the committee served the public good by discovering child molesters, "call boy" rings, and the like, it often botched investigations by obstructing duly constituted law enforcement agencies. Evans once boasted that the FLIC probed homosexuals because local police "exhibited little understanding of the problems involved or the techniques desirable in such investigations." Such a statement, coupled with the FLIC's willingness to allow known pedophiles to disappear after giving testimony, demonstrates the contempt the Johns Committee had for the separation of powers expressed in Florida's constitution, which clearly stated that the executive branch "shall take care that the laws be faithfully executed." [46]

Educators and other state employees offered an obvious target. While the committee probed Floridians from all walks of life, it quickly learned the McCarthyite ruse of purging from within. Investigators scrutinized the private lives of public servants to satisfy taxpayers such as prominent Tampa reactionary Sumter Lowry, who once asked, "Why shouldn't the people who are paying the bills have control over their state institutions?" Although Superintendent Thomas Bailey promised to conduct hearings with decorum and to protect the rights of the accused, he joined the committee and other state authorities in attempting to concoct a causal relationship between homosexuality and subversion. By inventing a connection between political and sexual "perversion," these officials transformed Communism and homosexuality into diseases that had infected American institutions. In this conspiratorial paradigm, gay and lesbian Floridians threatened the family, the church, and other bulwarks of democracy by eschewing the nuclear family—America's vanguard against internal subversion—as well as by living outside traditional Southern religious proscriptions. In the culture of the cold war, parents joined authorities in condemning homosexual teachers for fear that such educators might pollute the minds of children and convert them into juvenile delinquents or adolescent agitators. Indeed, the cult of consensus that pervaded American culture limited political, social, and intellectual debates in both the private and public spheres.[47]

Florida's homophobic witch-hunts served as a microcosm for cold war crackdowns throughout the nation. Politicians across America sought to bolster the family at a time when promiscuity, adult literature, changing gender roles, and birth control became more prominent in heterosexual circles. In addition to these redefinitions of heterosexuality, Floridians faced racial crises, animosity between urban and rural regions, and unparalleled demographic growth. As participants in the earlier congressional investigations of the comic book industry had attempted to do with alleged Communist sympathizers, FLIC investigators hoped to uncover "deviate" and "psychopathic" influences among homosexuals that might explain America's failure to contain external enemies or to preserve tranquillity on the home front. "Cold Warriors" thus fashioned gays and lesbians into traitorous beasts that placed sexual desires above national interests. Reinforced by a mass media and a popular culture that defined homosexuals as "perverts" and "sissies," authorities throughout America conducted comparable probes.[48]

Ironically, the excesses of the Johns Committee and similar bodies fostered a collective consciousness among lesbians and gays. Prior to World War II, most homosexuals viewed themselves as isolated, individuals guilty of "moral depravity" and worthy of societal and biblical condemnation. When Cold Warriors linked sexual practices with civic loyalty, they brought homosexuality into the public spotlight as never before. Like the African Americans who were questioned about their involvement in civil rights activities, gays and lesbians slowly began to see themselves as a distinct—and unjustly persecuted—minority. And while the culture of the cold war emphasized the trappings of consumerism as a means of sustaining the family, a homosexual identity and gay urban subcultures also grew out of the rise of consumption-oriented capitalism. Although Governor Reubin Askew proudly endorsed Anita Bryant in 1977 by boasting that he had "never viewed the homosexual lifestyle as something that approaches a constitutional right," neither he nor Anita Bryant could deny the growing economic clout of gay, lesbian, and bisexual Floridians. Barriers have fallen: The state supreme court overturned the vague "crimes against nature" statute in 1971, gay and lesbian student organizations appeared on college campuses, and calls for tolerance and diversity have permeated all levels of the government. Yet challenges still remain:

Groups such as the American Family Association and Take Back Tampa have continued to wage Bryant's homophobic crusade.[49]

Even as Floridians began to peer into the Johns Committee's closet of shame, former FLIC members refused to acknowledge the monstrosity they created. In a 1977 retrospective interview, Charley Johns, who died in 1990, told a reporter, "I'd wish I'd been naive and never knowed [sic] all that about homosexuals. I didn't know nothing [sic] about lesbianism before that." But Johns relished the notoriety his investigations received. Congressman Sam M. Gibbons, a supporter of the University of South Florida and Johns's contemporary in the state legislature, keenly assessed his rival's ability to blackmail others when he called Johns "the Christopher Columbus of homosexuality." Fellow Congressman C. W. "Bill" Young, a former member of the committee, has since attempted to distance himself from the agency's blatant homophobia by asserting that if the FLIC entrapped homosexuals, "it was done before my time." Two other members saw little purpose in opening the committee's records. While W. Cliff Herrell, a former vice chair on the committee, said, "I don't think there's anything sinister in those records," one-time chair William G. O'Neill considered the entire episode "ancient history" and added that condemning the agency is "like saying Columbus mistreated the natives when he came over." Former representative W. Randolph Hodges remarked, "I'm kind of from the old school. . . . I'm certainly not an admirer of sex perverts."[50]

Others remained silent. Farris Bryant, who placed many of his gubernatorial papers in the University of Florida's archives, continues to deny access to these public records until his passing. Before his death, Remus Strickland told one journalist, "I'm bound by secrecy to the Committee by sworn affidavit." The man who violated committee rules of confidentiality so blatantly during his life thus became something of an enigma after his death. In contrast, although the committee did force Sigismond Diettrich from his job, it failed to destroy his integrity. In the same letter that recounts his feelings of anger and uncertainty, he also expresses a ray of hope: "I have lost all I had, all I lived for in my proud vanity, but I gained infinitely more in the love and proved devotion of my family, my coworkers, my friends, and my students." The Purple Pamphlet once warned Floridians that "it behooves us all to come to know the nature of the homosexual, for he is with us in every area of the state." For Diettrich and the countless other victims of the Florida Legislative Investigation Committee, it behooves us to maintain eternal vigilance, to assure that such violations of our cherished freedoms never threaten any of us—gay, straight, or bisexual—again.[51]

NOTES

1. Chapter 93–405, Laws of Florida, restricts disclosure of the "identity of any witness, any person who was a subject of the inquiry, or any person referred to in testimony, documents, or evidence retained in the committee's records; however, this exemption does not apply to members of the committee, its staff, or any public official who was not a subject of the inquiry." To protect the many victims of the Johns Committee's investigations, this chapter includes only names already mentioned in newspapers and other sources. For a comprehensive history of the Florida Legislative Investigation Committee, see James A. Schnur, "Cold Warriors in the Hot Sunshine: The Johns Committee's Assault on Civil Liberties in Florida, 1956–1965" (M.A. thesis, University of South Florida, 1995).

2. Sigismond Diettrich to Raymond Crist, 24 March 1959, Sigismond de Rudesheim Diettrich Papers, 1933–1960, University of Florida Special Collections, Gainesville; Florida Legislative Investigation Committee Papers (hereafter cited as FLIC Papers), Doc. 4–43 (5 January 1959) and Doc. 2–76 (19 January 1959), Senate Office Building, Tallahassee. The document numbers mentioned above refer to the arrangement of the Johns Committee records in the Senate Office Building. Thus Document 4–43, appears as the forty-third document in the fourth box of the collection. Copies of the committee's records also reside in the State Archives (Record Group 940, Series 1486) with identical document and box headings. However, the archives rearranged the collection to impose provenance.

3. William C. Havard and Loren P. Beth, *The Politics of Mis-Representation: Rural-Urban Conflict in the Florida Legislature* (Baton Rouge: Louisiana State University Press, 1962), pp. 33–34; D. Stephen Kahn, letter to author, 17 June 1991.

4. *St. Petersburg Times,* 24 February 1993, 10A; 13 June 1993, 1B, 4B; 2 July 1993, 1A, 6A–7A; *Tampa Tribune,* 2 July 1993, 1A, 8A. Anita Bryant's 1977 campaign demonstrated that intolerance to gay and lesbian rights persisted long after the Johns Committee had disbanded. For Bryant's perspective, see Anita Bryant, *The Anita Bryant Story: The Survival of Our Nation's Families and the Threat of Militant Homosexuality* (Old Tappan, NJ: Fleming H. Revell Co., 1977), and her work with Bob Green, *At Any Cost* (Old Tappan, NJ: Fleming H. Revell Co., 1978). See also "Anita's Circle," *Time,* 2 May 1977, p. 76; "Confronting the Homosexual Issue," *Christianity Today* (8 July 1977): 36.

5. Bonnie S. Stark, "McCarthyism in Florida: Charley Johns and the Florida Legislative Investigation Committee, July 1956 to July 1965" (M.A. thesis, University of South Florida, 1985), pp. 2, 7–9, 16–18, 64; Chapter 31498 and Chapter 57–125, Laws of Florida; *Biennial Report of the Attorney General (1957–1958),* Declaration

057–36, p. 36; FLIC Meeting Minutes, 10 October 1956 and 18 October 1956, FLIC Papers, State Archives. For a thorough treatment of the NAACP investigations, see Steven F. Lawson, "The Florida Legislative Investigation Committee and the Constitutional Readjustment of Race Relations," in *An Uncertain Tradition: Constitutionalism and the History of the South*, ed. Kermit L. Hall and James W. Ely (Athens: University of Georgia, 1989), pp. 296–325.

6. Charles W. Arnade, interview with author, 29 November 1990, Tampa. Charles W. Arnade, interview for the University of South Florida Silver Anniversary Oral History Program (1985), Box 522, University of South Florida Special Collections, Tampa; Chapter 57–125, Laws of Florida.

7. *Tampa Tribune*, 21 December 1954, pp. 1, 8; Virgil M. Newton Jr., *Crusade for Democracy* (Ames: Iowa State University, 1961), pp. 144–45; Faculty Dead Files (Leathers, Robert, 1953–1955), Florida State University Special Collections, Tallahassee.

8. FLIC Papers, Doc. 3–92 (undated); Doc. 3–91 (24 May 1957); Doc. 4–12 (6 February 1959).

9. FLIC Papers, Doc. 2–77 (8 January 1959); Doc. 4–3 (9 January 1959); "Progress Report on the UF Investigation" (September/October 1958), FLIC Papers, Box 1, State Archives.

10. FLIC Papers, Doc. 1–68 (31 October 1958); Doc. 4–8 (7 January 1959); Doc. 4–3 (9 January 1959); Doc. 4–94 (20 November 1958); Doc. 4–43 (5 January 1959); Doc. 2–59 (20 October 1958).

11. FLIC Papers, Doc. 2–75 (22 January 1959); Doc. 4–8 (7 January 1959); Doc. 4–70 (6 December 1958); Doc. 2–77 (8 January 1959); Doc. 3–145 (25 May 1960).

12. Stark, "McCarthyism in Florida," pp. 96–97, 100–101; William G. Carleton, *Free Lancing through the Century: A Memoir* (Gainesville, FL: Carleton House, 1988), p. 147; Minutes of the Florida Legislative Investigation Committee, 27 September 1958, Box 9, Clerk of the House of Representatives Papers, Series 517, State Archives, Tallahassee; FLIC Papers, Doc. 4–11 (21 January 1959); Doc. 3–158 (19 August 1959); Doc. 1–180 (1 October 1958); Doc. 4–8 (7 January 1959); Doc. 3–153 (15 December 1958); Doc. 4–43 (5 January 1959).

13. J. Wayne Reitz to Charley Johns, 18 November 1961, Box 72L, J. Wayne Reitz Papers (hereafter cited as Reitz Papers), University of Florida Special Collections, Gainesville; FLIC Papers, Doc. 2–57 (4 November 1958); Doc. 1–36 (4 November 1958); Doc. 4–10 (undated); Doc. 13–26 (undated).

14. Tom R. Wagy, *Governor LeRoy Collins of Florida: Spokesman of the New South* (University: University of Alabama Press, 1985), pp. 108–9, 129–30; University of Florida *Alligator*, 20 February 1959, p. 1; 19 February 1960, pp. 1, 3; Stark, "McCarthyism in Florida," 109–11; Minutes of the FLIC, 27 September 1958 and 14 February 1959, Box 9, Clerk of the House Papers, State Archives. For example, see the FLIC transcripts labeled as Documents 4–43 and 4–44.

15. Report of the Florida Legislative Investigation Committee to the 1959 Ses-

sion of the Legislature, FLIC Papers, Doc. 10–19 (13 April 1959); Stark, "McCarthyism in Florida," pp. 109–11; Chapter 59–207, Laws of Florida. In a personal letter to UF president Reitz, Johns said, "I want you to know that you have my deepest sympathy in having to do all the dirty work that is done at the University of Florida. . . . It was your painful duty to call in those Professors, whom we exposed, whom you had known for years and have to fire them. . . . You did not shirk your responsibilities" (Charley Johns to J. Wayne Reitz, 12 December 1959, Box 39, Reitz Papers).

16. Florida State University *Flambeau* 13 March 1959, p. 2; Ellen McGarrahan, "Peeping Johns: Florida's Secret Shame," *Miami Herald Tropic Magazine,* 8 December 1991, pp. 9, 12, 15, 17.

17. FLIC Papers, Doc. 11–713 (23 January 1961); Doc. 11–1682 (22 March 1963); Doc. 2–104 (9 May 1960); Doc. 2–106 (19 May 1960); Stark, "McCarthyism in Florida," p. 93. See also McGarrahan, "Peeping Johns."

18. FLIC Papers, Doc. 3–65 (5 September 1961); Doc. 1–112 (9 May 1963); Doc. 1–113 (27 May 1963).

19. FLIC Papers, Doc. 1–95 (13 October 1960); Doc. 1–78 (13 October 1960); Doc. 1–79 (13 October 1960); *St. Petersburg Times,* 2 July 1993, 6A.

20. FLIC Papers, Doc. 11–256 (20 March 1962).

21. Karen M. Harbeck, "Gay and Lesbian Educators: Past History / Future Prospects," in *Coming Out of the Classroom Closet: Gay and Lesbian Students, Teachers, and Curricula,* ed. Karen M. Harbeck (New York: Harrington Park, 1992), pp. 123–25; FLIC Papers, Doc. 1–114 (19 September 1960); Doc. 11–1675 (7 October 1960); Doc. 4–48 (27 March 1961); memorandum from Remus J. Strickland to William O'Neill regarding Miami investigation (30 May 1961), FLIC Papers, Box 1, State Archives.

22. "Report of the Florida Legislative Investigation Committee to the 1961 Session of the Legislature," FLIC Papers, Doc. 10–58; Chapter 61–62, Laws of Florida.

23. FLIC Papers, Doc. 11–404 (9 November 1961); Doc. 10–37 (undated).

24. FLIC Papers, Doc. 11–1609 (13 November 1961); Doc. 11–1608 (9 February 1962); Doc. 11–1550 (22 November 1961); Doc. 11–1569 (12 December 1961); Doc. 11–823 (undated, 1962); Doc. 11–1153 (20 February 1962); J. Wayne Reitz to Charley Johns, 18 November 1961, Box 72L, Reitz Papers.

25. FLIC Papers, Doc. 11–122 (16 April 1962); Doc. 4–42 (16/17 April 1962); *St. Petersburg Times,* 17 April 1962, 7A.

26. *St. Petersburg Times,* 4 March 1962, "Sunday" magazine, p. 3; 12 March 1962, 1A, 8A; *St. Petersburg Independent,* 18 January 1962, 8B. FLIC Papers, Doc. 12–381 (7 March 1962); Memo from Board of Health to Florida Children's Commission's Advisory Committee on Homosexuality, 4 June 1962, with assorted clippings, Governor Farris Bryant Papers, Record Group 102, Series 756, Box 57, State Archives.

27. *St. Petersburg Times,* 3 September 1957, 1B; Arnade interview, 29 November 1990; Jack E. Fernandez, interview with author, 2 November 1993, Tampa; Sheldon

N. Grebstein, telephone interview with author, 15 November 1990; John W. Egerton, "The Controversity: One Man's View of Politics in the Making of a University" (unpublished manuscript, 1965), pp. 47–48, 50–57, 79, 86–88, John Egerton File on the Johns Committee, University of South Florida Special Collections, Tampa; Russell M. Cooper and Margaret B. Fisher, *The Vision of a Contemporary University: A Case Study of Expansion and Development in American Higher Education, 1950–1975* (Tampa: University of South Florida Press, 1982), p. 158; FLIC Papers, Doc. 9–78 (18 April 1962); Doc. 11–873 (23 April 1962); Doc. 1–94 (25 April 1962).

28. Phyllis P. Marshall, interview with author, 2 November 1993, Tampa; FLIC Papers, Doc. 1–190 (26 April 1962); Doc. 5–78 (10 May 1962); Doc. 3–134 (9 May 1962); Doc. 5–93 (14 May 1962).

29. FLIC Papers, Doc. 1–190 (19 May 1962); *St. Petersburg Times*, 25 May 1962, 1A; 7 June 1962, 20B; *Tampa Times* (USF edition), 21 May 1962, p. 1; Egerton, "Controversity," pp. 82, 85–88, 93; Stark, "McCarthyism in Florida," pp. 150–51; *Report from the Florida Legislative Investigative Committee to the State Board of Control and State Board of Education [on USF]* (hereafter cited as *FLIC Report*), pp. 1–4, 30–32, 41–42, Box 9, Clerk of the House Papers, State Archives. For a thorough treatment of the committee's probe at the University of South Florida, see James A. Schnur, "Cold Warriors in the Hot Sunshine: USF and the Johns Committee," *Sunland Tribune: Journal of the Tampa Historical Society* 18 (November 1992): 9–15.

30. *Clearwater Sun*, 26 August 1962, Johns Committee Scrapbooks, University of South Florida Special Collections, Tampa; Egerton, "Controversity," p. 117; *FLIC Report*, pp. 7–8, 11–12, 19–20, 26–27, 50–52; "Report of the Special Committee to the Board of Control," 14 September 1962, Vice President for Academic Affairs Administrative Policy Records, 1958–1974, Series 2A, Box 1, University of Florida Special Collections, Gainesville; FLIC Papers, Doc. 5–55 (6 June 1962); Emmett Peter Jr., "Florida's Sinner Safari," *New Republic*, 27 April 1963, p. 14. One professor feared the committee could not separate fact from fantasy. He had appeared as Flute the bellows-mender in a campus presentation of Shakespeare's *A Midsummer Night's Dream*, and worried that FLIC agents might call him in for testimony because of his acting part or costume (Fernandez interview, 2 November 1993).

31. Grebstein interview, 15 November 1990; University of Florida *Alligator*, 4 November 1962, pp. 1, 3; "Academic Freedom and Tenure: University of South Florida," *AAUP Bulletin* 50 (March 1964): 54; *St. Petersburg Times*, 3 November 1962, 1B; Egerton, "Controversity," pp. 169, 172.

32. Peter, "Florida's Sinner Safari," p. 15; "Still Another List," *The Nation*, 22 June 1964, p. 615; *St. Petersburg Times*, 29 January 1964, Johns Committee Scrapbooks, University of South Florida Special Collections. See also McGarrahan, "Peeping Johns."

33. *Neal v. Bryant*, 149 So.2d 529; *Gibson v. Florida Legislative Investigation Committee*, 108 So.2d 729; Harbeck, "Gay and Lesbian Educators," p. 126.

34. Chapter 63–545, Laws of Florida; *Tampa Tribune*, 25 January 1964, Johns

Committee Scrapbooks, University of South Florida Special Collections; *St. Petersburg Times* 23 January 1964, 1A. See also McGarrahan, "Peeping Johns."

35. FLIC Papers, Doc. 10–31 (undated); Doc. 4–77 (4 June 1964); Doc. 11–1639 (26 November 1963); Doc. 10–44 (undated); "Interim Report," Doc. 10–53 (March 1964); *St. Petersburg Times*, 23 November 1963, Johns Committee Scrapbooks, University of South Florida Special Collections.

36. See Florida Legislative Investigation Committee, *Homosexuality and Citizenship in Florida: A Report of the Florida Legislative Investigation Committee* (Tallahassee, January 1964).

37. Telegram from Richard Gerstein to the FLIC, 18 March 1964, Staff Report no. 15, 3 April 1964, Box 1, FLIC Papers, State Archives; John E. Evans to Stephen H. Jones (executive secretary, Florida Civil Liberties Union), 15 May 1964), Box 2, FLIC Papers, State Archives; *St. Petersburg Times*, 19 March 1964, 1A, 16A; *Tampa Tribune*, 20 March 1964, and *St. Petersburg Times*, 20 March 1964 and 31 March 1964, Johns Committee Scrapbooks, University of South Florida Special Collections.

38. *Tampa Tribune*, 30 January 1964, 4B; *St. Petersburg Times*, 19 March 1964, 1A, 16A; *St. Petersburg Independent*, 21 March 1964, Johns Committee Clippings, University of South Florida Special Collections; FLIC Papers, Doc. 4–73 (18 April 1964); "Homosex Report," 30 May 1964, Box 1, FLIC Papers, State Archives; Professor Anonymous [pseud.], "Perverts under the Palms," *Confidential Magazine* (February 1964): 48, found in Box 1, John Egerton File on the Johns Committee, University of South Florida Special Collections.

39. *Tampa Tribune*, 20 April 1964, 2B; FLIC Papers, Doc. 11–14 (6 April 1964); Doc. 11–16 (28 April 1964); Doc. 11–6 (22 April 1964); Doc. 11–17 (30 April 1964); Doc. 11–66 (13 July 1964); Doc. 11–68 (7 July 1964); Chapter 800.01, Florida Statutes; "Minutes of Advisory Committee," 15 May 1964, 29/30 June 1964, Box 1, FLIC Papers, State Archives.

40. *Mattachine Review* 10 (November–December 1964): 4–11; *St. Petersburg Independent*, 25 June 1964, 1A–2A; John D'Emilio, *Sexual Politics, Sexual Communities: The Making of a Homosexual Minority in the United States, 1940–1970* (Chicago: University of Chicago Press, 1983), p. 174.

41. Associated Press news release, 30 September 1964, Box 82, Bryant Papers, State Archives; "Resolution by St. Petersburg Post #14 of the American Legion," 12 October 1964, Governor Haydon Burns Papers, Record Group 102, Series 131, Box 38, State Archives; D. Stephen Kahn, letter to author, 17 June 1991.

42. FLIC Papers, Doc. 3–12 (undated); Doc. 3–60 (13 October 1958); Doc. 2–175 (24 May 1961); Doc. 4–36 (undated); Doc. 1–56 (undated). See also Dennis Altman, *The Homosexualization of America, the Americanization of the Homosexual* (New York: St. Martin's Press, 1982), p. 70.

43. FLIC Papers, Doc. 3–80 (24 June 1962); Doc. 1–49 (17 February 1961). See also Box 13 of FLIC Papers at the State Archives, for examples of the committee's "investigative leads."

44. FLIC Papers, Doc. 5–56 (25 June 1958); Doc. 5–90 (21 April 1958); Doc. 5–91 (5 May 1958); Doc. 3–156 (19 February 1959); Doc. 3–4 (13 June 1962); Doc. 11–197 (undated); Doc. 5–121 (16 October 1962).

45. FLIC Papers, Doc. 4–62 (13 June 1960), Doc. 2–19 (2 June 1962), Doc. 2–32 (11 October 1962), Doc. 2–27 (6 June 1962).

46. FLIC Papers, Doc. 4–11 (21 January 1959); Doc. 3–23 (28 June 1962); Doc. 1–146 (undated); Doc. 11–1678 (13 July 1964); Florida Constitution (1885), art. 4, sec. 6.

47. John D'Emilio and Estelle B. Freedman, *Intimate Matters: A History of Sexuality in America* (New York: Harper & Row, 1988), pp. 288–89; Sumter Lowry to Governor Farris Bryant, 14 March 1963, Box 27, Bryant Papers, State Archives; *St. Petersburg Times*, 4 March 1962, "Sunday" magazine, p. 3; Stephen J. Whitfield, *The Culture of the Cold War* (Baltimore: Johns Hopkins University Press, 1991), pp. 43–45; John D'Emilio, *Making Trouble: Essays on Gay History, Politics, and the University* (New York: Routledge, 1992), pp. 59–60; D'Emilio, *Sexual Politics*, pp. 17–18; James Gilbert, *A Cycle of Outrage: America's Reaction to the Juvenile Delinquent in the 1950s* (New York: Oxford University Press, 1986), pp. 7, 17–23, 72–76, 212–14; James T. Sears, *Growing Up Gay in the South: Race, Gender, and Journeys of the Spirit* (New York: Haworth Press, 1991), pp. 13, 64–65; Morris Dickstein, *Gates of Eden: American Culture in the Sixties* (New York: Penguin Books, 1989), pp. 26–29, 40.

48. D'Emilio, *Making Trouble*, pp. 62–66, D'Emilio and Freedman, *Intimate Matters*, pp. 282–84; Estelle B. Freedman, " 'Uncontrolled Desires:' The Response to the Sexual Psychopath, 1920–1960," *Journal of American History* 74 (June 1987): 84–85. Some examples of the media's treatment of homosexuals include: "Curable Disease?" *Time*, 10 December 1956, pp. 74, 76; "What Is a Homosexual?" *Time*, 16 June 1958, p. 11; Irving Bieber, "Speaking Frankly on a Once Taboo Subject," *New York Times Magazine*, 23 August 1964, p. 75. In the early 1960s, the governor of the U.S. Virgin Islands wanted to remove all homosexuals from the island. Other witch-hunts occurred on the mainland. See *Mattachine Review* 9 (February 1963): 33–34.

49. D'Emilio, *Sexual Politics*, pp. 9, 13; D'Emilio, *Making Trouble*, pp. 107–9, 183–84; Altman, *Homosexualization of America*, pp. 89, 110–11, 119; Elaine Tyler May, *Homeward Bound: American Families in the Cold War Era* (New York: Basic Books, 1988), 163–67; *St. Petersburg Times*, 12 May 1977, 1B; 4 May 1977, 1B; 21 December 1971, 2B.

50. *St. Petersburg Times*, 28 December 1977, 14B; Sam M. Gibbons, interview for the University of South Florida Silver Anniversary Oral History Program (1985), Box 522, University of South Florida Special Collections; *Tallahassee Democrat*, 1 July 1993, 6A. See also McGarrahan, "Peeping Johns."

51. Farris Bryant, letter to author, 17 February 1989; Diettrich to Crist, 24 March 1959, Diettrich Papers, University of Florida Special Collections; McGarrahan, "Peeping Johns."

Chapter Nine

Race, Class, Gender, and Sexuality in Pre-Stonewall Charleston

Perspectives on the Gordon Langley Hall Affair

James T. Sears

High birth is a form of congenital insanity, that the suf-
ferer merely inherits diseases of his ancestors, and en-
dures them, for the most part very stoically, in one of
those comfortably padded lunatic asylums which are
known, euphemistically, as the stately homes of England.
—Virginia Woolf, *The Common Reader* (1925)

Somewhere beneath the not-so-subtle messages of *The Birth of a Nation*
and *Song of the South,* the romantic relationships in *Gone with the Wind* and
Fried Green Tomatoes, and the raw emotionalism of *A Streetcar Named Desire*
and *Deliverance* is a scaffolding of race, gender, class, and sexuality that
has long contoured southern culture.

In many ways, Charleston is the epicenter of southern culture, whose
history and architecture occasionally expose this scaffolding. Located at
the tip of the peninsula formed by the meeting of Ashley and Cooper
Rivers, Charles Towne's legacy includes the ill-fated slave revolt led by
Denmark Vesey and the notorious abolitionist work of the Grimke sisters
a generation later. Spared by General William Tecumseh Sherman's long
march to the sea are a catfish row of brightly colored houses near the
wharves on East Bay Street, where cargoes of indigo and rice were readied
for their European journeys. Further along the water's edge, south of
Broad Street, majestically sit the mansions of the Manigaults, Blacklocks,

and Draytons, protected by ancient seawalls that form the Battery and overlook Fort Sumter, a not-too-distant reminder of Northern Aggression. On the other end of the city's peninsula lie eighteenth-century suburbs like Ansonborough, with historic homes purchased for renovation or resale by the Historic Charleston Foundation under the post–World War II leadership of Frances Edmunds.

Walking through the cobblestone streets of the "Holy City" takes one past the Dock Street Theatre, the first opera house in the United States, and Hibernian Hall, built in 1840 and the site of the exclusive St. Cecilia Cotillion, where Citadel cadets escort debutante Daughters of the Confederacy—just a stone's throw away from the old slave market, where the great-grandchildren of former slaves weave sweet-grass baskets and banter in Gullah. The streets made famous by the fictional black beggar Porgy also lead to the Greek revival architecture of the College of Charleston, the first municipal institution of higher education, and The Citadel, whose cadets and alumni struggled to preserve its all-male tradition.

Much as in previous decades, in the early 1960s

> Charleston was a city of thoroughly segregated neighborhoods, transportation systems, public schools, colleges and parks, churches, theaters, restaurants, and even shopping districts. Afro-Americans were expected to shop on King Street north of Calhoun Street, while whites shopped to the south. Even when the city's brown elite occasionally patronized the better stores south of Calhoun, they were not permitted to try on shoes and certain articles of clothing.[1]

By 1962, however, great changes were on the southern horizon. In the midst of tuning to new episodes of *Gunsmoke, The Defenders*, or *Have Gun, Will Travel* Saturday evenings on channel 5; viewing first-run movies like *Advise and Consent* (a political drama in which a senator with a homosexual past faces blackmail) at the Riviera Theater; or listening to Top 10 hits on WTMA 1250—Elvis Presley's "Return to Sender," Chubby Checker's "Limbo Rock," and the Four Seasons's "Big Girls Don't Cry"—Charlestonians faced a challenge to long-held social mores and cultural values.

The city's *News and Courier* juxtaposed state and national civil rights stories: the impending integration of Charleston lunch counters with southern senators blocking rules limiting filibusters; violence at the University of Mississippi (Ole Miss) as it integrated with threatened violence as Harvey Gantt registered at Clemson. Despite the polemics of die-hard segregationists such as Tom Waring, who editorialized against the "apostles of race mongrelization and socialism"[2] in the *News and Courier*, by 1962 peaceful integration had occurred in many public accommodations, although few blacks availed themselves of their new freedoms to shop, eat, and play in previously segregated areas.

And in a less noted although no less significant moment, 1962 was also marked by the arrival in Charleston of British-born Gordon Langley Hall.

The Early Years

Gordon was born to the aristocratic Marjorie Hall Ticehurst in Sussex, England, in 1937; his father, Jack Copper, was the chauffeur for Vita Sackville-West, the noted "transvestite" author depicted in Virginia Woolf's *Orlando*, a tale of a man transformed into a lovely woman. Becoming "a real live Orlando" is how Gordon remembers his life:

> I was the family black sheep in more ways than one: Marjorie, still unwed, had borne me when she was sixteen. . . . Shunned by most of her family. . . . Marjorie locked herself in a darkened room for most of the nine months. One close and sadistic relative saw fit to kick her in the stomach. . . . When I was eventually born at home with only a midwife in attendance, the clitoris was so swollen that the startled woman did not know whether I was a boy or a girl.[3]

One of Gordon's earliest memories was Vita reading his stories at Sissinghurst Castle; Gordon credits her with encouraging his writing. Effeminate in appearance, during adolescence he enjoyed playing with dolls and even reported occasional bleedings in his genital area.

Fearing embarrassment for himself and disgrace upon his family, Gordon fled his native England:

> I had been told by my doctor in England that a mistake had been made when I was born (I should have been twins) so I always took assignments that were very masculine (cut my hair short) because I thought it was something that could not be put right. . . . I lived a life of deception. As a child I never went to the bathroom with the other children, I would always run home. When I was in the choir my voice never broke like the other children. . . . I really lived in my own world.[4]

At age nineteen, Gordon journeyed to an obscure Ojibway Indian reservation in Gull Bay, Canada. There he taught, wrote, and served as a midwife. One of Gordon's novels, *Me Papoose Sitter*, is a humorous adult story based on those experiences, which he wrote during his years as an out-of-work writer living in New York City, after a brief stint as society editor for the *Nevada Daily Mail* in Missouri.

During his first New York summer, while living in a small apartment on West 103d Street, Gordon also wrote a modern morality play. *Saraband for a Saint* originated from the encouragement of the Episcopal rector at the nearby St. Martin's Church in Harlem. With Hall acknowledging that "most plays are somewhat autobiographical,"[5] it concerned the relationship and personal problems between two soldiers, an educated African American and a "talkative Englishman," who seek shelter in a bombed-out church during World War II. Bishop James Pike described the play:

> Here, a broken, wronged, and wrong man is met . . . by one outside his life who makes himself part of his life. The unacceptable is accepted and thus is able to accept himself and become more acceptable.[6]

After the play's performance, Hall fell ill. A "distant cousin"—Isabel Lydia Whitney, a member of the elite Pen and Brush Club in Greenwich Village—visited him in the hospital. A noted artist and heiress to her branch of the Whitney fortune, Miss Whitney was also a collateral descendant of William Penn and a relative of John Hay Whitney, then U.S. Ambassador to the Court of St. James, and Gertrude Vanderbilt Whitney, one of the founders of the New York Museum of Modern Art. Whitney and Hall became quick friends; they were, in effect, kindred spirits.

Then in her seventies, Isabel invited young Gordon to live in her forty-room mansion at 12 West Tenth Street, "where we could be company for each other and yet retain our individual independence."[7] Years later, Hall's fondness for Isabel has not diminished: "She was very kind to people lifting them out of their station in life."[8] At her express wish, she was buried beside his maternal grandmother in England.

Like the characters in Hall's morality play, Isabel and Gordon found strength in each other's company:

> Although my frustrating affliction was still with me, she had taught me how to live with it. No longer was I running away. . . . There was no need to prove I was strong and masculine when I really wasn't. As she had learned to live with her crippled leg, so she taught me to accept with resignation something that we thought could never be righted.[9]

During those six years living on the top floor of the Whitney mansion, Gordon wrote several other books and articles, including a feature on Princess Margaret that was published in *Look*. He quickly entered New York society, befriending the likes of Joan Crawford, Bette Davis, and

Dame Margaret Rutherford, stage star and Oscar-winning actress. According to Hall, Dame Margaret was so taken by reading *Me Papoose Sitter* and so heartsick over his "affliction" that she invited him to "join their family" during her New York visit in the fall of 1960: "Having no children of their own, Margaret and Stringer Davis [her husband] had picked out several young people whom they liked for their adopted children . . . and made me one of them."[10]

Falling ill with leukemia and advised to move south during the winters, Isabel Whitney encouraged Hall to tour the region in search of a fitting residence. Detailed letters and photographs followed his visits to southern cities such as Nashville, New Orleans, and Charleston. Independently, both Hall and Whitney chose a pink stucco mansion and the old high school on Society Street in the Ansonborough restoration area of Charleston. Hall purchased the home for $13,500 from his book club proceeds from *Golden Boats from Burma*.

Built between 1835 and 1840, the run-down mansion was residence to one of the South's finest medical scientists and an American patriot, Dr. Joseph Johnson. This typical period house had a large dining room with a drawing room opposite on the first floor; an upper drawing room and Victorian bedroom on the second; and several bedrooms on the third. A grand staircase joined the floors. Apart from the main house were a former slave quarters and kitchen. Hall recalls:

> The room that would be my bedroom was full of hay. The yard had old, broken motor cars and rubbish. The beautiful iron gates were lying in pieces. It reminded me of Sissinghurst Castle where my mentor, Vita Sackville-West, first found it and said, I think we could be very happy here.[11]

Restoration quickly commenced, with the renovation cost rising to $46,000, not including the cost for mantels, hardware, lighting fixtures, and marble washstands that Isabel brought from New York.[12] Isabel worked from photographs and drawings to direct the restoration. (Her bedroom, for example, incorporated an antebellum yellow, rose-flecked wallpaper.) Gordon traveled back and forth to Charleston to see it through.[13]

The Grand Arrival

After Whitney's untimely death in February 1962, Hall arrived in Charleston on September 2, right after a hurricane. In his British accent, Gordon greeted new friends with frequent references to his well-placed connections (Whitney's cousin, Rutherford's adopted son, Crawford's close friend). Using money inherited from Whitney's estate (estimated at $3 million, with Hall named as the alternate executor) and earnings from his books, he continued the restoration project:

> It was the first house that I restored to the specifications that had been taught me by my great-uncle and aunt in England, who restored big mansions and smaller houses to perfection. We even brought one mantelpiece that came from President Chester Arthur's White House.[14]

Frances Edmunds, longtime director of the Historic Charleston Foundation, which had sold Hall the Johnson mansion, was invited to select suitable furnishings. An acquaintance of Hall's recalls that the home "was absolutely a show place! These were museum pieces": an antique French harp; George Washington mirrors (Gordon claimed Jacqueline Kennedy Onassis had wanted these); a Joshua Lockwood tall clock; a gilded palmetto mirror; an early nineteenth-century portrait of Ann Judson, a collateral ancestor of Isabel Whitney, and a Washington Austin painting (both of which now hang in museums); one of the original knife boxes from Washington's Mount Vernon; a painting by Samuel B. Morse, completed while he was in Charleston; chairs once owned by Robert E. Lee.

When finished, the Johnson House joined the select group of Charleston homes open for public viewing each spring under the sponsorship of the foundation.

Hall epitomized good taste with a British flair and royal connections. One Christmas card sent to members of the Charleston elite, for example, included a drawing by Charleston artist Corrie McCallum of the Kuanyin sculpture in Hall's green-and-white garden dedicated to the memory of Vita Sackville-West.

Quickly accepted by the "south-of-Broad" society because of his pedigree, accent, and money, Hall was one of Charleston's most eligible bachelors. As Gordon tells it:

> The invitations from would-be matchmakers kept pouring in. One poor soul who would never see forty again, whose only asset was her family name and her illustrious forebear's sword, delighted in arriving at the Dr. Joseph Johnson House clad in white tennis shorts. . . . The Jewish society also seemed to like me. One of their leading hostesses gave suppers that I really dreaded. Always some poor husbandless girl was purposely placed beside me at the table. . . . When I showed no particular interest in the feminine sex

there were those who decided that I must be a homosexual. After more than one party I was driven home by the husband and practically had to fight for my "honour" at the doorstep.[15]

Frances Edmunds was responsible for introducing Gordon to the accomplished architect Read Barnes, who completed the restoration project. Barnes, as Gordon remembers,

was born a generation before his time because of his visionary views of modern architecture so detested in Charleston. He told me that every new owner of an old house should leave behind something of themselves in it. So we placed French doors in the dining room that opened onto the garden steps.[16]

Barnes's relationship with Gordon extended eventually into family life, as Gordon became godparent to the first child born by Read's wife, Ann— who always had a strained relationship with Gordon. Years later Ann claimed, "My husband never seemed to get all the money he was owed. But people just fell all over Hall."[17] Denying the accusation, Gordon recalled visiting the Barneses after bestowing his christening gift, a handsome piece of Whitney silver. "It was so immaculate when I had first seen the home with Mrs. Edmunds. This time it looked as if a hurricane had hit it, piles of dirty dishes, soiled diapers, and trash were everywhere."[18]

Later, after Read's suicide, Ann married Jack Leland, a reporter for the *News and Courier*. Leland's critical stories, none of which appeared in the Charleston paper, would eventually discredit Hall; Hall lambasted Leland as a henchman.[19]

Ann Leland also remembers Peter Manigault, whose family owned the *News and Courier*, befriending Gordon. Soon, stories written about Gordon began appearing in the newspaper. One of the first, printed in the "women's section," highlighted a tour of England by several prominent Charlestonians. A photograph chronicled their visit to the garden "on the country estate of author Gordon Langley Hall . . . an official biographer of the British royal family."[20] Another article, published in 1964, stated:

Years of planning and five months of actual preparation will be culminated Sunday with the opening of the Isabel Lydia Whitney Memorial Garden Gallery . . . housing the permanent collection of America's first woman fresco painter. . . . British-born author Gordon Langley Hall . . . will guide visitors through the historic house he restored in memory of his cousin.[21]

The newspaper also published features about Hall displaying pictures at the Gibbes Art Gallery—his art collection was valued at $250,000—as well as positive reviews of his books.[22] Stories such as that reporting on a coming-out gala at the Denver Hilton for Hall's two Chihuahuas, Miss Annabel and Miss Nelly (one black, one white), replete with dresses, were covered in *other* papers. In fact, according to Ann Leland, reporters from Charleston's *News and Courier* did not publish anything negative or questioning about Hall for fear of losing their jobs[23]—a policy that remained in effect three decades later, when a *News and Courier* reporter interested in writing a feature on Hall was forced to scuttle the project.[24]

Hall was also a contributor to the *News and Courier* and other publications. His 1964 *News and Courier* article "Twas the Night Before Christmas" described the origins of the famous poem and the reluctance of its author, an eighteenth-century professor of divinity, to claim credit. Hall's 1963 essay "Gleaning from the Confederate Museum: The Ladies Do It," published in *Preservation Progress,* described Civil War clothing on display, noting, "During the Confederate days, the men seemed to have been as handy with a needle as the ladies."[25] Another *News and Courier* essay described his experiences on the Ojibway reservation with an aging matriarch and reflected his penchant for older women, inner social circles, and aristocratic lineage. In part it read:

> Standing on the landing stage in front of the warehouse clutching her homemade bouquet of red paper roses, she greeted me upon arrival with a large Margaret Rutherford grin. . . . What I did not know then about this amazing woman was the fact that she was a great believer in protocol and that her heroine was none other than vivacious Princess Margaret. As I had come all the way from England to be their teacher, in Poor Old Grandmother's estimation I was Queen Elizabeth's own representative. . . . The Gull Bay Social Register was kept at the back of the school attendance chart on my desk. It made very interesting reading. Poor Old Grandmother was second in importance among the ladies of Gull Bay.[26]

Traveling the Seamy Side

Rumors

During his years in Charleston, rumors circulated about Hall's interest in animals, young black men, and a prominent aristocrat. Gordon, so the stories went, allowed animals to live in his house. Few faulted Hall for keeping Marilyn, his parrot; Jacqueline, his German shepherd; or Simon, his guinea pig, housebound. Ann Leland, however, later vividly retold stories of a pig and other barnyard animals residing on the third floor:

"When his home was sold that floor had to be gutted. The pig mess had seeped into the floorboards and they were beyond repair." In a letter to his father, Jack Copper, Hall wrote, "Our pig Frances is growing enormous. She is house trained to paper and she dances . . . and she bangs the toilet seat when she wants water. She thinks she is a dog. . . . She is the cleanest animal I ever had."[27]

More serious rumors abounded regarding his fondness for young black men. Ann Leland recalls the first significant event that called into question Gordon's "most eligible bachelor" status:

> The first hint was from Kessler's grocery store on Anson and Society Streets. The store used black delivery boys, so when Hall called to place an order, the owner would tell him the boy would have to stay on the sidewalk to deliver the groceries.[28]

Years later Hall characterized such stories as "typical jealous gossip." Politely responding to each of these rumors, he wrote:

> No barnyard animals lived on the third floor. I told John-Paul [whom he was dating] . . . that my sister and I had a pet pig as children in England. . . . I told him that they were wonderful watchdogs and the next thing I knew he brought a piglet to me as a gift. His name was Bono. As it was against the law to keep a pig or other barnyard animals within the confines of the city, I had to quickly find Bono a home. He stayed overnight in the old slave quarters which had a brick floor—and then went to live on John's Island with the agreement that he could be used for breeding but never killed.
>
> The Kessler grocery store incident first appeared in Stephen Birmingham's book, *America's Secret Aristocracy*, as told to the author by none other than Ann Leland's husband. . . . I did take counsel . . . who advised me that I had a clear case to sue Birmingham, his two publishers, and Leland for libel. A staff of five or six people, including the gardener, worked at 56 Society Street. Don't you think the housekeeper or butler would have dealt with Kessler's? . . . I had nothing to do with running the house, buying food supplies.[29]

Also rumored was a relationship with another male friend, Joe, who arrived in Charleston at about the same time as Gordon. "Dr. Leber," an aging gay man and longtime Charleston resident, reminisces, "Joe had a raspy voice. He was a very kind man who used to cook for everyone. He loved to cook!" Leber often found Hall at Joe's home with its distinctive green shutters. Alleging "there was some connection between the two of them," the doctor expressed his resentment and suspicion about Hall:

"Well, when Joe finally died he was to leave antiques for his many friends but the will was held up because Gordon contested it—well, no one ever got anything."[30]

While Hall acknowledges the connection with Joe, he describes a relationship far different from that rumored within the homosexual community at the time:

Joe came into Isabel's life when he worked for Coleman's Auction Gallery. She bought a tapestry. Joe came to deliver and hang the tapestry and she decided he should work for us! He more or less took over. Joe did all of the cooking; he got rid of the cook and the janitor. He really worked himself right in. He thought he was our bodyguard!

But, he was the bane of my life! One of the reasons I moved to Charleston was to make a completely new start. Unfortunately, Joe was very unhappy with Isabel gone and he caused a lien to be placed on the property there. I had to pay quite a bit of money.

Well, Joe turned up on my doorstep in Charleston. . . . In the end, to get him off my hands I set him up in business, renting an antique shop and giving him a great deal of stuff to sell. . . . When I wed . . . he spat in my face on King Street and painted my name off the antique shop.

I did not contest Joe's will. Before he died, he, in a macabre move, tagged all of his possessions—some of which were mine and Isabel's—with prices. . . . Not much sold since Joe's prices were too high. I did request that a table and four chairs that had belonged to Isabel's great-aunt, Lydia Wooster Harris, the Hudson River painter, be returned or for me to even buy them back. I heard no more.[31]

Unaware of or discounting Hall's perspective, the homosexuals frequenting Charleston's Wagon Wheel or the 49 Club, where gossip ran more freely than liquor, circulated these and other rumors. But, given Hall's background, wealth, and demeanor, they were overlooked by the well-heeled Charlestonian aristocracy.

The Ansonborough Homosexual Community

During the early 1960s there was a sizable homosexual community living in the historic Ansonborough area of Charleston. "Jeremy Morrow" was one of several longtime homosexual residents living near Gordon's home. He occasionally frequented the bars but preferred to attend small dinner parties among Charleston's gay elite or to steal away for a few weeks in Europe or Northern Africa to indulge his sexual fantasies.

In Ansonborough also lived "Russell," a former composer for the New York Metropolitan Opera, and his lover, "Tool," a Texas teenager. They moved to Charleston together in 1959, where they lived until the composer's death twenty years later. There also was Joe, Gordon's friend who followed him from New York. Joe's knowledge of antiques, his culinary talents, and his kindly demeanor endeared him to many in this close-knit community.

"Billy Camden" moved to Charleston in 1947 from a small South Carolina town and lived with "Heyward," his longtime companion. "The gay couples really restored Ansonborough," Billy relates. "I was on the Board of Directors for the Ansonborough Historic Foundation—it was made up of 80 percent gay men! There was a gay couple or gay person in almost every home." Pausing, Billy laughs: "They should have called it 'Queensborough' instead. . . . Now, they have all moved away or died."[32]

Next door to Billy and Heyward lived "Nicky" and "Tom," who were together nearly half a century. Now widowed and in his late seventies, Nicky recalls those pre-Stonewall years:

> We lived as "out" as possible for that time period. We were active socially: visiting other gay couples for dinner, going to one of the town's bars. We were also active in the larger Charleston community. We were always invited as a couple to Charleston's social events. Now, did other people know we were gay? Sure. Did we ever declare ourselves "gay"? No. Some younger people might look back at that time and ask, "How could you live in such a closeted world?" Well, as far as I am concerned it was the best of times! Back then you didn't have to carry that terrible label; you could be free to be yourself, enjoy your company of friends.

Billy remembers the social scene similarly to Nicky:

> One thing that was very nice about the sixties was our group of twelve couples—all professional people—who formed the "couples' club." Each couple entertained once a month in their home. You could invite whoever you wanted; it could be a formal dinner or a cocktail party.[33]

During this time cruising was common, as navy and air force men could be readily picked up along the Battery, in the town square, or at the Meeting Street bus stop. Negro homosexuals could also be found walking down Meeting Street. "Cruising was easy," Billy recollects. "Sex was easy in the fifties and sixties! They were just horny soldiers. If they had had a choice—a man or a woman—most would have taken the woman; but the choice, at the moment, was a man—so they took it! Of course, some of these men would want money before or after, and a lot of gay people got into trouble."

As a seaport, Charleston had long been a site for homosexual activity. Camden reminisces:

> There were always gay bars in Charleston. The first one I went to was in '47. Ratskellars was on Court House Square. Some of the bars were mixed, like the Anchor. It was not openly gay but a lot of bachelors would meet. Then there was the 49 Club where the front was gay, the back was mixed with couples, and the upstairs was gambling.

Being associated with the homosexual underground, however, posed dangers:

> Back then, for people who were in the military, teachers, government and state workers—if they found out you were gay [such people] would lose their jobs. So these people were very careful not to be seen in a place known as a "gay bar," which is why a lot of the bars were mixed. Those are the places where people went. Even if you were a civilian working for a private company but were hanging around military or government employees, the navy would investigate you. They'd go in and question you and your employers, trying to get people fired.

Billy recalls a visit he received from naval intelligence:

> They came in with a whole photo book of marines, navy, and air force men they suspected of being homosexuals. They wanted to see if I could identify any. Well, I wouldn't let them interview me at my business. I made them come to my house, making it as inconvenient as possible for them. But I was cordial and, of course, I did not recognize any as homosexuals. [Laughs.] "Sure are some good looking men," I commented to one of the investigators, "but I don't know any of them."

During this time Billy owned a gay bar, "Camden's Tavern," located in the heart of Charleston. Despite these and other terror tactics used by the government, he fondly remembers the pre-Stonewall homosexual community:

> Back then people all dressed. You never saw someone in those bars without a coat-and-tail or a tuxedo. It was a very nice time! Today, you have people wearing cutoffs; they look so grungy. To go out on a date you would put on a shirt, tie, and sports coat visiting restaurants like Henry's or the Cavalier Club. I go to the bars now, and you might see one or two young men and women dressed appropriately; the rest seem to be having a contest on who can look the worst. It's terrible!

Dangers other than government harassment and threats confronted homosexuals during this era. In the fall of 1956, Jack Dobbins was bludgeoned to death by a youth brandishing a silver candlestick from the fireplace mantel. This infamous "candlestick murder" sent a long-remembered message to Charleston's homosexual community. Jack had stayed with Billy and his partner for about a month when he first came to Charleston. Camden recalls:

> The guy that killed him got off scot-free because he said Jack had propositioned him for sex. Now, this kid had been in the gay bars; he knew what was going on! Yet he robbed and killed Jack, then turned himself in to a strong Catholic lawyer. "The boy was protecting his virginity," his counsel argued in court. Well, the boy got off with a slap on the wrist and a trip out of town. Dobbins's mother, who lived in Spartanburg, didn't pursue it because she was embarrassed and hurt. She just wanted it swept under the rug and forgot about. I'll never forget my mama saying at the time, "If that would have been you, I would have been fightin' up there like a wet hen for justice." But, you know, back then the gay community didn't get justice; we didn't expect it. Then gay people were often robbed and too embarrassed to report it. If they did report it, the person who was robbed was victimized again by the system: he was gay and, therefore, at fault.

Hall's Relationship with the Homosexual Community

Nicky first met Gordon at the Book Basement, a local bookstore, where Hall was promoting one of his biographies. He claims Gordon "patrolled Meeting Street at night. He loved black men almost as much as he liked old ladies with money." Distancing himself from Hall, Nicky asserts, "The man's *only* interest in gay life was picking black men up"—to which Gordon retorts, "Sheer poppycock! I didn't even promote a book in Charleston until 1993."[34]

Initially, Gordon was received politely and with interest by Charleston's gay elite. "When he first came, everyone accepted him," Camden remembers. "He was restoring that house with beautiful things from the Whitney estate." Yet this initial enchantment and hospitality quickly turned to disgust and social ostracism. Living around the corner from Gordon, Camden recalls:

> We saw him often, but he was not in our group. He was at my house several times, but I don't think I ever entertained him. When he first moved here, Joe brought him along to our beach house. He was a small-framed, very

effeminate guy with a very thick English accent. At the beginning, the people connected with historic Ansonborough included him. But as soon as it got out what was going on—with all the blacks he entertained—that was the end of it! He would always be with a group of black, screaming queens. Charleston people would have nothing to do with him. He was an insult to the gay community; we were *never* friends.

While Gordon has long resented those who wrongly labeled him homosexual or spread other vicious rumors, he had no animosity toward homosexuals and has long had "homosexual friends." Even as a child, "my mother had a lesbian cousin. We never ever rejected persons like that. In England we just accepted that part of her."[35] In Charleston, as Gordon acknowledged, "there were so many gay people that it was hard not to know them. In the arts you're always going to come across gay people, and they have a perfect right to their way of lives." He also observed:

> On the surface you would know a man and his wife, but you would also know about the other attachment. . . . In England, I grew up in that atmosphere with Vita Sackville-West and her husband, Harold Nicolson—two people who couldn't be more in love—going their separate ways with their sexual preference.[36]

Jeremy Morrow first met Gordon through another prominent Charleston family man who "spoke big, but wasn't monied." (Jeremy was quick to add "Gordon did both.") For Jeremy, Gordon Langley Hall was a titillating embarrassment; yet, unlike Nicky and Billy, he longed to enter Hall's social circle. With barely disguised bitterness Jeremy snaps, "I wasn't a celebrity! That was important for Gordon. He loved to boast of his friendship with famous or well-connected people." Jeremy had to content himself with eyeing the Society Street residence from a distance and gossiping with "a black male (maybe mixed)—funny, feminine, flaming—who worked for Gordon." Jeremy learned "about Gordon falling down stairs, wearing strange clothes, talking in a feminine voice, menstruating, and just being out-and-out flamboyant."[37]

From Hall's perspective, it was his fair treatment of blacks that underlay the antipathy toward him among his Ansonborough neighbors:

> In certain matters I was, perhaps, too liberal for Charleston. For instance, I got into trouble when I wanted to pay my cook her Social Security and went up to the Federal Building with her and arranged it. Some of my neighbors said I should have left "well enough alone because you are creating a

precedent." I just thought I was obeying the law! In the gay community, Joe hated Black people! The stories told about me are vicious with no foundation in fact: the black male referred to by Jeremy never worked for me; I never cruised King Street; the barnyard and Kessler Grocery stories are untrue; and I had friends who were not well-to-do or famous, such as the poor old cobbler on King Street.[38]

During one visit to the Joseph Johnson House, Nicky recalls several blacks in attendance; and Rita Smith, the sister of novelist Carson McCullers and the editor of *Redbook*, later described how "a young Negro man met them at the door, invited them in, mixed drinks, served them." The man then

> took his own off the tray and sat down to join in the conversation. Amazed at the familiarity of the servant, Miss Smith reportedly could hardly wait to tell Carson . . . about the experience. . . . Carson loved the story and delighted in hearing further evidence that fact is often much better than fantasy, but seldom believed unless cloaked in fiction.[39]

Hall entertained the grand dame of southern literature herself in the spring of 1963. In her biography of McCullers, Virginia Carr wrote of Carson's visit:

> Carson was intrigued by Hall, whom she later described as "a rather strange young British gentleman." . . . Always more of an observer than a participant, Carson had little to say to Hall throughout the evening. But just as [she and her escort] were about to leave, she turned suddenly toward the young man and said, "I want to talk to the *child* (referring to Hall). Please leave us together for a few minutes." Alone with the shy, rather diffident man who now sat beside her, Carson studied him closely without speaking. Then, with a bit of a smile, she said gently, "You're really a little girl." Hall looked at her, then nodded.[40]

Changing Times, Changing Bodies

By 1966, Gordon was tiring of Charleston's social life and "decided to retire from Charleston society. . . . Being an author I could always say that when I worked I liked to shut myself away from the world."[41]

As he began his newest biography on Lady Bird Johnson, Gordon began to feel physically different: "a sort of lethargy had crept into my life. Both body and mind seemed tired; they craved for rest. To add to my discomfort there were strange sensations in my breasts, as if, deep down, some seed long dormant was stirring." [42] Then, early one morning Gordon woke up in a pool of blood. His housekeeper

> panicked and called an ambulance that rushed me to the hospital. My secret was out! The gynecologist came in and said, "I guess you know what I am going to tell you. There is a vaginal tract that is blocked and if it is not put right, you will not live out the year." So, you see, I really had no choice. [43]

Hall visited a local physician, social activist, and friend Dr. Duncan Pringle. Her family had long been prominent in Charleston society: her grandfather owned the South Carolina and Pacific Railroad and a cotton mill; her father was a local banker; her mother was called a "communist" and a "nigger lover." Duncan had encouraged Hall to meet Margarita Childs, her sister. Margarita remembers Hall as a "nonstop talker who spoke intelligently against the death penalty." She also recalls the efforts of her sister, Duncan, to improve the lives of those on the margins of Charleston society:

> She worked awfully hard on her practice. The black class got a greater quality of medical treatment than they would [have] had she not been there. Back then, the white doctors would always say that the white patients wouldn't like it if they had blacks in the same waiting room and they couldn't afford two rooms. Duncan was the kind of person who, if she met a black couple in the park, she would invite them home for lunch or to stay a couple of days. [44]

On the recommendation of Dr. Pringle, Gordon visited the Medical College of Charleston, where a physician

> told me that I was a "transsexual." I can honestly say that I had never heard the word. Of course I had heard of sex-changes. The Christine Jorgenson story was universal. . . . I asked [him] exactly what a transsexual was. He explained that although I was not normal in the sense that other men or women might be normal, neither was I "a homosexual." This latter was interesting for although I had never felt at ease with so-called normal people, neither had I been happy in the company of the other kind. [45]

Contrary to the rumors circulating within the homosexual community, Gordon remembered that "even after the age of puberty I was like a vegetable; that I felt no sensual sensations at all in the sex organs as they were." [46]

Through the Medical College, Hall learned of the newly established Gender Identity Clinic, staffed by a team of doctors at Johns Hopkins

University. Formed in 1966, the clinic used surgical techniques learned during the two world wars and the clinical procedures developed by endocrinologist Harry Benjamin to perform sex reassignments.[47] Today there are about forty clinics specializing in sex-reassignment surgery in the United States, most adhering to Benjamin's step-by-step procedures of living the role of the other gender, participating in psychological tests, ingesting hormones, and enduring a series of progressive surgeries.

Gordon's vague awareness of the sexually different was not unusual for a person living during this era. It was not until the end of World War II that homosexuality, transsexuality, and sex-change procedures entered public awareness. The publication of the two Kinsey reports in 1948 and 1953, the extensive news coverage of Christine Jorgensen's "sex-change" surgery of 1953, the purges of "sexual perverts" in the government and military services throughout the McCarthy era, the popularization of castration therapy to cure homosexual men, the stereotyping of gay men as effeminate and lesbians as butch, and the linkage of parenting patterns to the development of homosexuality had a collective impact on alerting Americans to those roaming the sexual wilderness.

As sexual outsiders, however, many of Charleston's homosexuals during the 1950s and 1960s were assimilationists in orientation, reflecting the social conformity, self-hatred, or sexual inferiority epitomized in novels like Gore Vidal's *The City and the Pillar* (1948). Given this climate, as well as the confusion between homosexual and transgender issues, it's no surprise that Hall received little support within the gay community. The cruel taunts and jokes among some, like Jeremy, within Charleston's intimate homosexual community reflected the generations-old confusion of transsexuality with repressed homosexual tendencies[48] and the internalized homophobia so prevalent in the pre-Stonewall era. The maimed image of the "transvestite," popularized in the 1960s, was that of a person "trapped in the wrong body." Havelock Ellis first distinguished between two types of "aesthetic inverts": One simply wore the other gender's clothing (the transvestite), while the other "so identified himself with those of his physical and psychic traits which recall the opposite sex that he feels really to belong to that sex although he has no delusion regarding his anatomical conformation."[49]

Hall, however, did not fall into either the category of "cross-dresser" or that of "transsexual," in that his "anatomical conformation" was itself blurred. While Gordon's gender identity was male, he never considered himself a man. Until mid-adulthood, however, he accepted the "peculiar condition" fate had assigned him. As MacKenzie describes in *Transgender Nation*, individuals like Hall are

> intersexed individuals [who] are usually born sexually ambiguous at birth due to hormonal, gonadal, chromosomal, and/or genital contradictions. Some intersexed persons develop secondary sex characteristics of the "opposite" sex during puberty. In the U.S. transsexual surgery was developed from surgical techniques used on intersexed persons, who in some cases were raised as the wrong gender and after puberty had surgery to coincide with the gender of rearing.[50]

There had been no such opportunity for surgery when Gordon was growing up. However, in October 1967, at the age of thirty, Gordon was invited to a coveted screening interview at the Johns Hopkins Gender Identity Clinic through the auspices of Dr. Pringle and the Medical College of Charleston. A weeklong session of physical examinations followed in December. During this second visit, he met with the clinic's leading doctors, including psychiatrist John Money. Revealing that he had never engaged in sexual intercourse, Hall quoted his long-admired acquaintance Bette Davis: "The romance when mind meets mind—is quite as exciting as when boy meets girl."[51]

Gordon began growing his hair long (showing off his tight, natural curls well before such a style had become fashionable in the Holy City), taking prescribed hormone tablets, and dressing as a woman. When Jeremy Morrow asked about it, Gordon matter-of-factly replied, "I'm having a sex change." Morrow remembers, "Well, we all but fainted. We had never heard of such a thing! He said it was a 'medical necessity'; that was bullshit!" Nicky echoes this sentiment. The first time he saw Gordon dressed as a woman, "*he* had breasts; the next day, *she* was flat. Another day *he* would have breasts. I think he was stuffing himself with a pillow!" Billy recollects:

> Everyone reacted about the same way. She [Gordon] already [had] gone downhill, selling practically everything in the house. Her only contact or social life was with the black people. No one in the gay community wanted anything to do with her after that.

Not surprisingly, Hall preferred to remain secluded behind his well-manicured walled gardens and attended to by the Johnson House staff: Mr. James, the butler; Viola, the housekeeper; Irene, the cook. Ignoring the gossip among the well-heeled Charleston elite, as well as in the homosexual community, Hall found himself thinking about men and, in particular, one prominent gentleman:

> My doctors were glad to know that, where the now opposite sex were concerned, I was having normal reactions. Unmarried, he would have been a marvelous catch. As his wife I would one day have been chatelaine of one of the most famed historic mansions in the city. I might even have made the exclusive St. Cecilia's Ball.[52]

Finally, in the fall of 1968, Hall took the final step—gender-reassignment surgery, including opening the vaginal passage. Waiting for the bandages to be removed during those difficult weeks after surgery, Gordon—now Dawn—patiently edited her manuscript on Mary Todd Lincoln and sewed. As she was preparing to leave the hospital, one of the nurses told Dawn, "It's so good to see a real woman who sews and embroiders."[53]

Returning to Charleston in October as the 102-pound brunette Dawn Pepita Hall, she would write later in her biography:

> I knew now that Gordon was truly dead. What he had tried to do, all the years of frustration and worry, and fighting to prove that he was something that he was not, were over. To the new Dawn, Gordon was dead.[54]

The Less-than-Triumphant Return

Despite all of her social transgressions, Gordon was welcomed back into the bosom of the ladies of the Confederacy as Dawn. "It really didn't phase Charleston all that much. I had a lot of money then and a very good family background. They were more worried about who they would marry me off to. One very old family wined and dined me, but I refused them."[55]

Hall remained, however, the object of jokes, innuendo, and gossip among Charleston homosexuals. Jeremy Morrow simply declared, "He or she was not normal!"

There were rumors, now acknowledged by Dawn, of an affair with one prominent man in Charleston society, who would jump the fence to see her at night. Such rumors—according to Ann Leland, spread by Hall himself—later found their way into a national weekly tabloid:

> Before Dawn married . . . she was the mistress of one of Charleston's leading white aristocrats, a married man with children. This guy was like the study

in the old Hathaway shirt ads—tall, dignified, dashing, grey-of-temple, the quintessence of courtly grooviness, Southern style.[56]

There was also a rumor that Dawn was to marry a Mr. Simmons whom Gordon had met at a party held at one of the Battery mansions. The south-of-Broad elites' attitudes quickly changed, however, as Dawn announced her engagement to another Mr. Simmons—a local mechanic, sometime shrimper, sculptor, and, by that time, her "chauffeur," John-Paul Simmons, who also happened to be "a Negro":

> She is rich, he is poor. She is an intellectual and introvert. He is a boisterous and exuberant extrovert. He lives by his body, she by her mind. He is young, she is almost ten years his senior. He is a healthy heterosexual, she until their marriage had been sexually totally inexperienced.[57]

A generation later, Dawn's biographer echoed this newspaper's profile:

> Dawn taught John-Paul about art and ideas, antiques and life in Society. John-Paul taught Dawn about affection, spontaneity, adventure and uninhibited perception. Dawn saw John-Paul as an equal and encouraged his creativity. John-Paul saw Dawn as a woman with charm and grace and an uncanny humor.[58]

Dawn (a name chosen by John-Paul) first met her future husband midway through the sex-reassignment process. He knocked at Gordon's door one evening to escort Irene, the cook, on a date; she had already departed. Within a matter of days, John-Paul had

> forced entry into the house dressed in dirty old overalls, with his mechanic's cap over his eyes and his arms full of flowers. He had bought every flower he could find. He told me, "I'll never leave you again."[59]

With Dawn characterizing the meeting as "love at first sight," their relationship progressed. John-Paul "became an integral part" of Hall's path toward womanhood.[60] Describing John-Paul to her father, Jack Copper, Dawn later wrote, "You will like John-Paul as he is very clever with cars and is a natural born mechanic like yourself. . . . He is a rough diamond but his heart is in the right place and he is very good to me."[61]

It was not, however, an easy relationship, as evidenced by the sermonesque letter sent to John-Paul from his older brother, Alex:

> Why is it Johnnie that you still [sic] under the impression that you are sixteen years old? . . . The objective of this letter my bro is to bring to your attention the damage you are doing to yourself and to those who love you

very much. . . . If you hang around those places that's quite all right . . . but don't take my sisters with you having them subjected to degenerate abuses does not conform with the standard of a gentleman. . . . If you love her [Dawn] man, show more concern and consideration for her safety and well being. . . . Those people (your so called friends) are all parasites exploiting you. . . . They see that you've got a little something that's why they befriend you. . . . You're not even married yet and already you've violated one of the major codes by dealing in promiscuity. Listen, if the [sic] is all you have to offer this sweet girl, you'd be doing yourself and the family and her a great favor by just leaving her.[62]

During Dawn's recovery, she received her first love letter from John-Paul, which read, in part, "I love you even though I may not act like I do sometimes. I didn't realize it until you left me. I miss you very much and hope that you will be coming home to me soon."[63] Twenty years later, Dawn fondly remembered their budding relationship:

My good friend, Rita Mae Brown, the novelist, once wrote that you take the man that you want to marry to Charleston and if, after three days, he doesn't propose, then it is time to throw him into the crepe myrtle bushes. . . . We did all of our courting in the early hours of the morning driving over the Cooper River Bridge to a little Black cafe.[64]

As word spread among the Charleston elite, a group of concerned ladies of the Confederacy visited the Johnson mansion. One brought an apple pie for Dawn and a watermelon for John-Paul. Another warned Dawn that if the marriage took place, Dawn would find herself on the "cooling couch" (a bed or table on which the deceased is laid to air out). A third asked Dawn to consider the example of another local socialite with a fondness for the other color: "She fell in love with a nigger, but she married one of her own kind and they've all lived together for years in the old family mansion"[65]—to which Dawn replied, "A man worth lying down with is worth standing up with."[66]

Those within the gay community acquainted with Gordon were equally upset with Dawn's open relationship. "Back then," Morrow states, "gay men did not *date* blacks, and we certainly didn't 'marry' them. Sex between black and white men was *always* behind closed doors."

Not surprisingly, the entire affair, occurring in the milieu of the Civil Rights movement and the struggle for "gay power," caught the attention of the media.[67] Stories and photographs appeared in national and international magazines, tabloids, and newspapers, ranging from *Time* to *National Insider* and the *News of the World*.

Last week ... Hall, who claims to be 31 (other sources suggest he is 39), revealed an idiosyncrasy that Charleston could hardly ignore ... she was going to marry a 22-year-old Negro garage mechanic.[68]

According to Hall, these stories were instigated by someone with a long-standing grudge against her:

My engagement photograph was stolen from my living room at 56 Society on the Tuesday and appeared on the front page of London's *News of the World* on the following Sunday. Only someone with access to the media news services could have promoted it so quickly with the headline, "Royal Biographer Marries Her Butler." When Dena Crane [Simmons's biographer] was at UPI looking for photographs she found a glorious one of Dawn taken at this prominent gentleman's mansion. He had sold my photo to a news service![69]

Dawn remembers that such unwelcome publicity stirred others to action:

Mail arrived by the sackful at the mansion on Society Street; some letters kind and some vicious. I had fifteen Bibles from Born-again Christians and a rather nice leather-bound copy of the Koran from Saudi Arabia.... "Her Majesty, the Queen, was sympathetic," wrote Mother [Dame Rutherford]. Joan Crawford spoke up for me. "The heart knows why," she told Mother, at the same time sending me a bunch of yellow roses.[70]

Quickly dropped from Charleston's party lists and social registry, Dawn was abandoned by her "friends,"[71] and her enemies threatened to bomb the Shiloh African Methodist Episcopal (AME) Church where the wedding was to take place. On January 22, 1969, South Carolina's first mixed-marriage occurred—and the *News and Courier* placed the wedding announcement in the obituary section.

Due to threats against the Shiloh AME Church, the wedding ceremony was held in the lower drawing room at the Joseph Johnson House. After the area was checked for bombs, a group of twenty-five guests and journalists crowded into a small Victorian parlor to view the historic ceremony. ("The street was packed," reminisced Dawn, "their bodies rippling like waves.")[72] Escorted by her father-in-law, Dawn descended the huge staircase, wearing silver earrings, two ropes of pearls, and a white gown of candlelight lace with a twelve-foot train held by two children. The voice of Andy Williams sang the "Battle Hymn of the Republic" in the background as three black bridesmaids led the procession. During the ceremony Dawn's veil slipped several times (her mother-in-law fiddled with it repeatedly), and the black minister stumbled over his words, repeating entire paragraphs of the vows.[73] The reception was held at the Brooks Hotel—which mysteriously burned to the ground shortly afterward.

Jeremy wasn't invited to the wedding. Although Jack Leland attended, Ann later recalled, "Jack couldn't write about it for the *News and Courier* but he sold many stories to other papers"[74]—articles that Dawn would later denounce.

On learning that Dawn Simmons was denied a proper church wedding, Dame Rutherford spoke with the archbishop of Canterbury to arrange a Church of England ceremony.[75] The ceremony was held at the twelfth-century St. Clements Church in Hastings; Dawn wore "a gold brocade with leg of mutton sleeves and an enormous train of gold velvet. The veil was kept in place by Mother's [Dame Rutherford's] real diamond tiara which had been skillfully 'woven' into my hair by Princess Margaret's own hairdresser." As Dawn entered the church, the congregation rose to sing "O Perfect Love."[76]

But harassment intensified during the months following the marriage. Windows of their mansion were smashed. Three shots were fired at John-Paul. Dawn was run down by a car on Anson Street, injuring her left shoulder. The telephone rang incessantly with crank calls: one vowed, "Dawn, I'll kill you"; another warned Dawn that John-Paul was "consorting with other women"; and several callers sought Dawn for a 1960s version of phone sex. Charley, Dawn's Doberman pinscher, was poisoned, and their basset hound, Samantha, became a hit-and-run victim. These and other incidents led Dawn to query, "Am I in the middle of one of those Tennessee Williams plays where the innocent young man is literally destroyed by a parody of Southern justice?"[77]

Dawn's struggle occurred within a larger conflict over civil rights known in South Carolina as the "Charleston Movement."[78] Although race relations were considered good by southern standards, the underlying racial tension erupted during this time. March 1969 marked what the *New York Times* characterized as the "country's tensest Civil Rights struggle": the beginning of a more than one hundred-day strike of four hundred predominantly black, female hospital workers. As days turned into weeks, Governor Robert McNair ordered five thousand armed National Guard troops to Charleston, where they remained to enforce curfew until the mid-summer settlement.

During the height of the conflict, the AME Emanuel Church hosted a

9.1. Dawn Langley Hall following her marriage to John-Paul Simmons, 1969. From the collection of Dawn Langley Simmons.

meeting where the Reverend Ralph Abernathy, Andrew Young, and Coretta Scott King addressed the crowd. In violation of curfew a night march was held, during which hundreds of demonstrators—led by Abernathy—were arrested and detained:

> The strike had divided the white community. There had been fear abroad in Charleston during the dark nights of the curfew. Some were reminded of a much earlier era. The Charleston poetess Alice Cabiness wrote: "merchants lounging in doorways cursing ease, grouping angrily . . . patrolling windows, counting guardsmen going by / Denmark Vesey smiles with pleasure from another country / black shadows on the empty streets undo the handshakes of my friends."[79]

Dawn and John-Paul ventured out into the city on that fateful evening:

> I had a craving for pigs' feet and chocolate. But you could only get it in the coloreds' quarter of Charleston. There was a nine o'clock curfew. We were on the way back when the National Guard appeared not quite at nine o'clock. They chased us right up to our property at 56 Society Street and arrested us at bayonet [point]. They took us to the city jail, where they beat

us. The last time I saw John-Paul they were taking him upstairs with his hands and face all bloody. They took me into a cell—I can see the roaches crawling up the wall even now—where they kept my shoes. I had to stand on the bed to get away from all of the things crawling on the floor. But I pulled myself together and got my lawyer, who bailed us out. We appeared in court the next morning. Several black men were in their best Sunday churchgoing jackets. The judge dismissed our case because there was no case. Well, those men threw down their jackets for us to walk on—a very rare experience.[80]

In the midst of all of these controversies, Richia Atkinson Barloga, one of the few local aristocrats not abandoning Dawn, was selling her home on Gibbes Street, located south of Broad. She arranged for her real estate agent to put a clause in the agreement that allowed Dawn first priority to the property. The thought that Dawn and her Negro husband would take up residence at the epicenter of Charleston society drove one southern gentleman to offer the couple $5,000 not to move into the Gibbes Street home.

About this time, according to Hall, a group of wealthy Charlestonians conspired to remove Dawn from the city. When she was unable to receive money from Britain, due to a mail strike, the local bank foreclosed on the mortgage held for the former kitchen quarters (now a gallery) adjacent to the main house. As Dawn recollects:

> My lawyer told me that he had never known so rushed a foreclosure. At the last minute, an old friend [Richia] stepped in to say she would pay off the mortgage in full. . . . Unfortunately, she literally disappeared. . . . She had been drugged and taken by a man to a motel . . . emerging ten days later when our home had been sold for a pittance . . . on the steps of the Court House where so many of my husband's ancestors had also been.[81]

With less than twelve hours to leave the mansion, furniture and artwork set on the porch, John-Paul returned to his mother and Dawn left with Jackie, her German shepherd, for a nearby hotel.

After resettlement in a house on Thomas Street, located in one of the poorest areas of Charleston, Dawn's "pregnancy" became the next much talked-about affair in the long saga of Gordon Langley Hall. Even twenty years later, several persons who questioned Mrs. Simmons's authenticity as a "real woman" expressed the same skepticism felt in 1970. One reader of the *Charleston Chronicle* wrote to the editor of the black-owned newspaper:

The late Anna Montgomery, who worked at a baby store on King Street, said that he [Gordon] came into the store to make a purchase, and that the women were all laughing, because while looking like a pregnant woman, he forgot to tie down the strings of a pillow case stuffed with cotton. . . . Two months later Gordon or Dawn was seen pushing a baby carriage around town. There was a baby in the carriage, but, isn't Mrs. Simmons supposed to be white or British? The baby that several people saw was as Black as ten-midnights, not saying that dark skin children are not beautiful gifts from God, but . . . [82]

Dawn, however, is quick to point out that the *Charleston Chronicle* could never locate the "Mr. Brown" who penned this letter on College of Charleston letterhead. ("The president of the college wrote me a beautiful letter of apology.") Characterizing Brown's skin comment as "wicked," Dawn more graciously comments, "I can only smile at the pillow stories. I did use cotton wool pads at one point because of the burning in the breasts." [83]

On October 16, 1971, Dawn and John-Paul's daughter, Natasha Margi-nell Manigault Simmons, was born in a Philadelphia hospital, where Dawn had entered under an assumed name.[84] Returning to Charleston, Dawn often strolled along the city streets with Natasha in an "old fash-ioned British baby carriage (pram) just like the one that the Queen had for Prince Charles." [85] Yet Dawn and John-Paul's presence in Charleston was no less explosive in the years after the birth of their daughter. John-Paul's body hung in effigy on Society Street. Longtime British actor friend and Natasha's godfather, Anthony Dawson, strongly urged Dawn to

consider moving out of that atmosphere in Charleston. It is not a good atmosphere to bring up a child. Now that you are getting so much publicity moving to a more civilised part of the United States can do a lot to make look ridiculous and shameful and uncivilised the behaviour of those people.[86]

Dawn and John-Paul's explosive relationship behind the Society Street walls was less public. His frequent bouts with alcohol and related psycho-logical problems were sometimes too much for Dawn to bear. Finally, she departed for England with Natasha. Her letters from Europe reveal a dark, turbulent relationship that, a generation later, can be recognized as battered wife syndrome:

I am not upset with you as I know you were not yourself the other night. . . . For weeks you have known that you could continue with the house, that the payment only worked out to 25 dollars a week. I have no money left. You know that and you destroyed all of my work when I couldn't give you $30. . . . The British Consul sent you papers six weeks ago so that you could work in England. You are a good mechanic and you know that Cousin Peter has a garage. . . . I shall never stop you from seeing Baby as I love you and have always loved you. Nobody would love a man who had tried to kill them several times, gave them 45 stitches in their face, broke their nose and cheekbone and ruined the eyesight . . . but I never ever shut the door against you.[87]

A few of Dawn's Charleston friends were aware of their strained relationship, brought on by John-Paul's illness. In one letter to Dawn during her stay in England, Robert Holmes relayed "that the grocery store was visited last week by JPS, your husband and the father of your child, accompanied by several dogs. Nurse Mary was shocked by his appearance: nothing but skin and bone with great pouches beneath his eyes."[88]

As disturbing as these reports and John-Paul's treatment of Dawn were, she remained faithful and hopeful. Dawn's unremitting love for John-Paul and her deep anger over their treatment by Charleston society are well expressed in another summer 1972 letter:

As you said, everyone who wronged us would be punished. You say that you want a divorce. I'll not stand in your way . . . . There are only two ways I can divorce you . . . for adultery and for cruelty. . . . Cruelty would be the better. Nothing would be final for 4 months and you would have time to change your mind. . . . We have been through too much. You were the kindest man I ever knew before that woman who ruined you with drink. I am eternally thankful to you for the most beautiful baby in Charleston.[89]

Her unrelenting love and his deteriorating condition brought Dawn back across the ocean the following autumn into the sometimes loving and oftentimes hurtful arms of John-Paul.

A Footnote on Her Life after Charleston

In the summer of 1974, John-Paul, Dawn, and Natasha moved north of the Mason-Dixon line and rented a run-down, ten-room, eighteenth-century, brown stucco mansion in the Catskills. With promises of help with restoration (the home was the site of President Martin Van Buren's marriage ceremony), the community of eight thousand embraced them. The *New York Times* published a story under the title "Transsexual Starting New

Life in Catskills," and a controversial follow-up story summarized the chain of events from summer to winter:

> Today, the house is an empty wreck. The owner has sued for $800 in rent. As of last week, the Simonses [sic] were on welfare, living in a local motel. . . . [A] Catskill realty man who was handling the sale of the house, says the couple put down a $200 binder. Cash from the book that Mrs. Simmons was reported to be writing did not materialize. With no money for fuel, the family moved out "in the dead of winter," . . . and the pipes froze and burst, flooding the premises.[90]

Once again, Dawn's version is different: "The man who gave the *New York Times* the 'welfare' news was later jailed for stealing from Social Services. It was not true. The *New York Times* apologized to me."[91]

Shortly afterward, John-Paul abandoned Dawn for the fifth time. Living in a run-down Catskill motel, she contemplated divorce.[92] Although she finally departed the motel, she would not divorce John-Paul. In Hudson, New York, Dawn taught art at a Catholic school, became secretary and historian of the Presbyterian Women's Association, and served as secretary of the local Mental Health Association. In the words of Dawn's biographer:

> Her writing career was reduced to writing for *The National Enquirer.* She spent seven years in hunger, isolation, and poverty but never thought of herself as poor. She would collect broken objects and flowers and decorate her room with character and style. She devoted her life to Natasha and to giving her everything that money couldn't buy.[93]

Recently celebrating their twenty-fifth wedding anniversary, Dawn remains faithful to the rugged shrimper whose fateful knock on her Society Street door changed her life. Dawn speaks frequently with John-Paul by telephone and makes occasional visits to the mental health complex where he was admitted years ago. "I would never desert him," emphasizes Dawn. "I always see that he has clothes, pocket money, and everything he needs." This has not always been an easy task, during the lean years that have slowly progressed to more pleasant times:

> With John-Paul away most of the time and Natasha living in her own apartment, I am gradually picking up the pieces from nursing a husband with chronic schizophrenia for twelve years. The biography of my ["adoptive"] mother [Dame Margaret Rutherford] did very well indeed and now I am hard at work on a book about Mike Tyson.[94]

Dawn's thoughts nevertheless often return to the Holy City. "When I am lonely I dream of Charleston, of the congregation at Shiloh A.M.E., of a winter wind whistling through the palmettos and of Rosabelle Waite's good collard greens."[95]

Perspectives

Whereas Dawn and John-Paul left the South a generation ago, with Dawn returning to Charleston only for an occasional book signing, most of us have yet to depart from our fear of sexual diversity or to cross the boundaries of skin color, sexuality, social class, and gender that still contour the southern experience. The Gordon Langley Hall affair is more than a McCullersesque tale of southern social mores and lives fractured on the basis of sexuality, gender, race, and social class. The affair reveals individuals' predilections to reinterpret the past through the eyes of the present and the potential of history to lend insight into the future.

In the summer of 1994, six openly transsexual women attended the Nineteenth Annual Michigan Womyn's Music Festival, which for years had refused the entry of transsexuals on the basis of the festival's "womyn born womyn only" policy. Prior to the festival, protesters organized a series of workshops at "Camp Trans"—a set of pitched tents outside the festival's main gate. Among the topics explored were "How Many Genders Are There?"; "Transsexual Sexuality: Our Cunts Are Not the Same"; and "Primal Androgyny," the last led by a fifteen-year postoperative transsexual lesbian-feminist witch.

Within our community of sexual outsiders are many communities. Bound by our diversity, we rebel against the pre-Stonewall, black-and-white television world of sexual sameness—where right and wrong are defined by religious zealots like Pat Robertson; enforced by their political henchmen, such as Jesse Helms and Newt Gingrich; and practiced by thousands of Ozzies and Harriets committed to the prone position. To their credit, the women attending the 1994 music festival have acknowledged their fear of those who are sexually different by valuing dialogue over discord and prizing diversity above conformity.

This change in position reflects the growing number of persons identifying as transsexuals, cross-dressers, and transgendered persons and the increasing recognition by homosexual organizations of the interrelationship between these struggles.[96] Today individuals occasionally adopt the persona of the other gender (cross-dresser) or choose to live as the other gender on a continuing basis (transgenderist).

Despite a historical tolerance for eccentricity among the leisure classes on matters of sexual behavior in general and of transgenderism in particular (e.g., Henry III, who lived as a woman; Chevalier d'Eon, a transgenderist in the court of Louis XV), such behaviors were sharply reproved when the "offender" crossed social class or racial boundaries, as evidenced in the cases of Oscar Wilde or Gordon Langley Hall. The Gordon Langley Hall affair also demonstrates the historical dislike for transgenderists within the gay community. While this discomfort has lessened, it has not vanished. Part of this stems from the ideology of sexual essentialism accepted by modern-day homosexuals and evidenced in taken-for-granted statements like "I'm gay because I was born that way." The power of culture, language, and ideology to shape our perspectives of who we are transforms us into static sexual beings and denies our unique human capacity to choose our sexual, racial, class, and gender identities. Those who declare themselves sexually different not only must fight against the enforced conformity of heterosexism but must contend with many within the homosexual community who have defined themselves in terms of *what* they are *not*, rather than in *who* they have the potential of being. Gordon/Dawn, like Stephan in Virginia Woolf's *Orlando* and Cousin Lymon the hunchback in Carson McCullers's *The Ballad of the Sad Cafe*, presents us with such a challenge.

Finally, the Gordon Langley Hall affair also allows us to reflect on how differing social positions color our interpretation of events—past or present. For Ann Leland, whose two husbands enjoyed very different relations with Hall and who died a few weeks following her last interview, "Gordon really made me nervous; he was just plain strange. . . . He took everyone for a ride. He especially used older ladies for their money."[97] For Billy Camden, who operated one of Charleston's longstanding gay bars:

> She was a very sick woman or man or whatever. She was a pathetic figure who lives in her own world. She fabricates everything. In fact, she hurt a few very nice people here by writing stories which were just dreams. Just like her supposed relationship with a prominent southern gentleman that caused him and his wife to split up. That was just a lie. I don't know a *white* person who ever had sex with him. The only people he associated with were black men and boys; they ruined him. They stole everything out of the house. They would come up there by the carload and he would pay them for sex.[98]

In contrast, Alex Simmons, writing from prison to his younger brother, John-Paul, during the time of the controversial courtship, found Dawn

> a wonderful, sweet person and a real lady rating much more respect and consideration than you've shown. . . . I see in that sweet human being more then you are [sic] anyone else could ever hope to see. She loves you, passionately. However, there is a limit to how much hurt the human heart can withstand.[99]

For Jeremy Morrow, a Society Street neighbor and homosexual, Gordon was simply a "peculiar man" in a city where eccentricity was neither baneful nor unusual—provided that it had the protective coloration of southern euphemisms in the shadowy surrealism of southern culture.

For Nicky, who enjoyed nearly fifty years with his partner, Tom, Dawn wove fantasies to suit a world where she steadfastly braved misunderstanding, loathing, and scorn:

> One thing that really upset me was that *New York Times* article where Hall explained that when she lived in Charleston and had her mixed baby she couldn't walk on the Battery. This was simply untrue! Black people have always walked on the Battery. But I am afraid that, like so many things Hall has said, it will go down as fact. That's the problem with Hall, you can't separate fact from fancy. Despite all of her failings, though, one thing I admire about Hall was her courage. Even after all of those things happened to her, she still kept going.

And for Dawn, who is now a grandmother (Natasha, named after the heroine in Tolstoy's *War and Peace*, has two children of her own, Damian and Tamara Miquel):

> It has not been an easy life. . . . I had the misfortune of loving two men, perhaps not wisely, but too well. . . . I came from a small village in England where no black people lived. I was caught up in something I really didn't understand. . . . [100] I lost my home through chicanery and because of John-Paul's illness. I'm neither a widow nor divorced, yet I don't have my husband. It hurts to know he'll never get better. But I'm very grateful to Charleston for producing for me a wonderful husband. . . . [101] I have retained a great many friends in Charleston. It was very wonderful, when I went back for the book signing of *She Crab Soup*, that I signed books for three hours solid. They all turned out![102]

Despite her optimism, Dawn still expresses regrets: "Sometimes I think it would have been best had John-Paul never met or wanted me. He probably would have lived out his life in his cabin on Johns Island with his pig, Frances, fishing and hunting. It was so sad what happened." But a moment later Dawn's hopefulness returns, when she recalls how the new owners of her old Society Street house had "taken me out to the garden and offered to give me back the animals' tombstones which had all been cleaned. That was a great healing. If you wait long enough, it all comes out all right in the end."[103]

NOTES

This is a slightly different version of material that appears in *From Lonely Hunters to Lonely Hearts: Generations, A Cultural and Oral History of Lesbian and Gay Southern Life* (New York: Westview/HarperCollins, 1997). Copyright James T. Sears, 1997. The author acknowledges the contributions of Bill Briggman and Mark Grant, who served as paid research assistants for this essay; the substantive assistance of Dawn Pepita Langley Hall Simmons; and the help of Ginny Daley and others at Special Collections Library at Duke University, where the Simmons papers are housed. All other materials, including audiotaped interviews, collected for this article are now archived in the author's collection at Special Collections Library at Duke University.

1. W. Fraser, *Charleston! Charleston!* (Columbia: University of South Carolina Press, 1989), pp. 412–13.

2. Ibid., p. 412.

3. Dawn Langley Simmons, *Margaret Rutherford: A Blithe Spirit* (New York: McGraw-Hill Book Co., 1983), pp. xii–xiv.

4. Dawn Langley Simmons [Gordon Langley Hall], interview by telephone with B. Briggman, 10/19/94.

5. Dawn Langley Simmons, *Man into Woman* (New York: Macfadden, 1971), p. 69. Published by a friend of Rutherford, the original book title was changed and "sensational passages" inserted without the consent of Hall (Dawn Langley Simmons, personal correspondence to J. Sears, 1/1/95).

6. Ibid., pp. 62–63.

7. Simmons, *Margaret Rutherford*, p. xvi.

8. Simmons, interview with Briggman, 10/19/94.

9. Simmons, *Man into Woman*, p. 87.

10. Ibid., p. 80.

11. Dawn Langley Simmons [Gordon Langley Hall], interview with B. Briggman, 11/6/94.

12. Gordon Hall, letter to Irac C. Moore Jr., 4/5/63, in Dawn Pepita Simmons Papers, Correspondence, 1874–1970, Section 20, Special Collections Library, Duke University, Durham, NC.

13. Gordon Langley Hall, "Author Is Restoring Home in Memory of His Cousin," *Charleston News and Courier*, 11/8/64.

14. Simmons, interview with Briggman, 11/6/94.

15. Simmons, *Man into Woman*, p. 96.

16. Dawn Langley Simmons, personal correspondence to J. Sears, 1/12/95.

17. Ann Barnes Leland, interview with B. Briggman, 6/1/94.

18. Simmons, personal correspondence to Sears, 1/12/95.

19. Simmons, interview with Briggman, 10/19/94.

20. "Patlas Plant Tree of Friendship," *Charleston News and Courier*, 11/23/62.

21. "Memorial Gallery Opening Is Set," *Charleston News and Courier*, 12/11/64.

22. Jack Leland, "Gordon Langley Hall Scores with Novel for Juveniles," *Charleston News and Courier*, 12/23/62, 9C; Ripley, "Osceola's Story by Local Author," *Charleston News and Courier*, 11/13/64; "Johnson House Works Shown at Art Gallery," *Charleston News and Courier*, 11/5/64.

23. Ann Barnes Leland, interview with B. Briggman, 6/15/94. According to Hall, this account is evidence of further distortion by Leland: The trip to Denver "was to launch *Dear Vagabonds*, a book I had written for Denver socialite, Mrs. Brownie Adams, at which the Governor of Colorado attended" (Simmons, personal correspondence to Sears, 1/12/95). Hall also received some money following the death of Mrs. Adams. In a letter postmarked 31 March 1968 and sent to Hall after Adams's death, Mrs. Hugh March Andrews of New York City wrote, "She must have been a charming and interesting lady. Hope you are as far off on my age as you were on hers! Do you mean she left you *money* as well as things? How does it feel to be *left* something?" (Mrs. Hugh March Andrews, letter to Gordon Hall, in Dawn Pepita Simmons Papers, Correspondence, 1874–1970, Section 20).

24. Dawn Langley Simmons, personal correspondence to J. Sears, 2/27/95.

25. Gordon Hall, "Gleaning from the Confederate Museum: The Ladies Do It," *Preservation Progress* 8, 4 (November 1963): 6.

26. Gordon Hall, "Poor Old Grandmother and the Queen," *Charleston News and Courier*, 9/20/64.

27. Leland, interview with Briggman, 1/15/94; Gordon Hall, letter to Jack Copper, n.d., in Dawn Pepita Simmons Papers, Correspondence, 1874–1970, Section 20. However, "the pig belonged to John-Paul and was kept at his cabin on rural Johns Island, never at No. 56" (Simmons, personal correspondence to Sears, 2/27/95).

28. Leland, interview with Briggman, 6/15/94. See also S. Birmingham, *America's Secret Aristocracy* (Boston: Little, Brown & Co., 1987; reprint, New York: Berkeley, 1990), p. 149.

29. Simmons, personal correspondence to Sears, 1/12/95.

30. Dr. Leber, interview with B. Briggman, 9/15/94; Simmons, personal correspondence to Sears, 1/12/95.

31. Simmons, interview with Briggman, 10/19/94.

32. Billy Camden, interview with B. Briggman, 9/26/94.

33. Nicky, interview with B. Briggman, 9/13/94; Camden, interview with Briggman, 9/26/94. All further quotes from Camden are from this interview.

34. Nicky, interview with Briggman, 9/13/94 (all further quotations from Nicky are from this interview); Simmons, personal correspondence to Sears, 1/12/95.

35. Simmons, interview with Briggman, 10/19/94.

36. Simmons, interview with Briggman, 11/6/94.

37. Jeremy Morrow, interview with B. Briggman, 5/31/94. All further quotations from Morrow are from this interview.

38. Simmons, interview with Briggman, 10/19/94; Simmons, personal correspondence to Sears, 1/12/95.

39. Virginia Carr, *The Lonely Hunter: A Biography of Carson McCullers* (New York: Carroll & Graff, 1975), p. 520. Years later Hall elaborated, "The young man was probably Gussie, our under butler who later joined the Marines. . . . Gussie loved celebrities. . . . He acted more like family" (Simmons, personal correspondence to Sears, 2/27/95).

40. Carr, *The Lonely Hunter*, p. 519; Simmons, interview with Briggman, 10/19/94.

41. Simmons, *Man into Woman*, p. 97.

42. Ibid., p. 100.

43. Simmons, interview with Briggman, 10/19/94.

44. Margarita Childs, interview with B. Briggman, 8/16/94.

45. Simmons, *Man into Woman*, pp. 106–7.

46. Ibid., p. 148.

47. As Gordene Olga MacKenzie (*Transgender Nation* [Bowling Green, OH: Bowling Green State University Popular Press, 1994]) points out, isolated efforts to transform males into females surgically can be found as far back as Denmark of the 1920s and Germany of the 1930s.

48. An exception was Magnus Hirschfeld whose *Die Transvetiten* (1910) was one of the first to challenge this long-held stereotype. See M. Hirschfeld, *The Transvestite: An Investigation of the Erotic Drive to Cross Dress*, trans. M. Lombardi-Nash (Buffalo, NY: Prometheus, 1991).

49. Havelock Ellis, *Studies in the Psychology of Sex* (New York: Random House, 1906), part 2, p. 36.

50. MacKenzie, *Transgender Nation*, pp. 45–46.

51. Simmons, *Man into Woman*, p. 114.

52. Ibid., pp. 119–20.

53. Ibid., p. 152.

54. Ibid., p. 151.

55. Simmons, interview with Briggman, 10/19/94.

56. B. Riley, "Myra Breckinridge with a Twist," *National Insider*, 12/20/70, p. 11.

57. M. Parkin, "The Life and Love of a Trans-Sexual," *Sunday Times*, 3/7/71.

58. Dena Crane, personal correspondence to J. Sears, 10/31/94.

59. "Dawn's New Day," *Time*, 12/2/68, p. 34.

60. Simmons, *Man into Woman*, p. 108.

61. Dawn Simmons, letter to Jack Copper, 9/22/69, in Dawn Pepita Simmons Papers, Correspondence, 1874–1970, Section 20.

62. Alex Simmons, letter to John-Paul Simmons, 6/24/68, in Dawn Pepita Simmons Papers, Correspondence, 1874–1970, Section 20.

63. Simmons, *Man into Woman*, p. 123.

64. Dawn Langley Simmons, "Marriage That Shocked," *Charleston Chronicle*, 2/15/89, p. 1.

65. "New Book," *Charleston Chronicle*, 6/9/93, p. 2; Riley, "Myra Breckinridge with a Twist," p. 11.

66. Simmons, "Marriage That Shocked," p. 1.

67. Hall had already signed a contract on a " 'crash' schedule" with Doubleday "to take advantage of the publicity when the wedding takes place." This letter to Dawn from a senior editor continues, "It is especially reassuring to me that we have exactly the same book in mind and if we continue to think of the book as a medical documentary we will come up with something that will be so much more than a sensational flash-in-the-pan" (Lawrence P. Ashmead, letter to Dawn Simmons, 12/23/68, in Dawn Pepita Simmons Papers, Correspondence, 1874–1970, Section 20).

68. "Dawn's New Day," p. 34.

69. Dawn Langley Simmons, personal correspondence to J. Sears, 11/1/94.

70. Simmons, *Margaret Rutherford*, pp. 177–78.

71. Years later, in a letter penned to Charleston's African American paper, an unsigned apology for Dawn and John-Paul's treatment read, in part, "What is disturbing to me and many of the old-timers who were around at the time of their wedding, was that we refused to speak out at the mistreatment of two people obviously in love" (Letters to the Editor, *Charleston Chronicle*, 3/8/89, p. 5).

72. Simmons, personal correspondence to Sears, 1/12/95.

73. "Man Who Changed Sex, Husband on Honeymoon," *Columbia Record*, 1/23/69; "Dawn Hall Marries Her (His?) Ex-Chauffeur in Private Rites," *Greenville News*, 1/23/69; "Startling Bride Wants Children," *Raleigh News and Observer*, 1/23/69.

74. Leland, interview with Briggman, 6/15/94.

75. "New Book," pp. 1–2.

76. Dawn Langley Simmons, "Racism Scars Wedding," *Charleston Chronicle*, 2/22/89, p. 1.

77. Simmons, *Man into Woman*, p. 128.

78. Fraser, *Charleston!*, 413.

79. Ibid., pp. 422–23.

80. Simmons, interview with Briggman, 11/6/94.

81. Simmons, "Racism Scars Wedding," p. 2.

82. Mr. Brown, Letter to the Editor, *Charleston Chronicle*, 3/8/89, p. 5.

83. Simmons, personal correspondence to Sears, 1/12/95.

84. Dawn Langley Simmons, personal correspondence to J. Sears, 1/30/95.

85. Simmons, personal correspondence to Sears, 2/27/95.

86. Anthony Dawson, letter to Dawn Simmons, 9/14/72, in Dawn Pepita Simmons Papers, Correspondence, 1874–1970, Section 20.

87. Dawn Simmons, letter to John-Paul Simmons, Sunday [summer 1972], in Dawn Pepita Simmons Papers, Correspondence, June 1972–October 1972, Section 20, Special Collections Library, Duke Univerity, Durham, NC.

88. Robert Holmes, letter to Dawn Simmons, 9/18/72, in Dawn Pepita Simmons Papers, Correspondence, June 1972–October 1972, Section 20.

89. Dawn Simmons, letter to John-Paul Simmons, Saturday [summer 1972], in Dawn Pepita Simmons Papers, Correspondence, June 1972–October 1972, Section 20.

90. "Follow-Up on the News: Transsexual Life," *New York Times*, 11/23/75.

91. Simmons, personal correspondence to Sears, 1/12/95.

92. D. Siegelbaum, "Author, Socialite, Former Man and Now 'Mother' Faces Divorce," *Albany* (NY) *Sunday Times-Union*, 12/14/75.

93. Crane, personal correspondence to Sears, 10/31/94.

94. D. Simmons, "To John Paul: 20 Years of Marriage Is Like Yesterday," *Charleston Chronicle*, 3/8/89.

95. Ibid.

96. W. Blumenfeld, "Gender Politics: A Discussion among Transgender Activists," in J. Sears, *Bound by Diversity* (Columbia, SC: Sebastian Press, 1994), pp. 57–66; D. Denny, "You're Strange and We're Wonderful: The Gay/Lesbian and Transgender Communities," in Sears, *Bound by Diversity*, pp. 47–53; MacKenzie, *Transgender Nation*. By the mid-1980s, three sex-change operations occurred daily in the United States, with estimates of the ratio of transsexuals living in America ranging from one in ten thousand to one in five hundred. (MacKenzie, *Transgender Nation*, p. 16).

97. Leland, interview with Briggman, 6/15/94.

98. Camden, interview with B. Briggman, 9/26/94.

99. Alex Simmons, letter to John-Paul Simmons, 6/24/68. Years later Dawn wrote, "Brother Alex always called me 'his angel' as I was instrumental in getting his 15 year state prison sentence dismissed. As a naive young man he had driven to NYC from Charleston in his old car, lent it to friends who unbeknown to him returned it with a sawn-off shotgun in the trunk. The police found it. As a newly wed I took my mother-in-law . . . to see Alex in Dannemora Prison. . . . It upset me that in four years no member of the family had even been to see him" (Simmons, personal correspondence to Sears, 2/27/95).

100. Simmons, interview with Briggman, 10/19/94.

101. B. Blakeney, "Authoress Whose Marriage to Black Butler Shocked White Society, Says Charleston Has Changed," *Charleston Chronicle*, 12/8/91, pp. 1–2.

102. Simmons, interview with Briggman, 10/19/94.

103. Ibid.

INTERVIEWS

Billy Camden [pseud.], Charleston, SC, 9/26/94.

Margarita Childs, Charleston, SC, 8/16/94.

Dawn Langley Simmons, Hudson, NY, 10/19/94; 11/6/94.

Dr. Leber [pseud.], Charleston, SC, 9/15/94.

Nicky [pseud.], Charleston, SC, 9/13/94.

Ann Leland, Charleston, SC, 6/1/94; 6/15/94.

Jeremy Morrow [pseud.], Charleston, SC, 5/31/94; 8/8/94.

Lesbians, Communities

The Mid- to Late Twentieth Century

Chapter Ten

Softball and Alcohol

The Limits of Lesbian Community in Memphis from the 1940s through the 1960s

Daneel Buring

Before there was a national gay and lesbian culture, there were regional and urban ones. A small lesbian community, for example, developed between the 1940s and the 1960s in Memphis, Tennessee. During this period members of this community, many of them rural migrants to urban America, developed both an individual sense of lesbian consciousness and the shared interests and activities, as well as myth and folklore, that are necessary to establish communal identity.[1]

The continued growth of gay and lesbian history requires that the communities built by gays and lesbians become the focus of regional and local studies. Community studies such as this one are forming a broader base and stronger structure for a fuller understanding of gay and lesbian group identity, which developed slowly in large cities in the early twentieth century but stagnated, along with other progressive social developments, under the weight of the Great Depression of the 1930s. Gay and lesbian group identity began to coalesce as a result of two mid-century trends. First, World War II broke down boundaries, and as Allan Bérubé notes in *Coming out under Fire: The History of Gay Men and Women in World War Two*, it "propelled gay men and lesbians into the mainstream of American life."[2] Many gays and lesbians recognized a group identity while in the military or in war service industries and their related entertainment facilities. Urban centers of the North and West attracted gays and lesbians throughout World War II and in the years after. Those cities with large military bases and civilian support installations became the first to develop significant gay and lesbian communities. According to John D'Emilio, World War II served as a "nationwide coming out experience" for thousands of gays and lesbians.[3]

Second, gay community identity, however, remained an underground phenomenon because of social and, especially, military attitudes toward homosexuality; the emergence of the containment ethos, not only in foreign affairs but also in domestic relations; and the compulsory heterosexuality of 1950s culture, which limited its postwar development. At this critical juncture, gays and lesbians struggled to come to terms with their individual identities and to recognize their collective liminality, their existence between categories and outside established institutional frameworks—in short, their marginality. They found friends and colleagues and together responded to the hegemonic culture's construction of gender, carving out in the dim recesses of the larger community their own public space and constructing for themselves an alternative culture.

This chapter focuses on the Memphis lesbian community of the pre-liberation era. The birth of the national gay liberation movement, which has its roots in the civil rights and women's movements of the 1960s, is generally associated with the Stonewall Riot of 1969. The stigmatization of lesbians and the necessity of hiding their identities, particularly before the more open atmosphere of the post-Stonewall era, make tracing the history of sexuality-based communities difficult. Because of the lack of information available on the history of lesbian sexuality, many scholars have used oral history to document the existence of these communities.

Oral history, with its emphasis on individual lives, is particularly well suited to community studies. Within the field of gay and lesbian history, oral history interviews with individuals serve to widen the scope of history. Interviews themselves provide "an indispensable avenue into the lives of those who are otherwise hidden from history."[4] Gay and lesbian archives, oral history projects, and independent scholars across the country frequently approach community-based studies by employing the methodology of *ethno-history*, combining "ethnography—the intensive study of the culture and identity of a single community—with history—the analysis of forces that shaped how that community changed over time."[5] Among the cultural factors that contributed to the development of the Memphis lesbian community in the years before gay liberation were particular elements of Southern society.

Confronted with Southern conservatism and intolerance, many lesbians sought the anonymity of urban centers outside the South. Those who remained knew that too much openness would bring socially conservative or religiously fundamentalist responses. Such backlash could threaten social connections, jobs, and even physical safety. The South's distinctive regional character contributed to the invisibility of its lesbian communities.

The process of tracing the growth of the Memphis lesbian community through interviews with nine of its members highlights group characteristics and results in a compelling history. Participants in these interviews are referred to as narrators throughout this chapter. Their names and the names of individuals mentioned in the interviews have been changed to preserve the anonymity they prefer or require. The use of pseudonyms and the promise of anonymity were not enough to overcome the reluctance of several older lesbians who refused to participate in this study.[6] All of the narrators, white women born between 1918 and 1952, either were born in Memphis or migrated to the city as young adults. The migrants came from small towns in Mississippi, Kentucky, and Tennessee to seek employment and educational opportunities. The similar experiences of narrators born before and after 1950 illustrate how slowly the gains of the gay liberation movement affected the Memphis lesbian community. Topics covered in the course of each interview included coming out, sexuality, butch-femme definitions and roles, education, employment, socializing, friendships or interactions with gay men, bar life, the use of alcohol, the function or role of softball, oppression, and resistance.

Memphis lesbians of the pre-liberation era, like other older lesbians, often put off coming out to their parents and other family members. Few narrators did so at an early age. Some waited to discuss their sexual identity until they were adults, while others have never done so. For each one, coming out was fraught with anxiety and intense emotion, no matter how loving the family, how supportive the friends, or how independent the individual. One narrator, Irene, did not voluntarily come out to her family:

> I have to admit that the girl's husband that I was seeing did it for me. He told my family that I was wrecking his marriage. She was married and I was engaged, and it just happened. She had been married for seven years. We were just running around with each other. Neither one of us knew anything about gay life, but we just managed to find ourselves in bed together. . . . Not knowing anyone else and not understanding what I was doing except that it felt good . . . I talked to my fiancé and I told him that I thought that we shouldn't get married. . . . First of all, I told him I didn't want children

and I didn't tell him why of course, but I told him that I didn't think we should get married. He said, "But I love you enough for the both of us. Once we're married, you'll get over this fright and all this stuff." So, we went ahead and got married. In my own mind, too, I thought maybe this was a passing fad type thing. But it didn't work out that way. I was married almost three years, but he was in the service so we didn't see each other but every now and then. It just wasn't cut out for me.[7]

Coming out does not necessarily mean that one must acknowledge one's sexual identity to others. It also refers to awareness and acceptance of one's own identity. For many lesbians, this occurs during their teenage years and is often related to the peer pressure associated with dating. Alice says, "I always dated and it was okay. You did it because everybody else did and you'd be banished from high school if you didn't have a boyfriend." Loretta's high school years differed from Alice's. She says, "I didn't date much at all. I never felt comfortable with guys. . . . I didn't date in high school until almost the twelfth grade. I didn't know anything about sex and I can remember on my sixteenth birthday my uncle singing that thing about sweet sixteen and never been kissed. I cried because it was true." Shortly after her sixteenth birthday, Loretta and her brother's girlfriend began an affair. Her parents found out about her sexual identity two years later:

> When I was eighteen there were some questions. They basically accused me of being queer and you always denied it. My mother had found a note a girl had written me. There were questions at that point. Then I moved out and later, in my early twenties, my stepfather banned me from the house because I was gay. I didn't see my parents for three years. I was in a wreck and his sister told my mother that I was in the hospital and so my mom came to see me and then we slowly kind of reestablished a relationship.

Another narrator, Esther, recently celebrated fifty-three years of partnership with her lover. Neither one has ever acknowledged her sexual identity to family members.

Nancy began participating in the Memphis lesbian community at the age of nineteen but did not discuss it with her mother until she was forty-eight:

> I came out when I was nineteen [1957]. Even though I still dated men, that's when I realized exactly that there was a place for me, that there was a community, that I wasn't alone. . . . I'm sure my mother and father knew. We

didn't talk about it. I didn't really come out to my mother until . . . eight years ago and I'm fifty-six now. It just happened that she and my sister had come by that day and we were sitting there talking. I had just broken up with a relationship or was having a bad time and said something about how lonely I was and my sister said, "Nancy, mother knows." I went on with the conversation and I said, "Well, I've just been having a real hard time." She said, "Nancy, mother knows." And on the third "mother knows" I said, "Mother knows what?" And she said, "Mother knows everything. She knows everything about you." I said, "Everything, like what?" Well, we played this Mickey Mouse game and finally I said, "You know that I'm gay?" Mother said, "Yes, and have known." Well, I started crying. I said, "How long have you known?" She said, "Since you were about twenty-one." It felt like a ton of bricks had been lifted from my shoulder. Parents know. They don't have to be told. It would have made it easier a long time ago. I could have shared so much. "Hey, I'm really having a bad time." But I would just stay away when something was wrong.

As evidenced by the stories of Memphis narrators, coming out remained a very personal experience for many lesbians in the pre-liberation era. The coming-out stories recounted by Memphis lesbians indicate that these women share common experiences with other lesbians of this period, who often kept their sexual identities hidden from family members and the larger community.

Much lesbian life in the pre-liberation era was constructed around the categories of lesbian gender known as "butch" and "femme," which have served as both private and public expressions. Regarding the Buffalo, New York, lesbian community, Elizabeth L. Kennedy and Madeline D. Davis, authors of *Boots of Leather, Slippers of Gold: The History of a Lesbian Community*, refer to butch-femme roles as "the organizing principle for this community's relation to the outside world and for its members' relationship to one another."[8] Seven of the nine Memphis narrators identified, at some point in their lives, as butch. Some continue to distinguish themselves as butch or femme, while others contend that these identities no longer have a place in the lesbian community.

Referring to the period from the 1930s through the 1960s, Joan Nestle, in her introduction to *The Persistent Desire: A Femme-Butch Reader*, notes that "because of the surrounding oppression, ritual and code were often all we had to make public erotic connections. Dress, stance, gestures, even jewelry and hairstyles had to carry the weight of sexual communications."[9] Several Memphis narrators focused their discussions on dress rather than on the role-playing often associated with butch-femme identities. Shirley discusses her appearance and that of other butches:

> In my time it was strictly butch-femme. The butches looked like butches. I wore very short hair. I have to laugh about us because they wore blue jeans and as the typical butch, the plaid shirt and key chains hanging off the belt. I never liked blue jeans because they were always too heavy, but I just love plaid shirts and I love flannel shirts. I didn't have the key chain hanging off me. I can't stand that to this day, but most of them looked like little clones.

Nancy's description of butch appearance corresponds to Shirley's: "Being the dyke that I was then, and I have mellowed through the years, I dressed accordingly. When I first came out, I thought you had to look like you were a truck driver in order to be gay. That's kind of the way I looked with the short hair. . . . I wore men's pants, the tee shirt under it, even down to men's shoes and socks." Using the term *diesel dyke* synonymously with *butch,* Loretta portrays butches in the following way:

> Diesel dyke was the woman who dressed in men's clothing, boots, even to black leather a lot of times—rompin', stompin' dyke. A diesel dyke was typically one who didn't care who knew she was gay and had a very, very feminine woman, if she had a woman at all. The women who were with them thought of them more as men than as another woman.

Narrators' sketches of femmes refer to characteristically feminine appearance and style, as Shirley suggests:

> The femme women looked very feminine. I mean they might put on slacks, but they were women's slacks or shorts. They didn't wear masculine shirts or shorts at any time. I went with a woman for twenty-two years and as she went out the door in the morning she looked like she'd just stepped out of bandbox and when she'd come back in at 4:30 in the afternoon she still looked like it. Every hair was in place. Her makeup was to perfection. She was a lovely, lovely woman.

Memphis narrators' responses regarding the meaning of butch and femme roles are quite consistent. Irene, a femme, says, "What it meant to me at the time was essentially that I just took over the housekeeping roles in that particular relationship." Esther describes what butch and femme have meant to her and her partner in their fifty-three-year relationship:

> Initially, and up until fairly recently, there was a definite dividing line. Maybe always the woman didn't look butch, but she took the male attitude,

the male position of responsibility, productivity, protection, and doing the work. . . . There was always one that did like the man would do and one that did like the woman would do. In my case, I took care of everything. It's like this old joke about . . . my wife runs everything around the house except the lawnmower. The woman I live with does everything your mother would have done in a proper manner and I did everything that . . . your father would. That was the way a majority of our friends were. There was definitely a line. Now, at a point along the way I became aware of the fact that it had gradually changed, and that for the most part that dividing line had softened and it didn't make any difference who did what as long as it was agreeable to each one.

Other butches indicate that they, like Nancy, were "the dominant party of the relationship." The consensus among Memphis narrators reveals that butches identified as masculine in their behavior, while femmes identified as feminine in theirs.

The employment history of the narrators indicates that each began her career as a member of the working class. Although only three of the nine narrators—Sue, Loretta, and Gloria—attended and graduated from college, all of the participants in this study rose to become members of the middle class. Currently a paralegal, Sue has worked as a teacher, telemarketer, and bookkeeper. Loretta worked as a secretary before quitting to drive a chuck wagon while taking courses at Memphis State University at night. She was employed as a mental health professional for twenty years and now owns a small construction company. Three narrators—Shirley, Nancy, and Alice—purchased their own businesses. Shirley, who began her career as a tile setter, owned both gay and straight bars in the Memphis area. After many years as a butcher, Nancy began operating and later became the owner of several lesbian bars. Alice, who came to Memphis from a rural Tennessee town to go to beauty school, now owns a salon. Bea and Gloria maintained long-standing employment in the health professions, although Gloria eventually graduated from Memphis State University and became a librarian in the Memphis City Schools. Esther worked as an office manager at a local business for twenty-five years. Irene was employed as a systems analyst.

Other community studies have shown that working-class lesbians are more likely than middle-class lesbians to participate in public activities within the lesbian community.[10] The majority of narrators in this study reveal that as young working-class lesbians they participated in the lesbian community; however, some indicate that their rise in status paralleled their reluctance to risk exposure, which might threaten their jobs.

Growth and expansion in the pre-Stonewall era depended on the development of institutions that supported the lesbian community. In other cities, a lesbian bar culture facilitated such growth.[11] Although Memphis had no strictly lesbian bars prior to the 1960s, during the 1940s and 1950s lesbians who were interested in frequenting bars with other lesbians often went to mixed bars. Mixed bars were actually straight bars in which lesbians and gay men felt comfortable and whose owners were supportive and protective of their homosexual clientele. Esther remembers these bars, which she and other narrators call "mom-and-pop bars" or "juke joints":

> One I'm thinking about right now was called the Sombrero. It was out on Lamar and there was a couple that ran it. As a matter of fact, they referred to themselves as Mom and Pop. They knew that a lot of the people that came there were gay and they welcomed us because they liked the business. There was another place just before World War II that was part of an old warehouse on Jefferson, I think. It was called La Fiesta and it was a great place for gay people, and it continued to operate until the navy base opened up out there at Millington [Tennessee]. Then, when the navy people started coming in, of course, the cops came in and closed it down because it did become a drawing card for the gay boys from the navy.

According to several narrators, lesbians could sometimes dance together in these mom-and-pop bars. Shirley, who describes herself as masculine in appearance, even danced with other women at downtown hotels during World War II:

> There weren't too many men to dance with and the top bands came here then, so we went dancing and tea dancing. Every Saturday we went to the Claridge to a tea dance with top-name bands and I danced with women. There were times when I had girlfriends say, "How do you do it?" And I said, "I just walk proudly in and no one seems to give a toot who I am or what I am." Ninety percent of the women I danced with knew who I was. There might have been ten percent who didn't, but the thing about it was that the women came to me. I was a damn good dancer.

Some owners of mixed bars were particularly solicitous of gay and lesbian customers. Ben's, a popular mixed bar of the 1950s located on Highway 70 outside West Memphis, Arkansas, attracted scores of gay Memphians by remaining open exclusively to lesbians and gay men after hours.[12]

Irene recalls that Ben's had an upstairs barroom and dance floor where lesbians danced together in the mid-1950s.

In the early 1960s a few bars catering specifically to gay men and lesbians opened, but the frequency of police harassment and the concomitant threat of exposure often resulted in their closure. As public institutions, these gay and lesbian bars represent early attempts by the Memphis gay and lesbian community to claim a public space as its own. Seven of the nine narrators in this study have always maintained friendships with gay men; however, few recall sharing these public bar spaces with gay men. The first time Shirley remembers lesbians and gay men frequenting the same gay and lesbian bar was in the late 1960s when the Aristocrat and the Raven, two popular private clubs owned by a Memphis lesbian couple, opened in Tipton County, Tennessee. Loretta describes these clubs, which had a twenty-five-dollar annual membership fee:

> It was wonderful because it was way off the street. You drove down this long drive. They even had a bell cord, like service stations, so they knew when anybody was coming in because it got raided periodically, but they were always prepared because you had to go over this bell to get there. Those bars were great. They served food. Of course, none of these bars served mixed drinks. It was always just beer and soft drinks. You would bring your own bottle. The bars up there had a big room for dancing and they had tables in another room, and they even had a room upstairs with a bed in it that I understand got used periodically.

Memphis's first primarily lesbian bars opened in the late 1960s. Nancy, one of the narrators, entered into the lesbian bar business in 1969 when she took over the lease for a bar named the Famous Door. She subleased the Famous Door from the lesbian couple who had previously owned the Raven and the Aristocrat. The bar had originally opened as the Twilight Lounge Tavern. At that time, the Twilight Lounge catered to both gays and lesbians; however, when Nancy took it over as the Famous Door, lesbians predominated. After a short time Nancy gave up the lease on the Famous Door and opened the Psych-Out, which legally changed names several times throughout the 1970s but was always referred to as the Psych-Out by its patrons.

Whether mixed, gay and lesbian, or strictly lesbian, bars served as key meeting places for Memphis lesbians in the pre-liberation era. According to Irene, lesbians had virtually no other options for meeting other lesbians. Alice says that once she became old enough to go to bars, she "lived in them." Shirley indicates that bars provided a release for many lesbians:

> It was a lonely thing. You went to work and you sit with the straight people all day long and you listen to how their grandchildren and how their sons and their daughters [are] and all this good stuff—you couldn't very well say, "Well, hell, I'm in love with a woman." You couldn't really tell what you wanted to tell, what you wanted to scream, I'm sure. So many lesbians have said to me, "I wish to God I could just go and tell my family, 'Look, this is the woman I love.' " So, back then I think out of pure loneliness and wanting to be with their own kind they went to those little places.

Lesbians who frequented these different types of bars also occasionally had to deal with fighting. Fights sometimes broke out between straight men and lesbians or between lesbians and other lesbians. Butch and femme identities often played a role in these altercations. Loretta explains that with "the combination of alcohol and women and bars and all, it was real easy to get fights started. Typically, it started if somebody thought you were flirting with their girlfriend or . . . you looked at somebody's woman wrong." Shirley confirms Loretta's recollection that butches started fights with other butches who flirted with their femmes. At other times, some lesbians fought with straight men; however, narrators in this study did not often get involved. Nancy agrees with other narrators who were more likely to walk away from harassment:

> We have gone in groups of fifteen, twenty, twenty-five gay people to a straight bar. One in particular I can think of we used to go to down on Third Street was called the Little Black Book. We would go down there and bring a lot of tables together. Of course, the men would come over and immediately start hitting on the women to get up and dance. Some would. Some would refuse. Sometimes you left in a huff because they said, "You bunch of damned queers." I have encountered that.

Loretta, remembering that certain types of butches participated in barroom brawls, says, "Maybe some of the real diesel dykes did. I think most of us realized that we were outnumbered and we couldn't hold up to a guy. I'm real strong and do a lot of construction work and so forth, but I'm not likely to take on a man unless he's really threatening me and mine." Loretta and Nancy, both of whom consider themselves butches, confirm that while some butches willingly fought with straight men, others were reluctant to do so.

In addition to the lesbian bar culture that developed in Memphis in the pre-Stonewall era, softball emerged as a public institution that supported the lesbian community. Recognized as central to the community by all of the narrators, softball continually provided Memphis lesbians with a public space that served as an athletic and social gathering point. According to Yvonne Zipter, whose book *Diamonds Are a Dyke's Best Friend* traces the history of lesbian participation in softball from the early twentieth-century industrial softball leagues through the 1980s, "lesbians were drawn in greater numbers to softball teams because of their greater presence in the work force, because of social conditions, and because of their more independent natures."[13] For some of the participants softball was purely recreational, while for others it was highly competitive. Nancy remembers it as "more of an athletic outlet, perhaps because lesbians were athletic and that was the only outlet where you could display your prowess. I played in the Memphis Park Commission A-League. It was fast-pitch. These were *the* ballplayers of ballplayers. It wasn't like a church league or slow-pitch softball. This was blood-and-guts softball."

During Nancy's first year in the A-League, a regional softball tournament was held in Memphis. Nancy explains that she "thought there were going to be scouts there" and that she "was going to get drafted to play professional ball." She continues:

> The tournament started on a Friday afternoon. That day I told my boss I had to go. He said that if I left, I might not have a job when I came back. I told him I had to do it because the scouts were going to be there, and I had to be there too. He said I could lose my job, but I went to the back and got my softball uniform and I left the store. . . . Well, if the scouts were there, I didn't see them. I never did get to go professional, and sure enough I lost my job.

Softball offered players and spectators regular opportunities to meet other lesbians. According to Nancy, "It was predominantly *the* meeting place for me and so many others."

Softball became an important alternative to bars in the postwar era. Lillian Faderman addresses this phenomenon in *Odd Girls and Twilight Lovers*, a history of twentieth-century lesbian life in the United States, noting that "there were few attempts by working-class and young lesbians in the 1950s and 1960s to build institutions other than gay bars. The most notable was the softball team."[14] Women's softball leagues generally featured a few all-lesbian teams. The games also provided closeted lesbians and those who never went to bars with opportunities to participate in the lesbian culture. Zipter notes that "the softball game was one of the best, safest, and most socially acceptable places to meet and socialize."[15]

Shirley recalls that the games featuring teams such as the Memphis Belles drew large audiences:

> When we played here in Memphis it was nothing to have a thousand people come to watch. Every gay person in this city, whether they were in the closet or not, would be at the diamonds. We always played doubleheaders on Saturday nights. The first game was seven innings and the second was five innings. Sunday-afternoon crowds were huge, but Saturday night they'd be out there like crazy. You wouldn't believe the terrific teams Memphis had.

Loretta also remembers that "Memphis has always been one of the cities with the largest number of people playing softball."

One Memphis narrator claims that in the 1950s lesbians dominated softball teams. According to Nancy, "Back then they were almost all gay." Loretta, who played A-League in the 1960s, indicates that she, too, played on teams that were mostly lesbian. Several narrators' recollections contradict one another regarding the participation of femmes in softball. Loretta says that "butches played ball and femmes didn't." However, Shirley claims that femmes played just as much as butches: "One of the best ballplayers I've ever seen was . . . definitely a femme. I was a catcher and my pitcher was a precious girl, the most effeminate girl you've ever seen. We had a pretty good mixture of butches and femmes on the teams I played for. Some were even girls that went together."

For many Memphis lesbians, softball was the focal point of the lesbian community, and for some, it gave them access to the nationwide lesbian community. Shirley recalls that "softball was everything. I lived it, ate it, slept it, and played it. I loved every minute of it. It was my youth and it was great. . . . I played softball for a lot of years and I met a lot of people. I went all over the country playing ball and I made a lot of friends that I'm still, to this day, close with." Rather than come out in the bar scene, several narrators indicate that they came out after discovering a safe, comfortable lesbian environment at the softball fields. Loretta remembers that "through playing softball and getting out into the community more, I found out that there were other women who were lesbians. I think that softball fields were the only place that most of us felt comfortable."

For some lesbians, however, the softball fields, like the bars, were too public. Closeted lesbians, more often than those who participated in the bar and softball cultures, chose to socialize privately. This is not to say that those who frequented bars or played softball never attended the house parties so popular among members of the Memphis lesbian community. Each of the narrators recalls being present at numerous house parties. Most remember parties where they danced, drank, and played cards. Alice indicates that these house parties were not always planned events:

> I don't know if it was so much house parties all the time, as you always ended up at someone's house. "Let's call so and so, let's go see so and so," and people got together. You would say "party." You'd invite five people and by the time it spread out you didn't know all these people, but it was the only way you had of linking yourself with them. It was networking and trying to get everybody together.

Sometimes lesbians planned house parties to celebrate special occasions—such as one held in September 1960. Five of the nine narrators who participated in this study remember this particular party, during which the guests played poker and watched the Miss America Pageant. Held at the home of Ann, a lesbian who refused to be interviewed for this project, the party was raided by police. Several narrators recall other parties raided by the police in the oppressive postwar era; however, this party seems to have become part of the Memphis lesbian community's folklore. Only one of the five narrators who recounted the story actually attended the party, but five different stories regarding the cause of the raid emerged from the interviews. This incident therefore provides not only an example of homophobic oppression but also a folkloric focus for group support of oppressed peers.

According to Gloria, the narrator who attended the party and was arrested in the raid:

> The arrest was brought about by some other people coming in that were not invited. They knocked on the door and came in. We had not seen them in years. . . . They were being followed by the vice squad. They [vice squad] knocked and then they came in and they arrested us and them. The girls that had been followed admitted that it was their fault and they tried to get the vice squad not to bring anyone else in.

Gloria remembers that two of the three uninvited guests, Yvonne and Doris, "were sisters-in-law. Yvonne had been married to Doris's brother, but they were divorced. The two women got involved while Yvonne was still married and I think that Doris was named in the divorce suit." Although she is not sure, Gloria believes that some connection existed between the divorce and the women being followed. She says, "They could have followed them from anywhere back then. There was one guy who wasn't even on the vice squad who was riding with these guys just for fun. The vice captain had told one of these girls before this that if she was ever caught at a party of women she would be pulled in and he would have everybody arrested."

Two other narrators recall that the police were called by complaining neighbors. According to one story, the neighbors accused the guests of disturbing the peace, while another version has it that the next-door neighbor called the police because he objected to the slacks worn by the partygoers. Still another narrator contends that an ex-girlfriend of one of Ann's guests called the police. Gloria remembers that in cases where house parties were raided, "if you weren't at the party you were always suspected of calling the police." Finally, Shirley insists that one of the vice squad officers during this period seemed to have a personal vendetta against gays and lesbians:

> He arrested them on any occasion he could and he always made damned sure that the paper saw it—and for no reason at all. I remember one night that everybody—I think it was Ann's house—everybody went out there for the Miss America contest and they were playing penny poker at the table and watching and more were laying on the floor maybe drinking a few beers or whatever. All of the sudden the damn door's busted in and every one of them went downtown and, my God almighty, I think out of maybe twenty-five people all but four or five lost their jobs over this. And this went on all the time.

Gloria, the only narrator in attendance, does not corroborate Shirley's account of the raid. Shirley's exaggerated recollection of the number of guests and the number of women who subsequently lost their jobs is not unusual. Other narrators similarly overstate the details of this particular raid.

Those arrested were charged with disorderly conduct, a violation of section 22–12 of the City of Memphis Code of Ordinances.[16] Gloria's record of arrest also includes the words "suspected of homosexuality" and "involved with lesbians."[17] Of the ten lesbians arrested that night, only Gloria and one other woman appeared in city court to answer the charge. They paid a ten dollar fine in addition to one dollar for court costs. The eight lesbians arrested who did not appear in court each forfeited twenty-six dollars. An article appearing in the *Memphis Commercial*

Appeal on the Monday after the Saturday-evening arrests reported the charge of disorderly conduct and listed the names and addresses of all those arrested.[18] A similar article in the *Memphis Press Scimitar* stated the charge but listed only the names and addresses of the two individuals who appeared in court.[19] Both articles reported that complaints from neighbors about noise brought police to Ann's house.

For those arrested, the appearance of their names in the newspapers' articles meant that the effects of the raid went beyond merely having a police record. Gloria, a lab technician at the Veteran's Administration (VA) Hospital at the time, reconstructs the events following the raid:

> The day after the arrest it was in the paper and I went back to work. People looked at me and were curious, but I tried to act like nothing had happened. My uncle called me a few days later and told me that some agents had been by his house. That was where I lived when I first moved to Memphis. When he told me that, I knew that they would be out to the VA Hospital soon. They were there in a couple of days. They had been all around. I mean they had checked everywhere I'd lived, where I bought my gas, went to the grocery store, the neighbors in that area. They had done all that before they got to me. . . . They wanted to know what had happened and I told them. . . . They said they would take everything they had under consideration and get back to me in a couple of days. When they came back they told me that the record would be closed and that it would never be opened again and I was never to worry about that. The male investigator told me that the next time we had a party we should have some guys there.

Gloria does not remember what office of the federal government the two investigators represented. Not unusual during this era, similar institutional inquiries into private lives occurred frequently. Elaine Tyler May, in *Homeward Bound*, notes that "from private industry to the military, the sexual behavior of employees was considered to be a legitimate focus of investigation."[20] Sylvia, a civilian employee at the Naval Air Station in Millington, Tennessee, who was arrested in the raid at Ann's house, was subjected to an investigation, although Gloria cannot recall if Sylvia lost her job.[21] The fragmentation into folklore of the facts of this September 1960 incident allowed threatened individuals to feel a *frisson* of shared danger, to imagine the consequences of similar incidents in their own lives, and to structure methods of avoiding the generally negative possibilities.

Members of the Memphis lesbian community, like lesbians and gay men throughout the nation, lived with a significant fear of exposure during the pre-Stonewall era. This threat, particularly heightened in the years after World War II, resulted in a sort of paranoia for many lesbians and gay men. Nancy compares the postwar atmosphere to today's more liberal climate of acceptance:

> It [fear of exposure] was real serious. . . . That's the first thing that I'd tell somebody new. The first thing, being a lesbian or a gay person, you had to become a liar immediately. When I hear children say nowadays, "Oh, I wanna tell my mother and daddy" or "I just told my mother and daddy" or "I just came out" or "They all know at work"—that wasn't done then.

The anxiety felt by Nancy and others during that era was a reaction to what May describes as a "wave of officially sponsored homophobia." [22] During the 1950s, America's preoccupation with conformity encouraged the labeling of lesbians and gay men as degenerates, perverts, and deviants. Sexual conformity with narrowly defined gender roles became as important as political conformity. National institutions, by applying the containment ethos, sought to reconstruct the American family in order to preserve democracy. Homosexuals, particularly lesbians, did not conform to traditional roles and appeared to threaten the political and domestic order. The nationwide acceptance of antihomosexual feelings led to crackdowns and harassment by national, state, and local law enforcement officials. This period of hostility lasted well into the 1960s as many lesbians and gay men remained closeted in cities throughout the nation.

Several narrators refer to regular police harassment in their interviews, although Loretta recalls much more vigorous surveillance during local election years. Bea remembers that Memphis police officers vigilantly observed activity in and around gay and lesbian bars:

> They used to come into the Entre Nuit at night. A couple of times they would even take down your license number if your car was parked close to there. They would come into a lot of gay bars two or three times a night and then sit out there and watch as you went in and out, and if any strange crime happened they would, you know, call you or pick you up and ask you all kinds of questions.

Bea connects that surveillance at the Entre Nuit with an incident that occurred in 1967:

> I went to Kentucky to visit my relatives one time and while I was gone a detective kept calling my home. When I got back, my roommate informed me as to what had been going on. So, I called the detective back. They were

accusing me of bombing the statue of [former Mayor Edward H.] Crump in Overton Park and wanted to know where I was that night. Sometimes I'd go out there to watch softball games and read. That's about it. Anyway, I was taking one of my friends home at that time of night and I had about three verifications of it.

No official action followed Bea's questioning by the detective; however, she remains convinced that the police had a description of her car and knew her license plate number from watching her at the bar. From the dearth of narrators' specific recollections of police incidents, one can surmise that there was no broad Memphis consensus on homophobic oppression. Nevertheless, police may have found amusement and gratification in harassing these marginalized individuals.

The City of Memphis Code of Ordinances enforced during the 1950s and 1960s contained a provision prohibiting acts "of a gross, violent, or vulgar character" to be committed in a dance hall.[23] The Code also made it "unlawful for any person . . . to appear in public in the dress of the other sex."[24] The prohibition against "vulgar" acts committed in dance halls was used to harass and sometimes prosecute lesbians and gay men for dancing with members of the same sex. Butches appearing in public places in their regular masculine attire faced arrest under the cross-dressing ordinance. None of the butch narrators who participated in this study was ever prosecuted for cross-dressing, but several remember the anxiety they felt about going to the bars:

> If you pulled up in front of the Famous Door, and this was done many times, and you saw a police car there, you drove around and around and around. You wouldn't go in. If you were in there when they came in and . . . you had your arm around somebody, you dropped it. If you were sitting a little bit closer, you immediately tried to act straight. You wouldn't dare talk back.

As targets of persecution in America during the repressive, homophobic years of the postwar era, lesbians and gay men across the nation suffered enormously. The type of harassment and oppression described above became the norm as arrests and prosecutions increased.

Shaped by larger political and social forces, a Memphis lesbian community slowly developed in the pre-liberation era. Mid-South lesbians discovered in wartime Memphis not only employment opportunities but also lifestyle options with others like themselves. The repressive climate of the postwar years, which called attention to homosexuality in the public discourse, may have actually fostered the growth of this nascent community. For many Memphis lesbians, the recognition and acknowledgment of their sexual identities came through participation in the public institutions forged within the emerging lesbian community. There was a change from the belief expressed by Sue: "Alice and I thought that we were the only two people in the whole world at that time that were gay." A group consciousness and sense of belonging offered these women a clearer and broader social identity.

Although not entirely visible to others, Memphis lesbians did develop certain public institutions. As did lesbians in other cities across the nation during the pre-liberation era, members of the Memphis lesbian community found public spaces and co-opted them as their own. Attempts to keep their group identity hidden from the larger community, which police harassment encouraged, contributed to their collective marginality but may also have intensified their attachment to the group. But Memphis lesbians preferred remaining closeted over risking the loss of social connections or jobs. The constant fear of exposure kept many Memphis lesbians from participating in the bar or softball cultures so important to community growth.

Closeted lesbians built their own social networks through private parties; however, their lives often intertwined with more public lesbians who went to bars and played softball. Lesbians who did participate in the alternative worlds constructed by Memphis lesbians around the bar and softball cultures found a supportive community whose members shared a group identity. These cultures were, in fact, the limits of lesbian community in Memphis from the 1940s until the end of the 1960s.

NOTES

1. For discussions on community, see Denyse Lockard, "The Lesbian Community: An Anthropological Approach," in *The Many Faces of Homosexuality: Anthropological Approaches to Homosexual Behavior,* ed. Evelyn Blackwood (New York: Harrington Park Press, 1986), pp. 83–95; and Stephen O. Murray, "Components of Gay Community in San Francisco," in *Gay Culture in America: Essays from the Field,* ed. Gilbert Herdt (Boston: Beacon Press, 1992), pp. 107–46.

2. Allan Bérubé, *Coming out under Fire: The History of Gay Men and Women in World War II* (New York: Free Press, 1990), p. 255.

3. John D'Emilio, *Sexual Politics, Sexual Communities* (Chicago: University of Chicago Press, 1983), p. 24.

4. Jacquelyn Dowd Hall, "Documenting Diversity: The Southern Experience," in *Oral History*, ed. David K. Dunaway and Willa K. Baum (Nashville: American Association for State and Local History, 1984), p. 190.

5. Elizabeth L. Kennedy and Madeline D. Davis, *Boots of Leather, Slippers of Gold: The History of a Lesbian Community* (New York: Routledge, 1993), p. 2.

6. See Trisha Franzen, "Differences and Identities: Feminism and the Albuquerque Lesbian Community," *Signs* 18, 4 (summer 1993): 893, for her experience regarding the reluctance of older lesbians to be interviewed for community-based studies. According to Lillian Faderman, "The need to be covert became one of the chief manifestations of lesbian existence for an entire generation—until the 1970s and, for some women who do not trust recent changes to be permanent, until the present" (*Odd Girls and Twilight Lovers: A History of Lesbian Life in Twentieth Century America* [New York: Penguin Books, 1991], p. 157).

7. For information on narrators' quotations, see the section on "Sources Consulted" after the Notes.

8. Elizabeth L. Kennedy and Madeline D. Davis, "The Reproduction of Butch-Fem Roles: A Social Constructionist Approach," in *Passion and Power: Sexuality in History*, ed. Kathy Peiss and Christina Simmons (Philadelphia: Temple University Press, 1989), p. 244.

9. Joan Nestle, ed., *The Persistent Desire: A Femme-Butch Reader* (Boston: Alyson Publications, 1992), p. 15.

10. See, for example, Kennedy and Davis, *Boots of Leather, Slippers of Gold*, pp. 2–3, and Faderman, *Odd Girls and Twilight Lovers*, pp. 178–86.

11. See, for example, Kennedy and Davis, *Boots of Leather, Slippers of Gold*, p. 1; D'Emilio, *Sexual Politics, Sexual Communities*, p. 99.

12. "Gay Bars over the Years," *Memphis Gaze* (February 1989): 12.

13. Yvonne Zipter, *Diamonds Are a Dyke's Best Friend* (Ithaca, NY: Firebrand Books, 1988), p. 48.

14. Faderman, *Odd Girls and Twilight Lovers*, p. 161.

15. Zipter, *Diamonds Are a Dyke's Best Friend*, p. 48.

16. *Code of Ordinances, City of Memphis, Tennessee* (1967), sec. 22–12, pp. 970–72.

17. "Gloria," *Record of Arrest*, Memphis Police Department, 10 September 1960, photocopy in possession of author.

18. "Ten Women Arrested," *Memphis Commercial Appeal*, 12 September 1960, p. 24.

19. "Ten Women Pay after 'Noisy Party,' " *Memphis Press Scimitar*, 13 September 1960, p. 10.

20. Elaine Tyler May, *Homeward Bound: American Families in the Cold War Era* (New York: Basic Books, 1988), p. 95.

21. Sylvia no longer resides in Memphis. None of the other narrators remembers the results of this investigation.

22. May, *Homeward Bound*, p. 94.

23. *Code of Ordinances, City of Memphis, Tennessee* (1967), sec. 31–26, p. 1650.
24. Ibid., sec. 22–23, p. 974.

SOURCES CONSULTED

Alice [pseud.]. Interview by author. Tape recording and transcript in possession of author. Memphis, Tennessee, 14 September 1994.

Bea [pseud.]. Interview by author. Tape recording and transcript in possession of author. Memphis, Tennessee, 6 October 1994.

Esther [pseud.]. Interview by author. Tape recording and transcript in possession of author. Memphis, Tennessee, 19 August 1994.

Gloria [pseud.]. Interview by author. Tape recording and transcript in possession of author. Memphis, Tennessee, 28 October 1994.

Irene [pseud.]. Interview by author. Tape recording and transcript in possession of author. Memphis, Tennessee, 16 September 1994.

Loretta [pseud.]. Interview by author. Tape recording and transcript in possession of author. Memphis, Tennessee, 10 July 1994.

Nancy [pseud.]. Interviews by author. Tape recordings and transcripts in possession of author. Memphis, Tennessee, 7 October and 17 November 1994.

Shirley [pseud.]. Interviews by author. Tape recordings and transcripts in possession of author. Memphis, Tennessee, 8 July and 18 November 1994.

Sue [pseud.]. Interview by author. Tape recording and transcript in possession of author. Memphis, Tennessee, 14 September 1994.

OTHER SOURCES

Bérubé, Allan. *Coming out under Fire: The History of Gay Men and Lesbians in World War II.* New York: Free Press, 1990.

Code of Ordinances, City of Memphis, Tennessee. 1967.

D'Emilio, John. *Sexual Politics, Sexual Communities.* Chicago: University of Chicago Press, 1983.

Faderman, Lillian. *Odd Girls and Twilight Lovers: A History of Lesbian Life in Twentieth-Century America.* New York: Penguin Books, 1991.

Franzen, Trisha. "Differences and Identities: Feminism and the Albuquerque Lesbian Community." *Signs* 18, 4 (summer 1993): 891–906.

"Gay Bars over the Years." *Memphis Gaze* (February 1989): 12.

Gloria [pseud.]. *Record of Arrest.* 10 September 1960. Memphis Police Department. Photocopy in possession of author.

Hall, Jacquelyn Dowd. "Documenting Diversity: The Southern Experience." In *Oral History,* edited by David K. Dunaway and Willa K. Baum, pp. 189–94. Nashville: American Association for State and Local History, 1984.

Kennedy, Elizabeth L., and Madeline D. Davis. *Boots of Leather, Slippers of Gold: The History of a Lesbian Community.* New York: Routledge, 1993.

———. "The Reproduction of Butch-Fem Roles: A Social Constructionist Approach." In *Passion and Power: Sexuality in History,* edited by Kathy Peiss and Christina Simmons, pp. 241–56. Philadelphia: Temple University Press, 1989.

Lockard, Denyse. "The Lesbian Community: An Anthropological Approach." In *The Many Faces of Homosexuality: Anthropological Approaches to Homosexual Behavior,* edited by Evelyn Blackwood, pp. 83–95. New York: Harrington Park Press, 1986.

May, Elaine Tyler. *Homeward Bound: American Families in the Cold War Era.* New York: Basic Books, 1988.

Murray, Stephen O. "Components of Gay Community in San Francisco." In *Gay Culture in America: Essays from the Field,* edited by Gilbert Herdt, pp. 107–46. Boston: Beacon Press, 1992.

Nestle, Joan, ed. *The Persistent Desire: A Femme-Butch Reader.* Boston: Alyson Publications, 1992.

"Ten Women Arrested." *Memphis Commercial Appeal,* 12 September 1960, p. 24.

"Ten Women Pay after 'Noisy Party.'" *Memphis Press Scimitar,* 13 September 1960, p. 10.

Zipter, Yvonne. *Diamonds Are a Dyke's Best Friend.* Ithaca, NY: Firebrand Books, 1988.

Chapter Eleven

Louisville's Lesbian Feminist Union
A Study in Community Building

Kathie D. Williams

The 1960s and 1970s in this country marked a period of tremendous political, social, and cultural upheaval. The civil rights movement, the Vietnam War protests, the youth counterculture, the women's movement, and the gay liberation movement gathered momentum during these heady years, in which all kinds of social change seemed possible. For lesbians, the ideals that manifested themselves in the counterculture—including the beliefs that individuals become empowered through meaningful social participation and that a sense of community is crucial to any society—became incorporated into the desire to create a Lesbian Nation, a utopian society that honored women's values and rejected patriarchal ideals. At the same time, some lesbians began to recognize the gay liberation movement as sexist and the women's movement as homophobic. Calling themselves lesbian-feminists, these women set out to make the needs and concerns of lesbians primary by creating a political and social movement of their own and by founding such a Lesbian Nation.

This case study of Louisville's lesbian-feminist community demonstrates that lesbian-feminists of the 1970s were successful in their attempt to create a Lesbian Nation. The establishment of the Lesbian Feminist Union (LFU) in Louisville, Kentucky, in 1974 provided a foundation on which subsequent gay rights organizations in the city could build. Furthermore, the LFU helped foster a distinctly lesbian culture that both nurtured and grew out of lesbian politics. Although the LFU lasted just four and a half years, its impact on the city's homosexual community is inestimable.

Because this study is a work in progress, it does not address all of the elements connected with the development of Louisville's lesbian community. However, it does explore the Lesbian Feminist Union, its role in culture building, its effect on local politics, and its impact on subsequent gay rights organizations in the city.

Like lesbian-feminist communities nationally, Louisville's community grew out of other political organizations, such as those associated with the civil rights movement. As in many cities, Louisville's civil rights protests in the mid-1960s often began as a response to police brutality. In May 1968, a meeting was called in the city's primarily black West End to protest a flagrant case of brutality in which a black youth had been beaten by local police. All available police converged on the area, and violence broke out between police and the protesters. The next day Governor Louie B. Nunn sent two thousand National Guard troops to Louisville. The city imposed a curfew, and within two days of the incident, hundreds had been arrested and eight black residents had been shot.[1]

This 1968 uprising of Louisville's black community led to the development of many civil rights organizations in the city, the most visible being the group of Louisvillians associated with the Southern Conference Educational Fund (SCEF).[2] The organization sought an end to the conditions that led to the uprising but chose nonviolent means to achieve its goals. Activists who wanted to take a more aggressive approach to end racial discrimination viewed SCEF as too conservative and joined more militant civil rights groups. Some lesbians who would later become leaders in the local lesbian-feminist movement were members of the latter organizations. A longtime political activist and member of the LFU said of her experience in the civil rights movement, "We wanted racial equality and would stop at nothing to get it. Our goal was revolution and we were armed enough to succeed."[3] This LFU member was one of many local women who worked underground with revolution-minded members of militant civil rights groups. Women as well as men were armed, with both guns and the belief that revolution was possible. Their goal was radical change, and they were prepared to use violent means to achieve it. They bought guns on the black market, hid fugitives from the police, brought in outside "agitators," and organized many of the city's violent protests.[4]

Women were no less a part of the civil rights "revolution" than men, but Stokely Carmichael's assertion that the only position for women in the Student Nonviolent Coordinating Committee (SNCC) was "prone" echoed an attitude that prevailed in Louisville's civil rights movement as well. Women were frequently "protected" from the danger of civil rights work by being confined to office or educational duties. Yet women felt themselves to be involved in meaningful work, and the presence of sexism may have escaped them in the beginning because of the amount of personal and political growth they experienced. However, by 1970 few of the lesbians involved in Louisville's radical civil rights groups were still active, having learned that despite their devotion and hard work, their role in the civil rights movement was less important than that of men.

As lesbians questioned the sexism of the movement and looked for a place to voice their concerns as homosexual women, the almost simultaneous birth of the women's movement and of the gay liberation movement gave them a choice. Some lesbians felt that an alliance with men, even gay men, was not an option. They chose feminism as a means of achieving equality. But many did choose to align with gay men in the struggle for gay liberation. These lesbians helped establish Louisville's first gay liberation organization.

The Gay Alliance was established in 1971 as an organization of lesbians and gay men who worked jointly to fight oppression and ignorance in the Louisville area. The organization sponsored write-in campaigns to politicians, planned rallies, and tried to educate the public through open discussion about the oppression of homosexuals. The Gay Alliance, which lasted only two years, did not make a great change in the quality of life for homosexuals in Louisville, but it provided Louisville's homosexual community with their first stage from which to speak out against oppression. As with many other joint gay and lesbian organizations, the Gay Alliance was dominated by men. The majority of its members and all of its officers were men, and much like the homophile movement of the 1950s, men tended to exclude women's issues from their lists of concerns. By 1973, lesbians alienated by the group's sexism had begun to seek other alternatives.[5]

While some lesbians were working to establish a gay liberation movement in Louisville, others helped form one of the city's first feminist organizations, the Feminist Cell. These lesbian-feminists believed that the women's liberation movement would give them both a voice and a movement that would be willing to address their concerns. They began a consciousness-raising group made up of lesbians and straight feminists. The group was formed to give activist women a place to discuss their treatment in the civil rights movement and to explore their options as political activists. The Feminist Cell provided assertiveness training for women, shared stories of sexism, and sought alternatives to that treatment. The group used lessons learned from the civil rights movement and organized a protest against Dr. Martin Luther King Jr. to demonstrate the sexist nature of the civil rights movement.[6] The group also published a newsletter called *Woman Kind*, which was the first feminist-oriented newsletter in the Louisville area.[7]

When some of the Feminist Cell's straight members refused to support newly forming homosexual rights organizations in the city, its lesbian members began to search for other groups in which to work. Although the Feminist Cell dissolved after three years, it had given local lesbians their first chance to organize along gender lines and provided the foundation for future lesbian-feminist organizations.

Some of the lesbians who split from the Cell formed a circle of thirteen women who met to consider the needs of Louisville's growing lesbian-feminist community. This group included many women who made a political "choice" to become lesbians, and much of the group's discussion centered on what that choice meant to them as individuals, as well as on the necessity of making women central in all aspects of one's life, including the sexual.[8] They also debated the usefulness of aligning with the local chapter of the National Organization for Women (NOW) and whether straight feminists would be sensitive to their needs as lesbians, an issue that ultimately led to the circle's demise. One activist said of the debate, "This was the beginning of the lesbian-feminist movement in Louisville and many of us were starting to develop separatist attitudes. We were not sure who to trust—feminists, who actually offered us little support, or ourselves. We were not yet experienced enough to believe we could form a movement of our own, so the issue divided us."[9]

Some lesbians from the circle turned their energies to NOW, and others organized a group called Feminist Lesbians of America. The latter was a small group of six to ten women who primarily sought an alternative to the local bar scene. They organized as a social group that met to provide support and encouragement to lesbians. According to one member, the group was strongly feminist but resisted the political scene until three lesbians new to the Louisville area "infiltrated the group."[10] These women had been early organizers of lesbian-feminist groups in California and urged the Feminist Lesbians of America to become active members of the Lesbian Nation, defined as a separate women's culture based on superior female values and women's love for one another. The Lesbian Nation would be a nonhierarchical, spiritual, nonsexist, socially and economically equal world. It was to be pro-woman and pro-child and would reject anything that was part of the patriarchy. This Nation would have no geographic boundaries but would exist as a state of mind.[11]

Initially, the Feminist Lesbians of America resisted the notion of a Lesbian Nation. Louisville's lesbian community had spent the early years of its political involvement working for equal rights under the labels of "feminist" or "civil rights worker" and had not yet publicly organized as lesbian-feminists. However, after much debate within the group the Feminist Lesbians of America embraced the concept of the Lesbian Nation, and late in 1973 they decided to hold an open meeting to ascertain whether lesbians in Louisville would be interested in organizing a local lesbian-feminist movement. Flyers were sent to local universities and posted in bars throughout the city.[12] Lesbians from NOW and the Gay Alliance, as well as those not yet politically active, showed up to hear what amounted to strong testimony in support of a Lesbian Nation. Women who had worked within the women's movement spoke of NOW's homophobia; those involved with the Gay Alliance told stories of that group's sexism; and all shared their frustration over being treated like second-class citizens. They urged other women to "come out" and join them in establishing a lesbian-feminist movement in Louisville. Members of the Feminist Lesbians of America agreed that the time was right to take a stand, and Louisville's lesbian-feminist movement was born.

About a month later, at NOW's regular meeting, lesbians facilitated a discussion on the Lesbian Nation, and many of NOW's most dedicated members "came out" to the group. This was the start of a split between local lesbians and straight women within NOW in Louisville—a split that was also occurring nationally. In 1973, Betty Friedan, founder of NOW, told the *New York Times* that "lesbians were sent to infiltrate the women's movement by the CIA as a plot to discredit feminism."[13] However, in the same year, when a showdown between heterosexual feminists and lesbians actually occurred, most members of NOW agreed that the oppression of lesbians was a legitimate concern for feminism. NOW established a Lesbian Task Force to help repair the relationship between the organization and its lesbian members.

In Louisville lesbians participated in the Task Force and, for a brief time, worked to reunify the local chapter of NOW. Their frustration continued, however, when they were asked to be silent about their sexuality in favor of the greater cause: women's liberation. Lesbian members of NOW officially split from the local chapter in 1974 and established their own organization, the Lesbian Feminist Union (LFU).[14]

The Lesbian Feminist Union's stated purpose was "to establish a nation for lesbian feminists . . . where discovery and exploration of our evolving identities can come forth freely."[15] An editorial in the LFU newsletter in 1975 expressed lesbians' anger at the women's movement and their determination to be heard: "We are the heart and muscle of the womyn's movement, but we are still treated like dirty children told to be quiet if we can not be out of sight. But we will not hide and we will not be quiet. We will rise a stronger Nation of Amazons."[16] To foster the growth of their Nation, the LFU organized a land collective, hoping to buy property where members could live as a cohesive group free from the influence of men. While unsuccessful in that endeavor, the LFU eventually bought a house that served as a home to much of Louisville's lesbian community. A founder of the LFU remembers the group's move into the house: "We bought the house in March of 1976. We all pitched in and made it a space that helped to unify this community. Everyone from the most political lesbian to the butchest bar dyke came through those doors and they all felt welcome."[17] The LFU house, located on Brook Street in downtown Louisville, provided a meeting space, a library, and rooms that both local lesbians and visitors from other communities could rent.

The same spirit of cooperation that led to the purchase of the house encouraged twenty women to invest one hundred dollars each to become equal partners in a women's bar, Mother's Brew, which opened at 204 West Market Street in December 1976. Mother's Brew was Louisville's connection to the national lesbian-feminist movement. The bar was considered by the 1977 *Gaia's Guide* to be "an example to other lesbian-feminist communities of a bar that embraced the entire community."[18] Mother's Brew sponsored lectures by early lesbian-feminist leaders, such as Kathie Sarachild, and housed a lesbian resource center that provided women with information about the development of the Lesbian Nation.[19] One early member of the LFU said of the bar, "The Brew was the real center of our culture. In fact it may have been more unifying to this community than the LFU itself. The bar was a place for spiritual women, political women, and bar dykes. It was, in the beginning, like a greenhouse for our culture."[20]

Along with other lesbian-feminists, women of the LFU believed that to renew the matriarchy and allow the "Nation of Amazons" to rise, the patriarchal aspects of language, religion, culture, and politics would have to be challenged, redefined, and reclaimed. In this spirit, lesbians throughout the country founded magazines and newspapers, created publishing companies to print lesbian-oriented literature, opened their own book-stores, and established archives and libraries to gather and preserve their culture and history. Women's music, a vital element of lesbian culture in the 1970s, reached an ever-increasing audience through lesbian record companies and music festivals. Providing self-affirming lyrics about les-bian politics, love, and unity, the music helped create community by bringing women together and proselytizing for the lesbian-feminist move-ment. The songs echoed the anger of lesbians and provided them with an outlet for their frustration. In Louisville, the LFU played a central role in fostering this emerging and distinct lesbian culture.

Over the years Mother's Brew hosted nationally known lesbian musi-cians, such as Maxine Feldman, Alix Dobkin, Holly Near, Meg Christian, Cris Williamson, the Reel World String Band, and provided a regular stage for the local band River City Womin. An LFU member who reviewed a concert by Dobkin at Mother's Brew in 1977 addressed the "personal is political" concept and demonstrated the importance of women's music to lesbian-feminist politics:

> The Alix Dobkin concert at Mother's Brew was a not-to-be-believed combi-nation of high flying, full Moon light bathing, Dykenergy. Over 200 women attended the concert and were exposed to a woman who lives out the statement, "The personal is political." Alix speaks and sings directly of her life and politics and makes no apologies for either. As an energetic, woman-loving woman, she is a great spokesperson for our movement. The energy of her message will not soon be lost. The power of the evening continued with our own River City Womin.[21]

To many in Louisville's lesbian community, the band River City Womin was instrumental in the creation of a lesbian culture in the city. Formed in 1974, River City Womin's original members were Judy Paulsgrove, Betty Keeling, Joyce Hopkins, and Theresa Davis; within six months, Pauls-grove was replaced by Marge VanGilder. In addition to playing locally, the band gave concerts in Lexington, Kentucky, and Cincinnati, Ohio; performed at the Michigan Womyn's Music Festival; and recorded one album.[22] VanGilder talked about the band's beginning and its role in Louisville's lesbian-feminist culture: "The LFU had just begun and lesbi-ans in Louisville were hungry for the culture. They wanted to hear love songs about women loving women and about our struggle. I think we helped to create a sense of unity that led to a strong lesbian community in this city."[23]

When River City Womin played at Mother's Brew, their love songs and political messages reached a large cross section of women. A Louisville lesbian remembered her first experience with the band:

> I had heard of River City Womin and the bar [Mother's Brew] but I had never seen either. The first time I walked through the doors of the Brew and saw four strong, confident women performing love songs to other women, I cried. I had felt so alone, like I was the only one. I stood and listened to those songs as if I had never heard music before. I guess maybe I hadn't, at least not music for me. I returned every time they played. The energy was incredible.[24]

When Mother's Brew closed in 1978 and River City Womin split up the same year, it appeared that the lesbian-feminist movement in Louisville was waning. VanGilder said, "It seemed like many of the die-hard activists were getting tired and the money was running out. The gay circuit was drying up around here and when the Brew closed, we shaved our legs and became 'respectable.' We played at the Galt House and other local lounges. The LFU was in trouble, and many of us were questioning the movement."[25] Still, the impetus created by River City Womin was felt ten years later, when Louisville's lesbian community was able to rally around another all-women band. Laura Shine, Carol Kraemer, Phyllis Free, Patti O. Veranda, and Kathy Weissbach formed the band Yer Girlfriend. Lead singer Shine talked about the band, its significance to the local lesbian community, and its legacy from River City Womin:

> Our goal was to provide live women's music for the local community like River City Womin did in the 1970s. They paved the way for Yer Girlfriend. Our first concert drew one hundred women. The community support for the band was tremendous. Women from Louisville consider Yer Girlfriend "their band." We are their band. We exist because of this community and the women before us who created the culture we sing about.[26]

Like women's music, lesbian-oriented literature emerged in the 1970s to spread the lesbian-feminist message and culture. Lesbian-feminist newspapers, magazines, poetry anthologies, and novels came into being because lesbian-feminists believed they should control what was written for them and about them. From 1974 to 1978, Louisville's Lesbian Feminist Union published a newsletter with this mission in mind, providing a calendar of events and an editorial section that discussed a range of topics, from local politics to personal relationships. The newsletter also printed reviews of local concerts, a "lesbian herstory" section, interviews from lesbian-feminist leaders, and a column titled "Dykionary" that sought to educate the lesbian community on the correct terminology of the movement. For example, "Dykionary" changed the spelling of *woman* to *womyn* or *womun* in order to rid the word of *man* and made *history* into *herstory*. Men were called *boys* or *mutes* (short for mutation). *Gynergy* was "womun energy," *majik* was "womun powers," and a "rabid castrator" was an angry lesbian.[27] The vocabulary of the old lesbian culture was abandoned because it was seen as counter to lesbian-feminist politics. Lesbian-feminists no longer used the words *butch* or *femme*, which they viewed as imitation role stereotypes. Proper use of what lesbian-feminists called the "mother tongue" was vital if they were to be successful in creating a lesbian identity.

In addition to its monthly newsletter, the LFU sponsored a poetry group that included several published authors. The group met monthly at Mother's Brew and eventually published a collection of poetry entitled *Free Our Sisters*, dedicated to "sisters who are imprisoned in the jails and asylums of the patriarchy."[28] Not all of the poetry produced by the group focused on women in prison, however. Members of the poetry circle also wrote about love between women, the oppression of lesbians, and the rise of the matriarchy.

> Here is a dream I have . . .
> Dykes flank a line twenty feet wide
> down Broadway
> ten miles long down Broadway
> the East end Dykes join at Baxter
> the West end Dykes close the line at the Parkway.
> It is time. . . . A tremendous roar of Amazon strength
> Her vibrations heal all wimin. . . . Oppression
> has ended in Louisville. . . . End of a dream.
> Ah reality.[29]

The concept of the Lesbian Nation not only called for cultural independence; it called for economic independence as well. Lesbian-feminists believed that to create and control their own world, they would have to establish their own businesses and services. Louisville's lesbian community established a food co-op, where women worked in exchange for food. The LFU sponsored a women's resource center that included counseling and child-care services. Lesbians in the community opened the Bluegrass Feminist Credit Union in 1976, offering services to lesbians ranging from savings accounts to small loans.[30] Louisville's lesbian-feminists also supported many small, lesbian-run businesses. Two women in Louisville began a construction and renovation business called Woman Works, which proved to be a successful endeavor. Studio One, opened by a local jeweler, sold women's art of all kinds and provided a space for local lesbian artists to work and congregate, until its closing in 1982.

Lesbian-feminist culture was diverse and touched nearly every aspect of life. It created for lesbians a cohesive woman-identified world in which women could express their love, anger, dreams, and political goals. This culture still exists and is evidence of the strength and determination of lesbian-feminists.

Literature, music, language, and lesbian-run businesses were important elements of the lesbian-feminist community of the 1970s. But the politics of the lesbian community provided a common thread that ran through all elements of the culture. The music overtly encouraged political revolution, and lesbian literature embraced the "personal is political" theory by honoring love between women. Even lesbian language and spirituality had political overtones.

In Louisville, the LFU and its members were both the cultural and the political leaders in the early days of the lesbian-feminist movement. However, the LFU's role in political organization may be its most lasting contribution to Louisville's homosexual community. The LFU encouraged its members to voice their political and social concerns as they saw fit: "Our politics are those of individuals. We are diverse politically and are striving for the common goal, a Lesbian Nation where we can all be equal."[31] The organization felt it was important to reach out to all women and provide for them an alternative to an oppressive male-dominated world, regardless of their political views. The LFU staged political protests in support of the Equal Rights Amendment, participated in rallies at the state capitol, and helped organize a regional conference called "Building the Lesbian Nation."

By 1977 the LFU numbered over fifty members. A year later, the organization was forced to sell its house because of a decline in membership. Its financial situation worsened throughout the year, and in 1979 the LFU disbanded. The very foundation of the LFU and other lesbian-feminist organizations was sisterhood. When that feeling of likeness diminished, the organization suffered. Lesbian-feminists united because of their differences from gay men and straight women. But their differences from one another and the strain those differences put on their relationships with each other proved to be more than they could overcome. The LFU newsletter was published for the last time in the fall of 1978 and included this editorial on the community's future:

> Our sisterhood has served its purpose. We are a community now, diverse and at odds for sure, but a community nonetheless and if our accomplishments are to be realized by those sisters who come after us, then we must move on. We must continue to believe in and work for equality.[32]

Former LFU members went on to become active participants in numerous gay and lesbian organizations and have been responsible for bringing the issue of gay rights to the forefront in Louisville. Some of the lesbians who came out in the 1970s curtailed their political activities over the years, but many remain leaders in Louisville's gay and lesbian community. The social changes of the past two decades have allowed these women to integrate their lesbianism into other aspects of their lives and have caused them to broaden the scope of their political involvement. Lesbian-feminists in Louisville no longer seek a separate nation for lesbians; instead, they participate in coalition building to help bring about social, economic, and political equality for gays and lesbians.

Even though the Lesbian Feminist Union disbanded in 1979, its legacy remains. As that final LFU editorial stated, "Together we have accomplished a great deal. We united this community in a way it had never been before, but I fear that will not last. . . . Without a central, guiding force can our diverse community hold together?"[33] The answer to that question is both yes and no. Lesbian feminists were not successful in sustaining a separate, utopian Nation, but because of their courage, insight, and ability to compromise, the gay and lesbian community of Louisville did survive. In 1996 lesbians *and* gay men make up the strong, diverse, politically active community that currently exists in Louisville.

John D'Emilio observed that gay and lesbian organizations of the 1980s and 1990s were greatly influenced by the lesbian-feminist movement.[34] In Louisville, the four-and-a-half-year existence of the LFU changed the homosexual community forever. Eventually every oppressed group concludes that it deserves a say among the forces that decide its destiny. In *Two Tabloids Disseminated by Freedom's Heritage Forum,* David Williams contended that Louisville's gay and lesbian community did not reach that point until the 1980s. He said that Louisville's community did not organize politically in the 1970s; instead, "they were centered around bars, private social clubs, and public parks, which attracted closeted gay males."[35] While Williams might be correct in describing gay male social and political organizations before the 1980s, his description does not apply to lesbian organizations. The LFU created an organization, an all-women's bar, a culture, and a foundation on which future organizations could build.

In 1981, two years after the LFU folded, the firing of a local bank manager sparked the creation of a coalition among political-minded lesbian-feminists and gay men. Sam Dorr, a branch manager for Louisville's First National Bank, was asked by his employer to resign after he made it known that he was going to accept the presidency of the local Dignity/Integrity chapter, a Catholic gay and lesbian support group. The bank took exception to the fact that Dorr's responsibilities as president and spokesperson would make his sexual orientation public knowledge. Because employment discrimination based on sexual orientation was not protected by the civil rights laws of the time, Dorr challenged his dismissal with a lawsuit based on Title VII of the Civil Rights Act, which prohibits employment discrimination based on religion. The bank's statement that "homosexualism and religion seem like they're opposites" allowed Dorr's attorneys to argue that his freedom of religion and assembly had been violated.[36] Dorr's case was argued at the appellate level in the Sixth Circuit Court of Cincinnati. The court rejected the idea that involvement with gay religious groups should not be protected because such groups are geared toward the particular needs of homosexuals and ruled that Dorr's civil rights had been violated.

Dorr's case led to the unification of Louisville's homosexual community and was the catalyst for the formation of Gays and Lesbians United for Equality (GLUE), an organization responsible for educating the public on gay rights issues. GLUE was to be an umbrella organization for all Louisville-area nonprofit groups supportive of gay rights. Its members set as their purpose "to function as a liaison among all member groups and gay people in the community; to provide a forum for discussion of issues of importance to gays and lesbians; to provide help, assistance and support to any member of the gay and lesbian community; to strive to be an effective voice combating homophobia in the community." [37]

GLUE sponsored many community educational events and was responsible for creating a cable television show, *All Together Now,* which aired from 1984 to 1988. GLUE worked with the Pride committee to create Gay Pride Week events. GLUE members sponsored bar nights, picnics, theater productions, movie nights, and an awards banquet.

GLUE considered itself to be an organization of gays *and* lesbians, and for the most part that was true. However, a difference in focus and understanding of important issues led to an eventual split within the organization. GLUE was never meant to be a political organization and therefore did not provide the political representation that many lesbian-feminists wanted. Arising from this dissatisfaction, the Greater Louisville Human Rights Coalition (GLHRC) was established in 1984.

The GLHRC was not a lesbian organization, but some of its most active members were those women who for thirteen years had sought political representation for the entire homosexual community. GLHRC attempted to meet the needs of lesbians and gay men and was formed to fill the political void left by GLUE. A 1984 GLHRC newsletter defines the group's focus: "The GLHRC is a nonpartisan organization that was founded for the purpose of educating the public about the extent of discrimination against lesbians and gay men."[38] The leadership of the GLHRC was equally female and male. The group was distinctly political in nature and set out immediately to have the words "sexual or affectional orientation" added to the list of protected classes.

In 1985 the GLHRC surveyed more than three hundred lesbians and gay men living and working in the Louisville area. The results demonstrated the extent to which gays and lesbians were discriminated against and were used to convince the Human Relations Commission to pass a resolution urging the Louisville Board of Aldermen and the county's fiscal court to amend current nondiscrimination ordinances to include sexual orientation. In 1988 a resolution was passed by the Board that banned employment discrimination against persons with acquired immune deficiency syndrome (AIDS). Through the GLHRC, gay men and lesbians accomplished a great deal. But it was the confrontational attitude of a GLHRC planning committee known as March For Justice, Inc., that led to the community's most public display, an annual March for Justice, and ultimately their most important victory: the passage of a hate crimes ordinance that included protection for homosexuals.

Like GLHRC, March For Justice, Inc., was not a lesbian organization, but lesbian-feminists offered strong leadership to the group. Pam McMichael, a leader in GLHRC and March For Justice, Inc., stopped short of calling the latter a lesbian organization but made this comment about its members: "It was said that March For Justice was made up of radical lesbians and a few geeky men, and that Pride was comprised of wealthy gay men. It wasn't true, though—the men in March for Justice were *not* geeky."[39] March For Justice, Inc., was not only an outgrowth of the

GLHRC but also a response to Pride's reluctance to sponsor political and non-gender-specific events for Gay Pride Week. Pride, a predominantly male organization, had been planning Gay Pride Week events for several years, and members did not believe that a "March for Justice" was the appropriate way to celebrate Pride Week. They were not a political organization and wanted events of the week to remain social in nature. Many lesbians who had been involved in political organizing for over a decade did not agree. They had planned and participated in marches to protest racial and sexual discrimination, and they were now ready to do the same on their own behalf. Male members of GLUE saw this as a divisive event that would cause an even greater split between Pride and the "lesbian-ruled" March For Justice, Inc. Still, March For Justice, Inc., comprised primarily of lesbians, began planning its own Pride Week events.

Despite the split that March For Justice, Inc., caused within the gay and lesbian community, on June 27, 1987, more than three hundred people marched in Louisville's first Gay Pride march. Subsequently, through the determination of the GLHRC and March For Justice, Inc., four ordinances that either directly or indirectly affected the gay and lesbian community were introduced to the Board of Aldermen, between 1987 and 1991. In July 1990 a hate crimes ordinance was finally passed by the Louisville Board of Aldermen, marking the first time in Kentucky's history that the words *sexual orientation* were used in a piece of legislation. The new ordinance aided victims of "physical attacks and intimidation motivated by race, religion, sexual orientation, ethnicity, health condition, disability or gender." [40] The passage of this ordinance gave members of the March For Justice, Inc., the incentive to launch the next phase of Louisville's struggle for gay and lesbian rights, the "Fairness Campaign."

This campaign officially began at the Fifth Annual March for Justice in June 1991. March For Justice, Inc., initiated this campaign "in order to secure an ordinance that would ban discrimination based on sexual or affectional orientation in employment, housing and public accommodations." [41] Leaders of the Fairness Campaign were chosen from both March For Justice, Inc., and Pride, but some of the same lesbians who, seventeen years earlier, had begun Louisville's struggle for gay rights were among its most vocal leaders. Carla Wallace, member of GLHRC and March For Justice, Inc., and co-organizer of the Fairness Campaign, said, "This gay and lesbian community, after seventeen years of organizing, is ready to challenge the city on its proclaimed commitment to the fair treatment and inclusion of all its people." [42] This has proven to be the community's toughest, most unifying struggle to date. The city of Louisville still does not have legislation to protect the basic rights of homosexuals. However, the fight continues, and among the community's most vocal leaders are the women of the Lesbian Feminist Union.

Originally, LFU members were dedicated to the creation of the Lesbian Nation—a separate community where women's values and a lesbian culture would prevail. The separatist community envisioned by lesbian-feminists of the 1970s did not survive, but the Lesbian Nation they sought still exists. The Lesbian Nation has been transformed; it is more inclusive and has problems and concerns that its originators did not encounter. Lesbian-feminists no longer seek a world that would survive outside mainstream society; rather, they strive for a world that accepts them equally and allows them to live freely *within* mainstream society. Lesbian-feminists of the 1970s attempted to create a self-contained lesbian world in which lesbians looked alike, thought alike, and loved alike. As the 1980s progressed, moderation replaced this ideological rigidity. Lesbians became aware that politics through coalition was possible and, at times, beneficial. But more important, lesbians learned that change was necessary to the survival of their community.

Nearly twenty years after the demise of the LFU, the homosexual community in Louisville benefits from the foundation laid by the organization. Leaders of the Fairness Campaign would agree with singer Laura Shine's assertion that Louisville's gay and lesbian community owes a debt to the lesbian-feminists of the 1970s. The politically active homosexual community of Louisville still relies on the leadership of women who participated in the LFU, and the lesbian culture fostered by the women of the LFU continues to flourish through the efforts of lesbian business-women, writers, musicians, and political leaders.

NOTES

I would like to thank Nancy Theriot, Anne Swedberg, and Laura Shine for their support, encouragement, and endless editing in this ongoing project. My profound love and appreciation goes to the women of Louisville's lesbian community. Without them, this project would not have been possible or necessary.

The oral interviews and primary source material saved by individual Lesbian Feminist Union (LFU) members provided the foundation for this study. This collection, which consists of organizational newsletters, correspondence, and poetry, is in the process of being cataloged by the author for the Department of Rare Books and Special Collections at the University of Louisville Library.

1. Southern Conference Educational Fund (SCEF), *Lessons of Louisville: White Community Response to Black Rebellion* (Louisville: SCEF Press, 1972), pp. 2–5.

2. Ibid., pp. 2–5.

3. Anonymous interview no. 1 by author, February 1995, Louisville, Kentucky (no tape recording).

4. Ibid.

5. Ibid.

6. Anonymous interview no. 2 by author, June 1995, Louisville, Kentucky (no tape recording).

7. No copies of this newsletter have been found, but it was discussed by at least two of the interviewees.

8. Anonymous interview no. 1.

9. Anonymous interview no. 2.

10. Anonymous interview no. 1.

11. Lillian Faderman, *Odd Girls and Twilight Lovers* (New York: Penguin Books, 1991), p. 216.

12. Anonymous interview no. 1.

13. Cited in Faderman, *Odd Girls*, p. 212.

14. *LFU Newsletter* (1975), in LFU Collection, Department of Rare Books and Special Collections, University of Louisville Library, Kentucky.

15. LFU Charter, 1974, in LFU Collection.

16. *LFU Newsletter* (1975), in LFU Collection.

17. Yoni [pseud.], interview by author, December 1994, Louisville, Kentucky (no tape recording).

18. *Gaia's Guide* (San Francisco: Women In Distribution, 1977), p. 154.

19. *LFU Newsletter* (1975), in LFU Collection.

20. Anonymous interview no. 1.

21. *LFU Newsletter* (1977), in LFU Collection.

22. Marge VanGilder, interview by author, May 1995, Louisville, Kentucky (no tape recording).

23. Ibid.

24. Anonymous interview no. 3 by author, February 1995, Louisville, Kentucky (no tape recording).

25. VanGilder interview.

26. Laura Shine, interview by author, tape recording, May 1995, Louisville, Kentucky.

27. "Dykionary," *LFU Newsletter* (1976), in LFU Collection.

28. *LFU Newsletter* (1976), in LFU Collection.

29. Unsigned, LFU poetry circle, 1977.

30. These businesses were advertised in the LFU newsletter and were mentioned in interviews; however, there is little specific information available.

31. *LFU Newsletter* (1975), in LFU Collection.

32. *LFU Newsletter* (1978), in LFU Collection.

33. Ibid.

34. John D'Emilio, *Making Trouble* (New York: Routledge, 1992), pp. 254–56.

35. David Williams, *Two Tabloids Disseminated by Freedom's Heritage Forum* (Louisville, 1994), introduction.

36. Ibid.

37. Gays and Lesbians United for Equality (GLUE) Constitution (Louisville 1982), in LFU Collection.

38. *GLHRC [Greater Louisville Human Rights Coalition] Newsletter* (1984), in LFU Collection.

39. Pam McMichael, interview by author, October 1994, Louisville, Kentucky (no tape recording).

40. *GLHRC Newsletter* (1989); in LFU Collection.

41. Pam McMichael interview.

42. *The Lavender Letter,* 1978–1994, Gay History Archives, Louisville, Kentucky. Quote is from 1991.

Chapter Twelve

"Women Ran It"

Charis Books and More and Atlanta's Lesbian-Feminist Community, 1971–1981

Saralyn Chesnut and Amanda C. Gable

Introduction

Atlanta's feminist bookstore, Charis Books and More, founded in November 1974, remains today a central fixture of Atlanta's Little Five Points, a recently revitalized inner-city business district that spills over into the residential neighborhoods of Candler Park, Inman Park, and Lake Claire. As one of the older and most successful feminist bookstores in the country, Charis offers a window onto the history of the second-wave feminist movement, as well as of lesbians and lesbianism in the United States.

As the "and More" in Charis's name suggests, feminist bookstores typically do much more than sell books; they function as organizational structures within the feminist movement.[1] Furthermore, historically, the majority of such stores have been owned and operated by lesbians (as is the case with Charis).[2] On a more theoretical level, studying the history of a feminist bookstore offers a chance to study the relationship between what Terry Eagleton terms the "literary mode of production"—the "structures of production, distribution, exchange, and consumption" of written works—and the processes of social change (1978, 47). Implicit in a feminist bookstore's existence is the assumption that such a relationship does exist: that making certain types of books and other cultural products readily available makes a difference, since these products can affect individual readers and, through them, society. Moreover, because of the important role that written texts and their distribution have played (and play) in social movements, studies of feminist bookstores are crucial to an analysis of how feminist and lesbian-feminist ideas were (and are) developed and disseminated. Yet few studies to date of the feminist movement or of lesbian history have focused on institutions such as bookstores.[3] Our work on the history of Charis Books and More is meant, in part, to begin to fill this gap in our knowledge of our own history as feminists and lesbians. Our analysis of Charis's early history also adds our voices to the ongoing scholarly conversation (some might say debate) about the meanings and legacy of the early lesbian-feminist movement.[4]

We began our research on the history of Charis closely focused on the ways in which Charis might have effected social change both directly—through its role as a clearinghouse, meeting place, and resource center for feminists in Atlanta—and indirectly—through its role in disseminating certain types of texts.[5] Almost immediately, however, we began to realize that we needed to widen our angle of vision to encompass the confluence of social movements and forces that created a complicated and profoundly reciprocal relationship between Charis and the surrounding community. During the 1970s, members of the lesbian-feminist community centered in Little Five Points/Candler Park patronized Charis because, as one of our respondents put it, "it was in the neighborhood, and women ran it."[6] The "woman-identified" philosophy[7] that this statement describes, along with the importance of written texts to the lesbian-feminist movement, led Atlanta's lesbian feminists to visit Charis often to shop and to talk to the store's owners, and eventually to work there as volunteers. Charis's owners, as we will see, welcomed this type of community involvement. Over time the store itself, founded as a community bookstore with an emphasis on theology, women's fiction, and a large selection of nonsexist and nonracist children's books, became a part of the surrounding lesbian-feminist community and developed into a feminist bookstore featuring lesbian-feminist books and run predominantly by lesbians.

We argue, then, that in the 1970s the store-community relationship was reciprocal and dialectical, with each entity both supporting and being supported by the other in an ongoing process of change and growth. Here we will detail, as concretely as possible, how this relationship was played out. We begin with a discussion of lesbian feminism. As an ideology that emphasized female agency and autonomy, lesbian feminism in the 1970s found expression in a number of lesbian-feminist texts and gave rise to a proliferation of women's presses, printing collectives, and bookstores—what has come to be called the "women in print movement."[8] We give a

12.1. Charis Books and More storefront, one month after the store was founded (December 1974). Linda Bryant is standing out front.

brief overview of this movement, which helped disseminate feminist and lesbian-feminist ideas and thus helped shape the collective identity of a generation of mostly white, mostly middle-class lesbians, informing their social practices as well as the structure of their communities. We turn next to Atlanta's lesbian-feminist community of the 1970s, briefly outlining its history and structure in order to trace the circulation and enactment of lesbian-feminist ideology through its political, social, and cultural activities, organizations, and practices.

As we turn finally to the history of Charis Books during the years 1974–1981, we view the store as the site of two overlapping systems through which lesbian-feminist ideas circulated: a textual and a social system. We conclude by suggesting that the circuit of feminist writers, presses, and bookstores affected the degree to which new ideas could be generated, developed, and disseminated. In addition, feminist writers, presses, and bookstores supported the development of feminist and lesbian-feminist individuals, organizations, and communities and through them effected social change. Ultimately, we argue, the early lesbian-feminist movement, when examined in light of its creation of new social and cultural identities and spaces for women and especially for lesbians, can be seen not as a political cul-de-sac of disengagement from mainstream politics and culture but as a force that has significantly altered the socio-cultural, and thus the political, landscape in the United States.

"The Rage of All Women"

Nationally, the lesbian-feminist movement arose in the early 1970s as an offshoot of the women's and gay liberation movements of that era, which had themselves attracted many women who had been politicized via their participation in the civil rights or New Left (primarily the student and antiwar) movements. Lesbian feminists shared with their heterosexual feminist sisters a disenchantment with male domination of these earlier movements. However, they found themselves marginalized as lesbians within both radical and liberal feminist groups, where at best lesbianism was regarded as having nothing to do with feminism and at worst lesbians were viewed as hypersexual, role-playing, male-identified women whose open participation in the feminist movement would discredit it.[9] The earliest lesbian-feminist writings are best understood as responses to such views of lesbianism and as attempts to explain to heterosexual, feminists exactly how lesbianism relates to feminism. The Radicalesbians' position paper "The Woman Identified Woman," for example, begins by defining a lesbian in terms that de-emphasize her sexuality and stress her womanness and instinctive rejection of socially defined "femininity":

> What is a lesbian? A lesbian is the rage of all women condensed to the point of explosion. She is the woman who, often beginning at an extremely early age, acts in accordance with her inner compulsion to be a more complete and freer human being than her society—perhaps then, but certainly later— cares to allow her. . . . She may not be fully conscious of the political implications of what to her began as personal necessity, but on some level she has not been able to accept the limitations and oppression laid on her by the most basic role of her society—the female role.[10]

This definition clearly aligns lesbians more closely with feminist women than with gay men, who, as the writers go on to explain, can claim male privilege if they desire. In the 1970s, this alignment had the effect of helping resolve the split over lesbianism within the women's liberation movement and, in fact, positioned lesbians as the vanguard of that movement—they were feminists who not only espoused but lived their politics, giving their energy to other women instead of to men. Being "woman-identified" came to be the quintessential element of lesbian feminism as a political stance, regardless of one's sexual orientation or practices, and meant, as Charlotte Bunch explained it, "the life stance of self-affirmation and love for women; of primary identification with women that gives energy through a positive sense of self, developed with reference to ourselves, and not in relation to men" (1978, 180).[11]

Critics of lesbian-feminist theory have pointed out that as a globalizing theory that purported to define an all-inclusive identity, *the* lesbian feminist, lesbian feminism paradoxically excluded many women. Early lesbian-feminist theorists' left-wing politics; their emphasis on a countercultural lifestyle that included the ideals of androgyny, nonmonogamy, collective living, and downward mobility; and especially, some lesbian feminists' extension of the ideal of woman identification to its logical extreme, lesbian separatism, all alienated and excluded groups ranging from poor women and women of color to middle-class professional and working-class butch-femme lesbians. Historians—and lesbian feminists who remember the early movement—have also noted that lesbian-feminist writers' descriptions of a lesbian feminist as one "who acts and thinks in accordance with her inner compulsion" hardened over time into rigid prescriptions for how one should think and act in order to be a real lesbian feminist—prescriptions that, ironically, enforced conformity and denied differences of individual preference or racial or class identity. As Arlene Stein points out, it "was not so much that boundary-making took place—for it does in all identity-based movements—but that the discourse of the movement, rooted in notions of authenticity and inclusion, ran so completely counter to [the boundary-making]" (1995, 144). In addition, lesbian feminists have, in various academic accounts, been accused of essentialism, utopianism, an overemphasis on culture and lifestyle at the expense of politics, and a host of other, lesser evils ranging from bad taste in clothing to a lack of interest in sex.[12]

While many critiques of lesbian feminism have been warranted and have provided useful corrections, in particular to early lesbian feminists' focus on gender to the exclusion of race and class, many have suffered from the same shortcomings they pointed to in lesbian feminism: that is, they have ignored differences—this time within lesbian feminism. They have failed to inscribe in their accounts many lesbian-feminist individuals' and groups' dissent from the political orthodoxies laid out in lesbian-

12.2. Charis Books and More Staff in November 1994, the store's twentieth anniversary year. *From left to right:* Beryl Jackson, Linda Bryant, Sara Look, Sherry Emory. Courtesy of Bonnie Palter.

feminist theory.[13] This is true in part because historians and social critics have tended to focus on what lesbian feminists wrote rather than on what they did—on theory to the exclusion of practice. Many of these accounts have thus reduced lesbian feminism to a monolithic abstraction, a caricature of itself, detached from the day-to-day realities of lesbian-feminist women and communities as well as from the larger processes of history.[14]

Our intent here is not to make a sweeping argument for or against lesbian-feminist theory or practice, but we do feel strongly that more studies are needed of lesbian feminism both as sociopolitical theory and as the always-contested, always-evolving embodiment of that theory in the social practices and institutions of a specific community in a specific time and place. Along those lines, we hope that our discussion of the conflicts that ensued when the women in Charis Books attempted to put into practice the lesbian-feminist ideas they were reading gives some indication of the complex nature of lesbian feminism "on the ground."

However, our main focus here is on one contribution of lesbian feminism: its construction of a new lesbian identity. Totalizing though it may have been, this identity finally moved "the lesbian" out of the discursive realms of sickness and sin, where she had resided for much of the twenti-eth century in the United States, and placed her firmly in the political—and public—realm (Phelan 1989, 19–37; Stein 1995, 136–39). This new lesbian identity, with its emphasis, however conflicted, on individual agency and expressive authenticity, helped give rise to the women-in-print movement. The movement then reinforced the identity as it enabled the production and widespread dissemination of new and diverse repre-sentations of lesbian life and culture in works written by, about, and for lesbians.

It would be hard to overestimate the significance of this development. Perhaps it is easiest to grasp if we consider our country's history of censoring gay and lesbian texts that included positive portrayals of lesbi-anism, and that well into the 1960s, the most widespread representations of lesbian life were those in the "pulp novels," whose typical plots Bertha Harris summarizes as follows: "femme meets butch (usually in Greenwich Village); drunkenness, violence, and heavy (but very unspecified) sex ensues; femme ponders the problems of being 'different' and outcast; the young man in the background quickly replaces the butch in the fore-ground and we close on a vision of a heterosexual cottage covered with heterosexual ivy. The butch either commits suicide straight off, begins to drink herself to death or finds a new 'innocent' to corrupt" (Sisley and Harris 1977, 40).[15] In our view, among the most significant and lasting legacies of the early lesbian-feminist movement are the new lesbian sub-ject and the cultural products and institutions to which it gave rise. Stores like Charis, along with the writers whose work feminist presses and bookstores have nurtured, the ideas and images offered in the works produced, the cultural and social space both institutions and written works create and preserve, are manifestations of this legacy.

Women in Print: A Movement of Words

The second wave of the feminist movement and the concurrent bur-geoning lesbian-feminist movement were fueled by texts. In their guide to women's publishing, Polly Joan and Andrea Chesman wrote that "more than any other movement in history, feminism [was] identified with pub-lishing."[16] Radical feminist groups crafting manifestos, women's printing collectives producing newsletters, and poets writing chapbooks all gener-ated and disseminated the ideas and images that continued to propel the feminist and lesbian-feminist movements. Charlotte Bunch indicates the importance of texts to the feminist movement in her 1982 essay "Reading and Writing for a Feminist Future":

> Only in this century, and now only in some countries and among some classes, have significant numbers of women gained access to the tools of writing that Virginia Woolf explored in her essays—literacy, money, space of one's own, and admission to the 'public world' with its range of experiences. Women's struggles to write and to gain these and other attributes of freedom are connected. It is small wonder, then, that writing and publishing are passionate concerns for many feminists. The first large purchase of Washington, D.C., Women's Liberation in 1968, for example, was a mimeograph machine. Then, as now, women spread the word about feminism and argued its future course in everything from novels to political essays and personal diaries (1987, 217–18).[17]

Maria Lauret comments in her book on feminist fiction in America that "it would not be an exaggeration to say that Women's Liberation as a leaderless amalgam of dispersed groups and practices was held together not by organisation, but by an infrastructure of magazines, touring speakers, broadsheets, films and exhibitions and—last but not least—creative writing" (1994, 72). In an article reviewing twenty years of feminist criticism, Cora Kaplan notes that "in the 1970s those of us engaged in the feminist critical project . . . all read poetry and novels as they came out. . . . We read them because those texts were part of the ongoing debate of the social movement of which we were part" (1989, 18). And Bonnie Zimmerman, known for her pioneering lesbian-feminist criticism, proclaims that "no body of literature will ever have as strong an impact on my ideas as that produced in the first few years (roughly 1968 through 1972) of the women's movement" (1993, 115).[18]

The proliferation of written texts among feminists and lesbian feminists led logically to the formation of bookstores, presses, publishers, and periodicals. A good case in point is the Furies, a lesbian-feminist group who, in their short time together, produced many influential statements of feminist theory. When the Furies disbanded in April 1972, one year after the group had begun,[19] individual members went on to found a lesbian-feminist press (Diana Press—Coletta Reid), a journal (*Quest*—Charlotte Bunch), a book distributorship (Women in Distribution—Helaine Harris), a film company (Moonforce Media—Joan E. Biren), and a record company (Olivia—Ginny Berson and Helaine Harris). Two members became well known for other lesbian-feminist cultural contributions: Joan E.

Biren, for her photography of lesbians and lesbian/gay events, and Rita Mae Brown, for her poetry and best-selling lesbian novel *Rubyfruit Jungle*.[20] Significantly, Alice Echols (1989) marks 1973 as the year cultural feminism began to grow and eclipse radical feminism. The "ascendancy" of cultural feminism was thus accompanied by the growth of lesbian-feminist enterprises, such as the ones started by former Furies members, and by the founding of feminist bookstores.[21]

The oldest continuously operating feminist bookstore, Amazon Books in Minneapolis, Minnesota, began operating in 1970.[22] Others opened in succession: Common Language, in Ann Arbor, Michigan (1972); New Words, in Cambridge, Massachusetts, and Antigone, in Tucson, Arizona (1973); Charis Books, in Atlanta, Georgia (1974); and Old Wives' Tales, in San Francisco, California, and Lammas Books, in Washington, D.C. (1976). Shameless Hussy Press, the first U.S. feminist publisher, was founded in 1969 and printed the poems of its founder, Alta, as well as stories by Susan Griffin and poetry by Pat Parker. Many early feminist presses such as Women's Press Collective, begun in 1969, served as a print shops as well as publishers.[23] Women's Press Collective printed lesbian poetry by founder Judy Grahn and writers Pat Parker and Willyce Kim. The influential Daughters Press was founded in 1972 by novelist June Arnold and her partner Parke Bowman and soon published Rita Mae Brown's *Rubyfruit Jungle*, followed by groundbreaking experimental lesbian novels such as Arnold's own *The Cook and the Carpenter* (1973) and *Sister Gin* (1975); Elana Nachman's *Riverfinger Women* (1974); and Bertha Harris's *Lover* (1976). Diana Press (both printer and publisher) produced Rita Mae Brown's poetry, *The Hand That Cradles the Rock* (1971) and *Songs to a Handsome Woman* (1972), and an anthology of Furies articles, *Lesbianism and the Women's Movement* (1975). The Feminist Press was established in 1970 to publish reprints of women's writings. Naiad Press, founded in 1973–1974, pledged herself to publishing popular lesbian fiction. Other early presses include Out and Out Press, which published Jan Clausen's *After Touch* (1975), and Persephone Press (established in 1976), which first published Cherríe Moraga and Gloria Anzaldúa's *This Bridge Called My Back* in 1981. By 1976, June Arnold reported in her article "Feminist Presses and Feminist Politics" that more than 150 feminist presses or journals existed across some thirty states.[24]

In the 1970s, all of the feminist presses and most (if not all) of the journals were operated and edited by white, working- and middle-class feminists. Although women of color were published and most of the feminist presses and journals had an articulated antiracist stance, the defining presence in print was that of white feminists and lesbian feminists. To provide more writings by women of color, journals edited by white feminists most commonly published special issues devoted to women of color that were guest-edited by a woman of color. While this did provide more space for the voices of women of color, the locus of control still resided with the white women running the journal. In response to this situation, one such guest editor (and writer), Barbara Smith, along with the poet Audre Lorde, established Kitchen Table Press in 1981—the first lesbian-feminist press owned and operated by women of color. Currently, Kitchen Table is the only feminist press owned and operated by women of color.

Feminist bookstores and feminist presses from their beginnings were integrally connected. The first feminist bookstore, ICI (Information Center Incorporate)—A Woman's Place in Oakland, California (established in 1969),[25] shared a space with the Women's Press Collective, one of the first women's print presses.[26] To illustrate the interconnectedness of feminist bookstores and presses, Short begins her 1994 dissertation on feminist publishing with the story of Judy Grahn (poet) and Wendy Cadden (artist) producing the first all-woman anthology, *Woman to Woman,* and beginning the Women's Press Collective. In their travels from San Francisco to Boston before officially beginning the Women's Press Collective, they met Carol Wilson, who was in the process of starting A Woman's Place bookstore. As she traveled cross-country, Wilson sold books from her van, including *Woman to Woman.* This informal distribution system made it possible for Carol Seajay to buy *Woman to Woman* at the Michigan Woman's Liberation Retreat. Some years later, in 1976, Seajay, along with her lover Paula Wallace, (who had been a member of the Women's Press Collective), would start the first feminist bookstore in San Francisco, Old Wives' Tales. Also in 1976, the first Women in Print Conference was organized by June Arnold and Parke Bowman of Daughters Press. After returning from this conference,[27] where one hundred women involved in feminist publishing met in Omaha, Nebraska, at a Camp Fire Girls camp, Seajay began the *Feminist Bookstore Newsletter,* now called *Feminist Bookstore News.* Today this publication serves as the *Publishers' Weekly* for feminist bookstores.

The way these women's lives intersected was no accident. All were committed to the idea of women's liberation and to getting lesbian-femi-

12.3. Charis's current location on Euclid Avenue, just across from the old location on Moreland. Courtesy of Bonnie Palter.

nist writings into other women's hands. In their minds, no doubt, written texts were tools for effecting social change.

Echols argues that the rise of cultural feminism, which she defines as "a countercultural movement aimed at reversing the cultural valuation of the male and the devaluation of the female," meant the decline of radical feminism, "a political movement dedicated to eliminating the sex-class system" (1989, 6). In Echols's analysis, the cultural-feminist emphasis on creating woman-owned and -centered institutions and a "woman's culture" posed the danger of creating a politics in which "patriarchy was evaded rather than engaged" (5). However, in our view cultural feminism, at least in the case of women-owned and -operated feminist bookstores and presses, was essential to the development and maintenance of the feminist movement.[28] Both feminist bookstores and presses (as well as other cultural institutions) worked together to disseminate widely the ideas of individuals and groups. Feminist bookstores, as the name of the first bookstore—Information Center Incorporate—indicates, served as meeting places and resource centers for the community as well as locations to sell books and journals. Rather than short-circuiting the social-change agenda of radical feminists, in many ways the rise of feminist bookstores and presses allowed feminist ideas, including those of radical feminism, to continue to be developed and disseminated.

When analyses of cultural or lesbian feminism[29] fail to consider the relationship between cultural production and social change, they overlook what is arguably the most significant legacy of the lesbian-feminist movement: its creation of a new lesbian subject. Through the women-in-print movement, women were given access to a plethora of narratives and visual images that opened, not only for lesbians and soon-to-be-lesbian women but for the world at large, a new cultural space occupied by women whose primary social, emotional, and sexual bonds are with other women. "The lesbian," no longer inevitably a figure of shame and secrecy, sickness, and sin, emerged as a woman who is strong, independent, androgynous, romantic, sometimes charming and sometimes self-righteous, and explicitly or implicitly feminist. Once this figure entered the realm of public discourse, she could be argued over, qualified, modified, criticized, or even rejected—but she would never again be pushed back into the closet of silence and invisibility. For many women who came out or came of age during the lesbian-feminist movement, including those in Atlanta's Little Five Points neighborhood, the possibilities had never seemed so limitless.

"Little Five Points Was Just Crawling with Lesbians"

Atlanta's 1970s lesbian-feminist community was both a physical place— the Little Five Points neighborhood, ten minutes from downtown Atlanta—and a group of people who shared a set of values and a way of life: primarily young, white, middle-class lesbians.[30] This community was in many ways remarkably similar to lesbian-feminist communities in other parts of the United States; its emergence can be traced to at least as early as 1971, and its politics and lifestyle owed as much to 1960s-style radical politics and countercultural influences as to feminist and lesbian-feminist ideology.[31] Thus community members concentrated their time and commitment on political causes rather than on jobs (much less careers), were downwardly mobile, lived communally, and formed businesses and organizations with collective or cooperative, rather than hierarchical, structures. The Little Five Points neighborhood accommodated this style of living: The "white flight" phenomenon of the 1960s in Atlanta had left it, like many in-town neighborhoods, in transition, and there were few established businesses, mainstream organizations, or tradition-minded civic leaders around; there were, however, plenty of cheap rental properties available and an "anything is possible" view of the future.[32]

First one, then two, and eventually close to a dozen communal households of lesbians formed in Little Five Points, each consisting of five to seven residents and a stream of more or less transitory friends, lovers, and guests. Jane described her mid-1970s lifestyle as follows: "Most of [us] were young and jobless or just lived hand-to-mouth, so [we] had no ties to any establishment. . . . In every women's household there were different women who did different activities and then reported on them to the rest of the household members. . . . Everyone always went to any kind of demonstration."[33]

Atlanta's lesbian-feminist community was also similar to other feminist and lesbian-feminist organizations and communities in having its roots in New Left and women's liberation groups. Jane's narrative (Jane and Anne 1990) of her own personal-political evolution during the 1970s provides a good description as well of some of the movements and groups from which Atlanta's lesbian-feminist community evolved:

> I had become, by 1971, very involved with the beginnings of Atlanta Women's Liberation and with the first women's commune in Little Five Points, called Upstairs and Downstairs. The core of the people there were women who'd been on the Third Venceremos Brigade to Cuba—they were also coming out. In early 1971 no one in the house acknowledged she was a lesbian, and within six months *everyone* was a lesbian. We'd all been involved in Atlanta Women's Liberation, which met first at people's houses and then rented our own house, A Women's Center. Atlanta Women's Liberation was started by a number of women who were involved with the underground newspaper *The Great Speckled Bird* and other women who came back from the Second and Third Venceremos Brigades who weren't from Atlanta but stayed and helped start it. A number of the Atlanta Women's Lib people were lesbians as we all began to come out, and there began to be a split between the straight women and the lesbians, and that was the beginning of the end of Atlanta Women's Liberation. By this time there were several households of women in Little Five Points.

As this narrative makes clear, Atlanta Women's Liberation and the lesbian-feminist community that eventually split off from it were shaped, in part, by young leftist women who had joined the Venceremos Brigades and had come to Atlanta as one of the staging areas for the Brigades.[34] Atlanta's leftist alternative publication *The Great Speckled Bird* also played an important role in the genesis not only of Atlanta Women's Liberation but also of the city's first gay political group: A gay caucus organized by members of the nonsectarian leftist *Bird* staff provided the nucleus for an Atlanta Gay Liberation Front (GLF), founded in 1971 on the model of New York City's GLF, formed after the 1969 Stonewall Rebellion.[35]

With the founding of Atlanta's GLF and the emergence of all-lesbian communal households in Little Five Points, gay men and lesbians became public and even publicly political figures, for the first time in Atlanta's history.[36] This new visibility, along with political activities sponsored by the GLF and other organizations, soon captured the attention of young activists such as Anne, a Cuban-born woman who still lives in Little Five Points and who told us how she first became involved in the lesbian-feminist community there:

> I was a student at Georgia State University in 1972, where I became involved in antiwar activity and hung out with people who were sort of hippie-politicos. . . . At the same time I was dealing with this sexuality thing. . . . A friend who'd been in a Venceremos Brigade introduced me to some gay people and I ended up going to [a] gay march . . . and there I met a woman who really excited me. It turned out she lived in a women's commune in Little Five Points. . . . I had heard that Little Five Points was just crawling with lesbians and there was a lesbian press there and everything. So this woman invited me to her house and there I met all these women.[37]

The "gay march" Anne remembers was the 1972 Gay Pride march. Although lesbians obviously participated in this march, by that time many of them were fed up with the male domination of the GLF, symbolized for them by the omission of the word *lesbian* from the name of the group and the celebration. That year, a group of women including, according to Anne, "lesbians from Atlanta Women's Liberation and Gay Liberation [GLF], and some women who were middle-class lesbians who were interested, and some from the Socialist Workers' Party" met and decided to form a new, specifically lesbian-feminist organization: the Atlanta Lesbian Feminist Alliance, or ALFA. At last there was a home in Atlanta for lesbians who found the women's liberation movement too heterosexist and the gay liberation movement, as well as most leftist groups, too sexist.

ALFA eventually rented a house on McLendon Avenue in Little Five Points that served as the base of its operations and those of a number of other groups and activities.[38] Once the basic institutions around which the community was first organized—ALFA and the communal households—

were in place, lesbians not only from Atlanta but from other parts of the Southeast and even elsewhere in the United States moved into the area or began to participate in some of the wide range of activities happening there. For the first time in the history of lesbians in the South, there were social spaces outside the bars where lesbians could meet other lesbians and public activities in which they could participate as lesbians, without fear of persecution by police and with the knowledge that if they did encounter harassment or persecution from anyone, they had a community of strong, activist women to support and defend them.

The women we have talked to, most now in their forties and fifties, all remember the 1970s as a period of intense activity and excitement in the Little Five Points lesbian-feminist community—or the ALFA community, as it came to be called. ALFA had regular monthly meetings, published a monthly newsletter beginning in late 1973, and sponsored activities including talks by visiting authors and speakers, poetry and fiction readings, and workshops or panel discussions on political issues; potlucks, parties, and dances; and of course, softball teams. In 1974 the ALFA Omegas became the first out lesbian softball team ever to play in the city of Atlanta's recreational league. Several informal "rap groups" also met either at the ALFA house or in someone's home, simply to discuss current issues and ideas. And the idea of communality that underlay the organization of the multimember households was extended to the organization of eating co-ops—groups of women who took turns cooking dinner for one another on a given night of the week. In the mid-1970s, there was usually at least one eating co-op for each weeknight.

In addition to ALFA and its activities, several ALFA-related groups had memberships that overlapped with ALFA's, publicized their meetings and events in the *ALFA Newsletter*, and used the ALFA house for meetings and other activities. Some were explicitly political and leftist, including Dykes for a Second American Revolution (DARII) and the Socialist-Feminist Women's Union. ALFA women were also the driving force behind more mainstream women's rights and gay/lesbian rights organizations, including Georgians for the ERA (G-ERA), a coalition group that organized marches in 1974, 1975, and 1976 to urge ratification of the ERA (Equal Rights Amendment) by the Georgia legislature, and the Gay Rights Alliance, a gay and lesbian political group formed in 1976 after the demise of the GLF in 1973. A large contingent from the ALFA community could always be counted on to turn out for ERA marches and Gay Pride marches, as well as for other demonstrations, marches, and benefits for different causes. One such early "cause," for example, was to raise money for the legal defense of a community member who was in the Weather Underground and who had been arrested by the FBI while living in one of Little Five Points's communal households.[39]

In addition to these explicitly political groups, several groups with significant ALFA community involvement reflected the lesbian-feminist emphasis on individual empowerment. There were two lesbian-run counseling collectives, as well as a lesbian sex therapy group, Atthis, which held workshops designed to help participants "find new ways of owning our sexuality as lesbian women."[40] Jane taught self-defense and karate classes that many in the ALFA community attended, and even the ALFA softball team enacted principles that empowered all team members, including collective decision making (the entire team decided on the lineup for each game) and the provision that anyone who wanted to play could play, regardless of her level of athletic ability. Among the continuing debates within ALFA was the question of whether the organization should be primarily social or political, but in fact, many ALFA-related activities such as the softball team blurred the boundaries between the social and the political. Such activities introduced lesbian-feminist ideas and practices to women who were not necessarily aware of lesbian feminism as a political movement or theory, and who would not necessarily have engaged in something they perceived as purely political.[41]

In keeping with the lesbian-feminist agenda of developing a lesbian alternative culture, members of the ALFA community also organized or sponsored activities that were not only social and political but also cultural. Two lesbian-feminist theater groups—Red Dyke Theater and WomanSong—wrote short, humorous sketches and performed regularly for the rest of the community, and a music production group, Lucina's Music, brought to town the performers of the new "women's" music. However, writing and publishing in particular were central to the new women's community and culture emerging in Atlanta, as was true across the country. As we have seen, even before the founding of ALFA, women who would later become part of the ALFA community had worked on the staff of *The Great Speckled Bird*. Some of the same women were involved in a short-lived (1971–1972) women's press collective, Sojourner Truth Press, which printed, among other things, the Furies' newsletter.[42] Later, ALFA sponsored ongoing poetry and fiction-writing workshops and regularly held readings, sometimes featuring the writing of ALFA members, sometimes featuring lesbian-feminist writers whose work was being published by the newly emerging lesbian-feminist presses and publishing houses, including Rita Mae Brown, June Arnold, and Bertha Harris.

The *ALFA Newsletter/Atalanta* played an essential role in the development of the ALFA community by publicizing not only ALFA-sponsored but also other local and regional events and activities and by covering local, regional, and national news of interest to leftists, women, gays, and especially lesbians. From the beginning the newsletter carried lists of periodicals ALFA received, as well as, in the very early days, publications for sale through ALFA. Later, as ALFA developed a sizable library, the newsletter listed new acquisitions, and beginning around 1974, it also regularly featured members' reviews of newly published works considered of interest to the ALFA community.

Unlike lesbian-feminist communities and groups in other parts of the country, the ALFA community produced no body of theory, no articles or manifestos that have remained in print to be studied by subsequent generations of lesbians. Moreover, not every member of the ALFA community read works of lesbian-feminist theory or even the new lesbian-feminist fiction; these women were more likely to encounter lesbian-feminist ideas as they watched Red Dyke Theater perform, listened to the music of Cris Williamson, debated whether the softball teams should stress competition more, or took a date to a poetry reading. However, it remains true that the ALFA community, like lesbian-feminist communities across the country and the lesbian-feminist movement as a whole, was print-centered, dependent on the written word to generate, develop, and disseminate information and ideas. This fact, coupled with the lesbian-feminist ideals of giving one's energy to other women and supporting women's efforts to develop autonomous institutions, meant that ALFA women would inevitably be drawn to the new bookstore that opened in Little Five Points in 1974.

Early History of Charis Books and More: 1974–1981

Interestingly, the women who opened Charis Books on November 4, 1974, Linda Bryant and Barbara Borgman, initially did not identify the store as part of the feminist movement. Yet by 1979, and perhaps as early as 1977, it can be argued that Charis had an explicit lesbian-feminist ideology. Like many women who started feminist bookstores,[43] Linda and Barbara were activists involved in a social-change movement, but at the time they opened the store, their social-change work was focused on community work through a radical enclave of the nondenominational Christian youth group called Young Life.[44] Although Barbara remembers thinking of the store as a "radical social alternative bookstore," Linda remembers envisioning a store with a focus on women's books as well as children's books (Barbara's expertise) and radical theology books.[45] In a 1977 column in the *Atlanta Journal and Constitution*, local writer Carol Ashkinaze gives an indication of Linda's and Barbara's memories of the beginning of the store after it had been operating for almost three years: "[Linda and Barbara] envisioned a bookshop that would offer a full complement of Christian and Eastern religious literature, 'non-stereotypical, non-racist, non-sexist' children's books, books by and about women, books by local authors, plus a community bulletin board and a toy-laden loft/playpen to keep toddlers amused while their parents browsed. It would be a store where a woman with a budding interest in feminism or theology could drop by for advice on what to read first."

After graduating from the University of Florida in 1970, Linda Bryant had moved to Atlanta as a Young Life staff member to work at Avondale High School in the suburbs of Atlanta.[46] She immediately became involved in the Little Five Points area, in part out of her commitment to do inner-city work in this once prosperous but now marginal neighborhood.[47] A network of Young Life staffers already worked in Little Five Points as part of their urban ministry, and Linda took her Avondale High School students to tutor at Moreland Elementary School in the Little Five Points area. At this time, the corner space that would later become a part of Charis Books was a Young Life teen hangout called the Broken Wall.[48]

In January, 1974, although she no longer worked for Young Life and was teaching English at Walker High School, Linda went to a Young Life conference in Atlanta. There she talked to friends about starting a bookstore and reconnected with Barbara Borgman who, with her husband, was planning to move to Atlanta and live in an inner-city neighborhood in a communal house. Barbara and Linda had met one summer at a Young Life institute in Colorado that offered theology classes.[49] Now, when Linda talked over the bookstore idea with Barbara, they also found they shared a goal of living in a communal household. Linda relates, "I wanted to live with a family, live with a larger group of people and do that kind of experimental thing, and as I talked to Barbara Borgman about this idea [for the bookstore]. . . she said, 'Oh, I know about children's books. When I come [to Atlanta] I could do the children's books.' " That day Linda wrote a letter to a friend who had inherited money and asked for a loan to start the bookstore. The Borgmans moved to Atlanta, and they and Linda established a communal household in Grant Park, near Little Five Points. In November 1974 the two women opened Charis Books and More at its first location, 419 Moreland Avenue, in the heart of Little Five Points.

For Linda, opening the store felt like a calling: "It felt like it was a vision, that it wasn't just an idea—wouldn't that be a neat thing to do. See I come from a Christian background so those are the terms that are in my vocabulary for that time."[50] "Teaching [high] school [English] at the time was what I did for a living, but opening the bookstore was what I was called to do."[51] The name of the store, Charis (pronounced KA-riss), comes from Greek and means "grace" or "gift." Both women felt the name fit their philosophy of wanting the store to be a gift to the community, as well as acknowledging that their ability to open the store was a gift to them. Barbara explains that they also "picked the name because it [Charis] was a feminine aspect of God."[52]

At first Charis Books was set up as a nonprofit organization under the umbrella of an inner-city education project, Exodus, in which many former Young Life staff members were involved.[53] The decision to organize as a nonprofit was motivated in part by Linda's friend's desire to donate rather than lend the money for the project.[54] Barbara and Linda followed people's advice to set aside some of the donated money to live on, and their friends helped them renovate the space they had rented for the store. When they opened the store, the shelves were stocked with approximately two thousand dollars' worth of books. Linda worked full time and Barbara worked part time. In making decisions about the everyday operation of the store, Linda drew on her experience with her consciousness-raising group, and both women drew on their experience doing "contact work." Linda explains that to do "contact work" means to "be around, be available to the community you are interested in working with, and when they're ready they'll talk to you. That's what we started doing in Little Five Points. . . . We wanted to create an atmosphere of openness that would be healing. The books were just a part of that." Linda and Barbara reached out to communities they already knew about, operating a book table every Sunday at St. Luke's Episcopal Church in downtown Atlanta. Each Saturday morning they had a children's storytelling hour at the store. The children's section was and remains a distinctive feature of the store; Barbara had been a children's librarian and took care in providing nonsexist and nonracist children's books.

Neither woman had worked in a bookstore before, although before they opened Charis, Linda volunteered briefly at the Columbia Seminary bookstore to see how one was run.[55] To figure out what to stock, Linda wrote to a progressive Christian bookstore she liked, LOGOS in New Orleans, for their inventory list, and both women sent off for a variety of publishers' catalogs. At this time Linda was taking graduate English classes, and these courses influenced the fiction she chose. By the winter of 1975/76, Linda had entered a masters of theological studies program at Emory University's Candler School of Theology, and her course work continued to affect her choice of books that she and Barbara would carry in the store. For example, in 1978, Linda completed her master's thesis on Toni Morrison, Alice Walker, Tillie Olsen, and Rosellen Brown; Charis carried fiction by all these writers well before their widespread popularity.

Although Linda's course work and intellectual interests had a direct influence on the direction of the store, in January 1976 an important series of events changed Linda's personal life and, over the years, also influenced Charis's policies. That month, two friends called Linda, independently of each other, to tell her about a ten-month-old biracial (African American and Caucasian) boy who needed temporary care. Linda decided to care for Enoch, and although initially the boy's mother felt she could care for him again after a year or so, this did not prove possible. When Enoch was two and a half, Linda formally adopted him. Adopting and raising Enoch made Linda even more aware of racial issues and of how black people were (and are) treated by such institutions as the court system.[56] Having a son also affected her opinion of lesbian separatism, as did the influence of bisexual and heterosexual staff members at Charis over the years, and as a result, the store has always maintained a space for men who support feminist ideals. Linda's experience as a single working mother has also ensured that, over the years, the women running Charis have been aware of the needs of workers who are single mothers.

Gradually, as residents of Little Five Points/Candler Park began to frequent Charis, their interests and needs began to affect the store's focus and the books it offered for sale. Linda and Barbara's politics of inclusiveness, as well as their backgrounds as activists working in communities to improve education and social justice, gave them common ground with other neighborhood residents, including the lesbian feminists. Barbara Borgman describes their approach as "we'd say, 'Welcome. We want to meet you, we want you to come in here and sit down and have a cup of coffee, talk, and have a neighborhood meeting place.... What kind of books are you interested in?'. . . So it became quickly a place where people talked books and talked ideas."[57] For instance, Barbara remembers two gay men coming to the store and asking if Charis could carry particular gay-themed books. "Well, Linda had not come out as a lesbian at that time . . . this must have been 1975. . . . But we looked at each other and I can remember saying, 'We've gotta do this. This goes with it.' We were unanimous on it. . . . We got quite a bit of conversation from [our] conservative friends [for stocking these books]. 'What in the world are you doing? Do you know what you're doing?'"[58] Barbara felt they knew exactly what they were doing: They were providing books for people who wanted to be treated with dignity. Ultimately, however, the lesbian feminists in the neighborhood affected the store's overall direction more significantly than did any other group.

Former members of the ALFA community all recalled being aware of the store from the time they moved into the neighborhood. Jane and Anne, who were already living in Little Five Points, remember going to the store's opening "very cautiously. We were excited that there was a place where there were women's books . . . but then we got there and there were religious books. . . . But . . . it was something that was in the community, something that had potential. . . . The women in there seemed very subdued . . . not at all like the women we had been around. But on the other side we felt it was nice to be giving money to women" (Jane and Anne 1990). Jo Hartsoe remembers Charis before the women's section opened as "kind of a peace-and-happiness bookstore where you could get things like about antiwar stuff. . . . My memory is there was a lot of religious stuff too" (1990). Anne remembers the first book she bought there, Toni Morrison's *The Bluest Eye*, and the second, Margaret Randall's *Women in Cuba*. "We had a lot of study groups then, and we did a lot of reading," she said. "Charis was a good supplier of the material we wanted, and they weren't shocked when you came in and asked for material, whether it was lesbian or leftist or whatever. . . . Also if they didn't have a book you wanted, they'd order it and then they'd stock it" (Jane and Anne 1990).

All these women, when asked what they remember reading during the 1970s, said they read virtually anything and everything that had to do with feminism and lesbianism—in fact, they remembered being "hungry" for this material. Chris Carroll said she thinks this was because women- and lesbian-oriented writings were "sort of a reflection of ourselves that was very concrete . . . like to just get beyond the denial that's everywhere else . . . like we don't exist and we have no reality . . . and also there was a lot of testing of new ideas in these books, and we were interested in that" (1990).

When Charis first opened, neither Linda nor Barbara knew about the lesbian organization ALFA or the lesbian-feminist communal households in the Little Five Points area. Neither woman had been formally involved in the feminist movement in the early 1970s, although they were acquainted with feminist ideas through their studies in feminist theology and the influence of women's consciousness-raising groups. Linda said in a 1990 interview, "When the idea of the bookstore came to me I knew already that I wanted it to be involved with women's literature. I had been in my first women's group in 1971 [with wives of other Young Life staff members]. . . . We met every week for four years—met for three to four hours every time we met—and that was going on during the whole Young Life time and my teaching school time, that I was in this women's group and sorting things out and becoming a feminist really." [59] Soon after the store opened, Linda and Barbara began meeting the lesbians in the area. Linda remembers Chris Carroll and Karen Gold as the first self-identified lesbians from the Little Five Points neighborhood that she met; Chris was distributing Olivia records, and Charis began selling women's music early on. Linda also fondly recalls going to the favorite bar of the Little Five Points lesbians, The Tower, around 1975 to hear Olivia recording artists Cris Williamson and June Millington. Even though she identified as heterosexual at the time, she was thrilled by the experience. Around the time of this concert, Linda remembers becoming aware of the Atlanta Lesbian Feminist Alliance, which rented a house in the neighborhood.

Lesbians who frequented Charis in the early years remember the store as a welcoming place to them, even though they had little money to spend. Charis soon began to be a place where women could find out what was happening in the ALFA community—people posted flyers there for all the different events. Charis sold tickets to Lucina's Music concerts; they kept a listing of apartments or houses for rent in the neighborhood; and then, of course, people would run into one another there. Jane, who taught self-defense classes for women during this time, said that by 1978 she trusted Charis and Linda Bryant enough that when she began to get threatening phone calls at night, she asked Linda if she could list Charis's number on the posters advertising her classes, and for several months Charis took her calls during working hours. Jane also distributed a book list to the women in her classes, and Charis stocked the books. By 1977, when a third partner joined Linda and Barbara and brought with her an emphasis on lesbian books, Charis had become an integral part of the Little Five Points lesbian-feminist community.

In June 1977, Maya Smith added capital to the store and joined Linda and Barbara as a partner.[60] Identified as bisexual, Maya had been to the first Michigan Women's Music Festival in 1976, where she encountered many feminists and lesbian feminists, and she returned to Atlanta eager to start a women's business, preferably a bookstore. At the time she was a writer and was reading voraciously, getting most of her books from the Ansley Mall Book Store in Atlanta, where a few members of the ALFA community worked. Maya said in our 1990 interview, "I am really a believer that . . . the money . . . will pour back into the community if there are women's books being sold and women's presses. And so what I began to conceptualize was a women's bookstore . . . that if there was a women's movement and its books were being sold, we needed a place owned and run by women."

Barbara remembers that Maya came to visit her and Linda at Charis and asked for advice. It was an exciting meeting, and in the end, Barbara and Linda convinced Maya to join their business rather than start a separate (and competing) store of her own. At the time, the corner space on the block next to Charis was vacant, and with Maya's added capital and labor, this space was opened up and devoted, in part, to lesbian books. Maya not only brought to Charis an expertise in lesbian-feminist books; she also added science fiction, fantasy, astrology and nontraditional spirituality sections. She organized a system of volunteer workers, and women from the lesbian-feminist community began regularly volunteering at the store. Linda explains how Maya's joining the store fit into its evolution: "The way the store has grown in terms of what is there has to do with the people who work here and has a lot to do with the customers. If those women, like Chris [Carroll] and Karen [Gold] and other women, had not been coming in the store, had not been a part of the store, it wouldn't have made sense to do what Maya did. . . . Maya didn't bring in a whole new crowd of people—she satisfied some of the crowd that was already there."[61] Within a year after the new section of the store opened, Linda came out as a lesbian, thus moving the store further in the direction of its current identity.

Before Linda, Barbara, and Maya opened the new section of Charis Books, which Maya had accurately predicted would increase the visibility

of the store, the three women had many sessions discussing the philosophy of the store. Although these intentional sessions stopped as the
day-to-day grind of running the store intervened, informal political discussions continued. Like many other feminist enterprises, the store was
structured nonhierarchically and operated as a collective, with the three
workers making decisions by consensus. Their general guiding principles
were those of feminism, as they understood them, but the three partners
felt free to debate and disagree with specific feminist ideas and practices.
Maya remembers them discussing whether to carry tickets for a concert
by a woman performer who didn't allow male children to attend her
concerts. Maya also initiated discussions about reducing the number of
male-authored Christian books. In general, decisions about what books to
stock were made according to the ideas and values the books promoted
rather than simply based on whether the women felt the book would sell.

Because the store generated very little revenue, the women who
worked at Charis lived frugally on their savings or on the original donation. Over the years, many women who worked at the store had second
jobs on the side. This included Maya, even though she was a partner. By
1979, Maya's second career—her practice as a massage therapist—was
beginning to take off. As a result, she put in fewer and fewer hours at the
store, and the three partners decided to add two new employees. They
first discussed the power dynamics of adding employees to their group.
Maya describes their discussion:

> We realized there really was an imbalance of power; even though from a
> feminist perspective you might want to say we were all equal, we all weren't
> equal because the truth is it took you about six months to know the store.
> So we decided to name that, which felt important. . . . We'd try to bring [new
> employees] on like, oh yes, you're equal with us and that was all very good
> and fine, but they weren't. . . . We were explaining things to them. They
> couldn't work as fast. They didn't know the store. . . . So in naming it, that
> felt much better, because then we said to people, when you come in you're
> not full equal in the collective. . . . They came in at a lower pay with the
> [understanding] it was because they had less knowledge. That really felt like
> a fair way to do it. (Smith 1990)

Julia Strong, one of the store's new employees, began working at
Charis in 1979 and became the first woman who was out as a lesbian
when she joined the staff. (At that time, Linda had been out for approximately a year.) Julia had come out in 1977, during her first job after college

in rural Tennessee, and had moved to Little Five Points after she came to Atlanta in 1978 to attend the Third Annual Southeastern Conference of Gay Men and Lesbians.[62] Maya Smith was a close friend of Julia's lover, and through her, Julia heard that the collective of three at Charis had decided to expand. Julia describes Charis in those days as a place where women "were trying to create alternatives to the mainstream." She describes her relationship to Charis and the store's relationship to the community in the following way:

> Charis was my major community activity. . . . It was [a] hub of communication for so many individuals and groups. People would come in and say, "I have this idea for something and can I talk to you about it?" And Linda or one of us would spend two and a half hours helping someone think through whether this business or this idea that they had was a good thing for them to go ahead and pursue. So I think that we played a lot of different roles— providing published material was just another facet of that. Lots of intangible interaction and support [was] going on there too. (Strong 1995)

Julia likens being in the women-centered space of Charis to "being a seed in nice moist soil." It was a place in which she felt she and others had an opportunity to blossom.

Charis's other new employee, Judy Sanderson, like many of Charis's customers was drawn to Charis because she "knew it was run by women." When she joined the store in 1979, she identified as heterosexual, was married, and had a six-month-old baby. (She since has come out as a lesbian.) She sums up the sense of excitement that the women who worked for Charis had about the space itself and the books they carried: "The spirit of Charis at the time," she said, "was not a hit-you-over-the-head, you-have-to-be-like-anybody-else approach. It was an excitement . . . a learning about and celebration of women that was going on."[63] The women who worked for the store during the 1970s convey a strong sense that the store played an important role in the development of the feminist and lesbian-feminist community in Little Five Points and was an equally important part of their own personal growth. Judy told us she thinks of her experience at Charis as having been like "going to a safe place, getting knowledge about myself as a woman, and [knowledge] about what other people were doing. . . . There was a lot of laughter, but seriousness too— that nice kind of combination."

Lesbian Feminism and the Evolution of the Store's Identity

The history of the dynamics of the staff and the day-to-day operation of Charis Books and More reveals the realities—and difficulties—of trying to put feminist ideas into practice, especially of functioning effectively as a collective. At first, with only Linda and Barbara running the store, decisions were made with relative ease. However, as women were added to the staff and the identity of the store began to evolve, it became more difficult for the staff to come to a consensus on the direction of the store.[64] The individual women on staff in this early period, from 1974 to 1981, though all white and college educated, did represent a range of other differences—some had children and some did not; some were straight, others were bisexual, and still others were lesbian. These differences among the women, along with their differing individual understandings of how a collective should function, produced both strengths and conflicts.

The structure of decision making at the store changed as the staff changed and grew; overall, however, in keeping with feminist values, hierarchy was avoided, choice assignments or responsibilities were rotated, and decisions were made by consensus. After Maya Smith joined as a partner and more women worked at the store, an advisory board, which functioned much like a collective, was formed. Initially, the women working at the store constituted the board; but by 1980 the membership of the advisory board/collective who made decisions about store policy included women who were no longer working at the store on a regular basis. This created an imbalance of power in the collective, similar to the imbalance of power that Maya reported they had previously realized existed between new employees and "veterans."[65] In theory, members of a collective have equal say in decisions, but inevitably, in reality, some members are more articulate and therefore more persuasive than others, and some may have more knowledge or abilities pertaining to the matter at hand. Among other things, a balance of power and commitment among members is necessary for the collective to work. The women of Charis worked to deal with issues of power and how to allocate authority and responsibility fairly. However, making collective decisions was never easy or straightforward. Ongoing conflicts intensified, and a new one was added when Linda's lover, Kay Hagan, applied to work at the store and several in the collective opposed her hiring on the grounds that the dynamics of lovers working together would be disruptive. Although the collective ultimately did hire Kay, not long afterward another conflict erupted over the mission and identity of the store, with the result that in 1981 two collective members, Maya Smith and Julia Strong, resigned.

The conflicts at Charis resulted in part from the influence of lesbian feminism, particularly on Linda Bryant. As Charis evolved more as a women's bookstore and was integrated into the ALFA community, it became a place where lesbians worked without trying to hide their identity as lesbians. In this type of setting, however, as Kathleen Weston and Lisa Rofel (1985) point out, the public and private sphere merge more than in a typical work setting. Although this merging is positive in that it allows for the public expression of lesbian (or bisexual) identities, it also makes it difficult to distinguish between personal decisions and business decisions. As a result, romantic and sexual involvements can have a complicating effect on work relationships, particularly in terms of expectations and roles. For example, the merging of public and private can increase employees' commitment to the workplace, but it can also increase their disappointment when the workplace fails to meet their expectations.[66] In their excitement at being able to work with other women who share their ideals or at being able to be out at work, many women may not think through the consequences of conflict within such an environment. As the boundaries between public (work) and private (personal life) become blurred, conflicts that appear in one area also closely affect the other area, thereby complicating possible solutions. Thus, paradoxically, feminists who, like the women of Charis, are trying to create and maintain nonhierarchical institutions often find themselves having to work to solve conflicts in, and sometimes resulting from, the unique liberatory space they have created.

This proved to be the case with Charis. Shortly after Kay was hired over the objections of some women, the collective began to struggle over the store's evolving identity. At this time, the workforce of the bookstore included four regular workers, two of whom were lovers. As might be expected in a bookstore, lesbian-feminist ideas and books figured prominently in the struggle over the identity of the store. For example, although there is no clear cause-and-effect relationship, Linda and Kay had been seriously reading and discussing Mary Daly's *Gyn/Ecology* around the time the advisory board/collective began to try to draw up bylaws and a mission statement for the store. Maya remembers that Linda constantly quoted Mary Daly to her, and at the time she was angered and put off by Linda's fervor. Perhaps tensions were still high from the debate about whether lovers would be allowed to be hired. In hindsight, Maya told us she felt this was Linda's radicalizing period. It also seems possible that Maya felt her position as the store "expert" on lesbian feminism was being challenged as Linda developed a stronger lesbian-feminist stance. Undoubtedly, another factor involved was lesbian feminism's inherent tendency, as an identity-based politics, to lead to what Arlene Stein terms "boundary making" (1995, 144). In any case, in part as a result of the conflict among the collective, the store was evolving from a women's bookstore into a specifically feminist and lesbian-feminist one.

After several difficult meetings of the board/collective,[67] which were facilitated by a therapist to try to maintain the goal of collective decision making, the group reluctantly (in Linda's opinion) agreed that feminism was a concept informing the values of the store. Upset with the collective's hesitancy to define the store as feminist, Linda wrote a letter to the collective in which she articulated her idea of the driving principles of the store. In her letter she made a case for giving more power to the women who actually worked at the store, making it clear that these women (Linda, Judy, and Kay) agreed to strong feminist principles and a feminist identity for the store:

> We spent hours at the last meeting articulating our values.... When I walked away, I realized that we had only reluctantly agreed on a concept—feminism—as the informing voice for our values, and then could not/would not use that word. What I need to agree on with people with whom I work intimately—and the bookstore is, we've learned, intimate work—is the basic underlying frame/purpose/direction/focus of values.
>
> My focus is clear to me. I am committed to a definite, recognizable stance over against the patriarchy. My form of that stance, specifically, is keeping alive and en-couraging independent feminist voices. For me, that extends to writers, publishers, booksellers, and readers, customers, myself. I want to expedite the flow of cash among these people so that the support is tangible enough to realize the aim of not only survival, but also the infusion of courage. I want these independent feminist voices to speak/write and be heard and spoken again in many fields besides specifically-designated feminist thought or fiction by women. I want to en-courage the men who want to free themselves from the patriarchy. I want to offer an open path to our children. I want us to approach the earth and healing and systems holistically—and in all these fields (and more) I want to keep alive the voices that are not in submission to the white male system; voices that continually ask questions and un-think assumptions.[68]

The influence of Mary Daly's play with language is evident in Linda's letter, as is her own awareness of the thin line between public and private in a feminist (and increasingly lesbian) workplace. The women in the collective had strong reactions to the stance Linda articulated here. Although she didn't mention the letter in her interview with us, Maya did describe a facilitated meeting during which she felt Linda had framed the conflict in terms of which one of them (Linda or Maya) "got" the store. From Linda's perspective, as she related in interviews and stated in her letter, the issue was that the women running the store on a day-to-day basis should determine the ideology of the store.

Since no one remembers the exact discussions of the collective or why members were reluctant to identify the store as a feminist enterprise, it is possible only to speculate that had the mediation process continued, the collective might have agreed to and named feminist values similar to those that Linda articulated in her letter. However, since, as she explained in her letter, Linda felt she could not both give energy to the process of the board/collective and run the store full time, the process did not continue. In the end, two members, Maya Smith and Julia Strong, resigned from the board/collective, hurt and angry over what they perceived in part as a power struggle with Linda. Their strong feelings were still evident when we interviewed them some fifteen years later. In hindsight, Julia said, she now feels she had longed for Charis to be everything for her, which made the conflict more difficult. She also spoke to us of the difficulty of leaving the "womb" of lesbian feminism in Little Five Points and Charis and moving back into the "mainstream." Maya had a financial stake in Charis, and because of the extremely limited cash flow of the store, her original capital investment of three thousand dollars was paid back to her at forty dollars per month for over six years. However, even though she was angry at the time and the settlement didn't feel completely fair to her, Maya told us she still has great admiration for Linda's integrity in keeping her commitment always to give Maya credit for what she contributed to the store.

Struggles at the store were a working-out of feminist principles: The women were strongly committed to a collective model and, perhaps more important, to creating a workspace that was woman-centered and open to lesbians. Although such a space blurred public and private boundaries and therefore increased potential for conflict, it provided an unprecedented and unique opportunity for lesbian-feminist ideas to be circulated and further developed. In fact, the various conflicts at Charis (as in other feminist organizations) helped the store owners/workers develop new ways of running a feminist business as they put feminist theory into practice.

After Maya and Julia left, the women of Charis rethought the structure of the store's ownership and the makeup of the advisory board. Although an advisory board/collective structure was retained, the board's membership henceforth had to be active in the work of the store. A partnership model of ownership emerged again, and a series of documents were written to define more clearly the responsibilities of board members. Also at this time, Exodus decided Charis should no longer be under their nonprofit umbrella, and the board/collective began tackling the logistics of becoming a for-profit enterprise. During the next period of Charis's history, not only did the store become for-profit but it also took on the projects of sponsoring multi-media feminist artist Judy Chicago's "Dinner Party" exhibit in Atlanta and opening a temporary branch store next to the location of the exhibit. Charis's identity as a feminist and lesbian-feminist bookstore became increasingly known throughout the Southeast. Thus by 1981, Charis, having survived a series of conflicts and struggles, emerged as a specifically feminist bookstore, operated by lesbian feminists and enjoying a mutually supportive relationship with Little Five Points's lesbian-feminist community.

Conclusion

The early history of Charis Books and the lesbian-feminist community in Atlanta, Georgia, provides a concrete example of the interrelationship and dialectic between a feminist cultural institution and the lesbian-feminist movement, as manifested in a specific lesbian-feminist community. As we have seen, the Little Five Points lesbian-feminist community's adherence to the belief that they should support other women and women-centered institutions, coupled with their interest in books and ideas, influenced the store's development from a Christian-oriented bookstore with women's fiction and nonsexist and nonracist children's books to a feminist store run predominantly by lesbians. As Linda articulated it in her 1981 letter to the collective:

> The bookstore's identity has been evolving, its definition emerging from its experience. Each of us (on the current board) participated in the creation

of what the bookstore is today. Our commitments, values, directions, and personalities are primary influences on the shape of the store.

In addition, the bookstore has taken on its own identity in response to the community it serves. From a Christian bookstore with some women's and children's books to a feminist bookstore with a strong emphasis on alternative and children's books, is a jump which the bookstore made a few years ago.

In turn, Charis supported the community and played a pivotal role in its development, as well as in the personal growth of individual members of the community. Today, Charis Books still occupies a central place in the lives and activities of feminists, lesbians, and lesbian feminists in Atlanta. Whereas the long-standing lesbian-feminist organization in the community, ALFA (Atlanta Lesbian Feminist Alliance), disbanded in 1994, Charis recently bought a house, renovated it, and, despite threats from chain store competition, has continued to thrive.[69] When ALFA closed her doors in 1994, she donated a significant portion of her money (from the sale of a house and archives) to Charis Books. With this act, ALFA women acknowledged Charis's importance as a sister lesbian-feminist organization in the community and continued to support the store as they had when Linda and Barbara first opened in 1974.

The example of the relationship between Charis and Atlanta's lesbian-feminist movement and community also makes clear that written texts and the access to these texts play an essential role in the development of political ideas and social movements. An important aspect of this role is the relationship between readers and the sources of the texts they read. During the 1970s, when a woman bought, for example, Rita Mae Brown's *Rubyfruit Jungle* at a feminist bookstore, she would not only be exposed to a new, heroic image of a young lesbian; she might also see a flyer advertising a lesbian poetry reading to be held at the store. At this reading she would hear and meet other lesbians and connect with a larger community, providing her with a concrete, material context for the images and ideas in Brown's novel. The experience of our imagined reader would have been very different if she had bought her Rita Mae Brown novel at a grocery store, assuming she would even have been able to do so; there she would not have been able to connect with a larger community or become aware of ongoing discussions of lesbian issues. For this reason, the material history of feminist bookstores and presses and their interrelationships with their communities is a crucial part of the history of lesbian feminism: "Readers . . . are never confronted with abstract or ideal texts detached from all materiality; . . . reading is always a practice embodied in acts, spaces, and habits" (Chartier 1994, 3).

Finally, the early history of Charis Books and the lesbian-feminist community of Atlanta exists, as we have demonstrated, within the context of a larger lesbian-feminist movement that gave rise to the women-in-print movement. The lesbian-feminist movement, with its emphasis on female autonomy, independence, and woman-centered enterprises, spurred the rise of women's bookstores and continued to supply them with texts to sell. Without the confluence of lesbian-feminist writers and writings, publishers, and bookstores, any one of the three might have withered. The lesbian-feminist space created by feminist bookstores was an embodiment of the principles and theories of lesbian feminism. Conflicts that emerged in this exciting but unfamiliar space led to further understandings of how feminists could work together effectively. Studying the conflicts the women at Charis experienced as they tried to put feminist and lesbian-feminist ideas into practice thus provides a necessary corrective to the tendency to think of feminism or lesbian feminism as static or monolithic.

Once they were established, feminist presses helped provide materials for burgeoning women's studies programs and the earliest courses in lesbian and gay studies. The influence of lesbian feminists also affected the evolution of the larger movement for lesbian/gay/bisexual/transgender rights; no longer could the word *gay* subsume the names of the other groups or white gay males dominate the movement unchallenged. Moreover, despite the fact that many lesbian-feminist organizations have disbanded and the lesbian-feminist movement itself is now, as Stein puts it, "decentered" (1995, 133), the women-in-print branch of the movement has continued to grow. Currently, the impact of feminist and lesbian-feminist presses and feminist bookstores on our culture at large is evident on the shelves of any mainstream bookstore. Feminist presses together with feminist bookstores demonstrated that there was a significant market for feminist and lesbian material, and mainstream publishers and bookstores are now tapping into that market. It is clear, then, that cultural feminism, developed in large part by lesbians, has indeed engaged rather than evaded the patriarchy (see Echols 1989, 6), effecting cultural, social, and political change in the process.

NOTES

We have listed our names alphabetically and are each full authors of this chapter. Saralyn Chesnut was (and is) a member of the Little Five Points lesbian-feminist community, originally moving there in 1973. She was an early member of the Atlanta Lesbian Feminist Alliance (ALFA); played on the first out lesbian softball team in the city league, the ALFA-Omegas; and lived in the communal household called Hummingbird Heights. Amanda Gable regularly reads her fiction at Charis and is serving on an organizing committee for a nonprofit group, the Charis Circle, formed to help support the bookstore's programming. She was a member of ALFA from the mid-eighties and served on the library and archive committee for two years.

We thank Dee Terry and Julie Martin for transcription work and thank all the women of Charis and the Little Five Points lesbian-feminist community for their willingness to be interviewed and their generosity in sharing their files and memories with us. All women who have been interviewed are named in the section on "Sources Cited," following the Notes.

1. A recent fund-raising letter sent out by the Charis Circle, a group of women in Atlanta who have volunteered to raise money to fund the store's free Thursday-night programs, includes quotations from feminist authors Minnie Bruce Pratt, bell hooks, and Shay Youngblood, all attesting to the fact that Charis has been much more than a bookstore in their lives. Pratt writes that "Charis was the first women's bookstore I ever set foot in, twenty years ago, and she changed my life, as she's changed the lives of countless others. The bookstore has been a home-away-from-home, library, resource center, and cultural hot spot"; Youngblood says, "Charis isn't just a bookstore. It's been a kind of home/community for me for over 15 years. . . . I found my first apartment, my first real job, a massage therapist, a dentist, a doctor, and lots of new friends at Charis. Charis has been great for my social and intellectual life. I love Charis! I came out as a writer at Charis!"; and according to hooks, "Charis extends the work of multi-cultural women's studies as well as engaging in community activism on all levels."

2. Taylor and Rupp note that "since 1980 . . . , the alternative institutions founded by early radical feminists—including . . . bookstores, newspapers, publishing and recording companies . . . have increasingly come to be driven by the commitment of lesbians and women in the process of coming out" (1993, 38).

3. Some comprehensive studies, such as Lillian Faderman's *Odd Girls and Twilight Lovers* (1991), give brief attention to presses and bookstores in the second wave of the feminist movement, but the brevity of their information often leads to incorrect conclusions. For instance Faderman leads her readers to believe that the lesbian-feminist presses from the seventies do not continue to be a presence in publishing. As a quick perusal of *Feminist Bookstore News* shows, lesbian and feminist presses continue to publish widely and influentially.

4. For a review of current histories and critiques of lesbian feminism, see Taylor and Rupp 1993. They, like Arlene Stein (1995), treat lesbian feminism as an ongoing political philosophy, if not a movement. The former speak of lesbian-feminist communities as still in existence, while the latter contends that at this point it is more accurate to speak of a "decentered sense of community" and a " 'movement' (if one can call it that), [which] consists of a series of projects, often wildly disparate in approach, many of which incorporate radical and progressive elements" (1995, 134). We tend toward Stein's viewpoint: Lesbian-feminist communities no longer exist, to our knowledge, in the same forms in which they existed during the 1970s through the early 1980s. A more recent full-length historical study by Becki Ross (1995) provides a balanced and nuanced analysis of lesbian feminism by embedding it in a detailed history of a lesbian-feminist community and its organization, Lesbian Organization of Toronto (LOOT).

There are some indications that the ongoing critique of lesbian feminism and responses by those who identify as lesbian feminists are growing increasingly more contentious. For example, Bonnie Zimmerman, in a talk at Emory University in October 1995, reported that at the June 1995 National Women's Studies Association conference, pro- and anti-lesbian-feminist views were debated heatedly.

5. Our study of Charis's history is based on oral history interviews, personal files and memorabilia, local 1970s alternative publications, internal records and newsletters of various organizations, and store records.

6. Jane [pseud.], Jane and Anne 1990.

7. The term is taken from what is arguably the most-cited manifesto of lesbian feminism, "Woman Identified Woman," written by the Radicalesbians, first distributed as a "position paper" at the second Congress to Unite Women in May 1970, and first published in the *Ladder* 11/12 (August/September 1970).

8. Miller 1995.

9. For histories of the emergence of the lesbian-feminist movement, see Taylor and Rupp 1993, 37; Stein 1995, 133; Ross 1995, 23–40; and Echols 1989, 210–41. On heterosexual feminists' views of lesbians during the late 1960s and early 1970s, and on lesbians' reactions to these views, see especially Echols 1989, 210–20. On often-overlooked commonalities among the second-wave women's movement and the New Left and civil rights movements, see Echols 1995. Here Echols argues that women who had been involved in the earlier movements and later became feminists brought to the women's movement "the conviction that radicalism involved fighting one's own oppression; the commitment to both prefigurative politics [which, as Echols explains it, 'emphasized creating in the present the desired community of the future'] and participatory democracy; the genesis of identity politics; and . . . the idea that the 'personal is political' " (Echols 1995, 119; Echols 1989, 16). The terms *radical* and *liberal* feminism are used here to denote, respectively, a feminism that seeks to change the power structure and one that seeks to gain for women increased access to it.

10. Quoted by Penelope and Hoagland 1988, 17.

11. It is interesting to note the continuities between the concept of the woman-identified woman—who, according to Bunch, is not necessarily a lesbian in terms of sexuality but rather is a woman who "steps outside of society's assumptions of who she should be" as a woman—and the current concept of the "queer" as one who dissents from prevailing sex-gender arrangements, regardless of his or her sexual orientation. In fact, Bunch specifically uses the term *queer:* "The more any woman is already or steps outside of society's assumptions of who she should be, the more 'queer' she is" (1978, 182). On current deployments of the term *queer,* see Duggan 1995.

12. See note 4 above. In particular, Echols (1989), Phelan (1989), and Faderman (1991) level some or all of these charges against lesbian feminism. We have heard descriptions of some of the "lesser evils" of lesbian feminism from students in women's studies and lesbian/gay studies courses, who report having heard them from other professors. Especially baffling to those of us who came out in the context of the lesbian-feminist movement is the notion that lesbian feminists were not interested in sex. According to Faderman, "Lesbian-feminists . . . were too busy designing the Lesbian Nation to turn their attention to what they generally regarded as the triviality of sex" (1991, 247). One can only wonder where Faderman got her information on this.

13. The earliest criticism of the white, middle-class subject position from which lesbian separatists spoke, for example, was made by a group of black lesbian feminists, the Combahee River Collective, in their "Black Feminist Statement," dated 1977 (reprinted in Moraga and Anzaldúa 1983). More recently, although there were lesbian feminists on both sides of the so-called sex wars, characterizations of these encounters often portray them as having pitted sexually repressed and repressive lesbian feminists against "sex radicals." Faderman (1991), for example, treats lesbian feminists as a subgroup of "cultural feminists" (she offers no definition of cultural feminism but lists as another of its subgroups "middle-class lesbians") and depicts the sex wars as being between cultural feminists and "sexual radicals." Stein is virtually the only writer on lesbian feminism who describes a "revolt from within" the movement by "women of color, working-class women, and sexual minorities" (1995, 146). For a comprehensive and thought-provoking treatment of the sex wars, see Duggan and Hunter 1995.

14. Thus the early theoretical emphasis on woman identification rather than on any particular sexual activity as the defining element of lesbian feminism—an emphasis that was a response to heterosexual feminists' stereotypical views of lesbians and refusal to acknowledge a connection between lesbianism and feminism—has devolved into the notion that lesbian feminists were not sexual.

15. On images of lesbians and lesbianism in pre-1970s American culture, see also Phelan 1989, 19–35; Zimmerman 1990, especially the preface and chap. 1; and Faderman 1991, scattered references in chaps. 1 through 8.

16. Quoted by Short 1994, 3.

17. Becoming a part of public discourse through written documents has been an important act for minority populations throughout American history. Notable examples against all odds are slave narratives (see Gates 1988, 171).

18. We are indebted to Kim Loudermilk for the quotes from Lauret, Kaplan, and Zimmerman; we take them from chap. 1 of her unpublished dissertation-in-progress (1996). Loudermilk has also been generous in sharing with us her research on early women's periodicals.

19. Some members continued to put out the newspaper until summer of 1973 (Echols 1989, 238).

20. This list is developed from personal knowledge of the authors; Echols 1989; and Bunch 1987.

21. Only recently has study of the history of feminist bookstores and feminist presses begun. Recently published and in-progress works include Streitmatter 1995; Miller 1995; Short 1994; Eastland 1991; and Loudermilk 1996.

22. Miller 1995.

23. A panel presentation on "Living Proof: Lesbian Feminist Presses" at the 1993 Outwrite Conference gave firsthand information on the history of the presses, as well as on what they are currently doing. Included were women from Aunt Lute, Seal, Kitchen Table, and the *Feminist Bookstore News*. Panel sessions were tape-recorded; see Gates et al. 1993, tape 21.

24. Arnold's article appeared in the 1976 summer issue of *Quest*, a journal founded by former Furies member Charlotte Bunch. This article may have been written in anticipation of the first Women in Print Conference, held in August 1976 and organized by Arnold and Bowman.

25. Short 1994, 4–7.

26. Thanks to Mev Miller for sharing the long version of her article "Words Create a Movement: Women's Bookstores," which served as the basis for her radio documentary *A Labor of Love: A Tribute to Twenty-five years of Feminist and Lesbian Publishers and Bookstores* (1995), and for her e-mail correspondence with Amanda Gable (1996a, 1996b).

27. The location was chosen as a midpoint for women on either coast. This conference was the first of what became an annual event that served to put women in publishing across the nation in touch with one another. The women of Charis remember going for the first time in the early 1980s.

28. Taylor and Rupp (1993) also critique the analyses of cultural feminism developed by Echols and others. They examine the "consequences for feminist activism of lesbian feminist culture and communities" and suggest that "lesbian feminist communities preserve" the political agenda of radical feminism (34–60).

29. Taylor and Rupp note that "the boundary in common usage between cultural feminism and lesbian feminism is highly permeable, if it exits at all" (1993, 34).

30. A few members of this community were women of color or women from non-middle-class backgrounds. However, as Faderman notes with regard to young lesbians of this period who had been born into poor or working-class families, "the democratization of higher education in the 1960s meant that they might get an education (and the verbal and analytical skills that went with it) such as only women of middle-class backgrounds might have ha 1 earlier" (1991, 197). This was the case in the Little Five Points lesbian-feminist community; most of the young women who were part of it, even if they had been raised poor or working-class, had been to college by the time they joined the community. Some were students at the time, most at nearby Emory University or Georgia State University.

We might note also here the sense in which we use the term *community:* Susan Krieger notes that "some lesbian communities are geographically specific . . . ; some exist within institutions (e.g., prisons); some exist only in spirit; some are ideological (e.g., lesbian feminist); some primarily social. All are groups in which an individual may share her distinctively lesbian way of being with other lesbians" (1985, 224). Using Krieger's typology, Atlanta's Little Five Points lesbian community was, during the 1970s, at once geographical, ideological, and social.

31. Information about other communities is to be found in Echols 1989; Faderman 1991; and Ross 1995. Informal communications with lesbians who later moved to Atlanta from other parts of the country confirm these written sources with regard to the dates of emergence and the political and lifestyle characteristics of lesbian-feminist communities in other urban centers in the United States. It is worth noting that this information contradicts received wisdom about the South, which holds that "things happen later" here than in other parts of the country and often differ markedly in character.

32. According to Tina McElroy Ansa (1978), Little Five Points's decline had been caused by a combination of factors, including "the city's growth and suburban flight" as well as the "razing" of a number of houses "to prepare for expressways in that part of east Atlanta."

33. Jane [pseud.], Jane and Anne 1990.

34. The Venceremos Brigades were groups of volunteers who went to Cuba for periods of several months at a time to work in the sugar harvest or provide similar labor in support of Fidel Castro's government. The First Venceremos Brigade was in Cuba from November 1969 to February 1970.

35. Information about the early years of *The Great Speckled Bird* and the Gay Liberation Front is based on informal conversations between Saralyn Chesnut and two of the men involved in these groups during the early 1970s, Ted Brodek and David Hayward. The *Bird* was published from 1968 to 1978 by the Atlanta Cooperative News Project; its staff were, for the most part, unpaid volunteers. Brodek remembers that, although there were "big battles" about it among the staff, the publication covered feminist and then gay issues and had feminist writers as well as some who came out as gay after the gay liberation movement had emerged

nationally. There was always tension, however, especially around gay issues, and in later years some staffers were members of more doctrinaire Marxist-Leninist groups with explicitly antigay ideologies. Information on the early history of Atlanta's Pride celebrations and other gay rights activities has been compiled by Cal Gough and David Hayward (1991) along with other members of the Atlanta Lesbian and Gay History Thing, a grassroots organization.

36. Atlanta's first Gay Pride march was held in June 1970, even before the GLF was founded; 125 people, mostly gay men, marched, and the *Atlanta Journal and Constitution* refused to cover the event. The GLF did organize 1971's Gay Pride celebration.

37. Anne [pseud.], Jane and Anne 1990.

38. Information about ALFA and related groups and activities is based on vols. 1–8 (1973–1980) of the *ALFA Newsletter*, renamed the *Atalanta* beginning with vol. 5 (1977), as well as on interviews with Anne, Jane, Chris Carroll, Lorraine Fontana, Jo Angela Hartsoe, Sonya Jones, and Elizabeth Knowlton. The personal recollections of one of the authors, Saralyn Chesnut, also figure into this account. See also Gabriner and Wells 1978. At its height ALFA had about 125 members; women who never joined the organization but participated in its activities and attended lesbian-feminist events numbered an additional two hundred to three hundred.

39. See Gabriner 1974; Gough and Hayward 1991; and *Atalanta* 5, 2 (1977): 7. Gabriner's article details the internal struggles among groups working for ratification of the ERA in Georgia, which included labor unions, feminist organizations such as NOW, and women from the Socialist Workers' Party, as well as more mainstream women's rights groups such as the League of Women Voters and Church Women United. According to Gabriner, "the rabble," which "conservatives [working for the ERA] would like to keep in the closet," included "the lesbians, campus, radical, socialist, black, and uneducated women and even women's libbers" (1974, 64).

40. From an ad in the *Atalanta* 5, 5 (1977): 14. The name Atthis is taken from the name of the woman to whom some of Sappho's poems are addressed.

41. See Gabriner 1976 on the ALFA Omegas and the two teams that soon joined the Omegas in the city leagues: the ALFA Amazons and the Tower Hot Shots, the latter team sponsored by a local women's bar that included many ALFA members on its roster. Gabriner asserts that these softball teams were about more than sports or even socializing with other lesbians; they also "affirmed our lesbianism; . . . reinforced and developed positive attitudes about our bodies; . . . strengthened our ability to function collectively; . . . allowed us to reach women who otherwise would not be active politically, in some instances meaning we were able to cross class lines; . . . built ALFA as a political organization . . .[and] strengthened the lesbian-feminist community in several aspects" (54).

42. Another Atlanta lesbian, Sonya Jones, together with Lydia Ann Moore founded a short-lived independent press, Vanity Press, in 1975. Vanity published a

novel and a book of poetry by Jones, and Jones took copies of these works to Charis to sell. Jones considered herself an anomaly in that she was part of both the ALFA community and what was known as the "Ms. Garbo's crowd," the latter referring to the name of a women's bar that catered to lesbians who were, for the most part, more upwardly mobile than were members of the ALFA community.

43. Miller 1995.

44. Although at first we found Charis's initial ties to a religious group surprising, it makes sense historically: religious groups and churches have often played important roles in social movements in the United States, perhaps more so in the South than in other regions. As Sara Evans documents (1979), the roots of women's liberation and New Left movements were in the civil rights movement, and the civil rights movement, for both blacks and whites, had deep roots in the southern church. Looked at in this light, Charis provides an unexpected but crucial continuity among social movements in the South—from civil rights to feminism to lesbian/gay/bisexual rights. For instance, Evans points out that white southern Protestantism provided a space for a radical critique of segregation in the 1950s and that in her interviews and research, every white southern women who joined the civil rights movement did so through her involvement in the church (29–35). Linda's life fits this paradigm: She gained an analysis of racial oppression from a high school Young Life leader in Gainesville, Florida; was introduced to feminism through a Young Life feminist theology class; and became part of a consciousness-raising group started by her Young Life women friends in Atlanta. Later, she came out as a lesbian. Barbara Borgman's life has also combined religion and social activism. In 1995, when we interviewed Barbara Borgman, she had recently returned to the U.S. from teaching in Africa with her husband and children and was living in the Jubilee Partners community, a Christian-based community in Comer, Georgia, that in part helps refugees from countries such as Bosnia enter the U.S., learn English, and find work.

45. Linda remembers carrying Charis Clarence Jordan's *Cotton Patch Gospels* and books by Thomas Merton as well as women's novels by Toni Morrison, Alice Walker, Tillie Olsen, and Rosellen Brown.

46. Linda had been involved with Young Life since high school. Although she has spent her adult life in the South, she grew up as an "army brat," living all over the world.

47. Bo Emerson, in an article for the *Atlanta Journal and Constitution* (1994), gives a sidebar history of the neighborhood as follows: "1908—Little Five Points becomes city's first commercial district outside downtown, serving the town of Edgewood (later Candler Park); 1930s—Despite Depression, Little Five Points thrives; 1960s—Houses razed for the proposed Stone Mountain Tollway. The abandoned road project and the middle-class exodus to the suburbs lead to deterioration of the neighborhood; Early '70s—By this time storefronts are boarded up, two theaters close and a third becomes a methadone clinic; 1974—Charis Books

and More opens in Point Center Building; 1977—The Redwood Lounge is purchased by the Little Five Points Community Pub Inc. Gun and knife fights are replaced by sprout sandwiches" (M4).

48. In 1974, when Linda and Barbara drove around looking for a place to rent for the store, Barbara recognized that Little Five Points had once been a thriving commercial district and predicted that it would be again. In fact, Charis blazed the trail for the revival of this business district. In 1975 a health-food cooperative, Sevananda, moved from its Emory University location to Moreland Avenue, next door to Charis. In 1977 the Redwood Lounge was replaced by the Little Five Points Community Pub.

49. Barbara was there with her husband, who was taking classes; she was caring for their two children.

50. Bryant 1989.

51. Bryant 1990.

52. Later, in 1979 when *Womanspirit Rising* (edited by Carol P. Christ and Judith Plaskow) was published, Linda and Barbara were pleased to discover that Charis was an early designation of the mother goddess recognized by the Gnostics.

53. Barbara's husband worked with an arm of this group, Project Propinquity.

54. The relationship with Exodus and the store's nonprofit status remained until 1980/81, when Exodus decided it was too difficult (even unwieldy) to maintain the necessary financial records for Charis's separate operation.

55. She later learned that college bookstores function quite differently from retail stores.

56. In the 1989 interview, Linda discusses the adoption process. Despite an unconditional recommendation by a county agency, Family and Children Services, she had to go before eight judges before one would approve the adoption. The first judge based his refusal on racial reasons. Linda relates, "It was a place where I understood racism in a real deep way. That these judges had that kind of power and could use it against me and against my son . . . [my lawyer pointed out to me] how it must be to be black and go before those judges" (Bryant 1989).

57. Borgman 1995.

58. Ibid. Barbara couldn't remember the titles of the two gay books they stocked after the men requested them. She added in the interview that at that time that she didn't know very much about what to order for gay men or lesbians.

59. Bryant 1990.

60. Maya shared many interests with Barbara and Linda; she had finished her bachelor of arts in religion at Emory University in 1976 and was active in a health-food cooperative, Sevananda. As an undergraduate, she had written her senior thesis on feminist theology and was a member of a feminist women's theology group called The Becoming. This group was influenced by Mary Daly's *Beyond God the Father* (1973). At the time, Maya reports, there were only three books on women's spirituality in print.

61. Bryant 1990.

62. ALFA members were among the primary organizers of this conference. See Third Annual Southeastern Conference of Gay Men and Lesbians program, in possession of the authors.

63. Sanderson 1995.

64. Obviously, conflict is inevitable in all groups, although in hierarchical groups, those in authority typically decide how the conflict will be settled and enforce their views on the others involved. In a nonhierarchical group, the process to resolve a conflict can often be more creative but also more exhausting.

65. In Lynette Eastland's 1991 study of a Utah feminist bookstore, serious conflict was created by the fact that women in the collective worked differing numbers of hours but retained equal say in the operation of the store.

66. Carol Seajay (founder, with her lover Paula Wallace, of Old Wives' Tales bookstore in San Francisco) commented at the 1993 Outwrite Conference that someone should study how attractions and relationships have affected feminist projects.

67. The collective consisted of Linda Bryant, Barbara Borgman, Julia Strong, Maya Smith, and Judy Sanderson.

68. Linda Bryant, letter to the advisory board/collective of Charis Books and More, 4 July 1981, from store records in Linda Bryant's possession.

69. When ALFA closed her doors in 1994, she was the oldest continuously operating lesbian organization in the country.

SOURCES CITED

ALFA Newsletter/Atalanta, newsletter of the Atlanta Lesbian Feminist Alliance. 1973–1980. Vols. 1–8. Duke University Library Special Collection, Durham, NC.

Ansa, Tina McElroy. 1978. Reborn: Shops and businesses popping up. *Atlanta Journal and Constitution.* 23 August, B1, B4.

Arnold, June. 1976. Feminist presses and feminist politics. *Quest: A Feminist Quarterly* 3, 1 (summer): 18–26.

Ashkinaze, Carol. 1977. Charis was there first. *Atlanta Constitution.* 27 August, B4.

Borgman, Barbara. 1995. Interview by Amanda Gable and Saralyn Chesnut. Tape recording. Comer, GA, 2 February.

Bryant, Linda. 1989. Interview by Amanda Gable. Tape recording. Atlanta, GA, 14 July.

———. 1990. Interview by Saralyn Chesnut and Amanda Gable. Tape recording. Atlanta, GA, 10 May.

———. 1994. Interview by Saralyn Chesnut and Amanda Gable. Tape recording. Atlanta, GA, 13 September.

———. 1996. Interview by Amanda Gable. Atlanta, GA, 3 June.

Bryant, Linda, and Sherry Emory. 1994. Interview by Amanda Gable and Saralyn Chesnut. Tape recording. Atlanta, GA, 16 March.

Bunch, Charlotte. 1978. Lesbian-feminist theory. In *Our right to love: A lesbian resource book*, edited by Ginny Vida, pp. 180–82. Englewood Cliffs, NJ: Prentice-Hall.

———. 1987. *Passionate politics: Feminist theory in action, 1968–1986*. New York: St. Martin's Press.

Carroll, Chris. 1990. Interview by Saralyn Chesnut and Amanda Gable. Tape recording. Atlanta, GA, 24 May.

Chartier, Roger. 1994. *The order of books: readers, authors, and libraries in Europe between the fourteenth and eighteenth centuries.* Translated by Lydia G. Cochrane. Stanford, CA: Stanford University Press.

Duggan, Lisa. 1995. Making it perfectly queer. In *Sex wars: Sexual dissent and political culture*, edited by Lisa Duggan and Nan D. Hunter, pp. 155–72. 1992. Reprint, New York: Routledge.

Duggan, Lisa, and Nan D. Hunter, eds. 1995. *Sex wars: Sexual dissent and political culture.* New York: Routledge.

Eagleton, Terry. 1978. *Criticism and ideology: A study in Marxist literary theory.* 1976. Reprint, London: Verso Press.

Eastland, Lynette J. 1991. *Communication, organization, and change within a feminist context: An observation of a feminist collective.* Lewiston, NY: Edwin Mellen Press.

Echols, Alice. 1989. *Daring to be bad: Radical feminism in America 1967–1975.* Minneapolis: University of Minnesota Press.

———. 1995. We gotta get out of this place: Notes toward a "remapping" of the sixties. In *Cultural politics and social movements*, edited by Marcy Darnovsky, Barbara Epstein, and Richard Flacks, pp. 110–30. 1992. Reprint, Philadelphia: Temple University Press.

Emerson, Bo. 1994. The greening of Little Five Points. *Atlanta Journal and Constitution.* 22 May, M1, M4.

Emory, Sherry. 1994. Interview by Amanda Gable. Tape recording. Decatur, GA, 19 October.

Evans, Sara. 1979. *Personal politics: The roots of women's liberation in the civil rights movement and the New Left.* New York: Vintage Books.

Faderman, Lillian. 1991. *Odd girls and twilight lovers: A history of lesbian life in twentieth century America.* New York: Columbia University Press.

Fontana, Lorraine. 1995. Interview by Saralyn Chesnut. Tape recording. Atlanta, GA, 10 January.

Gabriner, Vicki. 1974. ERA: Year of the rabble. *Quest: A Feminist Quarterly* 1, 2 (fall): 62–73.

———. 1976. Come out slugging! *Quest: A Feminist Quarterly* 2, 3 (winter): 52–57.

Gabriner, Vicki, and Susan Wells. 1978. Nurturing a lesbian organization. In *Our right to love: A lesbian resource book,* edited by Ginny Vida, pp. 134–39. Englewood Cliffs, NJ: Prentice-Hall.

Gates, Henry Louis, Jr. 1988. *The signifying monkey: A theory of Afro-American literary criticism.* New York: Oxford University Press.

Gates, Bea, Carol Seajay, Makeda Silvera, Holly Morris, and Karin Aguilar-San Juan. 1993. Living proof: Lesbian feminist presses. Panel discussion, tape 21. Boston: Outwrite Writers' Conference.

Gough, Cal, and David Hayward. 1991. Pride '91: Twenty years of Atlanta gay and lesbian history. Special supplement to *Southern Voice,* Pride issue. June.

Hagan, Kay. 1995. Telephone interview by Amanda Gable. Tape recording. Santa Fe, NM, 27 January.

Hartsoe, Jo Angela. 1990. Interview by Amanda Gable. Tape recording. Atlanta, GA, 10 May.

Jackson, Beryl, Marlene Johnson, and Sara Look. 1994. Interview by Amanda Gable. Tape recording. Atlanta, GA, 16 March.

Jane and Anne [pseud.]. 1990. Interview by Saralyn Chesnut. Tape recording. Atlanta, GA, 20 May.

Jones, Sonya. 1996. Interview by Saralyn Chesnut and Amanda Gable. Tape recording. Atlanta, GA, 22 March.

Kaplan, Cora. 1989. Feminist criticism twenty years on. In *From my guy to sci-fi: Genre and women's writing in the postmodern world,* edited by Helen Carr, pp. 15–23. London: Pandora Press.

Knowlton, Elizabeth. 1995. Interview by Saralyn Chesnut. Tape recording. Atlanta, GA, 14 January.

Krieger, Susan. 1985. Review essay: Lesbian identity and community: Recent social science literature. In *The lesbian issue: Essays from* Signs, edited by Estelle B. Freedman, Barbara C. Gelpi, Susan L. Johnson, and Kathleen M. Weston, pp. 223–40. 1982. Reprint, Chicago: University of Chicago Press.

Lambert, Sandra. 1989. Interview by Saralyn Chesnut. Tape recording. Atlanta, GA, 17 April.

Lauret, Maria. 1994. *Liberating literature: Feminist fiction in America.* London: Routledge & Kegan Paul.

Loudermilk, Kim. 1996. Out of the seventies: Feminist politics and popular fiction. Ph.D. diss. (in progress), Emory University.

Miller, Mev (writer, narrator, and producer). 1995. *A labor of love: A tribute to twenty-five years of feminist and lesbian publishers and bookstores.* Minneapolis: Radio Studios of KFAI-FM. Radio documentary.

———. 1996a. E-mail interview by Amanda Gable. Minneapolis, MN, 15 March.

———. 1996b. Words create a movement: Women's bookstores. Text of an article sent in personal e-mail to Amanda Gable, 15 March.

Moraga, Cherríe and Gloria Anzaldúa, eds. 1983. *This bridge called my back: Writings by radical women of color.* 1981. 2d ed., New York: Kitchen Table, Women of Color Press.

Penelope, Julia, and Sarah Lucia Hoagland, eds. 1988. *For lesbians only: A separatist anthology.* London: Only Women Press.

Phelan, Shane. 1989. *Identity politics: Lesbian feminism and the limits of community.* Philadelphia: Temple University Press.

Rafi, Iris. 1995. Interview by Amanda Gable. Atlanta, GA, 23 June.

Ross, Becki. 1995. *The house that jill built: A lesbian nation in formation.* Toronto: University of Toronto Press.

Sanderson, Judy. 1995. Interview by Saralyn Chesnut and Amanda Gable. Tape recording. Atlanta, GA, 22 June.

Short, Kayann. 1994. Publishing feminism in the feminist press movement, 1969–1994. Ph.D. diss., University of Colorado.

Sisley, Emily, and Bertha Harris. 1977. *The joy of lesbian sex.* New York: Crown Publishers.

Smith, Maya. 1990. Interview by Amanda Gable and Saralyn Chesnut. Tape recording. Atlanta, GA, 24 May.

Stein, Arlene. 1995. Sisters and queers: The decentering of lesbian feminism. In *Cultural politics and social movements,* edited by Marcy Darnovsky, Barbara Epstein, and Richard Flacks, pp. 133–151. 1992. Reprint, Philadelphia: Temple University Press.

Streitmatter, Rodger. 1995. *Unspeakable: The rise of the gay and lesbian press in America.* Boston: Faber & Faber.

Strong, Julia. 1995. Interview by Amanda Gable and Saralyn Chesnut. Tape recording. Atlanta, GA, 22 June.

Taylor, Verta, and Leila J. Rupp. 1993. Women's culture and lesbian feminist activism: A reconsideration of cultural feminism. *Signs* 19, 1 (autumn): 34–60.

Weston, Kathleen M., and Lisa B. Rofel. 1985. Sexuality, class, and conflict in a lesbian workplace. In *The lesbian issue: Essays from* Signs, edited by Estelle B. Freedman, Barbara C. Gelpi, Susan L. Johnson, and Kathleen M. Weston, pp. 199–222. 1984. Reprint, Chicago: University of Chicago Press.

Zimmerman, Bonnie. 1990. *The safe sea of women: Lesbian fiction, 1969–1989.* Boston: Beacon Press.

———. 1993. In academia, and out: The experience of a lesbian feminist literary critic. In *Changing subjects: The making of feminist literary criticism,* edited by Gayle Greene and Coppélia Kahn, pp. 112–20. New York: Routledge.

Chapter Thirteen

Post-Lesbian-Feminism
Documenting "Those Cruddy Old Dykes of Yore"

'Becca Cragin

Introduction: Parallels

In the early eighties, a phenomenon arose: postfeminism. Feminists noted it, in academic and activist settings. News anchors proclaimed it. Conservative columnists celebrated it. People talked about the fact that people were talking about it. With each new iteration the thing grew, larger and more real. Soon the Death of Feminism became an entity in itself—something to respond to, incorporate, analyze, or deny. What was it? Was this thing real? Did it reflect economic, political, and cultural changes? Was it a fabrication of the media? A backlash? Was it a symptom of misogyny, or of fundamental flaws in feminist theories and strategies? Did we do something wrong?

In the early nineties, another phenomenon arose: lesbian chic. She bore a striking resemblance to her older sister. Suddenly, a new discourse materialized. Who are these new lesbians? Do they reject their older sisters? Are they feminists? Are they activists? Why are they all white, young, urban, and middle-class? Do these ones hate men too? The discourse turned in on itself. Did lesbian chic start with *Basic Instinct* or *L.A. Law?* Is it a fabrication of the media? How do lesbians feel about all this chic business?

Despite some disagreement on the ultimate meaning of postfeminism,[1] much feminist writing on the topic attributes this hostility or indifference toward feminism to an antifeminist backlash. When women reject the programs and strategies of feminism, this is often explained as a result of the media's distorting influence. The blame is not usually laid on feminism itself. Yet when lesbians reject the programs and strategies of lesbian-feminism, this is often represented within lesbian/feminist media as a rejection of "old-style" lesbianism because of purported flaws in lesbian-feminist politics and culture. The broad cultural and political shifts that have occurred in most U.S. lesbian communities in the last ten years have been widely interpreted as a (positive) renunciation of (failed) lesbian-feminism.

The postfeminist narrative tells us that feminism is dead, that women have rejected the movement because its goals are undesirable or, conversely, because its goals have been met. Similarly, I would suggest that in lesbian and feminist media there is a post-lesbian-feminist narrative in circulation, one which tells us that lesbian-feminism is (or should be) dead because it led feminism off track, toward undesirable goals. The motivations for these two narratives, however, appear to be quite different. In the mainstream media, this criticism of "old-style" lesbianism is obviously related to the general homophobia and antifeminism of the culture. In lesbian and feminist discourse, it seems linked to the political "wars" that have gone on since the early eighties, to disagreements about the goals of feminism, rather than constituting a rejection of feminism (or lesbians) per se. The discursive paths I will be tracing are very much parallel but in no way identical. It is also important to keep in mind that the mainstream media are much more powerful and widespread in their influence than are the lesbian/feminist media. This context makes it ever more crucial that "our" stories, the ones we tell ourselves within feminist circles and tell to interested others without, represent the complexity and diversity of feminist history.

Lesbian-feminism's time in the sun, as *the* representative lesbian culture, has now passed. Just as at one time a lesbian-feminist interpretation of butch-femme or pornography might have been most widely accepted, so now the pendulum has swung the other way and a "sex-positive" account dominates. Due to a variety of economic, political, and cultural factors, the number of women who self-identify as lesbians has grown substantially. A wide variety of sub-subcultures has developed, so that no one of them represents all lesbians anymore (if it ever did). As lesbian communities have become increasingly diverse, the "women's culture" that defined lesbian communities in the seventies and eighties is now frequently rejected in activist, academic, and social settings. This chapter addresses the anti-lesbian-feminist sentiment expressed in several academic accounts of 1970s U.S. lesbian/feminist history and offers an alternative interpretation of the apparent "death" of lesbian-feminism, based on interviews with former members of the Atlanta Lesbian Feminist Alliance (ALFA).

From Without: Mainstream Media Narratives

This section describes the general trend of recent cultural and political shifts within many lesbian communities across the United States, shifts that have, since the early 1990s, been the fodder for a proliferation of discourses around the topic of lesbian-feminism. In mainstream media, the discourse is framed around the phrase "lesbian chic." Within academic feminist discourse, similar dialogues usually center on issues of postfeminism, the "sex wars," and lesbian history. I think it is important to begin a discussion of academic representations by examining the social changes that have contributed to changes in political thinking for feminists. I also believe that mainstream media images have a significant and often understated impact on feminist self-representation. And because of the striking similarity to the postfeminism phenomenon, I think it is important to place debate about lesbian-feminism within the context of an explosion of anti-lesbian-feminist imagery in the larger culture. This contextualization allows us to consider at what points academic feminist discourse overlaps with or diverges from a general cultural antagonism toward lesbians, especially lesbian-feminists.

The term *lesbian chic* describes the members of a newly emerging subculture (of young, urban, fashion-conscious lesbians); a social phenomenon (a sudden fascination with and glamorization of lesbianism by the dominant culture); and a snowballing proliferation of media images. (The media tell us, media representations of chic lesbians are everywhere.) The distinctions among the three often blur: Do the constant images document or create a desire to see more images? Are young women coming out as a result of media-inspired fascination with chic lesbians? Do they come out because, once presented with the issues, they see the possibilities? Do they come out because these lesbians are chic (compatible with other media-inspired trajectories of desire and beauty)? Are these lesbians chic precisely because *we* are fascinated with *them?*

Despite the diversity of the media representations, they are motivated by a common set of sentiments: a voyeuristic excitement, behind which is the media's own self-conscious awareness of this voyeurism *as* a mediated, societal phenomenon. And there is a flip side to the curiosity: A strong anti-lesbian-feminism is expressed in the many magazine articles and talk-show episodes that have emerged in this era of Chic. Apart from instances in which the vilification of radical- or lesbian-feminism is made explicit, a subtle obscuring of marginal, troubling, and political aspects of lesbianism occurs through the representation of an ideal—the apolitical femme. Her valorization is almost always, for the sake of comparison, accompanied by the demonization of her opposite. Deb Schwartz explains:

> The recent flurry of articles on hip lesbians . . . isn't about documentation . . . it's about creation: building a better lesbian, one palatable enough for mainstream consumption. In order to show off the new and improved qualities of these lovely ladies, a line is drawn between the fab lesbians of today and those cruddy old dykes of yore. We meet the lesbian Goofus and Gallant. . . . The straight media is working overtime to cure the lesbian image problem we never knew we had. (1993)

The chic lesbian is valorized for being unlike her older lesbian counterpart. According to the image constructed by the media, she is sexy, young, high-fashion, and fairly apolitical. When she does participate in activism, it's usually toward achieving the most moderate liberal reforms. Schwartz argues that her public protests are heralded precisely because they don't upset mainstream values.

Schwartz's assertions hold true for the majority of magazine (cover) stories on lesbian chic that I've seen. Often extended, glowing descriptions of the chic lesbian's physical beauty and good fashion sense are contrasted with the "negative" stereotypes of the bulldyke and the radical-feminist. For example, in an article on lesbian chic by Jeanie Kasindorf for *New York Magazine*, we read a detailed description of the appearance of the elegant lesbians in an upscale New York City bar: their diamond rings, their pearls, their Armani suits. One woman's "Boycott Colorado" T-shirt is described as a fashion accessory, accentuating her "gorgeous brunette hair" and her "movie-star face" (1993, 33). This tony milieu is contrasted with the "sleaziness" of a butch-femme bar in Houston and the "angry feminism" and "hard-core separatism" of the women's movement (34). We learn of the "dogma" of 1970s feminist analyses of sexuality, but that eventually "erotica began to reign" (34). This section of the article ends with the crowning moment of the Lesbians Undoing Sexual Taboos Conference at New York University in 1992: "Former porn star Annie Sprinkle . . . had women climb up on stage, don rubber gloves, and find her G-spot" (35). The good lesbians, we are meant to understand, embody middle-classness and its corresponding standards of femininity. And good lesbians are interested not in political analyses of sexuality but simply in sex itself.[2]

We learn more about bad lesbians from a *Newsweek* cover story informing the general public about the "reemergence" of lesbians (Salholz 1993). Serving, as *Newsweek* so often does, as a vehicle for mainstream America's voyeuristic gaze down onto the margins, the article analyzes C-Span's live coverage of the 1993 Pride march in Washington, D.C., which included hours of footage of the brazen women of "the lesbian fringes" (56). We are told that these same types of women also stalked Northampton, Massachusetts, in the early eighties, which we learn was "a pretty radical, scary community. The politically correct uniform was flannel shirts and work boots" (56). Apparently, some college lesbians were even so politically correct (p.c.) that they became "four-year lesbians" or "LUGs . . . lesbians until graduation" (58). From all this chaos, the maelstrom of conflicting images of feminist fascists and pearl-laden homeowners (like the glowing gals next door on the cover), Salholz concludes that

> the desire to sleep with other women is perhaps the only common denominator in today's extraordinarily diverse lesbian culture. The pluralism is relatively new: in the 70s the prevailing outlook was separatist and even prudish. (59)

Thus we are told that sex is the most significant aspect of lesbianism (if it is the only thing lesbians have in common, it must be definitive), and that these new lesbians are praiseworthy because they are not like their older sisters—antisex and antimale.

What is most striking about these accounts is that they are so blatantly biased. In a medium that prides itself on getting "both sides" of the story, we are deluged with Gallant but never get to hear from Goofus, to extend Schwartz's analogy. We are not allowed access to lesbian-feminists' own interpretations of their history. Instead, their motivations and beliefs are characterized for them by less-than-friendly interpreters. So I decided to go to the source, as it were, and interviewed three women I knew who had been active in a small, lesbian-feminist subculture in Atlanta called the ALFA community.[3]

This community, based in the bohemian Little Five Points neighborhood of Atlanta, was the center of lesbian-feminist social and political activity in the 1970s.[4] It was organized around the Atlanta Lesbian Feminist Alliance, one of the oldest lesbian-feminist organizations in the United States, which was founded in 1972. The community was comprised of a core of regular members of ALFA and a larger group of lesbians who joined in at political and social events but were not consistently present as organizers. The community was at its largest and most vibrant in the mid- to late 1970s, when there were more than one hundred members of ALFA and several hundred others who regularly attended ALFA events. By the early 1980s the level of political activity had waned, and many of the original members left. In 1985 the Alliance bought a house, and the group directed much of their time and energy to renovations. After several years of waning membership and interest, ALFA eventually disbanded in 1994.

I spoke with Saralyn Chesnut, Esther "B" Connor, and Betty Irwin, women who were involved in ALFA at different points of its twenty-two-year history. Saralyn is in her late forties, joined ALFA in her twenties in 1973, and was a member until the early 1980s. B is in her late thirties, joined ALFA in 1979 at the age of twenty, and was an active member until the mid-1980s. Betty is in her late forties, joined ALFA in 1985 in her late thirties, and was an active member until the group disbanded in 1994. Saralyn is a native of Georgia, and Betty and B are native to Atlanta. All three women are white and middle-class. Clearly, a sample of this size cannot be representative of even a relatively small population such as ALFA; yet my intention in talking with the women was not to document the history of ALFA or the Atlanta lesbian-feminist community. Rather, I was interested in exploring ALFA members' perceptions of what their activism and membership in this community have meant to them, of what *they* believe they were doing during their time at ALFA, and of how they feel about the experience now.

I quickly found out that, even talking to just three women, their perceptions vary considerably. I discovered a much greater diversity of opinions on many subjects than the readers of *Newsweek* and *New York Magazine* might ever expect to find. For example, in the chic-infatuated articles I have discussed, a time line is implied in which a 1990s sex-positive celebration of eroticism evolved out of a 1970s prudishness and sexual dogmatism. But the interviews I conducted provided no indication of prudishness, asexuality, or any kind of enforced party line on sex. In fact, what seems to have occurred in Atlanta in the seventies was widespread nonmonogamy. The only theorizing of sexual relationships mentioned were discussions of s/m and nonmonogamy, which Saralyn described as casual conversations between friends. This categorizing of sexual positions, and attributing an antisex position to lesbian-feminists, has been depicted by lesbians/feminists and the mainstream media historically (back then, lesbians were antisex), generationally (older lesbians are antisex), and politically (lesbian-feminists are antisex). At least for Atlanta, it appears that none of the binaries—1970s/1990s, old/young, lesbianfeminist/non-lesbian-feminist—is accurate.

So why are these binaries so often repeated? What do they serve? I would argue that they assist two overlapping psychological functions among lesbians: the creation and celebration of a lesbian identity free from the conflicts and errors of the past (that is, an egoistic move to simplify and elevate self-perception) and the interpretation and explanation of the emergence of new lesbian subcultures. From what we know of U.S. lesbian history, it seems that lesbian communities here have often participated to some degree in what Jacquelyn Zita has dubbed "the Lesbian Olympics" (Ferguson, Zita, and Addelson 1982, 162), the debates over who count as the "real" or "truest" lesbians. Up until the last ten or fifteen years, most lesbian communities were smaller and more self-contained than they are now, and this debate centered on definitions of what it means to be lesbian or who a lesbian is. Now that there has been such a proliferation of styles and subcultures, to the point that no one group can be considered the *real* lesbians, the question has shifted to "Who are the good lesbians?"

As the newest generation of lesbians seeks its own self-definition, it has often been juxtaposed with a stereotype of the previous generation. When the contrast is made by those outside lesbian communities (the mainstream media), the focus is on what heterosexuals find striking—an apparent change in lesbian aesthetics and a new willingness to be part of the dominant culture. Although there have been notable shifts in these areas in many lesbian communities (Stein 1992, 431–32), what this dominant account lacks is an understanding of how what appears to be new is actually a continuation of, or reconfiguration of, many aspects of what is now old. Although the dominant culture may take pleasure in this change in lesbian imagery, and while young lesbians may take pleasure in considering themselves free of the problems of the past (homogeneity, racism, sexism, etc.), this kind of celebratory pronouncement of the death of lesbian-feminism distracts from the continuing problems lesbians face and distorts the contributions older lesbians have made to the possibility of a current flourishing of lesbian culture.

As prominent lesbian author and activist Sarah Schulman laments, the demonization of the seventies has contributed greatly to polarization between older and younger lesbians:

> [Younger lesbians] don't have a history of their movement. So many people don't know that there's anything before ACT UP. People who come to the Avengers are 20 years old. They've had a Women's Studies class in which they've learned a very revisionist version of what I consider to be reality. They learned that 1970s lesbians were prudish, moralistic, politically rigid; they've heard all this negative stuff about the gay women's movement that existed before the coming together of [lesbian] women and [gay] men. They've been given an incredibly negative view. (Metz 1994, 38)

It's worth noting that Schulman has been critical of political correctness in the past, so she would probably be the first to acknowledge that there have been instances of rigidity and intolerance among lesbians. What seems to concern her here is the complete dismissal of the earlier generation of radical activists, as if they played no part in the birth of the new activist movements of the eighties and nineties such as the Lesbian Avengers and ACT UP. Schulman herself is living proof that the dividing lines that are drawn between older and younger generations are false ones—there is continuity in the political values and personal styles of many lesbians. To separate an entire generation of people as being all alike and equally unlikable is a form of scapegoating that she feels will be disempowering for future lesbian activism.

That these dividing lines are both arbitrary and highly political becomes clear when one considers the kinds of categories that are drawn in the mainstream media representations. In the same column of the *New York Magazine* article that includes the claim "The new generation has challenged the seventies feminist dogma about lesbians and sex" (Kasindorf 1993, 35) are statements from Torie Osborn (National Gay and Lesbian Task Force director) and Rita Mae Brown (renowned lesbian-feminist) that are critical of gay men's sexism and espouse a need to separate from them politically. The statements reflect one of the core concepts of lesbian-feminist thought: that apart from a shared experience of homophobia, the feminist goals many lesbians work toward are often in contradiction with the sexism of many gay men. Yet it is presumed that these two women, who have stated that they celebrate the changes that have occurred in lesbian communities, are somehow very different from the "dogmatic" lesbians of old.

I suspect that one reason for Kasindorf's hostility toward the "dogma" of the seventies is that the sex lesbian-feminists were critiquing at that time (often quite fearlessly and unrepentantly) was heterosexual. Lesbian-feminists often described heterosexuality as a hopelessly sexist institution from which women needed to separate. To a heterosexual reader, Osborn's and Brown's critiques of gay male sexism may seem to be infighting, tangential to her own identity and life choices. Despite a generational and philosophical continuity between Brown, Osborn, and 1970s lesbian-feminists, Kasindorf feels a need to assert a polarization between the (young) chic lesbians of today and the (old) separatist lesbian-feminists of bygone days. The proof is doctored to fit the hypothesis, and what at first looks like simple description—younger lesbians reject lesbian-feminism— turns out to be not-so-subtle prescription: Younger lesbians, reject lesbian-feminism!

But the divide the media describe is not entirely a fiction. Debates about values and identity are taking place in many lesbian communities across the United States, and the issues are often redefined in ways that differ from their most common interpretations in the seventies. As one would expect, the twenty-year-olds of today often have different opinions from those forty-year-olds have today or did have when *they* were twenty. But the mainstream media's (and the mainstream culture's) concern with taking sides in the arguments and struggles that go on between lesbians seems disingenuous and arrogant at best and politically dangerous at worst—because the current heterosexual voyeurism is not disinterested; it parallels other historical moments when the dominant culture's attention turned toward marginal political communities. As Schwartz observes:

> Lesbian palatability exacts a price, the one required of most activism born in the 1960s and 1970s: to gain legitimacy, and be taken seriously in the 1990s, cultures outside the mainstream must prove they are free of the disruptive nature and threatening intent of activisms past. The media's invention of the term "postfeminism," its fascination with Camille Paglia and the star-studded glam factor of WAC [Women's Action Coalition], are all part of an attempt to clean up feminism for today's viewer. Hail the "new face of feminism": no longer angry, ugly, and badly dressed, she is, by the way, Radical Lite. "New" feminists and "new" lesbians are Stepford sisters, twin products of the sanitized '60s and '70s. (1993)

The media's postfeminist narrative tells us that radical-feminism is dead; it died of natural causes, and thankfully so. Similarly, in the 1990s young lesbians are represented as wisely and triumphantly exchanging the politics and personal styles of 1970s lesbian-feminists for the rational, reasonable, middle-of-the-road requests of liberal feminism. Rather than engage the heterogeneity of younger lesbians' attitudes toward older styles of lesbianism, the mainstream media assume and assert an antagonistic relationship between the generations.

From Within: Feminist Narratives

In academic feminist media, the story is familiar—less homophobic but equally damning. Despite very different motivations, a similar demonizing of lesbian-feminists and simplification of lesbian history occur in many historical and theoretical feminist texts. A general consensus seems to have developed, eventually solidifying into a historical narrative, that feminism went astray in the seventies when the predominance of politically extreme lesbian-feminists led to, or coincided with, waves of prudishness and dogmatism. An end to radical activism is asserted and attributed to the harsh personalities and flawed politics of the architects of 1970s and 1980s "women's culture," the "cultural feminists." This narrative has been articulated most succinctly and explicitly in the work of Alice Echols, but it is present very broadly, if more vaguely, in feminist culture.

In feminist literary theory it takes on a similar form: the dismissal of older (often lesbian) feminist texts, which are presumed to be unsophisticated and essentialist. Jane Gallop has linked this stance to the institutionalization of feminist studies, which she locates "around 1981" (1992, 23). By contrasting current work with older feminist writing, which they assumed was atheoretical, academic feminists were able to distinguish their writing as being properly theoretical, in order to assert the legitimacy of women's studies. What is assumed in this version of history is an inherent progress in the development of feminist thought over time:

> One striking feature of feminist metacriticism has been its attempt to describe the different types of feminist criticism . . . as constituting an evolutionary sequence. . . . This supersessional model of feminist criticism implies that feminism has progressed in a linear fashion, driven . . . by the demons of progress from early crudities to later sophistications. (Ruthven 1984, 20–21; as quoted in Gallop 1992, 79).

While the time lines Gallop and K. K. Ruthven describe are specifically related to literary theory, they strongly parallel the sentiments expressed in Lillian Faderman's *Odd Girls and Twilight Lovers* (1991).

Faderman: Humans without Penises

The last third of Faderman's overview of a century of U.S. lesbian history is dedicated to a scathing critique of the lesbian-feminist culture that emerged in the 1970s. Although each of the last four chapters of *Odd Girls* purports to describe a different population of lesbians in a different time period, each refers back constantly to the figure of the 1970s lesbian-feminist, as a way of constructing present difference. You can get an immediate sense of Faderman's attitude toward lesbian-feminism without even reading the book. Just by glancing at the index (Lesbian-feminists: drab-stylelessness of, 268; factionalism and, 235–44; political correctness and, 230–35) or by skimming an occasional paragraph, the reader meets with a deluge of pejorative descriptions. The phrases recur throughout her analysis: "doctrine . . . dreamt grandiosely . . . doomed . . . failure . . . utopian fantasies . . . fanaticism."

Even the captions under photographs reveal a similar disdain. Four of them strike me as particularly contemptuous. In the section between chapters 8 and 9, the first photo, of two young women sitting on a park bench, has a caption that reads: "1970s dyke style. Although butch-and-femme were 'politically incorrect' in the lesbian-feminist community, everyone looked butch." Aside from the fact that this is simply untrue ("androgyny was a widespread ideal" might be a more accurate statement), there are no corresponding pictures to illustrate the ostracization felt by women who weren't butch or femme in the 1940s and 1950s—the photographs at the beginning of the book selected to represent that era show groups of happy lesbians at parties, bars, and softball games.[5]

The derisive tone in Faderman's claim that "everyone looked butch" is even more apparent in the next caption. Under a photo of two women hard at work repairing an engine, Faderman writes, "Lesbian Nation required that women learn new skills so that they might be independent of 'the man' in all ways." The quotation marks around "the man" are meant to indicate the dubiousness of the lesbian-feminists' position. In relation to the earnestness of the women, the caption clearly mocks them. Rather than celebrating the opportunities feminism provided for women, Faderman explains that these opportunities were "required." Not only were they forced on women, but women were forced into thinking that they could build a Nation apart from a nonexistent enemy. The author speaks from a position of assumed superior wisdom, chuckling at the pipe dreams of some foolish women. This is quite different from other captions which inform us that "S/M lesbians believe that feminists have much to learn from sexual outlaws" and "Lesbian sexual radicals of the 1980s wanted to escape from 'politically correct sex' and expand lesbians' sexual horizons." Here there are no quotation marks that would create any kind of a distance between the author and the subjects. We should accept that these women are indeed sexual outlaws and sexual radicals. The only thing to doubt is the regime of "politically correct sex."

I have mentioned these issues of representation because they typify Faderman's account of lesbian-feminism. She expresses such hostility toward it that the heinousness of lesbian-feminism becomes the organizing principle for much of the book. Two themes that repeatedly surface are (1) that the political stances lesbian-feminists took were too radical (in particular, separatism), and so the kinds of social changes they envisioned were foolishly unrealistic, and (2) that lesbian-feminists were mercilessly doctrinaire, policing and politicizing other women's behavior (in particular, sex). My critique is not based on the fact that Faderman documents instances of extreme behavior, because it is inevitable that in studying groups of people, one will discover conflicts and cases of individuals who have behaved poorly. What is troubling to me is how these social facts are interpreted and presented. The same impulse I traced through mainstream media representations of lesbian chic, in which lesbian-feminists are distinguished as a specific type of lesbians—separate from the rest of "us"—who deserve disparagement, is present in *Odd Girls*. To achieve this seamless containment around the category "lesbian-feminist" and deposit within in it all things extreme and negative involves a lot of editorial work on Faderman's part.

For example, one of the most frequent characterizations of lesbian-feminists in *Odd Girls* is that they were always harshly criticizing the behavior of other women in their communities. This is presented as one of the distinguishing characteristics of the Lesbian Nation. However, Faderman's own interviews with lesbians who were out in the fifties reveal a great deal of policing of lesbians' behavior and dress during that decade as well. Although Faderman provides us with stories of women who were ostracized and even refused entrance to the community if they would not participate in butch-femme, she does not categorize that period in general as one of tyranny. Instead, she explains the need lesbians felt to be able to identify one another and build cultural traditions (through the development of a strict butch-femme model)[6] as a result of the constant homophobic pressures surrounding them. She could have interpreted the dynamics of lesbian-feminist communities with a similarly sympathetic,[7] multifaceted analysis. Instead, she attributes 1970s policing to one factor— the personalities of lesbian-feminists, whom she sees as young and idealistic (1991, 220). This allows her to make the highly dubious move of linking the "failure" of a community to its politics.

Reflecting the evolutionary model of history I described previously, Faderman seems to believe that the waning of a social movement's influence or the development of new ones should indicate to us that the movement didn't last because it was somehow inherently flawed. In the case of lesbian-feminism, the flaw seems to lie in the politics many lesbian-feminists shared: "Lesbian-feminists were true believers and destined, as true believers often are, for fanaticism and eventual disappointment" (217). We need to examine Faderman's interpretation of lesbian-feminist political values in order to see why, for her, the Reagan-Bush years heralded a "Shift to Moderation" (274).

One of the most obvious ways in which Faderman disagrees with lesbian-feminism is over the issue of separatism. She takes as its definition the most extreme form of separatism—total separation from and (from her perspective) hatred of men. This form was expressed by some lesbian-feminists in the seventies, although it represents just one out of a range of possible separatist positions. She does acknowledge that some women felt separatism was a useful strategy "for a specific struggle at a certain time" (293), but these women are placed in the 1980s on her time line. For the 1970s, her description of separatists' views is "They put out a call to 'explore with fact and imagination our dyke/amazon culture of the past, before there were parasitic male mutants, and to work toward our dyke/amazon culture of the future, when only xx's exist' " (237–38).

The "they" is crucial, because just as she glosses over the diversity in lesbian-feminist communities by repeatedly conflating lesbian-feminism and separatism, Faderman here glosses over the diversity among separatists by positing this statement by one individual as the voice of all separatists. This is *the* separatist position, which allows Faderman to conclude that the lesbian-feminist movement failed because it "was probably unrealizable without the help of a cataclysmic disaster that would somehow render the earth all xx" (244). Repeatedly she asserts that the single lesbian-feminist goal was to create an entirely separate society for women only. While many women unquestionably shared this goal, many did not. Like the more "moderate" lesbians of the eighties whom Faderman depicts, many in the seventies also saw separatism as a temporary strategy for political organizing, not a goal in itself. In my interviews with the ALFA members, I learned that the respondents had differing views on the purpose and value of separatism.

Saralyn believes strongly in the importance of separatism. She wrote an article about lesbian separatism for a local paper and for many years was separatist in the sense that most of the political and social activities she took part in involved lesbian-feminists. But her separatism does not appear to stem from a categorical hatred of men; rather, it emerged from a desire to be around people with similar values. In her experience, most men, including gay men, are sexist, and she found it more enjoyable and productive to be in an environment where feminism was a given:

> I wanted to spend my time with people who started off from the same premises that I started from. Who you didn't have to argue about feminism, for instance, or what it meant to be a feminist. You just worked with other people. (Chesnut 1993)

Although Saralyn spent most of her time with other lesbians, she and other members of ALFA worked in coalition with gay men, straight communists and socialists, and straight feminists. Despite the sexism of gay men and the homophobia of some of the communist and socialist groups, ALFA worked with them on some shared political projects and worked separately at other times.

Saralyn's view of separatism is intimately connected to her personal definition of lesbian-feminism as a commitment to women that stems from both lesbianism and feminism but that does not preclude supporting and working with others:

> So, I guess, lesbian-feminism, or—a woman who's a lesbian who has an analysis of being a lesbian that makes it clear, the relationship between lesbianism and feminism. You choose to make women your priority, to make your real commitments to other women. And you think about your relationship to straight women as well as you think about your relationship to gay men. They're both sort of parallel in certain ways, that you have certain things you have in common and certain things you don't have in common. But with other lesbians who are lesbian-feminists, that's who you have the most in common with, I would say. (Chesnut 1993)

Additionally, for her, lesbian-feminism means a commitment to radically change all of society, not only for lesbians:

> To me, it was also generally a leftist point of view. So you're not just concerned with, like liberal feminists, making it in the mainstream. That you're concerned with critiquing what we mean—what the values of main-stream America. You're concerned about issues like poverty and racism and things like that, just beyond helping white women get elected to office, or whatever. (Chesnut 1993)

This account does not match the stereotype of the lesbian-feminist, who is concerned only about gender inequality. And although Saralyn felt a lot of positive, lasting institutions came out of the ALFA community, she also is concerned that being too inwardly focused can lead to political stagnation:

> I think it's a danger that was always inherent in lesbian separatism, and in having these small, tight-knit communities. You know, you just get more and more ingrown until you're just spending time examining your own navel. Instead of looking outside yourself and seeing what needs to be done. Moving forward. (Chesnut 1993)

In terms of separatism, Esther "B" Connor does not consider herself to be a separatist, although she sees separatism as a useful political strategy, provided it's temporary. When I asked her whether she saw her lesbi-anism as being connected to feminism, her answer contained the follow-ing comments on separatism:

> I'm not a separatist in that, I know that separatism is empowering if you're able to get your power there and use it as a springboard to do things outside of your little cave. But if you stay in the cave, you have this self-imposed Neolithic period, you know? (Connor 1993)

She then continues her answer by discussing her relationship to men politically. Like Saralyn, she sees a danger in permanent, full separatism and defines lesbian-feminism as being inherently linked to social issues other than those affecting only lesbians:

> I guess it would mean lesbian-feminism is, by choice or biology, "Hey, I'm a lesbian," and it's a fusion of that with feminism and realizing that because we're women, we have social problems, concerns, goals that are real differ-ent and inextricably economic because we're women, because we're this down-pressed class of people, you know? We don't have penises.
>
> And if you think that if you have enough money, or you're white enough,

precisely the right age, you're driving the right car, you won't have these problems, then go ahead and think this. Just, you know, I'd hate to be around the day you get your head pulled out of your ass, 'cause it's gonna be very bright, and you're gonna need some cheap sunglasses. And you're gonna think, "Gee, I wish I was a lesbian-feminist all these years. Workin' on them social-economic issues." (Connor 1993)

Throughout her interview, B categorized ALFA women into two groups: those who, like herself, were more radical and wanted to be involved in political action, and those who were more mainstream in their political views and wanted to keep ALFA a safe space from the harmfulness of the outside world.

Betty Irwin is one of those women who believe that providing safe space is one of the most important roles ALFA played. She joined ALFA in 1985 when the membership and the amount of political activity was declining. In contrast to B's and Saralyn's descriptions of separatism as a way to avoid the frustration involved in continually engaging with sexist men, Betty describes the lesbian-only space of ALFA as "a place where women could go and always feel safe." Like the others, she also recognizes degrees of separatism and sees it as an issue of personal choice:

> To me, all lesbians are separatist, whether they want to say those words or not. Because they don't allow men in their bedrooms. I mean, it's the degree of separatism that you really have to look at. And you have to define where you want to cut that off. Whether it's that you have absolutely nothing to do with men, live in a separatist community where men just don't come at all.
>
> There are farms, like in Arkansas, and that kind of place. And there are women there that actually never see men. They just don't deal with them. [It ranges] to having a life like I do, where I work with men all day, see my brothers, see my nephews, but my political agenda and the majority of my social life are dealt just with women. So, you know, all lesbians are separatists, and they just have to decide where that line is for themselves. What do they need to protect themselves, to feel comfortable with themselves? (Irwin 1993)

Betty also distinguishes personal separation from men (not allowing men in the bedroom) from social separation but, unlike the other women, does not specifically mention political separation. I think this may be linked to her seeing separatism (in the way she words it, at least) as being a form of protection more than a political strategy. But, like the others, she also defines lesbian-feminism as a primary commitment to women that does not exclude commitments to other people:

> To me it means, to be a real lesbian-feminist means that you love all people, and that you consider everyone, but that's the feminism part of it. The lesbian part of it means that everyone only has so much energy, and I want to give my energy to women. Because that is my priority in life. That's basically what it means to me. We're all, we should all have the same opportunities, and that we should all have the same consideration. And that women are my priority. (Irwin 1993)

Unfortunately, it does not seem that ALFA provided that safe space for Betty. By the mid-1980s there were several debilitating political conflicts within ALFA.[8]

What these interviews indicate to me is that even within one organization, within one city, within a period of twenty years, there is evidence of a great variety of political activities and strategies, as well as political values and personalities. Just concerning the issue of separatism, just speaking with three women, I found three fairly distinct positions. Of course, there will be some degree of variety within any group that can never be encompassed by a political history. But it is not merely the personal variations in these three women's stories that call into question Faderman's assertions about lesbian-feminism. Looking at how B, Saralyn, and Betty understand the project of lesbian-feminism, how they describe their communities, makes it clear that Faderman has misunderstood their general intent in participating in a lesbian-feminist community. Even Betty, who desired ALFA to be a refuge from the larger society, never gives an indication that creating ALFA as a separate "world" is the goal in itself. She sees political action as an important component of social change and does not seem to believe that creating a safe space within ALFA will create that change. All three women felt the activities that centered in ALFA, even when they were "cultural," were also "political." The ALFA community was a center of political activity for years, and the social and the political were continually intertwined, to the extent that they were often indistinguishable.

Yet Faderman (1991) claims that lesbian-feminists were not interested in transforming society (216) but were instead trying to create a separate society (245) that would, apparently, be so wonderful that it would, "through its example" (217), encourage mainstream society to change. From this position, she is able to make absolutely false (and contradictory) generalizations about lesbian-feminists, which I believe are untrue not only for the ALFA community but probably for many other lesbian-feminist communities across the United States as well. She claims that lesbian-feminists only rarely worked in coalition with gay men (211); that many of them refused to do feminist political work, which they felt was irrelevant to them (238); and that they all "saw themselves as feminist rather than gay" (212). Clearly, for Faderman this last position is not the correct one to take. Her wording gives her away: These women "*denied* that they were 'gay.' They *insisted* on being called lesbian-feminist" (205; my emphases). The eventual return to coalitions with gay men during the AIDS activism of the eighties is roundly celebrated: "Progress, such as could only come about through a sense of community [between gay men and lesbians], was undeniable" (296). Faderman simply states that "activist gay men appear to have taken to heart lesbians' complaints in the 70s that they were insensitive to women's issues" (296), announcing for us an end to any need for separatism. This cheery assertion was not corroborated by Saralyn and Betty; they both feel that many gay men are still very sexist, which makes coalition work difficult.

Faderman seems to share the widespread belief that lesbian-feminist critiques of patriarchy reflect a hatred of men:

> Because a general disenchantment with and suspicion of all males was central to lesbian-feminist doctrine, the gay man was naturally seen as being no less an enemy than any other human with a penis, and lesbian-feminists could make no lasting coalition with gay men in a gay revolution (1991, 212).

Her interpretation is reflected in her word choice: The "any other human with a penis" remark is meant to indicate the irrationality and unfairness of a separatist position. It implies that lesbian-feminists believe all men are enemies by virtue of their biology, and that some men are unfairly judged, their only crime being the possession of penises.

In addition, Faderman's use of the word *doctrine* represents a systemic analysis of gender inequality as a requirement that lesbians exhibit specific emotional reactions toward men. A more accurate description might have been "Disenchantment with males was not infrequent"—or, as Saralyn suggested, "indifference":

> The idea of women being self-sufficient is very threatening, I think. Of course, indifference was what there was. There was indifference to men. And men I don't think can handle that. So it's turned into hostility. You know, it's true we thought a lot of things men did were totally stupid and

we didn't want to be bothered with them. But it was really profound indifference and this really self-sufficient culture. And I think that's real threatening and perceived as hostile. We spent a lot more time having fun with each other than being hostile towards them. (Chesnut 1993)

By describing this suspicion or indifference as "doctrine," Faderman conflates what was central to lesbian-feminist thought—the belief that an analysis of sexism is necessary for understanding and undoing homophobia—with what was perhaps common but by no means definitive or prescribed. She seems to be working off a cultural stereotype instead of a careful consideration of the analyses lesbian-feminists have developed of misogyny. From this position, the political work some lesbian-feminists did apart from gay men would seem not only unnecessary but an act of hostility.

Faderman seems to believe that lesbian-feminists are lesbians first, and that their feminism, which went too far in its critique of sexism, prevented their doing the "proper" kinds of coalition work that lead to real progress. This is why, for her, the eighties were a shift back into moderation. She even describes lesbians reuniting with gay men as a necessary condition for the former to be able to experience any happiness, friendship, or sense of community:

> The sense of family and the larger sense of community had not been easy to come by. It required ... that they accept the definition of themselves as "lesbian" and part of a sexual minority.... It required not only that they temper their views about how lesbianism should be lived as they did after the radical '70s, but that they learn to create coalitions with those who do not live it as they do. There was insufficient consciousness, moderation, and savvy to do all of that in the past.... In the course of the 1980s, however, lesbians who sought it were able to find all that was requisite to create among themselves both family and community (1991, 299).

Faderman suggests that lesbian-feminists would not admit that they were lesbian (?) and that they needed to face this fact. Otherwise they would be left sad and alone—that is, without men, families, or communities. No mention is made of gay men's need for lesbian community as a requisite of maturation and happiness. Nor does Faderman recognize that gay men's sexism has contributed substantially to some lesbians' desire to create separate social and political communities. The fault lay with the lesbians; therefore, it was the lesbians who needed to abandon their erroneous 1970s ways. Now, can you imagine for a moment a parallel statement, in heterosexual form? It might look something like this:

Why are you women so angry at men? They've learned from their mistakes. I mean, after all, this isn't the fifties anymore, it's the nineties. No need to be so hostile! You know you will never be happy until you come home to the men where you belong, instead of all this yelling and carrying on. LADIES, LIGHTEN UP!

That would look suspiciously like the classic postfeminist narrative.

The main weaknesses in Faderman's narrative are its generality and its tidiness. While she does acknowledge that, in each era she studied, lesbians differed from one another by virtue of their racial and class identities, she often attributes one set of attitudes to each subgroup she delineates— so, for example, lesbian-feminists hated men and wanted to build a separate society, and young lesbians in the 1980s rejected lesbian-feminism and wanted to work in coalition with gay men. In reality, there has been much more crossover between groups and over time. In Faderman's account, lesbian-feminism and lesbian-feminists are completely separated from other value systems and groups, historically and characteristically. She describes lesbian-feminism as a discrete entity that arose, dominated, and died in the 1970s, one that bore little resemblance to other periods and contributed little but provided much grief. A close look at her analysis, however, reveals that it is only her time line and her analytic categories that are clear-cut.

For example, when Faderman's analysis moves into the 1980s, a time when lesbian-feminism is supposed to have waned, she needs to explain why large numbers of lesbian-feminists are doing work in the antinuclear and environmental movements. This information complicates her earlier assertions that (1) lesbian-feminists didn't engage in political activity but preferred to stay separate from the rest of society; (2) they didn't involve themselves in activism that wasn't directly related to lesbianism; and (3) lesbian-feminism died in the late 1970s, as mass numbers of women defected from lesbian-feminist communities. Faderman deals with this incoherence in her model by informing us that now these lesbian-feminists are to be called "cultural feminists." The circularity of her argument becomes obvious when she explains that the reason for the name change is that they are engaged in political activism (1991, 281). So lesbian-feminists are lesbian-feminists who don't do political work (because lesbian-feminists don't do political work), but cultural feminists are lesbian-feminists who do political work. And of course, they only began this work in the eighties.

In her discussion of the 1980s sex wars, Faderman distinguishes lesbian-feminists from lesbian sex radicals by conflating lesbian-feminism with cultural feminism and cultural feminism with the antipornography movement. Katie King has noted that this is a common misconception in feminist discourse, which grossly exaggerates the importance of the pornography issue in lesbian communities (1990, 92). In some lesbian communities, debates over pornography and s/m were the cause of protracted, emotional arguments, whereas in other cities, such as Atlanta, they don't seem to have been an issue at all. In the ALFA community—and, I suspect, in most, if not all, lesbian-feminist communities—there were political lesbians, lesbian "essentialists," cultural feminists, radical feminists, socialist feminists, liberal feminists, and all these women were identified as lesbian-feminists. They were as diverse in their political views and as vociferous in their political conflicts as heterosexual feminists (indeed, as most leftist groups) are. Just as there is no single feminist position on what feminism is and is for, what it means to be a woman, or what needs to be done to improve women's lives, so there is no single lesbian-feminist position. Lesbians who were feminist and who held a variety of views on exactly what that might mean all participated in the "lesbian-feminist" community of ALFA.

To evaluate how and why the shape of lesbian communities changes over time, we need to look at many factors: societal changes, historical events, economies, regional differences, personalities, local particulars, core leaders versus general membership, political and legislative events. Apart from several asides, Faderman attributes the changes that have taken place in lesbian communities in the late 1980s and early 1990s to what she saw as the negative politics and personalities of lesbian-feminists. But in the case of ALFA, lesbians are now a part of other subcultures in Atlanta, for many reasons—including the success of lesbian-feminists' own efforts to create and maintain spaces to be lesbian.

Echols: Yins and Yangs

Alice Echols has written extensively on the lesbian/feminist seventies, and although her account of the period is much less vitriolic than Faderman's and comes from a position of commitment to radical feminism, she draws many of the same conclusions that Faderman does about lesbian-feminists. She and Faderman seem to agree (although for very different reasons) that the direction in which lesbian/feminist communities went in the 1970s was an undesirable one, marked by an apolitical women's culture that Echols has termed "cultural feminism." Although her work is much more responsible than Faderman's in its attention to the complexity of detail and historical context, Echols at times oversimplifies the variety of political projects and values to be found among lesbian-feminists.

Her 1983 article "The New Feminism of Yin and Yang" is perhaps the most widely read account of the rise of cultural feminism. According to Echols, by 1973 the radical feminist movement was waning, due to splits over lesbianism and class. Many heterosexual women left the movement, and by 1975, when the lesbian takeover was complete, lesbian-feminism devolved into cultural feminism (1983, 446). Cultural feminism killed off the radical feminist movement and left a burgeoning, apolitical "wimmin's culture" in its place; but it ultimately failed because of infighting, political correctness, sexual orthodoxy, and flawed theorizing that universalized women's experiences and made "male" values, rather than men, its political enemy.

I have simplified Echols's argument momentarily to illustrate how similar it is to "the narrative" I've discussed that circulates so widely in lesbian/feminist communities, and which Faderman utilized in structuring the second half of *Odd Girls*. This 1983 article is perhaps the definitive explanation of 1970s feminism, and the basic constellation Echols outlines, and later elaborates in *Daring to Be Bad* (1989), is an explicit articulation of more vague assumptions that underlie much feminist writing on the seventies.

Echols writes as a radical feminist committed to analyzing radical feminist history in a way that illuminates and educates rather than simply scapegoats. Although her work shares some interpretations of lesbian-feminism with Faderman's, I do not mean to imply that it shares the same degree of hostility. It is precisely because Echols's work has been important and influential and has become the base on which new narratives, such as Faderman's,[9] are built that its assumptions and conclusions must be examined. I will look at her earlier 1983 piece first, and then at its elaboration in *Daring to Be Bad*.

In "The New Feminism of Yin and Yang," Echols provides a definition of cultural feminism that has two components: a belief that gender differences are immutable and innate and a belief that building an alternative "women's" culture will lead to women's liberation (1983, 441). She sees cultural feminists' political project as being so at odds with the work of the earlier radical feminists that they must be distinguished linguistically as a separate category. To achieve this distinction, Echols must engage at times in what appear to be fairly selective readings of 1970s radical feminist work. She gives us snippets of quotations, here and there, out of context, as individual instances that illustrate a larger tendency among cultural feminists. Yet a closer look at how she uses the quotations reveals that she sometimes stretches her interpretation to fit the writers she has labeled "cultural feminists" squarely into an essentialist mode.

For example, one aspect of her charge of essentialism involves the assertion that cultural feminists are unable to distinguish biological maleness from masculinity; they assume men are incapable of reform and, just by virtue of being male, are oppressive. As evidence of this position, she cites Adrienne Rich as an example of a cultural feminist who believes that socialism is a masculinist project that has no usefulness for feminists (Echols 1983, 443). Note 18 in Echols's essay supports this assertion by citing a passage from Rich's *Of Woman Born* (1976, 285) that reads "The repossession by women of our bodies will bring far more essential change to human society than the seizing of the means of production by workers." Especially in the context of the rest of Rich's book, there is no need to read this passage as a claim that masculinity is the only problem women face. Rich is simply asserting that, in her opinion, sexual/reproductive autonomy for women will bring women more freedom than socialism-without-a-critique-of-sexism will. While not the focus of the book, *Of Woman Born* does discuss the economic difficulties women face, especially in relation to motherhood, and she does not seem in any way to see socialism as "irrelevant" to women.

Additionally, many of the themes Rich addresses in this work do not fit Echols's model of cultural feminism. Just two pages before the passage Echols cites, Rich provides a lengthy warning to her readers that she is not implying that women have special nurturing abilities (Rich 1976, 283). She discusses the desirability of men taking a larger role in nurturing children (216, 282), as well as the possibility of raising male children to be feminists (215–17). *Of Woman Born* challenges feminists to explore the possibilities for strength and resistance, as well as pain and oppression, that we experience in our relationship to our bodies, rather than rejecting the body outright as a kind of misogynist trap society has set for us:

Patriarchal thought has limited the female body to its own narrow specifications. The feminist vision has recoiled for these reasons; it will, I believe, come to view our physicality as a resource, rather than a destiny (Rich 1976, 40).

Other writers not usually saddled with the title "cultural feminist" have called for this same reexamination.[10] For most women, this physicality includes reproduction, and although Rich is addressing the particular differences women face due to biology, it does not follow that exploring this difference is automatically an essentialist project. While Echols defines *Of Woman Born* as "a major cultural feminist text" (Echols 1983, 441 n. 7), I see it as an exploration of the socially constructed experience of motherhood as both a culturally enforced institution that oppresses women and a relationship that provides mothers the opportunity for transformation.

Other moments where I feel Echols is overreading to fit Rich's work into her model of cultural feminism occur in her analysis of Rich's "Compulsory Heterosexuality and Lesbian Existence" (1980). Echols attributes to Rich the position that "the actions of the Marquis de Sade or Son of Sam come to symbolize the murderousness of male sexuality, and sexual intercourse becomes a mere euphemism for rape" (Echols 1983, 449). In a fairly confusing note 47, Echols backs up her claim by citing a section of "Compulsory" in which Rich praises Catharine MacKinnon for criticizing Susan Brownmiller for saying, "Rape is violence, intercourse is sexuality" (Rich 1986, 235). Brownmiller was arguing that sex between men and women isn't inherently degrading, and so Echols implies that Rich is so obsessed with a notion of male sexuality as an oppressive force that she is unable to imagine consensual intercourse as anything other than violation.

However, when we place Rich's comments in the context of her argument—that heterosexuality is a pervasive, coercive institution, which means that feminists should be problematizing the notion of "natural" sexual orientations that exist free from the pressures of economics, homophobia, and violence—the meaning of the passage Echols refers to changes dramatically. Rich uses MacKinnon's argument to call for an examination of the extent to which "normal" courting rituals and beliefs about sexuality are rife with images and expectations of male domination. She suggests that it is meaningless to separate any discussion of rape from discussions of cultural beliefs about women and sexuality; to see rape as being only about violence is to ignore the spectrum of sexual coercion that women negotiate.

Echols seems to misinterpret the purpose of Rich's article, seeing it as a glorification of lesbianism that requires a vilification of heterosexuality. While there seems to be a good deal of evidence that many lesbians did consider themselves to be more feminist than heterosexual women (typified in Rita Mae Brown's accusation that straight women betray feminism by "fucking the oppressor"; Echols 1983, 446), this does not appear to be the point of Rich's article. The article might be more accurately described as a rhetorical strategy to assert the right of lesbians to claim the title "feminist," as well as a call for all feminists to explore the relationship between patriarchy and the construction of sexuality. Echols takes the Rich quote "For women heterosexuality might not be a 'preference' at all but something that has to be imposed, managed, organized, propagandized, and maintained by force" (Rich 1980, 648) to mean that "for women, heterosexuality is neither fully chosen nor pleasurable" (Echols 1983, 450). It is here that she distinguishes lesbian-feminists from cultural feminists: while a lesbian-feminist (Rita Mae Brown) would call a straight woman the enemy, a cultural feminist (Adrienne Rich) would feel sorry for the straight woman and would explain her free choice of heterosexuality as the result of a heavy-handed coercion.

Not only is this distinction that Echols draws highly tenuous (both Brown and Rich would probably call themselves lesbian-feminists), it also misrepresents the subtlety of Rich's argument. "Compulsory Heterosexuality" is, I would argue, one of the earliest, most thought-provoking, and most influential calls for a study of the social construction of sexuality. As Jacquelyn Zita has pointed out, in this article Rich was the first to articulate the coercive aspects of heterosexism. Before this, radical-feminists who supported the "pro-woman line" explained that the reason women stayed in unequal relationships with men was the (primarily economic) privilege they received (Ferguson, Zita, and Addelson 1982, 164 n. 26). That explanation grants too much agency to women, overestimating the degree of conscious thought put into the "choice" of heterosexuality. Rich's argument forced feminists to reconceptualize the degree to which heterosexuality is either a "natural" sexual preference or a calculated, "free" choice.

Given Echols's condemnation of what she sees as a tendency among lesbians to accuse heterosexual women of being the enemies of feminism, one would expect that she would appreciate an argument that does not condemn individual heterosexual women for being with men but that instead examines the structures of heterosexuality itself. But because

Echols's project in this 1983 article is to identify a distinct strand of thought called "cultural feminism," and to illustrate the ways in which it has been a largely negative development for feminism, she seems to map what may or may not have been a widely held community discourse (lesbian chauvinism) onto a complex textual examination of lesbianism.

In essence, Echols is slotting examples of lesbian-feminist thinking into a prefabricated explanation—cultural feminism—in a way that shores up her argument but does not do justice to the complexity of the examples. In this sense, her work reflects a common trend in the narratives we tell ourselves of our feminist history: the construction of binary opposites, mutually exclusive positions from which feminists are supposed to choose. The most common categorization, most simply expressed as the debate over "equality" versus "difference," has been present from the beginnings of feminist movement, and according to Ann Snitow, an "oscillation" between these two positions is the definitive characteristic of feminism (1990, 13). However, Snitow describes this oscillation not as a simple swing back and forth between two discrete positions but as a negotiation of aspects of both; feminists who are represented as being entirely opposed often incorporate aspects of the "other side's" argument but still retain a preference for the strategies of their "side" (13). There is a long history of infighting among feminists in which, at different historical periods, one side of a (constructed) binarism is considered the vanguard and the other regressive (25). While feminists may gain some rhetorical mileage out of constructing and declaiming sides of issues, how those issues are conceptualized has always been much more complex.

For example, although feminists work for "equality," it does not necessarily follow that there are literally no differences between men and women (such as the fact that women give birth). As Joan Scott has argued, a call for equality is an implicit acknowledgment of difference: Let this group be treated the same as another (1990, 143). Equality is the call not for sameness but for "the irrelevance of categorical differences" (145). Similarly, because some feminists attempt to theorize ways in which women may be different from men, it does not follow that they believe these differences are inherent, immutable, or necessitate unequal treatment. It is our society that has defined equality and difference as opposites, and if we accept this binary logic, we are placed in the impossible position of having to prove sameness in order to deserve equality (Scott 1990, 144).

And it is not that feminists have believed in only equality or difference;

the dilemma is made up of the strategical conflicts between deconstructing "woman" and mobilizing for political action. The tension is between feminist strategies, because no one strategy will fit all situations, in a society that resists a complex understanding of equality/difference. As Teresa de Lauretis puts it, the problem is not an internal conflict but the difficulty of "engagement with the social" (1990, 267). She argues we need to take a closer look at what appear, at first glance, to be essentialist statements from feminists: Given the context of feminists fighting to change the category of "woman," essentialism is usually "a project of revision," not a description of reality or biology (257).

Echols often relies on these binaries to describe differences between cultural feminists and radical feminists, placing cultural feminists on the side of "difference" and the earlier radical feminists on the side of "equality." When lesbian-feminists are discussing nonsexual aspects of lesbianism or re-visioning and reinterpreting lesbianism as something other than merely sexual behavior, Echols assumes that they deny *any* sexual element to it or display "an unwillingness to accept that within the larger culture lesbianism is viewed as a perversion" (Echols 1983, 452). I am sure that most lesbians were well aware of this fact, and their choice to celebrate lesbianism was not delusion or stubbornness but resistance to that devaluation. Similarly, Echols assumes that, because some lesbian-feminists made distinctions between themselves and gay men, they are hostile to gay male sexuality, which is seen as a contaminating influence when put in close proximity to lesbians (450).

While there is no question that there has been animosity between many lesbian-feminists and gay men (in *both* directions, I might add), it was an important rhetorical move for lesbians to acknowledge the differences between the two groups. It is frustrating to be associated, in the dominant cultural imagination, with practices in which you take no part, simply because heterosexuals are unable to distinguish between groups of minorities. If the most significant thing society notices about me is that I do not have sex with men, they may lump me together with other people with whom I have nothing in common except that they, too, are having their sex "improperly." If I believe that lesbianism is about something more than the fact that I do not have sex with men, however, then my resentfulness toward the culture's myopia would not necessarily imply that I wish to be seen as distinct from gay men *because I am hostile to them*. As Saralyn said, there are things lesbians do have in common with gay men, as well as things we do not. But Echols, like Faderman, interprets an expansion of the understanding of lesbianism to include more than same-sex genital contact as a hostile gesture against gay men that also reflects prudishness toward questions of sexuality.

As with Faderman, Echols's wording illustrates her bias: "Their insistence that lesbianism is an issue of 'radical female friendship' rather than sexual preference reflects an unwillingness . . ." (1983, 452). The choice of the word *insistence* implies that lesbian-feminists are doing something they shouldn't—stubbornly clinging to an association that is not rightly theirs. The use of "rather than" reflects Echols's inability to acknowledge that lesbianism *can be both*. Echols claims that this "desexualizing" move that lesbian-feminists made precipitated the rise of cultural feminism. She explains that lesbians politicized lesbian identity as a means of responding to the homophobic assumption among some heterosexual feminists that lesbianism was a sexual perversion and that lesbians were "male-identified" (446). The lesbian separatist stance that defined heterosexual women as traitors to feminism became "reincarnated" as the cultural feminist stance, which promoted "woman-bonding" rather than lesbianism (446). Echols says this move allowed some degree of unity between straight and lesbian feminists, but it also led to many unfortunate developments, such as the antipornography movement.

While there is little to argue with in Echols's criticism of the antipornography movement, the other aspect of cultural feminism she outlined, culture-building, goes largely unexamined in "The New Feminism of Yin and Yang." A closer examination of "women's culture" would reveal to an even greater extent the arbitrariness of her categories. She concludes the article confidently, asserting:

> By equating feminism with the so-called reassertion of a female identity and culture, cultural feminism seems to promise an immediate solution to women's powerlessness in the culture at large. Its growth is attributable to the frustrating fragmentation of the women's movement and the erosion of feminist gains in the recent past. Cultural feminism represents a retreat from the difficulties of political struggle into the self-validation that community-building offers. It further substitutes the fantasy of a united sisterhood for political theory. (1983, 455)

The polarities surface again: politics versus culture, fantasy (cultural feminism) versus reality (radical feminism). Given the context in which Echols's article appears to have been written (the infamous Barnard College conference on sexuality), the urgency of the argument in "Yin and Yang" and the rhetorical use of binarisms seem more understandable. Yet she went on several years later to expand on this same model in much greater detail. Her next project, *Daring to Be Bad* (1989), serves as a case study for the premises outlined in her 1983 article and, like the earlier work, illustrates the extent to which the historian's search for yins and yangs will reveal just that.

Echols: Woman-Identified Lesbians

To put this critique in perspective, I first want to say that, overall, *Daring to Be Bad* is an excellent book. It was a long-awaited (King 1990, 90) and important contribution to our understanding of second-wave feminism. Particularly impressive is Echols's ability to analyze closely and assimilate huge amounts of information about many of the early radical feminist groups. She has provided documentation of many political events and personalities that would otherwise be lost to the next feminist generation. With her very close readings of interviews, newsletters, and manifestos, she distinguishes between different strands of radical feminism, making apparent the complexity and contradiction of the period. Unlike Faderman, she looks from within the ideology of a group, making a best-case argument for their beliefs, and she looks at their political positioning within the context of inter- and intragroup dynamics, as rhetorical exchanges and strategies intimately related to their historical moment. She offers multiple causes for the rise and fall of various groups—personality conflicts, infiltration, economics, political disagreement—and gives a sense that there were diverse personalities, political values, and styles within each group of radical feminists. This complexity falters, however, in her final chapter on cultural feminism.

"The Ascendance of Cultural Feminism" is an elaboration of the ideas articulated by Echols in "The New Feminism of Yin and Yang." Essentially, Echols argues in this chapter that cultural feminism began when lesbian-feminists started defining the lesbian as the "woman-identified woman" (1989, 217). She states that radical feminism began to wane as cultural feminism grew in strength, during the painful gay/straight split that took place from 1970 to 1972. By 1973 the cultural feminist takeover was complete. Cultural feminism, again characterized by essentialism and institution building, led to the decline of feminist activism. Although most of *Daring to Be Bad* is a wonderful account of the period, the post-1973 section of her analysis contains many of the same binaristic generalizations found in her "Yin and Yang" article.

For example, Echols attributes great power to the rhetorical shift from "lesbian" to "woman-identified woman." She describes how the renaming was an imperative that defined lesbians as the only true feminists. This drove the radical (read "heterosexual") women out of the movement (1989, 239–40). Her analysis is somewhat confusing because, although she does attempt to separate lesbian-feminism from cultural feminism, at least momentarily, the distinct process she describes does not quite make sense. Echols says this politicized definition of lesbianism drove straight women away but then argues that it watered down lesbianism, making it palatable to heterosexual feminists. She distinguishes lesbian-feminism from cultural feminism by saying that lesbian-feminists believed lesbians were different from straight women but that cultural feminists believed women were all the same. One might think from her argument that lesbian-feminism (defined by her as divisive and prescriptive) would be depoliticizing by pushing feminists away and cultural feminism would increase activism by welcoming heterosexual women into the movement, but she seems to be making the opposite claim.

The problem is that at first Echols conflates lesbian-feminism (the belief that feminism is necessary for lesbian liberation) with political lesbianism (the belief that women can choose to be lesbian or call themselves lesbian as a way of resisting patriarchy). So lesbian-feminists would support "The Woman Identified Woman" manifesto (Radicalesbians 1973), which is seen as prescriptive and alienating, because it tells straight women they are not real feminists. But then Echols explains that lesbian-feminists are essentialists who believe that lesbians are different from other women. It is the cultural feminists who insist on an apolitical definition: woman-identified woman. Her difficulty in distinguishing between lesbian-feminists and cultural feminists is that she has already defined lesbians as politically prescriptive (lesbian-feminist) and at the same time apolitical (woman-identified women), as well as both sexual (lesbian-feminist) and at the same time asexual (cultural feminist). Although she wants to, she is unable to back out of the assertion that it is strictly the lesbians who are cultural feminists, and that it was the emergence of a lesbian presence in the feminist movement that led to the fall into cultural feminism and political apathy. But this model does not work. Echols defines the emergence of lesbian-feminism as the denial of a sexual aspect to lesbianism, and so she conflates lesbian-feminism with an antisex cultural feminism. The reason for this blurring of categories is her reliance on the binarism sexuality/politics.

As with her use of culture/politics, Echols can represent the assertion of one only as a refutation of the other. As I mentioned in my critique of her reading of Rich, it is not at all clear that articulating a political aspect to lesbianism implies it is only political. Rich isn't saying lesbianism and feminism are the same thing; she's saying the two are not mutually exclusive. That is, in an environment in which lesbianism was routinely dismissed as something sexual or aberrant or outside feminist concerns, Rich makes the argument that lesbianism does have something to do with feminism. Echols's assertion that this politicized-desexualized definition, separating lesbian-feminism from politics and sex, was used to gloss over differences between straight and gay women so that they would work together creates a similar problem. It is not self-evident that simply calling oneself a "woman-identified woman" rather than a "lesbian" would change a straight woman's feelings about you as a lesbian, or that a group of feminists wouldn't be distinguishing between their gay and straight members. Did this change in self-definition truly lead to an assumption of sameness? Echols implies that it was this rhetorical move that led to the rise of an apolitical "women's culture," in which lifestyle and self-improvement became more important than political activism:

> With the rise of lesbian-feminism, the conflation of the personal with the political, long in the making, was complete and unassailable. More than ever, how one lived one's life, not one's commitment to political struggle, became the salient factor. One can even see this illustrated in the increasingly popular term "woman-identified," which seemed to suggest that one's attitude and behavior mattered more than one's political philosophy and stance (1989, 240).

According to Echols, the shift into lesbian-feminism, symbolized by the new self-definition, paved the way for cultural feminism (1989, 243). Her description of this second shift is revealing:

> Cultural feminism succeeded in large measure because it promised an end to the gay-straight split. Cultural feminism modified lesbian-feminism so that male values rather than men were vilified and female bonding rather than lesbianism was valorized, thus making it acceptable to heterosexual feminists (244).

Because she saw lesbian-feminists' claim to feminist legitimacy as an assertion of superiority and their critique of sexism as a vilification of men, she can trace the direct development of cultural feminism from these positions. I wonder, though, who the straight women were that the cultural feminists were supposed to be bonding with (lesbian = feminist = bonding), since, according to Echols, they were already driven out of the movement (because lesbian = feminist = prescriptiveness).

As I mentioned earlier, this narrative does not squarely fit with the history of lesbian-feminists in Atlanta. Although according to Echols' time line they should have been (or were) cultural feminists, many of the women involved in the ALFA community did not fit the stereotype of the cultural feminist: They were not asexual (according to B, the ALFA community was one long revolving game of "musical beds"); they weren't apolitical; and they didn't see themselves as being indistinguishable from heterosexual women. This lack of congruence with Echols's account suggests not only the variance from a generalized model that inevitably occurs but that the model itself is oversimplified in the way it slices up complex dialogues into concrete, oppositional categories, attributing them to discrete groups of people at discrete moments in history.

B's interview (Connor 1993) illustrates this nicely, because although she sees her own lesbian identity as a sexual one and expressed hostility toward ALFAns who were "political lesbians" (women whose identification changed later in life from heterosexual to lesbian, as a result of their contact with feminism), she considers herself a lesbian-feminist and sees feminism as a part of her identity as a lesbian who is concerned with political issues. She does not see politics and sexuality as two distinct, unrelated entities, but neither does she conflate the two to the extent that they are indistinguishable. She rejects the "cultural feminist" notion that simply socializing together as lesbians is sufficiently political, yet she saw the culture they built together at ALFA as a political one. She does not believe that women who are not having sex with other women should identify as lesbians, but neither does she believe that straight women should not be a part of the ALFA community. And within her account, and across all three accounts, one gets a sense of the diversity of opinion within the community, at any given moment as well as over time.

This points to a criticism of Echols's work raised by Verta Taylor and Leila Rupp in "Women's Culture and Lesbian Feminist Activism: A Reconsideration of Cultural Feminism" (1993). Although, as they point out, in many people's minds cultural feminism and lesbian-feminism are virtually synonymous, in fact the values associated with cultural feminism (essentialism, separatism, spirituality, etc.) are constantly debated within lesbian-feminist communities (34). That is, although there are women within lesbian communities whose beliefs might appear to be cultural feminist, there are many other lesbians whose beliefs are not. Focusing as they do on the history of a specific lesbian-feminist community (in Columbus, Ohio) rather than on an abstract ideological position (the category of "cultural feminism," as distilled from aspects of lesbian-feminist writing) they are able to express a complexity that escapes a simple either-or analysis of politics/culture or essentialism/social constructionism.

Taylor and Rupp explore the overlap and gap between what might be seen as the "formal ideological position" of cultural feminism (1993, 34) and how common beliefs that lesbian-feminists hold are operating in the community. For example, although one might, in the abstract, describe institution building as a retreat from direct political confrontation, they investigate the ways in which apparently nonpolitical activities, such as music festivals, sustain political activity by providing support and a shared political identity. Similarly, the growth of social service organizations (such as rape prevention workshops) could be seen as a shift from radicalism to reformism, but they describe the ways in which many of the support organizations in the area incorporate into their work an explicitly politicized understanding of the social problems they address.

In examining a specific community, Taylor and Rupp are unable to generalize about the values the group shares. Although there are general values that most lesbian-feminists in the area have in common, how those values are applied and to what degree vary considerably. Taylor and Rupp distinguish a generalized belief that men and women are to some degree different (hence the need for a "women's community" rather than a "people's community") from a belief that these differences are inherent (1993, 41). While only some in the community trace "female values" to women's reproductive capacities, all in the community believe to some extent that there is value in joining together as women, socially and politically; otherwise, they would not be there.

Unlike Echols's reduction of culture-building to an automatic separatism and essentialism, Taylor and Rupp distinguish among many degrees of separatism, from the annual National Women's Studies Association (NWSA) conference all the way to the complete separation from men (1993, 44). The example of the NWSA conference stands as a challenge to their audience to resist the scapegoating that occurs when previously held values that we come to feel are undesirable, such as essentialism, are projected onto a single group: If we can accuse lesbian-feminists of being essentialists obsessed with building an alternative culture, for instance, we can rid ourselves of the possibility that there is some degree of essentialism in our own thinking. To cite another example, women's studies could, I suppose, be identified as a cultural institution built as a way of avoiding political conflict, but it is not usually spoken of in this way. Many feminists attend NWSA; many feminists believe in the importance of meeting apart from men to discuss their interests; many feminists value their relationships with women and see them as qualitatively different from their relationships with men. Yet when lesbian-feminists express these same values, they are often interpreted as expressions of an extreme, concrete belief in essential female superiority or of a hatred of men.

That so many feminists are able to be this dismissive of the lesbians whose work, at times, seems to comprise the bulk of feminist cultural and political activity (Taylor and Rupp 1993, 38; King 1990, 92; Echols 1989, 240) is a testament to the lingering traces of an unreconciled gay/straight split (that is, homophobia), as well as to the emotional appeal of historical narratives that give us one direction in which to point the finger (backward, at the past), a chance to vent our uncertainty (and even embarrassment?) about the radicalism of the past, and an answer to why things went wrong, why feminism didn't conquer the patriarchy. A narrative that fobs off the mistakes of the past onto the doorstep of one faction of the movement, that sets one group apart as being entirely distinct from the rest, provides just such appeal. Because Echols's argument is structured around a rigid model of radical/cultural feminism, where cultural feminism is credited with the theoretical and strategical flaws of the movement (when those same flaws occur before 1973, they are labeled "proto-cultural-feminist"),[11] it allows for, and at times even encourages, this type of scapegoating.

Conclusion: Paradoxes

Most of the women I know who are my age or younger are cynical and alienated. They don't have any cogent analysis of where they stand in the world except that everyone should own a black bra. One side of me wants to say, "Can't you stop calling us girls for one second?" At the same time, when I encounter older women who are rigid, I want to give them the finger and put on red lipstick.

—Maria Maggenti, in Solomon 1993, 214

On the one hand, the new lesbianism deconstructs the old, perhaps overly politicized or prescriptive notion of lesbianism by refusing ghettoization, acknowledging internal group differences, and affirming the value of individual choice when it comes to style and political and sexual expression. On the other hand, it comes perilously close to depoliticizing lesbian identity and perpetuating our invisibility by failing, frequently, to name itself to others. —Stein 1992, 437

In the early 80s I was trashing lesbian feminism and brandishing "incorrect" politics at every turn. My criticisms are more tempered now, and my enthusiasms less blind. For one thing, lesbian feminism has become an easy target, and easy targets are no fun. But more to the point, those things that are real dangers—random, vicious violence against women and gay men and people of color, the decimation of a generation from AIDS and complacency ... the misery of urban poverty, and the latest wars—weren't created by lesbian feminists. Increasingly, I wonder whether we take each other on because we've lost faith in our ability to fight the big fights. —Whisman 1993, 55

What are we to make of the changes that have taken place in much academic and activist lesbianism? I myself feel stuck in the middle. I do feel distanced from those younger lesbians who lack political and historical insight, but also from those older lesbians whose differing cultural styles (although it usually feels like mistrust of my cultural difference) can be alienating. However, I recognize, as Arlene Stein does, that the lesbian-feminists of the 1970s made substantial, lasting, courageous contributions to the quality—and even the possibility—of lesbian living. She writes:

> By struggling to destigmatize lesbianism, and by forging institutional spaces within which it could flourish, lesbian-feminism was largely responsible for creating the conditions under which a new, more mainstream and less radical lesbianism would eventually take root. . . . This new lesbian freedom is testimony to the success, rather than the failure, of the old. (1992, 438)

Stein edited the anthology *Sisters, Sexperts, Queers: Beyond the Lesbian Nation* (1993), which (despite the tone of triumph in its subtitle) is one of the few recently published books on the changes in U.S. lesbian cultures that deals in a fairly complex way with the relationship between 1970s lesbian-feminism and more recent lesbian styles. Apart from a few dissenting voices, such as Stein's, Taylor and Rupp's, and Katie King's, there seems to be a widespread view, at least in academic feminist print, that lesbian-feminism is dying or dead. In the postfeminist narrative found in most mainstream media representations of the newest generation of lesbians, lesbian-feminists were "antisex," "antimale," bossy, and dogmatic. Their movement died because it was radical—that is, they let politics get in the way of fun. In the (overlapping) post-lesbian-feminist narrative found in much academic and activist lesbian/feminist discourse, lesbian-feminists were too separatist, too essentialist, too p.c. Their movement failed because they weren't radical enough—that is, they let culture-building (fun?) get in the way of politics.

The lesbian-feminists I spoke with had different ideas about why the level of activism in their community waned in the 1980s. Saralyn described "a stagnation" that occurred in ALFA, which she attributes not to separatism but to the general waning of radicalism in the Reagan eighties, the proliferation of other gay and lesbian organizations, and the maturation of the generation:

> ALFA didn't seem, we were no longer having ERA marches, there just didn't seem to be as much going on, or as much focus to the group. It got larger. Some of the things we had done . . . those were over by then. Times just really changed, and I think a lot of us changed. We were growing up, we had careers by then, we were buying houses, we were in couples, you know? And all that was true for me. My priorities really changed.
>
> It had a lot to do with getting older. I mean, most of us were in our twenties in the seventies. If we had jobs, they were just jobs, they weren't careers. That was true for many people. Our priority was really being lesbians, being lesbian-feminists. That was really the center of our lives. And that changed somewhat over the years for most people, I think. It was a core of your life, and then you sort of went on, and grew up and dealt with your issues.
>
> It bothers me sometimes that me and my friends have gone on, but I don't know what else you can do, except just go on and live your life. And do what you can. It would have been ridiculous for us to go on living in broken-down old houses and not making much money. I mean, that doesn't really accomplish anything. I think we had this sort of romanticized notion about that at some point in our lives that we don't have anymore. (Chesnut 1993)

B also felt that ALFA had begun to stagnate in the early 1980s, but she attributed the decline in political activity to a shift in the membership as a middle-class, less political crowd came to dominate:

> One of the things that I think happened to ALFA is that it became less working-class and more bourgeois. And there was like this understated class war that went on at ALFA. Working-class women—even though in the South they're kind of kept from doing this—are likely to be more group-identified, and bourgeois women are like, you know, "Well, I need a diploma, I need a BMW." They're more into accumulation for themselves. Or they think of merit in a solitary kind of way.
>
> I guess it manifested itself in the kind of deviation away from politics. ... A lot of the stuff we could've [been] involved as a group in, that a lot of people went off and did individually, there wasn't enough stuff at ALFA to get people together on. Like the U.S. intervention in Central America. Or the Atlanta Murdered and Missing debacle. At that point, women were more into this bourgeois thing, like "Why should we do that as lesbians?"
>
> And it is really hard when you have a group, whether it's a bowling group, or a group of people that all fuck the same way, and you try to come together and say we're all like-minded, like on the issue of abortion. Do you think you could make a bowling team that was all pro-choice and make it last for twenty years or so? ... It's very tricky. Especially when some of them are into becoming accountants and real estate [agents], and other ones who are lifetime people who are committed to social change. They just had totally different goals. (Connor 1993)

According to B, ALFA started to become less political in the eighties, not when it turned to "cultural feminism" but when political women began leaving the organization and apolitical women remained behind.

When I asked Betty what ALFA was like when she first joined, she began discussing the decline in its prominence in the community and gave a variety of causes:

> At the time, ALFA was at the point where they were just buying the house. They really, since I've been a member (this is a terrible thing), they really have declined. So I came in after their heyday. So I came in just right when they bought the house. And the house has really been a drain for ALFA. It's a wonderful thing, but it's also been a terrible thing, because it needed all this work, all this renovation. And also during that period, during those Reagan years and Bush years, all of the separatist—that kind of stuff—just went by the wayside.
>
> Groups like Fourth Tuesday [a local networking group for "professional"

lesbians], which, you know, I'm not saying bad things about, kind of rose, and it was more important to be social than it was to be political. And so a lot of political theory hasn't been discussed. And so a lot of the members left to go do other things. One of the problems that ALFA has had is that it hasn't been able to attract younger membership. And as the members got older, even though they may not have gone off and joined a group like Fourth Tuesday that's social, they may have become so involved in their own lives that their political activism is taking a backseat. And it just didn't seem like that new crop, the next wave of women that should be really holding things together in their thirties now, didn't happen.

When ALFA first started, they were the only game in town. I mean, you had, like, two choices: You either went to the bar, or you went to ALFA. And there wasn't any place else to go to. There wasn't a Fourth Tuesday, there wasn't a WOW [Women of Wisdom], there wasn't a WINK [Women in Kahoots], or the [Atlanta Feminist Women's] Chorus. The Chorus came out of ALFA. So there wasn't many games in town to go to. And so, you know; even if you weren't political, you still came to ALFA, to meet women. So you know, I think as other groups formed to achieve different things than what ALFA was trying to achieve, then it was easy just to move along. (Irwin 1993)

While it is difficult to know exactly which factors are most responsible for ALFA's decline, clearly the process was generated by much more than the politics and personalities of its members, since both of these fluctuated quite substantially over time.

I conclude by pointing out that it is not just that feminism is misrepresented in the mainstream media; we feminists have our tidy narratives, too. What the narratives of lesbian chic and post-lesbian-feminism lack, in my opinion, is a more complex, more sociological explanation of the experiences of 1970s lesbian-feminist activists in their specific communities, rather than general, abstract "positions" drawn across nations and periods or from theoretical texts alone. As the quotes at the beginning of this section suggest, the reasons that lesbian-feminism is rejected by many lesbians and feminists are highly complex and contestable. Lesbian-feminism in the seventies was sometimes excessive in its theorizing and practices, but it also has been roundly scapegoated as a movement doomed to failure by its radicalism or as encompassing the women who doomed the radical feminist movement. Among nonfeminist lesbians, especially younger ones, a rejection of lesbian-feminism seems related to the homophobia and sexism directed at women who don't conform to our culture's notions of what is important, sexy, powerful, or interesting. Among lesbian/feminist activists and academics, I would argue that the circulation of this narrative stems from at least two factors (besides, of course, the fact that the negative behaviors attributed to lesbian-feminists have been warranted in some instances).

First, as I've said, in the struggle over lesbian identity, which has always occurred in lesbian communities but is now accelerated by the growth and diversification of the lesbian population, there is a need to construct an older, negative identity against which to compose a newer, positive one. Although I know many women of my age (twenty-seven) who are lesbian and feminist and who share many "lesbian-feminist" values, I know almost no one other than myself who *calls* herself a lesbian-feminist. And since there do not seem to be many lesbians willing to admit that they were there in 1973, that they were or are "those women," to dispel the generalizations or clarify what lesbian-feminism means to them, the stereotype continues, growing larger each time it is passed on.

The second reason I tentatively put forward is one that strangely parallels Echols's account of the rise of cultural feminism. Just as she says that the 1970s were racked with political division and that cultural feminism arose as a way of avoiding internal conflict, I believe that within academic feminism there exists the same type of need to come together, after a decade and a half of heated arguments, and agree that someone else, out there, is responsible for feminism's troubles. *They* were essential-ist, racist, naively utopian, unsophisticated. *We* are multicultural, post-modern, social constructionist. Just as cultural feminists united in their distance from "the man," feminist scholars can unite around their opposi-tion to the "Lesbian Nation." There seems to be a lot of emotional, finan-cial, and professional profit accruing in the accounts of those who do.

Psychologizing? Yes. Oversimplified? Maybe. But still, comparing Lil-lian Faderman's glowing descriptions of lesbian-feminism in the early 1980s[12] to her thorough demonization of it ten years later, one wonders what exactly is at stake in such an abrupt and emphatic reversal. This reversal highlights starkly, I think, the pressures that seem to hang over the heads of those too closely associated with lesbian-feminism.

Every decade or so the political tide shifts, and different lesbian/ feminist communities are corrected, responded to, and, at times, scape-goated for present difficulties. In the 1970s, the "new" lesbians rebelling against the "old" were the lesbian-feminists. They often villainized older butch-femme lesbians.[13] Now they are grown, and the new vanguard is after them. Instead of endlessly recirculating the same overarching narratives about lesbian/feminist history, we need to strive for complexity and specificity in our discussions. We should be accounting for what feminists have done and how they have felt about it, rather than projecting political positions, theoretical commitments, or generalized, media-fed images onto the past. For the sake of truth, if nothing else, history should not be told from only the winner's point of view.

NOTES

1. By *lesbian/feminist media* I mean lesbian and feminist theory, criticism, journalism, teaching, art, conferences, and so forth—the vehicles by which we communicate to ourselves and others the events of importance to our communities. Throughout this essay I have sometimes used an unconventional phrasing: *lesbian/feminism*, rather than *lesbian-feminism*. My intention is both to emphasize the overlap between lesbian and feminist arenas and to suggest an alternative way of thinking about lesbian-feminism.

To me, the hyphen in *lesbian-feminism* evokes images of a political faction sharing a set of specifically articulated tenets and strategies. I have always understood the term *lesbian-feminism* to mean, quite simply, a feminist who is lesbian and believes that sexism and heterosexism are intricately connected. In this essay I am calling for a reconceptualization of lesbian-feminism that acknowledges that the same degree of diversity is present in the category "lesbian-feminist" as in "lesbian" or "feminist." To that end the term *lesbian/feminist* serves as a kind of grammatical reminder that the meaning of *lesbian-feminism* varies widely and is subject to constant renegotiation.

2. Schwartz argues that the image of the chic lesbian is a desexualized one, but I would argue the opposite. Although it would be difficult to generalize about which depoliticizing impulse—diffusing the threat of homosexuality by eliding sexuality or diffusing the threat of lesbianism by sexualizing it—predominates in these representations, clearly the chic lesbian represents a sexual possibility to the mainstream audience (at least those schooled in the pornographic vernacular) in a way that the figure of the "short-haired bulldagger" and the "hairy-legged, bra-burning, porn-hating 'angry feminist' " (Schwartz 1993) do not.

3. See Saralyn Chesnut and Amanda C. Gable, " 'Women Ran It': Charis Books and More and Atlanta's Lesbian-Feminist Community, 1971–1981," chapter 12 in this book, for a much fuller description of this community.

4. There were, of course, other lesbian communities in the Atlanta area at this time, including social networks for upscale "Buckhead dykes" and the outlying rural areas' lesbians. The predominantly white and leftist ALFA community was the most visible site of specifically lesbian-feminist activity.

5. See Audre Lorde's *Zami* (1982) for her account of the ostracization "ki-ki" women like herself faced in the 1950s.

6. She also attributes butch-femme to 1950s lesbians' inability to understand their identity in some other way than in relation to (or as a replication of) heterosexuality. This reading, interestingly, mirrors what could be considered the standard lesbian-feminist critique. (See Nestle 1981, for a critique of that critique.)

7. By "sympathetic," I mean not necessarily uncritically supportive but something more like ethnographic, in the sense of trying to understand a group's actions according to their value system, rather than simply describing them within the terms of your own.

8. Most notably, the argument in 1988 over whether alcohol should be stored in the ALFA house and provided at ALFA functions. After an extensive period of argument, both sides eventually compromised, but, according to Betty, they all felt unhappy with the resolution, and some members left the group because of this.

9. Another example is Linda Alcoff's "Cultural Feminism versus Post-Structuralism: The Identity Crisis in Feminist Theory," in which, as Teresa de Lauretis points out, Alcoff senses that Echols is oversimplifying but uses her analysis anyway (de Lauretis 1990, 263).

10. Audre Lorde, "The Uses of the Erotic" (1984), among others.

11. For example, Echols's discussions of the Feminists (1989, 183–84), or of the New York Radical Feminists (188).

12. For example, *Surpassing the Love of Men* (Faderman 1981), and "The 'New Gay' Lesbians" (Faderman 1984).

13. Although it's worth remembering that lesbian-feminists themselves were also mocked, as "fake" lesbians. Many of them originally identified as heterosexual and came out as lesbian after they became involved with feminism. Those who felt they chose lesbianism stood in close proximity, symbolically, to those heterosexual feminists who did not have relationships with men on political principle and called themselves "political lesbians." Because political lesbianism arose out of radical feminism, because many lesbian-feminists were radical feminists who originally identified as heterosexual, and because beliefs about lesbianism are often based on essentialist, biological understandings of sexuality, there has been a widespread tendency to depict lesbian-feminists as fake lesbians, in contrast to nonfeminist, older, butch/femme or s/m lesbians.

As I have shown, this attitude is shared by both Echols and Faderman (in their chiding of lesbian-feminists for failing to define lesbianism in sexual rather than social terms), and was also expressed by B (Esther) throughout her interview. Even though B and I are good friends, and she knows that I feel lesbianism was a choice for me, her contempt for this position is so strong that she repeatedly referred to the ALFA lesbians who've shared my experience as "heterosexuals," even blaming them at times for the downfall of the organization.

SOURCES CITED

Alcoff, Linda. Cultural feminism versus post-structuralism: The identity crisis in feminist theory. *Signs* 13, 3 (spring 1988): 405–36.

Chesnut, Saralyn. 1993. Interview by author. Atlanta, Georgia. July.

Connor, Esther "B." 1993. Interview by author. Decatur, Georgia. July.

de Lauretis, Teresa. 1990. Upping the anti (sic) in feminist theory. In *Conflicts in feminism*, edited by Marianne Hirsch and Evelyn Fox Keller. New York: Routledge.

Echols, Alice. 1983. The new feminism of yin and yang. In *Powers of desire: The politics of sexuality*, edited by Ann Snitow, Christine Stansell, and Sharon Thompson. New York: Monthly Review Press.

———. 1989. *Daring to be bad: Radical feminism in America 1967–1975*. Minneapolis: University of Minnesota Press.

Faderman, Lillian. 1981. *Surpassing the love of men: Romantic friendship and the love between women from the renaissance to the present*. New York: William & Morrow.

———. 1984. The "new gay" lesbians. *Journal of Homosexuality* 10, nos. 3–4: 85–95.

———. 1991. *Odd girls and twilight lovers: A history of lesbian life in twentieth-century America*. New York: Penguin Books.

Ferguson, Ann, Jacquelyn Zita, and Kathryn Addelson. 1982. On "compulsory heterosexuality and lesbian existence": Defining the issues. In *Feminist theory: A critique of ideology*, edited by Nannerl Keohane, Michelle Rosaldo, and Barbara Gelpi. Chicago: University of Chicago Press.

Gallop, Jane. 1992. *Around 1981: Academic feminist literary theory*. New York: Routledge.

Irwin, Betty. 1993. Interview by author. Atlanta, Georgia. July.

Kasindorf, Jeanie R. 1993. Lesbian chic: The bold, brave new world of gay women. *New York Magazine*, 10 May, 31–37.

King, Katie. 1990. Producing sex, theory, and culture: Gay/straight remappings in contemporary feminism. In *Conflicts in feminism*, edited by Marianne Hirsch and Evelyn Fox Keller. New York: Routledge.

Lorde, Audre. 1982. *Zami: A new spelling of my name*. Freedom, CA: Crossing Press.

———. 1984. The uses of the erotic: The erotic as power. In *Sister Outsider*. Freedom, CA: Crossing Press.

Metz, Holly. 1994. Interview with Sarah Schulman. *The Progressive* (October): 37–41.

Nestle, Joan. 1981. Butch-fem relationships: Sexual courage in the 1950s. *Heresies* 3, 4: 22–24.

Radicalesbians. 1973. The woman identified woman. In *Radical feminism*, edited by Anne Koedt, Ellen Levine, and Anita Rapone. New York: Quadrangle.

Rich, Adrienne. 1976. *Of woman born*. New York: W. W. Norton & Co.

———. 1980. Compulsory heterosexuality and lesbian existence. *Signs* 5, 4: 631–60.

————. 1986. Compulsory heterosexuality and lesbian existence. In *Blood, bread, and poetry: Selected prose, 1979–1985*. New York: W. W. Norton & Co.

Ruthven, K. K. 1984. *Feminist literary studies*. Cambridge: Cambridge University Press.

Salholz, Eloise. 1993. Lesbians: The power and the pride. *Newsweek*, 21 June, 54–60.

Schwartz, Deb. 1993. The days of wine and poses: The media presents homosexuality lite. *Village Voice*, 8 June, 34.

Scott, Joan. 1990. Deconstructing equality-versus-difference. In *Conflicts in feminism*, edited by Marianne Hirsch and Evelyn Fox Keller. New York: Routledge.

Snitow, Ann. 1990. A gender diary. In *Conflicts in feminism*, edited by Marianne Hirsch and Evelyn Fox Keller. New York: Routledge.

Solomon, Alisa. 1993. Dykotomies: Scents and sensibility. In *Sisters, sexperts, queers: Beyond the Lesbian Nation*, edited by Arlene Stein. New York: Plume.

Stein, Arlene. 1992. All dressed up, but no place to go? Style wars and the new lesbianism. In *The persistent desire: A femme-butch reader*, edited by Joan Nestle. Boston: Alyson Publications.

Taylor, Verta, and Leila Rupp. 1993. Women's culture and lesbian feminist activism: A reconsideration of cultural feminism. *Signs* 19, 1: 32–61.

Whisman, Vera. 1993. Identity crises: Who is a lesbian, anyway? In *Sisters, sexperts, queers: Beyond the Lesbian Nation*, edited by Arlene Stein. New York: Plume.

Aids and Beyond

Chapter Fourteen

Dateline *Atlanta*

Place and the Social Construction of AIDS

Meredith Raimondo

We Must Distinguish between the Unique and the Seemingly Universal.[1]

There is a story that people tell about the founding of AID Atlanta, Atlanta's largest AIDS service organization, that functions as a local variant on the narrative of how the "gay community" became aware of AIDS, a moment symbolized in many accounts by the 1981 *New York Times* report about a new cancer in gay men.[2] A group of gay men in Atlanta were concerned with the impact of this new illness on gay men in the "ground zero" of New York City and raised a sum of money to send to an organization called Gay Men's Health Crisis. At least in this way, Atlantans could contribute to the effort to address what was being experienced as a catastrophe. With profound thanks, Gay Men's Health Crisis returned the uncashed check and advised the men to keep the money, for if Atlanta did not have immediate need for the funds, soon it most certainly would. These funds became the seed money for AID Atlanta.[3]

This story strikes a chord because it so vividly captures a moment in Atlanta in which AIDS still seemed distant. Identifying AIDS as something present in Atlanta was a process that quickly became a central political issue in local responses to AIDS. Indeed, over the last decade and a half, American AIDS activists and educators have wrestled with the challenge of helping variously framed constituencies recognize that AIDS is an immediate part of their individual and social worlds. For the most part, these efforts have transpired in and through identity politics.[4] What has been less well articulated in these conversations is the crucial role of geography in defining the perception of AIDS as a threat, a crisis, a lived reality, or all of these. As we look back at the early and mid-1980s and the initial struggles to recognize, understand, and respond to AIDS, we find in the stories we tell about this time both the importance of place and the absence of any sustained understanding of its effects. By mapping the cultural politics of place in the early history of AIDS in the United States, we can identify important and often unacknowledged variations in Americans' experiences with AIDS.

In the mid-1980s, the places of AIDS would not have been hard to name: New York City, San Francisco, Los Angeles. These cities played prominent roles in Randy Shilts's *And the Band Played On*, one of the first histories of AIDS. Shilts, the first journalist to be assigned to the "AIDS beat" in the 1980s, mapped the course of acquired immune deficiency syndrome across and between the two U.S. coasts. While these three cities were his primary settings, the moral of his story concerned the country as a whole. In his prologue, Shilts argued that

> from 1980, when the first isolated gay men began falling ill from strange and exotic ailments, nearly five passed before all these institutions— medicine, public health, the federal and private scientific research establish- ments, the mass media, and the gay community's leadership—mobilized the way they should in a time of crisis. The story of these first five years of AIDS in America is a drama of national failure, played out against a back- drop of needless death.[5]

For Shilts, the key geographic dimensions of AIDS were national bound- aries. In his view, the United States had a vast wealth of resources, unique among the world's nations; but faced with AIDS, it squandered them. The consequences of this failure were clearest in New York City, San Francisco, and Los Angeles, where death and suffering reached such catastrophic proportions that people used metaphors such as "holocaust" and "ground zero" to describe them.

If these cities were the places of AIDS, then to be elsewhere was to be—for the moment—"safe." For example, the characters in Harlan Greene's *What the Dead Remember*, set in Charleston, South Carolina, seized on this geography of risk. In their eyes, AIDS was happening somewhere else:

Fall brought a chill to the air; but it was the news that set people shivering. There was more and more talk of the strange new disease; its mere mention distilled unease. People got up and moved, changed the conversation even though they felt it had nothing to do with them. The nameless thing only got those glamorous boys in San Francisco and New York City. Yet men started recasting their histories. As AIDS was named, it was like being inside, in Charleston, listening to the first stirring of a storm.[6]

This novel addresses a social experience of AIDS in a place far from ones evoked in *And the Band Played On,* suggesting that the equation of those coastal cities with the nation effaces important differences in Americans' experiences with AIDS. Greene's unnamed narrator was distant from AIDS; he felt "inside," momentarily protected from the gathering "storm." Even when he grappled with his own illness at the end of *What the Dead Remember,* it was to reflect that "Charleston has no use for people like us. They treat us as if we are beyond help, dead already. . . . In a world apart, we are like ghosts or creatures undersea, a different species."[7] Within the world of the story, the narrator's experience was shaped by the fact that while people experienced the effects of the human immunodeficiency virus (HIV) in their lives, in a very real sense, neither the "AIDS epidemic" nor the "AIDS crisis" existed in Greene's Charleston.[8]

The differences between these two narratives suggest that place plays a key role in social experiences of AIDS. Yet in much of the writing about AIDS, region is an invisible factor.[9] If it is acknowledged, it often surfaces as an urban/rural distinction between the ultramodern metropolises and the American "heartland."[10] So where does a city like Atlanta fit? This formulation leaves such a place a curious and contradictory discursive position in the social construction of AIDS. Atlanta shares many features with the "modern metropolises" of New York, San Francisco, and Los Angeles, but it is also in the "South," an amorphous and sprawling section of the United States that is, like the Midwest, constructed as a rural and particularly antimodern space. To propose looking at a unified South in order to add a measure of geographic analysis also poses problems, for this section of the country contains several distinct regions. Thus we cannot assume that Greene's novel captured *the* Southern AIDS experience of the early and mid-1980s, for Charleston and Atlanta are very different places. However, *What the Dead Remember* raises a question about the histories we construct about the emergence of AIDS in the United States: Was Atlanta "inside" during this stirring storm? Its location as a "Southern" city might imply that it was, but its structural similarities to urban centers like New York City, San Francisco, and Los Angeles suggest that it could be one of the places where AIDS began. To explore this contradiction, we must confront the complicated politics involved in historicizing and spatializing AIDS. There is no way to answer definitively the question of how Atlanta came to see AIDS as something local, for such a process is as complex and varied as the millions of people who make up the city's population. We can, however, begin to reconstruct the broad outlines of such a history and the issues and controversies that helped shape it by approaching the subject of location and AIDS from multiple directions. I will explore a series of questions in order to consider the implications and effects of regional analysis of AIDS: How did epidemiologists' and medical geographers' approach to the mapping of AIDS use geography in such as way as to construct AIDS in the United States as a national phenomenon, without regional variation? How did the connections between scientific research and the commercial media result in the popularization of this approach? If the commercial media have served as "scriptwriters" for cultural interpretations of AIDS in the United States, then what story or stories were Atlanta's daily newspapers, the *Atlanta Journal* and the *Atlanta Constitution*, telling about AIDS in the early and mid-1980s? While the newspapers' reporting represents only a fraction of the stories it is possible to tell about AIDS in Atlanta in this period, both their interests and their silences suggest some of the factors that structured Atlanta's social experience(s) of AIDS. As this coverage clearly demonstrates, in the first half of the 1980s, Atlanta was indeed struggling with AIDS. However, the city's efforts to understand and respond were profoundly influenced by regional issues.

"The Inadequate Metaphors": AIDS, History, and Narrative

To describe the processes through which interpretations of AIDS in the 1980s acquired coherence and power is to confront the political uses and limitations of history as a narrative form. Many AIDS critics have feared that historical inquiry as it is traditionally practiced constitutes a form that cannot reflect adequately the complexity of AIDS. This concern derives in part from an attentiveness to the political implications of language. For example, AIDS has been commonly described as an "epidemic," the modern "plague." The use of these terms has helped perpetuate fears about the unchecked spread of contagious disease. However, the virus believed to cause AIDS is infectious, not contagious. Nor is AIDS a "disease," according to its medical definition. In the 1980s, a person was diagnosed with this syndrome only if he or she exhibited one of several opportunistic infections as specified by the Centers for Disease Control (CDC). A person with HIV who had other opportunistic infections was not diagnosed with AIDS, which helps explain the underrepresentation of broad demographic categories, such as women, in the initial counts. When the CDC revised its definition in 1992 to address such omissions, a whole group of people suddenly became people with AIDS who had not been the day before, including people who were asymptomatic and healthy but exhibited low T-cell counts.[11] Further, different infections have been variably visible in different parts of the country. Doctors in New York City were first struck by the unusual number of people with Kaposi's sarcoma, a skin cancer. Doctors in Los Angeles were puzzled by a sudden rise in cases of Pneumocystis pneumonia.[12]

These contradictions and confusions led cultural critic Douglas Crimp to suggest that "AIDS does not exist apart from the practices that conceptualize it, represent it, and respond to it." He did not deny that AIDS has material consequences: "This assertion does not contest the existence of viruses, antibodies, infection, or transmission routes" or "the reality of illness, suffering, and death." However, Crimp argued that we cannot separate those "facts" of AIDS from cultural meanings and politics. There is, he said, no "underlying reality of AIDS, upon which are constructed the representations." Biology and culture are too deeply intertwined to be separated. If anything, *culture* is the privileged term, as it is through social values that understandings of biology are produced.[13]

The production of meaning occurs in part when names invoke cultural narratives. The term *epidemic* is a good example of the narrative logic of language. Charles Rosenberg argues that in Western culture, epidemics have "dramaturgic forms." That is, they begin, build momentum toward a climax that is a crisis of "individual and collective character, then drift toward closure." This formulation is particularly helpful in understanding the ways in which societies shape fragmented incidents into a coherent story, utilizing the conventional plotting devices of beginning, middle, and end. Rosenberg explains that the dramaturgic form of epidemics begins with a state of "progressive revelation," in which the community in question "discovers" the epidemic at the point at which it becomes "unavoidable." From there, the community explores ways to "manag[e]

randomness," imposing order or narrative coherency on revealed information. Finally, there is a period of "negotiating public response," by
which appropriate response is contested and ultimately defined.[14]

Crimp and Rosenberg both suggest that traditional narrative forms,
such as those favored by journalists and historians, have a tendency to
suggest false unities, efface difference and contradiction, and suggest
closure in ways that do indeed "exaggerate and diminish" the complexities of AIDS.[15] Hayden White argues that this inclination is the result of
our cultural preoccupation with the "real" in historical accounts. In modes
of storytelling such as myth that do not pose the "imaginary" and the
"real" as exclusive categories, narrative is not a "problem." Conflicts
emerge only when "we wish to give to real events the form of story . . .
because real events do not offer themselves as stories." That is, "real
events" do not typically "display the coherence, integrity, fullness, and
closure" that narrative suggests we hope to find.[16]

Even the word *AIDS* has narrative implications. As Rosenberg points
out, we can only understand "it" as an epidemic because of modern
medicine's ability to unify a wide range of illnesses through a single viral
agent[17]—and in some circles, even the relationship of HIV to the collection of illnesses labeled "AIDS" remains in dispute.[18] To talk about AIDS
is to participate in the construction of its meanings and, as such, to engage
in a highly political act. Cultural analysts have demonstrated that terms
such as *general public* and *innocent victim* have been used to manage and
justify social responses to people who are sick, dying, or, in some cases,
healthy.[19] Thus cultural critic and AIDS activist Simon Watney argues that
while a historical perspective is necessary, the dispassionate and objective
stance of historical narratives is incapable of recognizing these political
implications. Therefore history is an unacceptable epistemological approach for someone who defines her- or himself as an activist: "We cannot
afford the luxurious delusion of some ultimate recognition of the scale of
injustice perpetrated at all levels of the management of the epidemic,
because we don't have time. Too many lives are still at stake." For these
reasons, Watney concludes that "for those actively involved in HIV/AIDS
work, the time has not yet arrived for the writing of history."[20]

These arguments illustrate that "history" represents a highly charged
and contested mode of thinking about the complex of issues, experiences,
and actions that cohere around the sign "AIDS." Because AIDS is so
acutely a material and symbolic feature of the "present," casting it in
terms of "history" is a political as well as an intellectual move. Given this

knowledge, one might well question the utility of trying to construct a narrative history of AIDS in Atlanta in the early and mid-1980s, even if it is presented in the guise of complicating the existing story about the geography of AIDS's emergence in the United States. However, historical narrative is not without its uses. In the introduction to *AIDS: The Burdens of History*, Elizabeth Fee and Daniel Fox argue that public policy discussion about AIDS could be greatly enriched by historical analysis. Without history, our attempts to understand AIDS are greatly limited: We cannot escape the "burdens of history," which Fee and Fox define as "the inescapable significance of events in the past for the present." [21]

Without accounting for the ways in which past events influence meaning and action in the present context of AIDS, we lose a critical position from which to articulate and evaluate public policy alternatives. And while we must carefully interrogate our histories for the tendency to efface difference and elide contradiction, narrative remains a powerful form of representation for addressing Fee and Fox's concern. As White points out, narrative has tremendous force and "moral authority" in "social reality." [22] Despite its flaws, it can be put to use as one part of the broader political struggle. Cindy Patton argues in *Inventing AIDS* that

> we must speak about our experience, participate in public debate, make available medical test results, and render as data the individual social experiences out of which broader scientific and pedagogical strategies may be created. We must use the inadequate metaphors available to construct a cultural space from which those people most affected in the epidemic, as well as those observing its radical ruptures from afar, can make sense out of HIV and AIDS and make the necessary personal and social choices and resistances. [23]

It is the very difficulty of representing AIDS that necessitates its representation, particularly by those who seek more just responses from institutions and individuals in a position to address the needs of those affected by HIV. If the inadequacies of current representations of AIDS are not challenged, naturalized social fictions threaten to claim authority. If the most effective way to challenge narratives that obscure important dimensions of AIDS is to provide alternative narratives, then we must take up these "inadequate metaphors" and, while utilizing their power, not forget to demonstrate their limits as well.

Mapping the Origins of AIDS: Medical Geography and National Borders

The histories of AIDS's beginnings in the United States do not account for the meaning of region in social experiences of AIDS.[24] In part, this omission reflects the hegemonic role of epidemiological explanations for the origins of AIDS in the United States, as popularized in the commercial media. But given the centrality of geography to the practice of epidemiology, how did this research help efface regional differences in the experiences of AIDS? As the case of Atlanta illustrates, epidemiological constructions of AIDS's origins invoked geographic narratives that allowed many places to be overlooked.

As is the case with newly identified "epidemics," one of the initial tasks epidemiologists faced was understanding the spread of AIDS. Gary Shannon and Gerald Pyle offered a model of this process in their 1989 article "The Origin and Diffusion of AIDS" and further developed it in their 1991 book with Rashid Bashshur, *The Geography of AIDS*. Their diffusion model investigated global origins for AIDS by calling into play continental and national borders. To map the spread of AIDS over time, Shannon and Pyle looked at where and when cases were diagnosed and hypothesized causal relationships between the clusters. They interpreted the early identification of many cases on the continent of Africa as suggesting that HIV had African origins and spread from that continent to the rest of the world.[25] In critiquing this model, Renee Sabatier argued that the African origins theory was based on proposed "African links" to early European cases and the assumption that "it was [un]likely that such an unusual disease could have gone unnoticed for long in the United States."[26] This belief in the efficacy of U.S. scientific and medical establishments did not account for factors such as racism, homophobia, sexism, and class interest that affected these institutions' definition of a phenomenon as an acceptable object of study.[27] Further, the diffusion model did not address the conditions that make epidemics possible. For example, Sabatier pointed out that while "Western" researchers were quick to look for "Third World" origins, they appeared unwilling to consider the possibility that AIDS spread from the United States to the rest of the world in exported blood products, which were then used in ways that resulted in the rapid dissemination of HIV in some African nations.[28]

Even more disturbing, prominent versions of the African origins theory were founded on the theory that simian immunodeficiency virus (SIV), an HIV-like virus found in the green monkey, was transmitted to humans and mutated into HIV. However, no scientific research has been able to demonstrate how this process might come to pass. In *AIDS, Africa, and Racism,* Richard and Rosalind Chirimuuta pointed out that "such ideas cohabit easily with racist notions that Africans are evolutionarily closer to sub-human primates, or with images gleaned from Tarzan movies of Africans living in trees like monkeys."[29] Shannon, Pyle, and Bashshur responded to these sorts of criticisms by carefully contrasting three theories of origin: the Haitian theory, the Euro-American theory, and the African theory. They concluded that "to date, there exists no conclusive scientific evidence for locating the exact origin of HIV." However, they also noted that "it does appear plausible to suggest that HIV infection in the United States resulted from tourism and travel to Haiti and Europe," intimating that in their eyes, a U.S. origin theory was not probable.[30]

The question of origins illustrates the ways in which "objective science" helped construct a racialized, nationalized narrative for AIDS: for even when science began to explore alternative possibilities, these purportedly "factual" constructions remained alive in popular culture, as with the green monkey. There is no doubt that the continued prominence of the question of origins has emphasized the geography of U.S. national borders as a contrast to the undifferentiated continent of Africa.

Although the global origins debate treated the United States as a undifferentiated unit of analysis, diffusion patterns within the United States serve as one place to begin examining regional differences. Shannon and Pyle suggested that AIDS arrived in the American South through Miami via the Caribbean.[31] They confirmed this finding in their 1991 study, identifying " 'incubator' neighborhoods" in New York City, San Francisco, Los Angeles, Miami, and Houston.[32] In this analysis, Atlanta was not a site of entry or origin for AIDS in the United States; rather, it was a site of secondary expansion. Their map suggested a causal link in diffusion between the Atlantic seaboard and the West Coast but did not identify a similar link between New York City and Atlanta, despite the clear transportation corridor that exists between the two cities. Although their 1991 study argues that "travel by air, and therefore, airline network connections were involved in the early diffusion of the HIV and the subsequent development of AIDS in not only large metropolitan centers, but also major resort areas," they never discussed Atlanta as one of the "incubator" sites, despite the presence of Hartsfield International, one of the country's busiest airports. Atlanta was not one of the cities in which AIDS originated, according to this model, despite the fact that by 1983, Georgia, whose initial cases were located mostly in Atlanta, was among the states with the top ten caseloads.[33]

Shannon, Pyle, and Bashshur's "travel by air" diffusion theory utilized the "Patient Zero" hypothesis. This idea, popularized by Randy Shilts, proposed that the inconceivable promiscuity of Canadian flight attendant Gaetan Dugas was the primary cause of the "gay-related immune deficiency" (GRID) epidemic, the first scientific construction to describe the strange cluster of illnesses appearing among gay men.[34] In *And the Band Played On*, Dugas roamed the transportation corridors of the United States, malevolently spreading his strange illness to as many men as he could to satisfy both his insatiable sexual appetite and his need to avenge his infection. Many researchers and critics have debunked Shilts's scientifically unsound but culturally resonant myth about Dugas's role as an individual in the dissemination of HIV.[35] However, the story does suggest that transportation corridors were critical to this process. For example, Abraham Verghese discovered that interstate highways represented an important connection between urban areas and seemingly isolated cities and towns in rural Tennessee, Kentucky, and Virginia.[36] But Shannon, Pyle, and Bashshur's diffusion model did not identify a seemingly obvious link between New York City and Atlanta, focusing instead on the "travel of homosexual males from the United States to Haiti—as Patient Zero had on occasion—and the migration of infected Haitians to the United States" to explain what they call "a substantial Gulf Coast pattern," the key geographic feature of AIDS diffusion in the Southern United States.[37] Identity, whether sexual or national, is set up as the cause of AIDS, a strategy of blame that would become all too familiar through the CDC's articulation of "risk groups."[38]

This description of AIDS's movement in the South had several problems. For one, the misguided focus on Dugas returned analysis to a national focus, mapping his travels to illustrate how he affected the United States as a whole. Further, the preoccupation with the Haitian origins of AIDS in parts of the South, to the exclusion of links between places such as New York City and Atlanta, recapitulated the politics of the search for AIDS's African origins by targeting a seemingly geographically distant, racially despised "Other." Shannon, Pyle, and Bashshur's model failed to explore the movement between the South and other sections of the country and within regions of the South itself.

Ashok Dutt and his colleagues offered a national diffusion model more sensitive to regional analysis in "Geographical Patterns of AIDS in the United States." Their mapping of the data demonstrated that Georgia's caseload developed quickly and remained comparatively high, and they contended therefore that AIDS was not simply a West Coast–East Coast phenomenon.[39] They did identify New York City, as well as the Caribbean, as contributing to the high incidence of AIDS in Florida, presenting a more sophisticated analysis of AIDS in the Southern United States by focusing on intersectional as well as international relationships.[40] As they explored the geography of AIDS, they attempted to provide demographic data by region. However, their regionalization patterns were based on a South so sprawling and diverse as to be almost useless, ranging from the Atlantic Ocean to the Arizona–New Mexico border.[41] In their 1981–1987 comparisons, the South seemed to exhibit typical mortality rates, a patient group with high rates of sexual transmission (as opposed to intravenous needle sharing or other transmission modes), a higher number of people of African or Haitian birth than other regions, a relatively large number of young people with AIDS, and a patient group whose racial composition was close to the national aggregate, with far fewer people of color than the Northeast but far more than the West.[42] This attempt at regionalization was important but questionable given the definitions of region they used.

Shannon, Pyle, and Bashshur suggested that it was possible to chart the geography of AIDS "relatively accurately" from 1984, when the CDC began to chart statistics by state.[43] However, these accounts from the 1980s constructed the origins of AIDS in a way that resulted in an emphasis on AIDS as primarily a national phenomenon. A model to describe the different patterns of caseloads within a broadly defined South has yet to be developed.[44] The omission of Atlanta—seemingly the most "modern" city of the South in its similarity to the urban industrial Northeast—from a theory which proposed that such cities were the sites of origin of AIDS in America points to the inadequacies of this work.

Dateline Nowhere: *The Commercial Media, the Construction of Knowledge, and the Search for Regional Identity*

The paradigm of origins suggested by these diffusion models was not merely a subject of debate among scientists involved in epidemiological research but was widely popularized by the commercial media in the

United States. The entry of such theories into these popular outlets represents an important moment in the history of AIDS, especially given the
media's significant role in the construction of Americans' knowledge,
ideas, and beliefs about AIDS. As with medical geography, the cultural
implications of location seldom surfaced in the commercial media, except
to define a geography of risk. In Atlanta, the daily newspapers' reliance
on epidemiological paradigms for AIDS set up a fundamental contradiction about place that reflected a broader tension about the significance of
region to the stories the *Atlanta Journal* and *Atlanta Constitution* were
telling about the city in which they are located.

The media have had a profound influence on both perceptions of and
policies about AIDS. As Charles Rosenberg argued, the "AIDS epidemic"
existed only in the media for many people who had no lived experiences
with AIDS:

> For most Americans—insofar as this epidemic can be construed as a na-
> tional phenomenon—it is a media reality, both exaggerated and diminished
> as it is articulated in forms suitable for mass consumption. The great major-
> ity of Americans have been spectators, in but not of the epidemic.[45]

Certainly, the media did not represent an exclusive source of information
or narrative authority. For example, in his discussion of AIDS and African
Americans, Harlon Dalton pointed out that "the mass media are scarcely
the only avenues of communication in the black community," citing the
example of the African American church as an alternative site for education.[46] Conversations, storytelling, and oral traditions remain important,
informal modes of communication and instruction for many Southerners—in fact, in some cases they may be more important methods, for
newspapers and other print forms continue to face the challenge of high
rates of illiteracy in parts of the South. However, Gary Moore sees a
connection between print and oral communication in the South: "Southerners like a good story, and they like a good story well told, and they like
to see it in the newspaper."[47] There is a relationship between the stories
people tell and the stories they read. Joseph Goodwin explored this connection in his study of AIDS jokes. Many of the jokes he collected followed "waves" of media coverage: a 1984 media blitz identifying the
syndrome, the 1985 announcement of Rock Hudson's illness, and a lesser
wave surrounding Ryan White's attempts to go to school in Kokomo,
Indiana.[48] As Goodwin's work demonstrated, media narrative has a great
deal of influence on other kinds of knowledge and communication in a

culture saturated with information technology and may produce values that help frame debate as information travels from print into oral tradition.

One of the ideas popularized by the media was the notion that once AIDS had arrived somewhere, its "experience" had no important regional variation. This assumption emerged out of the earliest AIDS reporting in the 1980s. According to James Kinsella, the greatest initial coverage of AIDS came from the Associated Press (AP) Wire Service, a service that seems to cover everywhere while having no location of its own.[49] AP writers work under great deadline stress, with little time for detailed research. So in covering this curiosity, a disease picking away at society's marginal groups (the way the AP first covered AIDS), there was one stationary, constant, and reliable source of information: the CDC in Atlanta, which publishes the *Morbidity and Mortality Weekly Report*.[50] The focus on the CDC foregrounded a construction of AIDS as an undifferentiated national phenomenon because of the CDC's primary unit of analysis in 1980s: the risk group. While such groups may have been found in specific locations, within this framework these locations had no culturally significant regional specificity.

In addition to explaining what was happening, the media in the 1980s struggled with how to feel about AIDS. James Kinsella used Vincent Coppola's work to illustrate this process. A writer covering the Southeast from Atlanta for the national news magazine *Newsweek*, Coppola was one of the reporters most active in the early coverage of AIDS. He had a personal stake in his reporting: His brother Thomas, a resident of New York City, had AIDS. Anxious for information that could help his brother, Coppola focused on the medical mystery being tackled at the CDC. Kinsella noted that to justify the time he was spending there, Coppola had to "generate more interest" in the AIDS story. He created an emotional hook for his stories by describing what he saw during his visits to New York to see his brother, where he witnessed "the horror" of "men battling death." Kinsella argues that the function of the weekly news magazines, with their seven-day publishing cycle, is "to put the news in perspective" rather than to break stories.[51] Coppola created perspective by providing an emotional structure for the "disease."

The problem is that place plays a part in determining social experiences of AIDS, creating variation even among the cities considered most alike. For example, Philip Kayal noted this difference between New York City and San Francisco:

While the urgency of dealing with AIDS was the same in San Francisco, gays there had achieved a modicum of political power. Hence AIDS has been less a political crisis and more a health and service issue in that city. In New York, gay political impotence, relatively indifferent mayors, and the power of the Catholic archbishop there clearly make AIDS a continuous political crisis.[52]

If such structural factors so dramatically affected the social experience of AIDS, they must have affected emotional experiences as well. Coppola's work, while important as one of the early sources of coverage, helped create an emotional discourse for the "AIDS experience" that did not reflect the specificities of regional experiences. In the absence of awareness of the role of place, a structure of feeling that reflected a specific class position in a specific location was generalized into a universal national experience.[53]

In the 1980s, the dateline *Atlanta* marked a contradictory discursive space, for in the print media this place name was almost always a reference to a federal institution: the CDC.[54] This replacement of local with national meaning effectively eclipsed local experiences of AIDS in the city's daily newspapers until 1985.[55] The dearth of local coverage was not unique to the AIDS story. In Atlanta, the tendency of the daily newspapers to focus on the region-blind approach of the CDC was exacerbated by conflicts around the meaning of place. According to Gary Moore in the *Columbia Journalism Review,* reporters at the *Atlanta Journal* and *Atlanta Constitution (AJC)* in the early and mid-1980s were writing during a period in which the regional identity of Southern journalism was very much contested. Moore stated that

> the story of the South's quest to know (or not know) itself, through its journalism, could make a monumental narrative, particularly timely now when a lot of people are saying that whatever it was that may or may not have been special—or horrible—about the South, and about its journalism, is gone with the wind. Begun among the chains of slavery, the rambunctiousness of southern journalism may now be dissipating like exhausted swamp gas among the info boxes and migratory managers of the newspaper chains.[56]

In Moore's eyes, a unique, historic tension between affirmation and self-reflection had marked the mission of Southern journalists since sectional conflict about slavery and racial segregation. On the one hand, Southern newspapers were supposed to "make the community feel good about itself—because nobody else was." On the other hand, "the 'crusading country editor' syndrome" demonstrated the opposite impulse: to name, record, and confront injustice.[57]

In the Reagan "Sunbelt" of the 1980s, the rise of big newspaper chains—such as Cox Enterprises, owner of the *AJC*—seemed to signal the demise of this kind of Southern journalism. Moore characterized the struggle as follows:

> The soul of southern journalism today may be said to be under contest by two main camps—those who see the South as basically no place special anymore, with southern journalism being like any shiny sprocket in chain news; and those who say, Well, yeah, okay—but the South still *breathes*. Its essence may be hard to write down as a broad "I" or a narrowed eye, but it's there, despite the difficulty of digitizing it.[58]

At the *AJC* in the early to mid-1980s, proponents of the "no place special" position were clearly in power, for this era in the paper's history was a time when self-critical "crusading" was shunned. According to Bill Cutler in another *Columbia Journalism Review* piece, Jim Minter, editor of the *AJC* from 1980 to late 1986, was perceived as being "far too respectful of local authorities and institutions." His deference to local power, both political and economic, led reporters to feel they were supposed to "back off from controversy," thus compromising the spirit of investigative journalism. As a result, morale plummeted and many good writers left for other papers. An outside evaluator in 1985 described the *AJC* as "one of the most unhappy papers I've been in." John Fleming, a former senior editor at the *AJC*, characterized the papers under Minter as "asleep."[59] What Moore described as a "national trend 'toward comfort journalism' " had the effect at the *AJC* of discouraging aggressive, challenging investigative reporting into local issues.[60] This situation reached a point of crisis in the late 1980s, when Bill Kovach was hired as editor. Eric Guthey argues that for a short-lived moment between 1986 and 1988, Kovach lifted the paper out of the "haven for mediocrity and soft business coverage it had become." But Kovach's resistance to New South boosterism proved his undoing, and he was fired in the *AJC*'s push to look and read more like *USA Today*.[61]

This history suggests that the *AJC* should be a suspect source of local narrativity because it is a product of a vision in which the South retains a distinct regional identity only as a kind of titillating curiosity (exemplified by the *AJC*'s problematic "Dixie Living" section). Although it may be true that the *AJC* resembles *USA Today* more than anything else, the absence of a self-articulated regional identity informed by the history of Southern journalism that Moore describes does not mean that the *AJC* cannot be a source of information about the role of region in local experiences of AIDS. While not the only available AIDS narrative in Atlanta, because it commanded so large an audience it served as the theater for the people Rosenberg described as "spectators in but not of the epidemic"—those who had little or no personal experiences with AIDS. As the *AJC* constructed a drama about AIDS in Atlanta in the 1980s, it created the players, both heroes and villains; the critical moments; and the moral lessons. Although the *AJC*'s stories cannot be taken to represent anything other than what they are—one of many possible narratives produced by a complex of individuals operating within a system with a clear social relationship to the status quo—the framing of local issues by this "mainstream" paper reveals some of the dynamics of power operating in Atlanta's experiences of AIDS.

"It's Hard to Ignore Something like That": AIDS and the AJC

The complex politics of location in Atlanta's daily papers make them a particularly useful site for exploring how place affected perceptions of AIDS.[62] It is impossible to point to a moment in which Atlanta claimed AIDS as its own. Rather, we find many such moments in the stories of individuals and institutions. The narrative about AID Atlanta's founding is an example of one version of how a group of Atlantans came to experience AIDS as something local in the early and mid-1980s.

When and how did the *AJC* recognize that AIDS was a concern in the city of Atlanta? Obviously, such a realization took place gradually. If we accept Rosenberg's formulation of epidemics as narrative, then 1985 represents the turning point in this process, as the significant jump in the amount of coverage shows.[63]

By that year, the *AJC* was describing AIDS as a feature of Atlanta's "gay community" and, having "diagnosed" and defined that "epidemic," contemplated uneasily the signs that sexual identity bounded it falsely. The development of this narrative in the *AJC*'s AIDS reporting in the early and mid-1980s allows us to see some of the ways in which regional characteristics affected social experience(s) of AIDS in Atlanta.

The earliest stories about AIDS published by the *AJC* were CDC reports of "gay cancer" in New York, San Francisco, and Los Angeles. Most of those stories came from the wire services. When *AJC* science and medicine

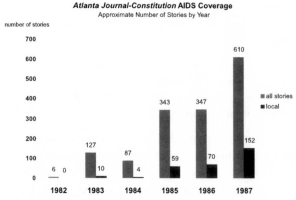

Local is defined as discussing some aspect of AIDS and Georgia, including Georgia federal legislators but excluding the CDC.

reporter Charles Seabrook did write a brief piece in June 1982, it was to note that "a rare type of deadly cancer that has reached epidemic proportions among homosexual men now is occurring in alarming numbers among heterosexuals, the U.S. Centers for Disease Control reported today."[64] It was the "heterosexual threat" that apparently motivated the paper to research its own story. As a science and medicine reporter, Seabrook focused on the CDC's efforts to define and understand AIDS, which offered few tools for regional analysis.

The wire service stories began to articulate "lifestyle" as a cause, which ultimately developed into the distinction between the "innocent victims" of AIDS and those who, by implication, were guilty.[65] For example, a 5 March 1982 story explained that researchers were exploring the possibility that "drug habits common in the gay community play a part in the development of Kaposi's sarcoma."[66] A March 31 story pointed out that these men had been diagnosed with "a rare form of skin cancer usually seen mostly in Africa," foreshadowing the origins debate.[67] In June the *AJC* reported that "scientists . . . are unsure what role, if any, homosexual activity has in triggering the diseases."[68] These stories illustrate the genesis of the elements of blame as they appeared, before a coherent narrative existed to unite them.

By contrast, the *AJC*'s coverage of Atlanta's "gay community" in the first half of 1982 did not even mention these health issues.[69] The key topics discussed in a meeting between the mayor and lesbians and gay men in April 1982 were police brutality and the appointment of openly gay men and women to the city and police force.[70] Several articles discussed the political battle concerning a city proclamation of Gay Pride Day, which Mayor Andrew Young refused to sign. Said the mayor by way of explanation:

> I believe that it is inappropriate for governments to proclaim or comment on the sexuality of private individuals. . . . I do not think it is necessary or desirable to single out groups of people based on their sexual preference, whatever their contributions may be.[71]

This strategy of silence contrasted vividly with the approach being consolidated at the CDC, whose litany of risk groups "singled out" this very group of people by their sexuality again and again. AIDS would force Atlanta to confront the differences between Young's stance and the CDC's tactics, particularly during the bathhouse controversy of 1985.

In 1983, reports that AIDS could be spread by casual contact sparked the first of three media peaks identified by James Kinsella. The *AJC* joined in with a dramatic increase in AIDS coverage, focusing on the safety of the blood supply and the "Haitian connection." It also brought AIDS home with a front-page feature in the February 13 Sunday paper about the experiences of Charles, a resident of Atlanta and a gay man living with AIDS.[72] The article reported that 409 Americans had died of AIDS and that "most of its victims—about 75 percent—have been homosexual males, like Charles." It then noted, "The nation's gay communities therefore have been dealing for almost two years with an epidemic that researchers say could soon attack the public at large." This language suggested that "homosexual males," as well as "hemophiliacs, Haitians, intravenous drug users and a few infants," were not part of that "public." The article did attempt to address the question of homophobia:

> Homosexuals are understandably defensive about the disease, which for a time was informally called the "gay plague." Theirs is a subculture already plagued with stigmas from a larger society that regards their sexual habits as unconventional. To them, the prevalence of the disease in homosexuals— and the backlash from groups like the hemophiliac foundation—stigmatizes them further.

The story attempted to treat Charles with respect and allowed him to speak in his own voice. However, its use of the risk-group structure also safely contained him, undermining the writers' attempts to counteract prejudice.

In this piece, the *AJC* considered the relationship of AIDS and region for the first time. The authors offered the following speculation:

Some authorities on Atlanta's gay community cite a sexual conservatism
bred of Southern culture as one reason the disease has not hit hard here.
Many Atlanta gays are from small Southern towns, where promiscuity—
whether it be homosexual or heterosexual—is frowned upon. Others say
the disease simply has not landed here in full force yet . . . Atlanta, after all,
is a national crossroads.

This story recognized the travel corridors in which geographers were
interested. It also raised important questions about the Atlanta gay community's experiences with AIDS, insofar as one "gay community" exists.
When this construction appeared in the *AJC*, it referred generally to white
men in urban areas with enough class privilege to gain access to medical
and social service institutions. But this article suggested that within this
group, the relationship of sexuality to gay liberation may have been
figured differently in the predominantly rural and historically religious
South than in other places. At the time of this article, there were fifteen
reported cases of AIDS in Georgia, and nine deaths.[73]

In June 1983, the newspaper covered the remarks of Seventh District
congressman and John Birch Society national chair Larry McDonald at a
meeting of the North Georgia John Birch Society at a Cobb County hotel,
where McDonald suggested a "user tax" on participants in AIDS research
programs as a way to finance such investigations.[74] Then controversy over
zoning for a proposed all-male health club was reported as splitting the
gay community, particularly because a gay man with AIDS initiated the
protests. This coverage specified the local geography of AIDS even further
when the *Atlanta Journal* reported that Charles Barden, "the 30-year-old
Atlanta hairdresser," lived "in the Virginia-Highland area," thereby invoking an important local unit of distinction: the neighborhood.[75] The *Atlanta
Constitution* divulged even more details: "He has been crusading to block
the opening of an all-male health club about 150 feet from his home on
Amsterdam Avenue."[76]

In July the *AJC* reported that "AIDS fear [was] increasing among gays,"
as the Georgia caseload rose to twenty-seven, and described "paranoia"
among the estimated 125,000 gay residents of the metropolitan Atlanta
area. As evidence of changes in the "gay community," the authors cited
an organization meeting for AID Atlanta attended by "a crowd of 80 gay
men—most of whom . . . had never before joined a gay organization of
any type." One of the attendees, David Harris, described an increase in
monogamous relationships among gay men as "shot-gun marriages," an
interesting metaphor that may suggest the beginnings of a kind of re-

gional imagery. The article also suggested that Atlanta was less concerned about AIDS than was San Francisco or New York, citing the previously mentioned zoning struggle as the only time that "AIDS has sparked public debate here."[77] Clearly, this feature limited AIDS in Atlanta to gay men, although it did mention that lesbians were also organizing to raise money for AIDS. And while AIDS had certainly become a local issue, it had not reached the scale of other cities.

At the end of the year, AID Atlanta approached the county and city with a funding request. The group wanted to establish "a 10-hour daily AIDS hotline and a screening clinic" and asked the Fulton County Board of Health "to formally declare AIDS . . . a public health emergency in Atlanta."[78] City councilwoman Mary Davis supported the proposed program, which "focused primarily on homosexual males, but . . . also serve[d] intravenous drug users and Haitians," but in September the request for $10,000 was tabled. Some city council members apparently felt such programs should be the province of the Fulton County Health Department.[79] The possibility of public funding for the year-old group was raised again at the end of the month. The *AJC* noted that twenty-five of Georgia's twenty-eight cases of AIDS were in Atlanta. Ten people had died. The Fulton County Board of Health recommended that the funding be made available.[80]

This incident illustrates two important issues. First of all, it reveals the beginnings of an official reaction to AIDS and suggests some of the bureaucratic dimensions that would define public response, such as the relationship between Fulton County and the City of Atlanta. Second, it demonstrates the constructed exclusions in the *AJC's* narrative. Intravenous drug users and Haitians, two of the CDC's key "risk groups," were mentioned in the last sentence of the article describing the funding request. However, discussions of individuals' experiences of living with AIDS were situated entirely in a "gay community" of white men with economic privilege. In September, the *AJC* ran a major front-page feature on AIDS in Haiti, the pinnacle of its coverage of the island nation.[81] Like others before it, this article makes no mention of Atlanta's immigrant Haitian community, although their brief mention in the funding request article suggests that AIDS was impacting on some of them. In the *AJC's* narrative, AIDS in the United States (as opposed to African or Haitian AIDS) was thus far a white experience. This misrepresentation may reflect either judgments about "newsworthiness" or racial and class barriers to the services that caused AIDS to be publicly recognized. However, the demographic data from the *Geographic Review* suggest that there were many Atlantans whose stories were left untold.

Coverage dropped off in 1984 nationally as fears about casual transmission quieted, and the *AJC* followed suit, running 87 articles about AIDS compared to the previous year's 127. Local reporting also declined—whereas ten articles in 1983 discussed local experiences of AIDS, only four did in 1984. As in 1983, the *AJC*'s stories continued to concentrate on gay men and services in the gay community. However, its coverage changed dramatically in 1985. Kinsella has argued that 1985, the year of Rock Hudson, was the year America "discovered" AIDS.[82] It was certainly the year that the *AJC* discovered it—through a "celebrity" of its own.

The first part of 1985 witnessed a few isolated controversies about AIDS in the *AJC*. With a street specificity that enabled further local mapping of AIDS, the *AJC* described Fulton County's suit to close two bathhouses, the Locker Room Health Club on Cheshire Bridge Road and Club Atlanta on Fourth Street, both targets of vice squad investigations for violations of sodomy law, as well as health risks.[83] Delta Air Lines, headquartered in Atlanta, considered and rejected a proposal to bar people with AIDS from its planes.[84] Two inmates in the Georgia prison system were diagnosed with AIDS and "isolated before they reached the general population in a prison." This article pointed out that "seventy-three percent of reported cases occur in homosexual men; another 17 percent of AIDS victims are intravenous drug users, and a small number of cases are linked to blood transfusion," reflecting the CDC's revision of its "risk group" list to remove Haitians and hemophiliacs.[85] At the end of June, AID Atlanta held a service at All Saints' Episcopal Church on West Peachtree, attended by three hundred people, in the memory of those who had died.[86] In late July, the Rock Hudson diagnosis was revealed in the national media.

But Atlanta had a story of its own, indicating clearly that the city had developed a local AIDS narrative distinct from the national one—although the two remained oddly conjoined. On July 30, the wire services broke a story revealing that a cancer clinic in the Bahamas was using blood products that were possibly infected with HIV in cancer treatments. The most well known American patient was former Georgia governor Lester Maddox.[87] The *Atlanta Constitution* ran the story in a local news summary on page 18. The next day Maddox was on the front page of the *Constitution*, praising the clinic and revealing his intent to test for the virus, despite his belief that he had not contracted it.[88] He was back on the front page on August 1, when a report indicated that serum he had used had tested positive for HIV.[89] On August 28 he was on the front page of the C section, "grinning broadly" because his own blood test was "clean as a whistle."[90]

AIDS was no longer isolated in Atlanta's gay community in the story being told by the two papers. In the national media, Rock Hudson made AIDS real for Americans otherwise untouched by lived experience of it. For the first time, everyone "knew" someone who had AIDS. Likewise, many Georgians could now identify someone they "knew" whose life had been touched by AIDS. There is a key difference between the two stories, however. Until 1985, the majority of *AJC* reports associated AIDS with gay men. The Rock Hudson story fit this pattern: Revelations of the popular actor's sexuality positioned him as one more "homosexual" undone by his lifestyle. Maddox, in contrast, was being treated in a medical clinic. In the rhetoric of AIDS discourse, that made him an "innocent victim"—an especially ironic twist, given Maddox's staunch defense of segregation during his political career. Although the *AJC* did not use this phrase, enough stories had run in the paper that distinguished between people who acquired the virus through "passive" means, such as blood transfusions, and those whose "improper" or criminalized behavior had resulted in HIV infection to suggest this possibility. Maddox represented the threat of AIDS to the "general population" and the end of the safety that some readers could find in not belonging to any of the CDC's risk groups.

Perhaps not incidentally, the state apparatus began to move into gear in 1985, with the formation of a state task force on AIDS in the fall. By September, Georgia had 216 cases of AIDS, with almost 75 percent concentrated in the metropolitan Atlanta area, moving the state from eleventh to ninth in state totals.[91] The task force was charged with recommending policies to limit the spread of disease. The state government under Governor Joe Frank Harris remained largely unresponsive, with the exception of metropolitan Atlanta representatives such as Jim Martin.[92] And in the *AJC* fear still ran high, as exemplified by high-profile coverage of the confusion over how to "decontaminate" a police car in which a person with AIDS had had a nosebleed. Officials contacted a hazardous waste disposal company and were told that "the material and equipment used [would] have to be disposed of."[93] A state epidemiologist finally volunteered to clean the car in order to demonstrate that fears about touching it were unfounded.[94]

In 1986, local coverage continued to increase and change character. The most-reported issues concerned the school attendance of children with AIDS, despite the fact that, by August, "only three children in Georgia [were] currently known to have AIDS."[95] AID Atlanta (whose director, Ken South, emerged in the paper as the voice of the "AIDS community"), the state task force, and the legislature struggled with legislation introduced by Representative Billy McKinney of Atlanta that, in its original form, would have permitted quarantine, required testing for all pregnant women, and empowered the state to test and isolate "at-risk" individuals at will.[96] Atlanta pastor Charles Stanley, president of the Southern Baptist Convention, described AIDS as God's displeasure at America for its tolerance of homosexuals, spawning controversy and protest.[97] The legislature considered and rejected a mandatory reporting bill.[98] The Atlanta arts community rallied to the cause, producing both AIDS-themed productions and fund-raisers.[99] The governor's office blocked a grant to AID Atlanta because protesters argued that allocation of money for an explicit same-sex education pamphlet would amount to state funding for illegal sodomy.[100] The Georgia AIDS Task Force released a report in June which advocated that children and employees with AIDS remain in their schools and workplaces.[101] Delta removed Mark Sigers, a San Francisco man with AIDS who was visiting family in Atlanta, from one of its planes, apologizing to avoid a boycott.[102] By early September, Georgia had 495 reported cases of AIDS. The chair of the state task force suggested that as many as 49,500 Georgians might be infected.[103] The *AJC* began to consider AIDS in the metropolitan Atlanta area.[104]

One indication of the changes in coverage was the emergence of gender as an issue in the *AJC*. In these stories, women represented the threat of AIDS to the presumptively male heterosexual "general public." For example, Atlanta municipal court judges took it upon themselves to counsel "johns"—men accused of soliciting prostitution—of the dangers they faced and of their potential to spread the disease to their wives and to the heterosexual population at large.[105] There was a great deal of discussion about the mandatory testing of convicted prostitutes, despite the fact that studies designed to test the rates of HIV infection among sex workers in Atlanta showed very low results. The debate about prostitution also raised the possibility of requiring testing for "high-risk" pregnant women.[106]

Self-conscious discussions of race also entered the *AJC* for the first time since interest in the origins of AIDS had faded, when the paper reported on the Southern Christian Leadership Conference's (SCLC's) concern with

the rate of AIDS among African Americans. Spokesperson Sandra Mc-
Donald blamed the media for underreporting, noting that while African
Americans comprised around 25 percent of the national caseload, they
accounted for 29 percent of Georgia's caseload.[107] The SCLC's challenge
reveals that more than one AIDS "epidemic" was present in Atlanta, and
this one had been unnoticed or ignored by the *AJC* and by the power
structures on which the newspaper reported. The failures in its AIDS
coverage reflected the larger context of the *AJC*'s difficulty in reporting
constructively on African Americans. According to Bill Cutler, in the past
the *AJC* had had a "troubled relationship with the city's black community," alternating between "overly harsh criticism of local black leaders
and overly scrupulous reluctance to find fault with them." Under President David Easterly, who came to the *AJC* in 1982, the paper attempted to
be more "careful" and less "reckless" in its writing on Atlanta's African
American community.[108] In the case of AIDS, this caution was taken to a
dangerous extreme. Where there was no coverage, there could be no
controversy about content. The *AJC* clearly distorted the story of AIDS in
Atlanta by omitting the voices of African Americans from its reports.

   In the *AJC* in the 1980s, AIDS emerged as a feature of Atlanta's presumptively white "gay community." In constructing certain "victims" the
AJC erased others, which may partially explain the absence of self-conscious discussions of race. Silences on the subject of race in the *AJC* also
reflected a broader cultural anxiety about how to address the history of
racism in science. As Georgia State University psychologist Dr. Roger
Bakerman pointed out to the *AJC*, "Researchers have been 'afraid to talk
racially' about the disease. After all . . . we have had a century of scholarship where whites have studied blacks not to their benefit." However, he
suggested that the generic use of the term *gay* hid the disproportionate
impact AIDS had on African American gay men: In 1986, gay white men
accounted for sixty-five cases per million, whereas gay African American
men accounted for ninety-three cases per million.[109] The white face of
AIDS in Atlanta in the *AJC* clearly obscured the actual demographics of
disease, as well as indicating both what "newsworthy" meant and the
problems of access to medical care for many Atlantans.

What Region Reveals

What does the *AJC*'s coverage of the emergence of AIDS as a local issue
suggest about the importance of region in understanding the social expe-

riences of AIDS in Atlanta? In many ways, the *AJC*'s narrative seemed to follow the structure of the national media's narrative: For example, when Ryan White struggled to go to school in Indiana, Georgia schools struggled with AIDS policies. However, to dismiss any regional effect is to overlook complex and important factors that structured experiences of AIDS in Atlanta. In most mainstream newspapers in the United States in the 1980s, AIDS was perceived as a "gay disease." While the *AJC*'s narrative certainly reflects this general assumption, the primacy of sexual orientation in its analysis of AIDS also reflects two specifically regional factors: the strong influence of religion and the state sodomy law.

The prominent role that Christianity plays in cultural life in the South may have helped focus discussions of AIDS on sexual identity, given the preoccupation of some American Christians with issues of sexuality and sin. But while religion clearly fueled homophobia, as in the case of Rev. Stanley, it also energized AIDS activism. Actions often took the form of memorial services, prayer services, and protests in which ministers spoke. For example, religion represented a powerful source of resistance in the *AJC*'s description of a "healing service" at St. Philip Episcopal Church, attended by four hundred people, the first such service in Atlanta: " 'My faith in the institutional church has been restored,' said George Leich, a resident of Atlanta who said he has been suffering from AIDS-related viruses for more than four years."[110] Religion served as a basis for political organization as well as personal strength. To challenge Rev. Stanley's homophobic remarks, 350 people formed "a 'circle of prayer' around his downtown Atlanta church." They then held "a service of their own with some Baptist-style testifying, a collection and songs."[111]

Even the *AJC*'s constant identification of Ken South with the title "Reverend" indicated a religious dimension to local responses to AIDS in the 1980s, given AID Atlanta's prominent role in the *AJC*. Philip Kayal locates the private response to AIDS represented by AIDS service organizations in the "rebirth of American volunteer ideology under President Ronald Reagan."[112] This political analysis helpfully illuminates volunteerism in the context of the failure of federal response. However, the visibility of churches and religion in the *AJC* as not just the enemy but also a source of strength and resources suggests that the increased religiosity of life in the South may inform the politics of volunteerism with an additional dimension. Gay men with AIDS were not just coming home to their families—they were coming home to their churches as well, churches that may have played significant roles in their lives. When those churches chose to welcome them, people with AIDS found a much-needed support network. This kind of activism may not seem "political" from the vantage of New York–style activist street theater, but in Atlanta's social context it often proved a courageous response, as gay activists and AIDS activists explored political strategies effective within the cultural environment of Atlanta and the Deep South. To equate religion only with homophobia and AIDSphobia distorts its role in the construction of local responses to AIDS.

As for the state sodomy law, it was clearly a barrier to the efforts of AIDS activists to educate Atlantans about safer sex. It also served as an unspoken but critical subtext to the "homosexual" as high-risk group. Because HIV can be sexually transmitted, to identify as a gay man with AIDS was to admit to breaking the law. As Haitians and hemophiliacs were withdrawn from the CDC's list of risk groups, homosexuals and intravenous (IV) drug users were left. In the state of Georgia, unlike California or New York, both are criminals. The focus on female prostitutes as the harbingers of heterosexual AIDS makes sense in the context of a narrative logic that links AIDS and criminalized sexualities. Charles Rosenberg's model for epidemics proposed that the "progressive revelation" of an epidemic was followed by a period of "managing randomness." In Georgia, this management was accomplished through the social identification of groups whose criminal status served as a key justification for the abrogation of their rights as individuals, in order to protect the law-abiding "general public." Representative McKinney's quarantine, test-at-will bill was ultimately dropped by the legislature when the state attorney general ruled that the bill was redundant, because the state *already held* such powers.

Rosenberg's theory could also explain the tremendous interest in the issue of children with AIDS in 1986, despite the very low incidence of actual cases. This interest demonstrates that Atlanta, like the rest of the United States, was constructing multiple narratives about AIDS. In Georgia, the establishment of a discourse of criminality served to contain the original threat. Because children were assumed to have acquired HIV through "noncriminal" means, such as blood transfusion, birth, or breast-feeding, they fell outside this discourse. The school attendance controversy in 1986 represents the progressive revelation of another epidemic, which the discourse of criminality could not explain.

Just as the sodomy law affected responses to AIDS, AIDS affected responses to the sodomy law. The year 1986 was the one in which the U.S.

Supreme Court upheld Georgia's statute in *Bowers v. Hardwick*, which was wending its way through the courts in 1985. In a 1985 article on the case, *AJC* political editor Frederick Allen pointed out that

> a new element has stormed to the top of the barricades: the threat of acquired immune deficiency syndrome. The old argument centered on moral philosophy and a question of whether the Constitution could be interpreted to contain a "right of privacy" that protected adults in the pursuit of consensual sexual encounter. The new argument ignores morality and asks whether certain homosexual practices, as a medically proven source of AIDS, constitute a public health menace.[113]

Interestingly enough, the state of Georgia chose not to include AIDS as a justification when it defended the sodomy law before the Supreme Court. The issue was raised in amicus briefs filed by people such as David Robinson Jr., a professor of law at George Washington University. In an October 1986 article in *Commentary*, a conservative monthly opinion magazine, Robinson expressed outrage that Georgia would decline to include AIDS in its justification, for the threat of AIDS provided a clear, compelling state interest in the regulation of private behavior. His connection of the legal issue of sodomy to public health was evident in this criticism of the American Psychological Association's support for repeal of Georgia's statute:

> I could understand how an organization dedicated to placing the highest value on civil liberties [the American Civil Liberties Union] . . . might well support a constitutional right to engage in sodomous behavior. . . . I could not understand how an organization dedicated to safeguarding the nation's health could do so.[114]

The proximity of AIDS and criminalization of sexuality—Georgia state law prohibits certain acts, regardless of the genders of the partners—produced a situation in which certain basic rights, such as freedom from government interference, could be set aside. The Georgia example demonstrates the importance of understanding AIDS regionally. To rely on solutions that are effective in California or New York, where structural barriers like the sodomy law are absent, invites failure. Strategies must address regional and local situations.

The *AJC*'s coverage reveals the struggle of a city to come to terms with AIDS in the early and mid-1980s. Although AIDS was new, it was experienced through ideologies of race, class, and gender as well as sexuality and religion—ideologies that were, at least in part, the product of local histories. To understand the process by which AIDS acquired meaning(s) requires an analysis not just of the present but of the past and of social context as well, such as the ways in which Atlanta is a Southern city as well as a major metropolitan area. Unfortunately, it was precisely this sense of history that was under contest within the leadership of the *AJC* in the early and mid-1980s.

By the end of the decade, the *AJC* attempted to assume greater responsibility. In 1989, it ran a long feature called "When AIDS Comes Home," recording "the life and death of Tom Fox," an advertising account representative for the paper. Like the recent film *Philadelphia,* this well-intentioned piece was designed to raise sympathy and awareness about an experience of living with AIDS. Such pieces may represent the greatest achievements possible in the commercial media, which seldom adopt the radical politics of street activists and community organizers. What is most ironic, however, is that the feature brought AIDS home without a full accounting of what "home" means. What continued to be absent was any kind of analysis of how living in Atlanta affected Tom Fox's experiences with AIDS.

In its struggle to understand AIDS as a local issue, the *AJC*'s story reveals some of the complications of region in the United States in the late twentieth century. AIDS has been called a postmodern epidemic, and if "postmodern" is taken to represent, in part, the collapse of binary oppositions, it certainly applies here.[115] The distinction between national and local is tenuous at best, and always in danger of disintegration. Atlanta is a specific place. It is also the location of national federal institutions. And local issues about the American Red Cross Atlanta chapter policies are inseparable from the policies of the national American Red Cross leadership. Delta is headquartered in Atlanta but is an international carrier. The Lester Maddox story was first reported with a *New York* dateline by one of the national wire services and was carried in newspapers around the country, much like the Rock Hudson story. And in 1986, Georgia's sodomy law was a national issue before the Supreme Court, setting policy for the nation. Even defining who an Atlantan is becomes confusing. Like most urban spaces, Atlanta has a mobile population of people from all over the country and, increasingly, the world.

This is not to suggest that region is a concept inappropriate to modern, or postmodern, urban settings. Rather, it is to conclude that like AIDS itself, region is not just a material phenomenon but a constructed social experience, which can be illuminated as it illuminates. Clearly, region is critical to understanding the factors that structured the unique local experiences of AIDS in Atlanta—factors that must be addressed in order to create the best and most just responses possible. Such responses are desperately needed. According to the CDC, 13,343 people in Georgia had been diagnosed with AIDS through June 1995. More than five thousand people were reported to be living with AIDS.[116] Despite the dramaturgic closure AIDS narratives may exhibit, lived experiences of AIDS continue as a very real part of our present.

To return to the initial question: In the early and mid-1980s, was Atlanta "inside," listening to a distant, gathering storm? The obvious answer is no. The more accurate answer is that in a space like Atlanta, distinctions between inside and outside are always in the process of collapse. The narrative of AIDS in the *AJC* suggests that although there were some similarities, Atlanta had qualitatively different experiences from places like San Francisco, Los Angeles, or New York City. It also suggests that Atlanta was not like the Charleston that Harlan Greene described. Perhaps the clearest lesson of all is that terms developed in other places will not adequately explain the ways in which AIDS was experienced in Atlanta. For Atlanta and the South, as well as for all the other places where social experiences of AIDS have been unarticulated or misarticulated, the task is to tell the stories of how it happened there. Then, perhaps, we can begin to share our stories and find what common ground may exist—not by translating those stories into our own terms, for that represents the writing of another, new story, but by developing metaphors that are as respectful of the ways in which we differ as they are of the ways in which we are the same.

NOTES

1. Charles Rosenberg, "What Is an Epidemic? AIDS in Historical Perspective," *Dædalus* 118, 3 (summer 1989): 2.

2. For example, Norman Rene's film *Longtime Companion* (Santa Monica, CA: Vidmark Entertainment, 1990) uses the *New York Times* article in this fashion. See also Allen Barnett's story "The *Times* as It Knows Us," in *The Body and Its Dangers and Other Stories* (New York: St. Martin's Press, 1990), pp. 62–117; and Randy Shilts, *And the Band Played On* (New York: Penguin Books, 1988), pp. 76–77.

3. As recounted by a speaker from AID Atlanta at the Candlelight AIDS Vigil during Lesbian, Gay, and Bisexual Pride Weekend, Atlanta, GA, 1994.

4. Thomas Yingling, "AIDS in America: Postmodern Governance, Identity, and

Experience," in *Inside/Out,* ed. Diana Fuss (New York: Routledge, 1991), p. 303: "Myths of identity have framed the interpretation of AIDS, and it remains a disease that attaches itself—rightly or wrongly—to identities."

5. Shilts, *And the Band Played On,* xxii. Shilts attempts to establish that AIDS traveled from Africa to Europe and then to the United States, but his interest in this theory is not to understand AIDS's effects in Africa but the path AIDS took to the United States. Simon Watney offers a critique of this preoccupation in *Practices of Freedom* (Durham, NC: Duke University Press, 1994), pp. 98–101.

6. Harlan Greene, *What the Dead Remember* (New York: E. P. Dutton, 1991), p. 145.

7. Ibid., p. 179.

8. The complex politics of the language(s) of AIDS are evident in the struggle to find terms to describe the experiences we are discussing. We now have an acute awareness of the (political) effects of language and the power of names in the context of AIDS. The label "epidemic" was displaced in AIDS activist circles in the 1980s by "crisis" in order to call attention to the horrific failings of city, state, and federal service providers and to the active role of homophobia and AIDSphobia in preventing people's needs from being addressed. But reminding us that AIDS has become for some a part of daily life, activist and critic Cindy Patton questions in whose interests and in what contexts it is useful to characterize AIDS as a crisis. For more, see Cindy Patton, *Inventing AIDS* (New York: Routledge, 1990), pp. 106–7. Given this shifting terrain, I will use simply the term *AIDS* to refer to social experiences of living with HIV disease. The danger is that this word will be read as a clinical term rather than a socially constructed phenomenon of multiple and, at times, contradictory meanings, but it seems to be the most accurate and careful for now.

9. There are a number of interesting recent works that address questions of geography. Cindy Patton has consistently addressed spatial aspects of the epidemic in her work, particularly in her recent piece "Performativity and Spatial Distinction: The End of AIDS Epidemiology," in *Performativity and Performance,* edited by Andrew Parker and Eve Kosofsky Sedgwick (New York: Routledge, 1995), 173–96. Peter Gould's *The Slow Plague: A Geography of the HIV Pandemic* (Oxford: Blackwell Publishers, 1993) is commendable for its attempt to illustrate the wide range of AIDS geographies, from the micro- to macroscopic, but remains problematically committed to the African origins theory. Finally, essays in the recent collection *Mapping Desire,* edited by David Bell and Gill Valentine (London: Routledge, 1995), offer important models for incorporating place as well as space into geographical analyses of AIDS, a necessary move in order to address concepts like region.

10. Gary W. Shannon, Gerald F. Pyle, and Rashid L. Bashshur, *The Geography of AIDS: Origins and Course of an Epidemic* (New York: Guilford Press, 1991), p. 118: "It is notable that the 'interior' of the United States did not experience substantial numbers of AIDS cases."

11. See U.S. Department of Health and Human Services, *HIV/AIDS Surveillance Report* 6, 2 (year-end 1994): 36, for a description of the revised surveillance case definition. Cindy Patton's *Last Served? Gendering the HIV Pandemic* (London: Taylor & Francis, 1994) is an excellent source on the gender(ed) politics of AIDS.

12. Shilts, *And the Band Played On*, pp. 56, 64.

13. Douglas Crimp, "AIDS: Cultural Analysis/Cultural Activism," in *AIDS: Cultural Analysis/Cultural Activism*, ed. Douglas Crimp (Cambridge, MA: MIT Press, 1988), p. 3.

14. Rosenberg, "What Is an Epidemic?" pp. 2–5.

15. Ibid., p. 12.

16. Hayden White, *The Content of the Form: Narrative Discourse and Historical Representation* (Baltimore: Johns Hopkins University Press, 1987), pp. 3–4, 24.

17. Rosenberg, "What Is an Epidemic?" p. 12.

18. Dr. Peter Duesberg is the scientist most well known for challenging the relationship of HIV and AIDS. Simon Watney offers a critique of Duesberg's position in *Practices of Freedom*. Whatever the problems in Duesberg's work, AIDS activists such as Michael Callen (*Surviving AIDS* [New York: HarperCollins, 1991]) have also voiced concern about the sufficiency of HIV in explaining AIDS. Although I am aware of this controversy and the many unanswered scientific questions about acquired immune deficiency, in this chapter, I assume that HIV is related or connected enough to AIDS that we can speak of people affected by HIV and include people living with AIDS among them.

19. Good examples of this kind of discourse analysis are Jan Zita Grover, "AIDS: Keywords," and Paula A. Treichler, "AIDS, Homophobia, and Biomedical Discourse: An Epidemic of Signification," in *AIDS*, ed. Crimp.

20. Watney, *Practices of Freedom*, p. 256.

21. Elizabeth Fee and Daniel Fox, "Introduction: AIDS, Public Policy, and Historical Inquiry," in *AIDS: The Burdens of History*, ed. Elizabeth Fee and Daniel Fox (Berkeley: University of California Press, 1988), p. 4.

22. White, *Content of the Form*, p. 25.

23. Patton, *Inventing AIDS*, p. 2.

24. *Experience* is another one of the terms that cultural critics have interrogated. I use it provisionally to indicate that living is material and "real" but also socially constructed. For more, see Joan Scott, "Experience," in *Feminists Theorize the Political*, ed. Judith Butler and Joan Scott (New York: Routledge, 1992), pp. 22–40.

25. Gary W. Shannon and Gerald F. Pyle, "The Origin and Diffusion of AIDS: A View from Medical Geography," *Annals of the Association of American Geographers* 79, 1 (March 1989): 12. It is important to note that they do not conclude with finality that AIDS originated in Africa but rather propose this possibility based on a model that can locate no evidence of movement of HIV into Africa from elsewhere.

26. Renee Sabatier, *Blaming Others: Prejudice, Race, and Worldwide AIDS* (Philadelphia: New Society Publishers, 1988), p. 38.

27. Despite its many problems, one of the contributions of *And the Band Played On* was to demonstrate irrefutably the inefficacy of U.S. scientific and social service institutions in the face of AIDS.

28. Sabatier, *Blaming Others*, p. 63.

29. Richard C. Chirimuuta and Rosalind J. Chirimuuta, *AIDS, Africa, and Racism* (London: Free Association Books, 1989), p. 71. There are various viruses that cause immune suppression in animals, such as SIV in monkeys and feline immunodeficiency virus (FIV) in cats, but to date there is no evidence that any of them can affect humans. However, they have been the subject of much research because some scientists are hopeful that understanding these viruses may provide clues for slowing or stopping HIV.

30. Shannon, Pyle, and Bashshur, *Geography of AIDS*, p. 112.

31. Shannon and Pyle, "Origin and Diffusion," pp. 13–17.

32. Shannon, Pyle, and Bashshur, *Geography of AIDS*, p. 112.

33. Ron Taylor, "Fear of AIDS Leads Some to Postpone Elective Surgery," *Atlanta Constitution*, 27 April 1983, sec. A, p. 1, col. 2, for Georgia statistics. Shannon, Pyle and Bashshur do include Atlanta in a table of cumulative AIDS rates, listing a case load of 2,316, the tenth highest of the metropolitan statistical areas mentioned. This table represents the only mention of Atlanta in their book. See *Geography of AIDS*, 130–31.

34. Shilts, *And the Band Played On*, p. 147: "A CDC statistician calculated the odds on whether it could be coincidental that 40 of the first 248 gay men to get GRID might all have had sex either with the same man or with men sexually linked to him. The statistician figured that the chance did not approach zero—it was zero."

35. For an excellent if brief critique of Shilts's use of Patient Zero, see Simon Watney, "Politics, People, and the AIDS Epidemic: *And the Band Played On*," in *Practices of Freedom*, pp. 98–100. For an equally pointed take, see the John Greyson film *Zero Patience* (New York: Cinevista, Inc., 1994), a musical about a love affair between an immortal Sir Richard Burton and the ghost of Patient Zero.

36. Abraham Verghese, *My Own Country* (New York: Simon & Schuster, 1994), pp. 94–96.

37. Shannon, Pyle, and Bashshur, *Geography of AIDS*, p. 118.

38. AIDS educators have countered this problem by pointing out that viruses cannot recognize social identities, and that it is behaviors involving the exchange of some body fluids that allow the virus to be transmitted.

39. Ashok K. Dutt, Charles B. Monroe, Hiran M. Dutta, and Barbara Prince, "Geographical Patterns of AIDS in the United States," *Geographic Review* 77, 4 (October 1987): 456–71.

40. Ibid., p. 458.

41. Ibid., p. 461. Dutt and his colleagues use the CDC's regionalization pattern.

42. Ibid., pp. 463–69. It is important to remember that this article was published in 1987 and that the demographics of AIDS in the South have changed in significant ways since, especially as reporting has improved based on changes in the diagnostic definition. More recent information can be obtained from the U.S. Department of Health and Human Services' *HIV/AIDS Surveillance Report*, published twice annually.

43. Shannon, Pyle, and Bashshur, *Geography of AIDS*, p. 111.

44. One of the very few exceptions can be found in a brief, speculative article by Abraham Verghese, Steven Berk, and Felix Sarubbi, "*Urbs in Rure:* Human Immunodeficiency Virus Infection in Rural Tennessee," *Journal of Infectious Diseases* 160, 6 (December 1989): 1051–55.

45. Rosenberg, "What Is an Epidemic?" p. 12.

46. Harlon L. Dalton, "AIDS in Blackface," *Dædalus* 118, 3 (summer 1989): 210. Dalton is aware that *community* in the singular is a problematic term, and he uses it provisionally.

47. Gary Moore, "Southern Journalism: Gone with the Wind? Seems like Nobody Is Left to Name Names and Kick Ass," *Columbia Journalism Review* 30, 5 (January/February 1992): 32. Moore identifies the roots of Southern oral traditions in both African and Celtic culture.

48. Joseph P. Goodwin, "Unprintable Reactions to All the News That's Fit to Print," *Southern Folklore* 46, 1 (1989): 20. Goodwin does not attempt a regional analysis of these jokes, but his extensive index documents where they were collected.

49. James Kinsella, *Covering the Plague: AIDS and the American Media* (New Brunswick, NJ: Rutgers University Press, 1989), p. 3.

50. Ibid., pp. 48–50.

51. Ibid., pp. 88–93.

52. Philip M. Kayal, *Bearing Witness: Gay Men's Health Crisis and the Politics of AIDS* (Boulder, CO: Westview Press, 1993), p. 9.

53. Class is significant, because Kinsella suggests that Coppola saw a good part of this "horror" accompanying Thomas to Sloan-Kettering for treatment. For people without clear access to health care, the "experience" might have been quite different.

54. For example, Atlanta makes many appearances in *And the Band Played On* as the setting for dramas played out at the CDC.

55. The *Atlanta Journal* and *Atlanta Constitution* can be treated as a single unit, the *AJC*, due to both corporate structure and a joint weekend edition. In the context of AIDS, their shared staff is particularly apparent, for much of the early reporting was done by the same writers, Charles Seabrook and Ron Taylor.

56. Moore, "Southern Journalism," pp. 31–32.

57. Ibid., p. 31.

58. Ibid., p. 34.

59. Bill Cutler, "Trying to Make Atlanta's Papers 'World-Class,'" *Columbia Journalism Review* 26, 6 (March/April 1988): 40–41.

60. Moore, "Southern Journalism," p. 32.

61. Eric Guthey, "The Press as Company Store, Atlanta Style," *Southern Changes* (December 1988): 8–10.

62. The quotation in the head to this section is from Hal Straus, "AIDS Fear Increasing among Gays," *Atlanta Journal-Constitution*, 10 July 1983, sec. D, p. 1, col. 2.

63. Source: *Atlanta Journal-Constitution* subject index, January–July 1982, 1983–1987; see search term *Acquired Immune Deficiency Syndrome* (except for 1982, see *gay cancer*; AIDS not in use. Published indexing of the *AJC* is not available for 1981 or the second half of 1982. The stories discussed here were published between January and July 1982).

64. Charles Seabrook, "Rare Cancer on Increase," *Atlanta Journal*, 11 June 1982, sec. A, p. 6, col. 1.

65. For more on the politics of "lifestyles," see Paula Treichler, "AIDS, Homophobia, and Biomedical Discourse: An Epidemic of Signification," in *AIDS*, ed. Crimp, pp. 31–70.

66. "Medicine," *Atlanta Journal*, 5 March 1982, sec. B, p. 6.

67. "Rare Cancer Found Among Homosexuals," *Atlanta Journal*, 31 March 1982, sec. A, p. 8.

68. Associated Press, "New Homosexual Cancer Link," *Atlanta Journal-Constitution*, 5 June 1982, sec. B, p. 3, col. 4.

69. The *AJC* used the term *gay community* in the singular, but clearly, socially salient differences such as race, class, and gender have produced more than one such community in Atlanta.

70. Lynne Anderson, "Gay Crowd Hails Mayor's Speech," *Atlanta Journal*, 13 April 1982, sec. C, p. 2, col. 1.

71. Gail Epstein, "Gay Pride Day Fails to Win Young's OK," *Atlanta Constitution*, 16 June 1982, sec. A, p. 12, col. 4.

72. Ron Taylor and Charles Seabrook, "AIDS: The Killer That No One Understands," *Atlanta Journal-Constitution*, 13 February 1983, sec. A, p. 1, col. 3, p. 14, col. 2.

73. I have some hesitation about adopting the *AJC*'s measurement of AIDS through the number of cases, a strategy popularized by Randy Shilts. Some activists, particularly those associated with the Names Project Memorial Quilt, have responded with a "names not numbers" strategy, in order to personalize the incomprehensibility of such counts. However, the *AJC* faithfully reported these figures, and it does serve as one limited point of comparison with other cities.

74. Ron Taylor and Ellie Susman, "McDonald Suggests 'User Tax' to Pay for Research on AIDS," *Atlanta Constitution*, 7 June 1983, sec. A, p. 12, col. 3. The name

Cobb County may be familiar from recent national coverage of its antigay "family values" resolution and the successful protest launched by Olympics Out of Cobb to remove an Olympic volleyball event from a venue there.

75. John Lancaster and Connie Green, "Foes Fighting All-Male Club, Citing Fears about AIDS," *Atlanta Journal*, 13 June 1983, sec. A, p. 10, col. 2.

76. Connie Green and John Lancaster, "Gay Health Club Foes Fear Spread of AIDS," *Atlanta Constitution*, 16 June 1983, sec. A, p. 29, col. 1.

77. Hal Straus, "AIDS Fear Increasing among Gays," *Atlanta Journal-Constitution*, 10 July 1983, sec. D, p. 1, col. 2, p. 3, col. 1.

78. Nathan McCall, "AIDS Group Appeals to Fulton for Help," *Atlanta Constitution*, 28 July 1983, sec. A, p. 28, col. 1.

79. Katheryn Hayes, "Davis Loses in Bid for AIDS Plan," *Atlanta Constitution*, 16 September 1983, sec. A, p. 19, col. 2.

80. Scott Thurston, "AIDS Counseling Agency Asking Government for Help," *Atlanta Constitution*, 30 September 1983, sec. A, p. 23, col. 2.

81. Ron Taylor, "AIDS Adds to Haiti's Woes," *Atlanta Journal-Constitution*, 11 September 1983, sec. A, p. 1, col. 3.

82. Kinsella, *Covering the Plague*, p. 4.

83. James Alexander Jr., "Fulton Plans Suits in Effort to Close Two Male Bathhouses," *Atlanta Constitution*, 7 February 1985. sec. B, p. 17, col. 1.

84. Rob Levin, "Delta Ends Plan to Deny Flights to AIDS Victims," *Atlanta Constitution*, 18 February 1985, sec. A, p. 3, col. 2.

85. Bill Montgomery, "Two Inmates Have AIDS, Officials Say," *Atlanta Journal*, 19 April 1985, sec. D, p. 16, col. 6.

86. Ron Taylor, "Memorial Service Held for AIDS Victims," *Atlanta Constitution*, 1 July 1985, sec. D, p. 3, col. 1.

87. "Cancer Clinic Has AIDS Scare," *Atlanta Constitution*, 30 July 1985, sec. A, p. 18, col. 1.

88. Nancy White, "Cancer Patients Urge Reopening of Bahamas Clinic," *Atlanta Constitution*, 31 July 1985, sec. A, p. 1, col. 2.

89. David Corvette, "Maddox Says His Serum Tested Positive for AIDS, Hepatitis," *Atlanta Constitution*, 1 August 1985, sec. A, p. 1, col. 2.

90. David K. Secrest, "AIDS Examination Reveals Maddox Is 'Clean as a Whistle,' " *Atlanta Constitution*, 28 August 1985, sec. C, p. 1, col. 4.

91. Connie Green, "Task Force to Examine Funding AIDS Treatment," *Atlanta Journal*, 13 September 1985, sec. C, p. 4, col. 2.

92. Jim Galloway, "AIDS Panel to Tackle Tough Task," *Atlanta Journal-Constitution*, 22 September 1985, sec. B, p. 1, col. 4, p. 9, col. 1.

93. Connie Green, "Police Uncertain How to Decontaminate Car Where Arrested AIDS Victim Had Nosebleed," *Atlanta Journal-Constitution*, 28 September 1984, sec. B, p. 7, col. 1.

94. Connie Green, "Health Official Offers to Clean AIDS-Contaminated Squad

Car," *Atlanta Constitution*, 2 October 1985, sec. A, p. 10, col. 5; Larry Copeland, "AIDS-Infested Car Gets a Good Scrubbing," *Atlanta Constitution*, 3 October 1985, sec. A, p. 29, col. 1.

95. Charles Walston, "School Boards Try to Deal with Subject of AIDS in the Classroom," *Atlanta Constitution*, 11 August 1986, sec. E, p. 1, col. 1, p. 3, col. 4.

96. "AIDS Task Force Says Legislator Misled Group," *Atlanta Journal-Constitution*, 5 January 1986, sec. B, p. 2, col. 5; Ann Woolner, "McKinney Defends Proposed AIDS Bill," *Atlanta Constitution*, 7 January 1986, sec. A, p. 24, col. 1; Ron Taylor, "Task Force on AIDS against Bill Requiring Disease to Be Reported," *Atlanta Journal*, 3 February 1986, sec. D, p. 8, col. 5; idem, "AIDS Test Reporting Bill Opposed by Task Force," *Atlanta Constitution*, 4 February 1986, sec. A, p. 13, col. 4; Jim Galloway, "Panel OKs Bill Requiring List of AIDS Carriers," *Atlanta Constitution*, 5 February 1986, sec. A, p. 8, col. 1; idem, "House Panel Rejects Having State Collect Names of AIDS Carriers," *Atlanta Constitution*, 6 February 1986, sec. A, p. 50, col. 1; idem, "House Approves Bill to Require Reporting AIDS Cases to State," *Atlanta Constitution*, 14 February 1986, sec. A, p. 12, col. 4; "Senate Panel's Cuts in AIDS Bill Anger Task Force Members," *Atlanta Constitution*, 28 February 1986, sec. A, p. 11, col. 1.

97. Associated Press, "Stanley: God Is Using AIDS to Punish Gays," *Atlanta Journal-Constitution*, 18 January 1986, sec. A, p. 2, col. 3; Ron Taylor, "Stanley Calls AIDS 'Judgment upon Sin, Not Homosexuals,'" *Atlanta Journal-Constitution*, 2 February 1986, sec. C, p. 1, col. 2, p. 8, col. 6; Priscilla Painton, "Stanley's Remarks on Gays, AIDS Draw Protesters at Church," *Atlanta Constitution*, 10 February 1986, sec. E, p. 1, col. 2.

98. See note 96, above.

99. Linda Sherbert, "AIDS Theme Is Challenge to Dramatists," *Atlanta Journal-Constitution*, 27 July 1986, sec. J, p. 1, col. 1, p. 4, col. 5; idem, "AIDS Benefit Will Pull Your 'Heart Strings,'" *Atlanta Constitution*, 20 February 1986, sec. C, p. 1, col. 2, p. 2, col. 1.

100. Ron Taylor, "AID Atlanta Official Protests Loss of Grant," *Atlanta Journal*, 21 March 1986, sec. A, p. 16, col. 1.

101. Renee D. Turner, "Task Force Winds Up AIDS Study," *Atlanta Constitution*, 27 June 1986, sec. A, p. 18, col. 1.

102. Burt Roughton Jr., "AIDS Victim Tries to Find a Way Home," *Atlanta Constitution*, 7 August 1986, sec. C, p. 1, col. 1, p. 6; idem, "Eastern Lets Stranded AIDS Victim Fly Home," *Atlanta Constitution*, 8 August 1986, sec. A, p. 14, col. 1, p. 18, col. 1.

103. Ron Taylor, "Almost 50,000 in Georgia May Be Infected with AIDS Virus," *Atlanta Constitution*, 17 September 1986, sec. A, p. 10, col. 1.

104. Jan Hillings Gable, "Few Cases of AIDS Reported by Area Hospitals," *Atlanta Journal-Constitution*, 28 November 1985, sec. IX (Clayton Co. Extra ed.), p. 1, col. 1, p. 6, col. 2.

105. James Alexander Jr., "Judges Warning 'Johns' against Danger of AIDS," *Atlanta Constitution*, 10 July 1985, sec. A, p. 9, col. 1.

106. James Alexander Jr., "Judge Offers Deal for AIDS Tests in Sex Crimes," *Atlanta Constitution*, 18 March 1986, sec. C, p. 2, col. 1; Charles Seabrook, "Results from Tests of Atlanta Prostitutes Show No Signs of AIDS Virus," *Atlanta Journal-Constitution*, 26 April 1986, sec. B, p. 2, col. 1; Fran Hesser, "Judges Should Order AIDS Tests for Prostitutes, Board Says," *Atlanta Constitution*, 18 December 1986, sec. C, no. 4, col. 1.

107. Donna Williams Lewis, "Blacks and AIDS Are the Main Focus of National SCLC Forum Being Held Here," *Atlanta Journal-Constitution*, 22 May 1986, sec. XE (Intown Extra ed.), p. 7, col. 1; Ron Taylor, "Blacks High AIDS Risk Spurs Push for Warning Campaign," *Atlanta Journal-Constitution*, 5 October 1986, sec. D, p. 1, col. 1, p. 8.

108. Cutler, "Atlanta's Papers," p. 40.

109. Taylor, "Blacks High AIDS Risk," sec. D, p. 1, col. 1, p. 8.

110. Gustav Neibuhr, "Four Hundred Attend Special Healing Service for AIDS Victims," *Atlanta Constitution*, 23 June 1986, sec. E, p. 1, col. 1.

111. Priscilla Painton, "Stanley's Remarks on Gays, AIDS Draw Protesters at Church," *Atlanta Constitution*, 10 February 1986, sec. E, p. 1, col. 2.

112. Kayal, *Bearing Witness*, p. 5.

113. Frederick Allen, "AIDS Threat New Factor in Sodomy Fight," *Atlanta Constitution*, 3 September 1985, sec. A, p. 2, col. 1.

114. David Robinson Jr., "Sodomy and the Supreme Court," *Commentary* 82, 4 (October 1986): 59.

115. Rosenberg, "What Is an Epidemic?" pp. 13–14.

116. U.S. Department of Health and Human Services, *HIV/AIDS Surveillance Report* 7, 1 (mid-year 1995): 5, 29.

SOURCES

Bell, David, and Gill Valentine, eds. *Mapping Desire: Geographies of Sexuality.* London and New York: Routledge, 1995.

Callen, Michael. *Surviving AIDS.* New York: HarperCollins, 1991.

Chirimuuta, Richard C., and Rosalind J. Chirimuuta. *AIDS, Africa, and Racism.* London: Free Association Books, 1989.

Crimp, Douglas, ed. *AIDS: Cultural Analysis/Cultural Activism.* Cambridge, MA: MIT Press, 1989.

Cutler, Bill. "Trying to Make Atlanta's Papers 'World-Class.' " *Columbia Journalism Review* 26, 6 (March/April 1988): 40–45.

Dalton, Harlon L. "AIDS in Blackface." *Dædalus* 118, 3 (summer 1989): 205–28.

Dutt, Ashok K., Charles B. Monroe, Hiran M. Dutta, and Barbara Prince. "Geographical Patterns of AIDS in the United States." *Geographic Review* 77, 4 (October 1987): 456–71.

Fee, Elizabeth, and Daniel Fox, eds. *AIDS: The Burdens of History.* Berkeley: University of California Press, 1988.

Goodwin, Joseph P. "Unprintable Reactions to All the News That's Fit to Print." *Southern Folklore* 46, 1 (1989): 15–39.

Greene, Harlan. *What the Dead Remember.* New York: E. P. Dutton, 1991.

Greyson, John. *Zero Patience.* Zero Patience Productions, Inc., 1993; New York: Cinevista Inc., 1994.

Guthey, Eric. "The Press as Company Store, Atlanta Style." *Southern Changes* (December 1988): 8–10.

Kayal, Philip M. *Bearing Witness: Gay Men's Health Crisis and the Politics of AIDS.* Boulder, CO: Westview Press, 1993.

Kinsella, James. *Covering the Plague: AIDS and the American Media.* New Brunswick, NJ: Rutgers University Press, 1989.

Moore, Gary. "Southern Journalism: Gone with the Wind? Seems like Nobody Is Left to Name Names and Kick Ass." *Columbia Journalism Review* 30, 5 (January/February 1992): 30–34.

Patton, Cindy. *Inventing AIDS.* New York: Routledge, 1990.

———. *Last Served? Gendering the HIV Pandemic.* London: Taylor & Francis, 1994.

Robinson, David, Jr. "Sodomy and the Supreme Court." *Commentary* 82, 4 (October 1986): 57–61.

Rosenberg, Charles E. "What Is an Epidemic? AIDS in Historical Perspective." *Dædalus* 118, 2 (summer 1989): 1–17.

Sabatier, Renee. *Blaming Others: Prejudice, Race, and Worldwide AIDS.* Philadelphia: New Society Publishers, 1988.

Scott, Joan. "Experience." In *Feminists Theorize the Political,* edited by Judith Butler and Joan Scott, pp. 22–40. New York: Routledge, 1992.

Shannon, Gary W., and Gerald F. Pyle. "The Origin and Diffusion of AIDS: A View from Medical Geography." *Annals of the Association of American Geographers* 79, 1 (March 1989): 1–24.

Shannon, Gary W., Gerald F. Pyle, and Rashid L. Bashshur. *The Geography of AIDS: Origins and Course of an Epidemic.* New York: Guilford Press, 1991.

Shilts, Randy. *And the Band Played On: Politics, People, and the AIDS Epidemic.* New York: Penguin Books, 1988.

Tannen, Holly, and David Morris. "AIDS Jokes: Punishment, Retribution, and Renegotiation." *Southern Folklore* 46, 2 (1989): 147–58.

U.S. Department of Health and Human Services. *HIV/AIDS Surveillance Report* 6, 2 (year-end 1994); 7, 1 (mid-year 1995).

Verghese, Abraham. *My Own Country.* New York: Simon & Schuster, 1994.

Verghese, Abraham, Steven Berk, and Felix Sarubbi. "*Urbs in Rure:* Human Immunodeficiency Virus Infection in Rural Tennessee." *Journal of Infectious Diseases* 160, 6 (December 1989): 1051–55.

Watney, Simon. *Practices of Freedom*. Durham, NC: Duke University Press, 1994.

White, Hayden. *The Content of the Form: Narrative Discourse and Historical Representation*. Baltimore: Johns Hopkins University Press, 1987.

Yingling, Thomas. "AIDS in America: Postmodern Governance, Identity, and Experience." In *Inside/Out,* edited by Diana Fuss, pp. 291–310. New York: Routledge, 1991.

Chapter Fifteen

Queering the South

Constructions of Southern/Queer Identity

Donna Jo Smith

The terms *southern* and *queer*[1] both come laden with a host of stereotypes, which we have all internalized to one degree or another. When combined, these stereotypes tend to conflict or conflate, depending on perspective. For some, the notion of a "southern queer" is an oxymoron, conjuring up images of a drag queen with a pickup truck and gun rack or of a dyke with big hair and Birkenstocks. For others, the term *southern queer* is redundant: Since the South is already an aberration, what is a southern queer but deviance multiplied? In other words, did Truman Capote really need to tell the world that he was a pervert? After all, he was from south Alabama. These varied conceptions of southern queer and the internal contradictions they reveal suggest some of the complexities involved in the development of historical projects such as *Carryin' On in the Lesbian and Gay South.*

With the publication of this anthology, we see region added as a category of analysis in the history of same-sex desire in the United States—a move that begins to address the obvious bias toward East and West Coast urban centers in queer U.S. history to date. Yet this anthology doesn't simply reflect a new subfield called "southern queer history"; it creates and defines that field as well, which suggests that it is not too soon to ask ourselves what is implied in the formation of specifically "southern" queer history projects.

For several years now, I have been exploring southern queer experiences through the life stories of older lesbians and gays in the South. This task has led me through the discontinuous terrains of lesbian/gay studies and southern studies, in search of an analytical framework that best illuminates these narrators' experiences. More often than not it has left me stymied, but it has raised a number of questions that I would like to sketch briefly here, in hope less of providing definitive answers than of opening up a much-needed dialogue. Foremost is the question of how "southern lesbian/gay" studies projects will define "southern" and "lesbian/gay." In other words, who and what are our subjects? What are we assuming about the relationship between "southern" and "lesbian/gay"? What are the identity models we will draw on to theorize "southern lesbian/gay" identity?

As paradoxical as some might find it, lesbian/gay studies and southern studies do have something in common: Scholars in both fields have expended a great deal of energy searching for the distinctiveness of their subjects, and both searches are mired in quicksand. Just when we're convinced we know what defines "southernness"—let's say, southerners have a stronger sense of place—we are confronted with the evidence that, historically, great numbers of southerners have packed up and left the region without a backward glance (O'Brien 1988, 216). And just when we think we have lesbian/gay identity boiled down to its essential ingredient—say, the specificity of same-sex desire in our subjects—these same subjects confess opposite-sex dalliances or enter heterosexual marriages.

But ... my readers might protest, It still means something to be "queer" or "southern," no? Even if we're not sure what? To which I would answer yes, it still means *something* to be queer and it still means *something* to be from the South or to identify as "southern." That we find it difficult to answer *what* in any conclusive sense does not undermine the effects these identities have in the world. It is our assumptions about this "what" that could prove difficult for us to negotiate, however.

As historian Donna Penn reminds us, "To the extent that the practice of history interprets and explains social, cultural, and political change, it must also delineate how those changes are produced, when and by whom, if they are to serve as 'lessons of history' " (1995, 40). As historians, our present concerns have everything to do with the interpretive frameworks we bring to our projects. It would be disingenuous for me to imply by omission that my motivations for creating southern lesbian/gay studies projects were not deeply personal and political. At base, I tell myself, my goal is to revise what gets constituted as southern, so that those definitions will include me—a project with great political import. It is also, however, an attempt to reconcile the incongruities, more apparent than real, in my own identities. As a white woman born and raised in a working-class, "respectable," fundamentalist Christian family in Pawnee, Alabama, who is now middle-class (in status if not materially), highly educated, and "out" in the academy as a radical lesbian-feminist and political activist, I don't easily fit into any of the definitions that are conventionally attached to "southern." And yet, of course, because I am from the South, I will be read within definitions of southern whether I choose to be or not, unless I were to attempt to hide this part of my experience or mask the telltale accent.

At one level, my interest in the historical experiences of queers in the South reflects a desire to create a narrative that would allow me to bring the seemingly disparate parts of my identity together, if only for a textual moment. Yet I am leery of this desire for synthesis, for given the normative definitions that coalesce around "the South" and "southern," (i.e., the South as more racist, sexist, heterosexist, etc. than the rest of the country), this desire seems suspect. I have had to ask myself what this "togetherness" would symbolize. Is reconciliation necessary, desirable, or even possible? The impulse to distance myself from dominant definitions of southern seems as suspect as the desire to create a definition of southern that could include me, however. Is this impulse a wish for a benign vision of my regional identity—one that would place me outside the oppressive structures of power that shape normative definitions of southern? Is it a search for a place of innocence? Whom would a potential reconciliation serve, and whom would it serve best? And perhaps most important (to return to the issue of my own assumptions about what constitutes "southern") who is this "we" I wish to make visible?

Because those of us creating southern queer histories will undoubtedly look to lesbian/gay U.S. histories and histories focused on the U.S. South as models, it seems critical that we examine carefully the definitions of lesbian/gay and southern implicit in these projects as we undertake the task of historicizing queer experiences in the South. To explore these questions in more detail, I will briefly outline some issues that complicate our notions of both queer identity and southern identity, before turning to an investigation of their intersections.

Lesbian/Gay Identity and the "Coming-out" Narrative as Model

In an act of self-reflexive criticism, historian Allan Bérubé notes that the identity model implicit in many of our historical narratives to date[2] closely resembles that seen in the "coming-out" narrative, which, in a crude form, goes something like this:

> People who are gay grow up in a heterosexual world, discover that they are gay, feel isolation and face the hostility of society, protect themselves inside a closet, leave home to come out of the closet, go to a city where they find and become a part of a gay and/or lesbian community and a gay movement.... (Bérubé 1990a, 1)

As Allan Bérubé has argued, our dependence on this identity model has led our histories to privilege certain kinds of visibility over others. Those who participated in institutions such as urban bar cultures and political organizations most closely fit the parameters of gay/lesbian experience modeled in the coming-out narrative and are thus more identifiable as "gay." Subjects whose lives have been lived outside those subcultures, whose other identities competed with or superseded their "gay" identities, or whose "gay" or "lesbian" identities are more ambiguously defined are marginalized by historical projects that focus on urban gay experiences and the political achievements of those communities.

The exclusions and omissions evident in this narrative illuminate the degree to which the coming-out model of lesbian/gay identity is predicated on modern notions of the autonomous individual. The assumption that subjects hold complete agency to construct their experience is evident throughout this narrative, whose "happy ending," or movement into lesbian/gay community, depends on the subjects' ability to clear a daunting set of obstacles. Ironically, lesbian/gay liberation movements, like civil rights and feminist movements, have argued strenuously that assumptions of the autonomous individual serve to mask the actual dynamics of power that effect our marginalization.

Why, then, do we accept as foundational for our political struggles and our histories a narrative that credits us with more power than we hold? Certainly, this concept appeals not only to lesbians and gays; in fact, it provides the bedrock for American ideology at large, as is seen in the "bootstrap" theory and Horatio Alger stories. Yet I think our attachment to the coming-out narrative as identity model serves political goals specific to our community. The act of coming out and the coming-out narrative have been considered foundational to the development of a lesbian/gay group consciousness. As Biddy Martin notes in her work on lesbian autobiography, "Self-worth, identity and a sense of community have fundamentally depended on the production of a shared narrative or life history and on the assimilation of individuals' life histories into the history of the group" (1993, 279). Since Stonewall, coming out has been used as an effective political tool, based on the logic that until gays and lesbians are "seen" as a significant minority voting group, we will not have access to civil or human rights. Dependence on this narrative reflects our efforts to fit the lesbian/gay experience into the preexisting group-identity models delineated by ethnic minorities, whose identities are thought to be displayed on their bodies, or publicly legible. Within this model, one has to be visible to *have* an identity.

Yet the extent to which the narrative conflates lesbian/gay identity with the ability, desire, or willingness to be "public" about one's same-sex desire presents problems for historians. While "outness" is valorized as a political act that signals one's maturity as a gay person, the coming-out narrative as identity model attaches the pejorative connotation of cowardice to those who aren't visible in the required ways (Bérubé 1990a, 1). Our notions of outness, however, need to be carefully historicized when theorizing lesbian/gay identity pre-Stonewall. As John D'Emilio observes in *Sexual Politics, Sexual Communities,* the term *coming out* was not widely used in the 1940s and 1950s, and when it was used, it was defined quite differently (1983, 20). To "come out" was not then conceptualized as a public or political act but rather described the process of acknowledging to oneself and to a select group of others one's same-sex desire. In this period, when a group lesbian/gay identity was yet to become visible in American culture, to either the heterosexual majority or to gays and lesbians, the act of making one's same-sex desire "public" was virtually unthinkable. Because U.S. culture lacked a frame of reference with which to politicize sexuality, to come out in this era would have simply meant acknowledging oneself a sexual pervert, making oneself a social pariah.

Also problematic is that the coming-out model invites us to believe that outness is a permanently obtainable state. But as Eve Sedgwick has observed, "The deadly elasticity of heterosexist assumption means that . . . people find new walls springing up around them even as they drowse" (1990, 68). Because the closet reproduces itself again and again in each new setting in which gay/lesbian subjects find themselves, we must "come out" repeatedly to attain even a provisional visibility. This imperative for repetition contradicts another notion inherent in the coming-out model: the presumed stability of lesbian/gay identity. As Judith Butler asserts, the fact that we must "perform" our sexual identities through repeated acts of outness establishes the *instability* of lesbian/gay identity.

Both the necessity of repetition and the fact that these performances cannot completely define us reveal the instability of the very identity category we are investigating (1991, 18).

That lesbian/gay identity, like all identity categories, is fundamentally unstable signals the ways in which the coming-out narrative as model doesn't even adequately contain the experiences of those it seems to privilege—urban, white, middle-class gay men—for this model reflects only what has been deemed "gay" about our subjects or what our subjects deem "gay" about themselves. Allan Bérubé illustrates the gaps that arise, both for historians and subjects, when we presume a stability in identity that doesn't exist. Describing an interview with a World War II veteran, Bérubé recalls that when he turned the tape recorder off, the veteran began discussing his grandchildren (1990b, 4). He had edited out those parts of his life that didn't fit his and his interviewer's preconceptions of "gayness." Bérubé makes visible some of this veteran's gay experiences in World War II, yet we learn little about how this veteran conceptualizes his heterosexual experience in relation to his "gay" identity. As historian Joan Scott has argued, the presumption that the identities of our subjects are self-evident leads us to naturalize their difference and reify the categories of "homosexual" and "heterosexual" that we set out to question (1993, 399).

Scott notes that our attempts to "make visible" the previously hidden experiences of marginalized groups elide the fact that our conceptions of experience are also constructed. While our histories have demonstrated the effects of repression and exploitation on marginalized groups, they have failed to examine the internal dynamics of the ideological systems that create the "categories of representation (homosexual/heterosexual, man/woman, black/white as fixed, immutable identities)" (1993, 400). Using histories of homosexuality as an example, Scott observes how these foundationalist assumptions have shaped our projects:

> In these stories homosexuality is presented as repressed desire (experience denied), made to seem invisible, abnormal, and silenced by a "society" that legislates heterosexuality as the only normal practice.... Resistance and agency are presented as driven by uncontainable desire; emancipation is a teleological story in which desire ultimately overcomes social control and becomes visible. (400)

While histories of homosexuality have made visible the regulatory effects of science, church, and state on the lives of gays and lesbians, in these works the categories "heterosexual" and "homosexual" are often treated as dichotomous rather than dialectical. Furthermore, our continued dependence on the "authority of experience" allows us to retain modern notions of the autonomous individual through the unproblematized assumption that "desire" simply constructs the agency necessary for our liberation, even as social constructionist theory challenges this assumption.

Ironically, it has been the successes of the gay liberation movement, grounded in an ethnic model of identity, that have created the cultural space in which to make gay/lesbian history. Assertions of the instability of lesbian/gay identity have raised fears among some scholars and political activists that this move will contribute to the heterosexist imperative to further erase us, an effort lesbian and gay historians have fiercely battled. But as Judith Butler has noted:

> Ought such threats of obliteration dictate the terms of the political resistance to them, and if they do, do such homophobic efforts to that extent win the battle from the start? . . . Which version of lesbian or gay ought to be rendered visible, and which internal exclusions will that rendering visible institute? . . . There is a political necessity to use some sign now, and we do, but how to use it in such a way that its futural significations are not foreclosed? (1991, 19)

Clearly, if we lived in a society where the gender of one's sexual partner was genuinely not at issue, then lesbian/gay identity or heterosexual identity would have no meaning or necessity. The instability of lesbian/ gay identity and heterosexual identity doesn't prevent the need to operate under these signs. But it is, perhaps, more useful to think about lesbian/ gay *identities*, as plural rather than singular, for an insistence on impossible levels of stability and visibility in our subjects will only distort histories of same-sex desire.

Southern Distinctions

If the voluminous literature on southern distinctiveness has proven anything, it is that in-group differences are at least as great as between-group differences. Whatever commonalities the Appalachian and the Charlestonian have around their regional identity are more than outweighed by their differences. Michael O'Brien argues that, "as usually practiced, the search for southern distinctiveness is a logical nightmare" (1988, 215). He asserts that the works that attempt to establish regional cohesion most often define "by taking the significant and crucial step of deciding upon value, that one thing matters more than another, that the Black Belt matters more than Knoxville, fundamentalism more than urban sociology, honor more than racism, white more than black, black more than white" (215). Historians engaged in this search for southern distinctiveness tend to find what they look for, aided by value judgments that determine which "facts" count the most.

This scholarship tends either to celebrate the South's "distinctions" or to disassociate itself from them. The work of sociologist John Shelton Reed does both. In the span of a single essay, "The South's Mid-Life Crisis," he both reinforces and dismantles the notion that the South is significantly different from the rest of the nation, concluding with the assertion that "to the extent that the South is held together—southerners' belief that they have distinctive things in common supplies the glue" (1993, 42–53). Surveying this literature on southern distinctiveness, one begins to suspect that the scholarship itself has provided a sizable proportion of the "glue." Reed himself is something of a "one-man industry" in that marketing niche which thrives on southern distinctiveness, for his creative mappings of southernisms have found a wide audience, both academic and popular.

Other historians have sidestepped the problems presented by this search for southern distinctiveness and declared that myths of "southernness" are as significant as any "realities" we could hope to define. While the South is both different from and similar to the rest of the country, and while separating myth from reality can serve useful purposes, it might be more fruitful for our historical projects to begin by examining how these myths have functioned. As George Tindal has observed, there are times when "a myth itself becomes one of the realities of history, significantly influencing the course of human action" (in Smith 1985, 5). Southerners and non-southerners, queers and straights alike, have all internalized these myths and stereotypes in varying degrees, and the myths have helped shape our definitions of *southern*. The literature on myth in southern history invites us to ask why, given that in-group differences have been found to be at least as great as between-group differences, southerners and non-southerners alike insist on seeing the South as so distinct.

Clearly, the South doesn't function simply as a region that we can demarcate on a map but operates as a "state of mind." What we often forget, however, is that "the North" is also a state of mind, for when placed in opposition to "the South," it exceeds its literal demarcations to include every non-southern region in the United States.[3] To understand how these myths function, it might be useful to think of them as ideological constructs set within binary oppositions. While the South is subordinated to the North in the cultural imaginary, the North depends for its meanings on the normative definitions attached to the South. John Shelton Reed has observed that "lurking in the background of almost any statement about the South, if not stated outright, is a comparison to the rest of the United States. If people say Southerners are lazy, or violent, or religious, they mean: compared to Northerners—not to Mexicans, to Martians, or to some absolute standard" (Reed 1993, 46). However, the opposite is also true: Northerners become efficient, energetic, and self-restrained only in opposition to southerners.[4]

Race is, of course, central to the maintenance of this North/South binary opposition. Although we know that people of color, and in particular African Americans, form a sizable percentage of the American South's population, southern identity is often discussed as if it were explicitly a white identity, revealing again the degree to which "southern" functions as an ideological construct. In the cultural imaginary, it is generally assumed that African Americans' ethnic identity will supersede any impulse they feel for a regional affiliation. Yet African Americans within the South are incorporated into definitions of *southern* when it suits the marketing purposes of "New South" chambers of commerce, often with images that correlate their presence with other natural assets, such as Spanish moss gracing the live oaks on the coastal plains.

As Eve Sedgwick suggests, "Contests for discursive power can be specified as competitions for the material or rhetorical leverage required to set the terms of, and to profit in some way from, the operations of such an incoherence of definition" (1990, 9). That the South is frequently characterized by qualities of both negative and positive excess (as more racist, more sexist, more classist, more heterosexist, and more violent, as well as more passionate, more religious, more polite, and more generous, than the rest of the nation) suggests that we must ask ourselves: Whom do these incoherences of definition around a North/South binary opposition serve, and whom do they serve best?[5]

America has long projected its "Queer Other" onto the South. And in the national cultural imaginary, definitions of the southern are regularly utilized to maintain myths of American innocence. We should question this North/South binary opposition, because it maintains structures of

power that oppress all historically marginalized groups: Popular definitions of *southern* depend on a political conservatism that marginalizes
queers, radicals, feminists, and non-Christians, as well as people of color
and working-class whites. Obviously, the South doesn't hold a patent on
the catalog of social ills attributed to it; yet it is also true, as Mab Segrest
has observed, that "white southerners—as American Family Freaks, racist
and immoral—have acted out our pathology at times with great zest"
(1985, 26).

Myths Southern and Queer

Theorizing the relationship between the southern and the lesbian/gay
requires us immediately to confront the fact that, as popularly defined,
these identity categories are ideological opposites. Mythic conceptions of
southern identity assume that southerners have greater attachments to
home, family, place, religion, and traditional gender roles, as interpreted
within a conservative discourse that defines family as exclusively heterosexual, same-sex desire as evil, and gender roles as essential. This version
of "southern" would seem to be a recipe for "queer" exclusion. Ironically,
myths of queer identity generally assume that any allegiances queers
(southern and non-southern alike) feel to home, family, place, region, and
religion should be secondary to our same-sex desire and/or identity. As
discussed earlier, the coming-out narrative as identity model assumes that
queer identity is inimical to the nuclear family and incompatible with
rural or small-town existence. This mythic narrative of lesbian/gay identity also implies that we all have relative amounts of agency and desire
with which to make these moves. Media representations of queers often
present us as urban, sophisticated, and upwardly mobile: This version of
queer would seem to be a recipe for southern exclusion, according to its
mythic definitions.

Of course, neither of these mythic models of southern and queer reflects our realities. Some queers from the South leave home, move to New
York City, and join Queer Nation. Other queers stay home, buy a double-
wide trailer, park it out back of their mama's place, and continue to direct
the church choir on Sundays. Some southern queers are Lesbian Avengers,
and some are fund-raisers for the Religious Right. Just as the coming-out
narrative and its implicit assumptions have helped create and sustain
notions of a unified lesbian/gay identity, myths and narratives of southernness help create and sustain notions of a unified southern identity.

Recalling once more George Tindal's assertion that the myths themselves often become "one of the realities of history, significantly influencing the course of human action," my point is not that we can usefully separate southern/queer myths from southern/queer realities but that because these myths will have a shaping effect on the lives of our subjects, they must be considered in our analyses (Smith 1985, 5).

One of the dangers for specifically southern lesbian/gay studies projects is that we will privilege an oversimplified visibility and stability in both *queer* and *southern* identity—that we will find what we go looking for and ignore those experiences that don't fit our preconcieved notions of the southern queer. For instance, one might reasonably assume that queers in the South would have no investment in identifying as southern. Like southern white radicals and progressives in general, however, many southern white queers share a perverse ambivalence about their region. The notion that one must return regularly "to renew the sense of horror," by now a cliché, has been variably attributed to both Carson McCullers and Tennessee Williams—southern queer writers and friends. (One can just imagine those two on the beach at Fire Island, scotched to the gills, arguing over who said it first.) Implicit in this anecdote is the assumption that these are white queers who are progressive on issues of social change. I suspect that many of us engaged in queering southern history will be more comfortable with subjects who hold this ideological perspective. There are, however, white southern queers who seem unfazed by such ambivalences: They are from the South, they like the South, and they will fly the Confederate flag proudly if they feel like it. "After all," they argue, "it's a part of our history. Sure, slavery and segregation were evil, but that's over now."

These are responses particularly marked as white, however. Again, we see the tendency of white southerners to respond to their regional identity in ways defensive, celebratory, and/or disassociative. I can't quite imagine a black queer southerner of Williams's and McCullers's generation wanting to "return regularly to renew the sense of horror," since that horror was frequently all too real.

I don't mean to suggest however, that southern queers of color have uncomplicated relationships to this region (the works of Randall Keenan and Shay Youngblood, to pick two examples, certainly suggest otherwise); only that we can't assume that a "perverse ambivalence" will characterize the experience of *all* queers in the South. In other words, we cannot assume that our subjects will share any particular ideological perspective regarding southern identity. While we obviously don't want to create all-white southern queer studies projects, if we allow "southern queer" to mean "white southern queer," if we do not fully "race" ourselves and our subjects, we will not decenter the white southern subject as "norm" and will end up reifying the myth that the South is white.

One myth that is particularly southern *and* queer reflects the notion that it's harder to be queer in the South than in the rest of the nation. Southern and non-southern queers alike have internalized this myth to the degree that it has had a significant effect on southern queer experiences. I have seen this myth surface dozens of times in conversations between both southern and non-southern queers, and it seems virtually impermeable to logical analysis. What could be more apparent, this myth assumes, than that queers in the South not only would want to leave home but literally would be *required* to leave home, as a matter of survival? And of course, like all myths, this one contains its grain of truth, reflecting some southern queer realities. Even the most cursory attention to current events, however, suggests that queers are made the target of hate crimes everywhere, and that hateful rhetoric toward queers is not only spewed by southern politicians. So one danger that our projects face is that we will reify myths both queer and southern, which once more function to maintain notions of national innocence.

If the lesbian/gay cultural imaginary has mapped visibility or outness onto urban bar cultures, it has mapped the closet onto rural areas, small towns, and small cities. These sites, which predominated in the South at the mid-twentieth century, are conceptualized as spaces of uniform, hegemonic oppression, with minimal, if any, lesbian/gay visibility and community. But one narrative I have collected vehemently resists these assumptions, raising questions about what kind of communities we are expecting to find and to whom they should be visible.

Eddie Sandifer's life story challenges popular conceptions of both southern and lesbian/gay identity (1991). Sandifer grew up in McComb, Mississippi, as the son of a Methodist minister, and moved to Jackson, Mississippi, as a young adult. He declares that he was always "open" about his same-sex desire and that his family was supportive. During the 1940s and 1950s, he argues, he received more harassment for being Communist than for his sexuality. Sandifer described dancing openly with men in a Jackson supper club as early as the late 1940s, with no negative repercussions: "The women would come in the front door with their husbands, and we would go out the back with them." His openness about his gay identity was, during this period, treated more as a novelty than as a serious transgression, and his experience was more typical than not for that area of Mississippi, he asserts. Sandifer's assertion here raises questions about regional variations in the rate at which binarized conceptions of sexual identity were culturally transmitted.

In contrast to Sandifer's experience in McComb and Jackson, police harassment of lesbians and gays in New Orleans and in Memphis was much more consistent and pronounced, Sandifer notes, based on his experiences there during frequent visits and those of friends who lived in these cities. Interestingly, Sandifer asserts that he first experienced harassment based on his sexuality during the early 1960s, when his involvement in the Civil Rights movement became known after he began housing Freedom Riders in his Jackson home. His account of the ways in which his sexuality was used as a weapon in local battles to maintain white dominance parallels similar reports surfacing in research on lesbian/gay experience throughout the South during the 1960s and reveals how ideologies of race and sex have been inextricably intertwined in the South.

I would argue that to best illuminate southern queer experiences, we must leave open questions of identity, both queer and southern, and explore how our subjects have negotiated their same-sex desire within this region and how that experience has been mediated by complex, intersecting identities. We should carefully consider how demands for visibility and stability in a southern/queer context could proscribe our historical vision and avoid assuming that our subjects experienced "outness" and the "closet" as dichotomous, or that they conceptualized urban bar cultures as inherently liberatory and community-building institutions. While projects that explore the development of public/political institutions and group consciousness are important, we need to avoid privileging such projects over studies that focus on the nuances of identity construction within individuals or specific locales.

Our projects will be stronger if we consider our subjects' *relationships* to popular definitions of the South and inquire about *their* definitions of *southern*, rather than presuming or requiring regional identification. We should ask ourselves: Where and with whom could queers be visible? How does each "where" differ or compare? What forces shape a sense of individual and group identities? When is one identity prioritized over another? Projects that use region as a prism through which to analyze how gender, race, class, and religious identities intersect in the formation of queer identity will eventually produce a more complex understanding of U.S. queer experiences and illuminate our understanding of how sexuality is constituted more generally in American culture and politics.

NOTES

1. My use of the term *queer* is meant to circumvent the limitations to our historical projects effected by the narrow model of lesbian/gay identity that has been utilized in many U.S. histories to date, so that identities and behaviors such as "bisexual" and "transgendered" and desires as yet unmapped and perhaps "unmappable" can be considered within my discussion. For a more complete discussion of both the assets and the liabilities reflected in the conceptual shift implied by the use of the term *queer* in historical projects, see Donna Penn's essay "Queer: Theorizing Politics and History," *Radical History Review* 62 (1995): 24–42.

2. Most useful for my purposes have been John D'Emilio's groundbreaking study *Sexual Politics, Sexual Communities: The Making of a Homosexual Minority in the United States, 1940–1970* (1983); Elizabeth Kennedy and Madeline Davis's *Boots of Leather, Slippers of Gold: The History of a Lesbian Community* (1993); Allan Bérubé's *Coming out under Fire: The History of Gay Men and Women in World War Two* (1990b); and Lillian Faderman's *Odd Girls and Twilight Lovers: A History of Lesbian Life in Twentieth-Century America* (1991).

3. While it is true that other regions of the United States are also conceptualized in opposition to the North or Northeast, I would argue that the North/South binary both supersedes and subsumes these regional oppositions. For instance, midwesterners usually suffer in comparison to northeasterners, who regard them with a certain amount of disdain, and vice versa; but those same midwesterners can still thankfully claim that at least they are not southern.

4. That the North both excludes and subsumes the South is further illustrated by an exercise Reed conducted with students, in which he asked them to list typical southern and American traits. What he found was that "southern traits" were the mirror image of the "northern" ones: "slow, not fast; generous, not greedy; religious, not materialistic; conservative, not progressive; and so forth." But significantly, when the point of comparison became the rest of the world, southerners suddenly became Americans: "progressive, efficient, and all the rest" (1993, 46).

5. To the degree that these myths are characterized by qualities of excess, they overlap with stereotypes of southern locales in a variety of geographical locations.

For instance, again in the U.S. context, similar myths and stereotypes circle around images of southern Europeans and Latin Americans.

BIBLIOGRAPHY

Bérubé, Allan. 1990a. "Fitting in": Expanding queer studies beyond the "closet" and "coming out." Unpublished speech presented at the Contested Zone Conference, Pitzer College, Claremont, CA, April.

———. 1990b. *Coming out under fire: The history of gay men and women in World War Two.* New York: Free Press.

Butler, Judith. 1991. Imitation and gender insubordination. In *Inside/out: Lesbian theories, gay theories,* edited by Diana Fuss. New York and London: Routledge.

D'Emilio, John. 1983. *Sexual politics, sexual communities: The making of a homosexual minority in the United States, 1940–1970.* Chicago and London: University of Chicago Press.

———. 1993. Capitalism and gay identity. In *The lesbian and gay studies reader,* edited by Henry Abelove, Michèle Aina Barale, and David M. Halperin. New York and London: Routledge.

Faderman, Lillian. 1991. *Odd girls and twilight lovers: A history of lesbian life in twentieth-century America.* New York: Columbia University Press.

Gerster, Patrick, and Nicholas Cords, eds. 1989. *Myth and Southern history.* 2 vols. Urbana and Chicago: University of Illinois Press.

Kennedy, Elizabeth, and Madeline Davis. 1993. *Boots of leather, slippers of gold: The history of a lesbian community.* New York: Routledge.

Martin, Biddy. 1993. Lesbian identity and autobiographical difference[s]. In *The lesbian and gay studies reader,* edited by Henry Abelove, Michèle Aina Barale, and David M. Halperin. New York and London: Routledge.

O'Brien, Michael. 1988. *Rethinking the South: Essays in intellectual history.* Baltimore and London: Johns Hopkins University Press.

Penn, Donna. 1995. Queer: Theorizing politics and history. *Radical History Review* 62: 24–42.

Reed, John Shelton. 1993. *My tears spoiled my aim, and other reflections on Southern culture.* Columbia and London: University of Missouri Press.

Sandifer, Eddie. 1991. Interview by author. Jackson, MS: 30 March.

Scott, Joan. 1993. The evidence of experience. In *The lesbian and gay studies reader,* edited by Henry Abelove, Michèle Aina Barale, and David M. Halperin. New York and London: Routledge.

Sedgwick, Eve Kosofsky. 1990. *Epistemology of the closet.* Berkeley and Los Angeles: University of California Press.

Segrest, Mab. 1985. *My mama's dead squirrel: Lesbian essays on Southern culture.* Ithaca, NY: Firebrand Books.

Seidman, Steven. 1993. Identity and politics in a "postmodern" gay culture: Some historical and conceptual notes. In *Fear of a queer planet: Queer politics and social theory,* edited by Michael Warner. Minneapolis and London: University of Minnesota Press.

Smith, Stephen A. 1985. *Myth, media and the Southern mind.* Fayetteville: University of Arkansas Press.

Contributors

Daneel Buring teaches in the Department of History at Savannah State University in Savannah, Georgia. She has published "Gay Activism behind the Magnolia Curtain: The Memphis Gay Coalition, 1979–1991" in the *Journal of Homosexuality, 32,* 1 (1996). Her dissertation, "Building Gay Community behind the Magnolia Curtain: Memphis from the 1940s through the 1980s," analyzes the history of Memphis's gay and lesbian communities and focuses on the members, their institutions, their activities, and their values, as well as the forces that have shaped each of them.

Saralyn Chesnut, a Georgia native, directs the Office of Lesbian/Gay/Bisexual Life and teaches women's studies and interdisciplinary studies at Emory University, where she received her Ph.D. in liberal arts. She taught the first course in lesbian history offered at Emory and recently co-taught the school's first Introduction to Lesbian and Gay Studies course. An activist and an academic, she has been active in the women's movement and the movement for lesbian, gay, bisexual, and transgender rights for more than twenty years. Her academic interests center on the relationship between cultural production and social change movements and between scholarship and activism; she has an essay forthcoming on the relationship between lesbian and gay studies programs and co-curricular programs (like the one she directs) that are intended to improve campus climates for lesbian/gay/bisexual/transgender students and employees.

Katy Coyle is a doctoral candidate in U.S. women's history at Tulane University in New Orleans, Louisiana. Her dissertation focuses on Storyville prostitutes, lesbianism, and the sexual landscape of New Orleans at the turn of the century. She currently lives in Philadelphia with her partner, Shannon McGuire.

'Becca Cragin is a graduate student in the Institute for Women's Studies at Emory University. She is currently writing a dissertation on gay, lesbian, and bisexual viewers of daytime talk shows.

Martin Duberman, Distinguished Professor of History at Lehman College and the Graduate School of the City University of New York, is the founding director of the Center for Lesbian and Gay Studies. He is the author of seventeen books, including *Black Mountain, Paul Robeson, In White America, Cures, Stonewall,* and, most recently, *Midlife Queer.* He is also the editor of *A Queer World: The Center for Lesbian and Gay Studies Reader* and of *Queer Representations: Reading Lives, Reading Cultures* (also available from New York University Press). As both historian and playwright he has received numerous awards, including the Bancroft Prize, two Lambda Literary Awards, the George Freedly Memorial Award, and a Special Citation from the National Academy of Arts and Letters for his "contributions to literature."

Amanda C. Gable, after receiving her Ph.D. from Emory University, taught literature and creative writing at Denison University. Her short stories have been published in *Sinister Wisdom, Quarry West, Other Voices, Crescent Review, North American Review,* and elsewhere. Her scholarly interests include the politics of the production and distribution of printed texts, particularly the interconnected history of feminist publishing and feminist bookstores. She is currently working on a book about contemporary Southern lesbian fiction, of which an excerpt, "Bertha Harris's *Lover:* Lesbian *and* Postmodern," is forthcoming in a special issue of the *Journal of Homosexuality.* A native of Georgia, she coordinates a graduate writing program for the Georgia Institute of Technology.

Margaret Rose Gladney, native of Homer, Louisiana, is an associate professor of American studies at the University of Alabama in Tuscaloosa, where she teaches courses on women in the South, the civil rights movement, and lesbian and gay cultures.

John Howard, a native of Brandon, Mississippi, holds degrees from the Universities of Alabama, Mississippi, and Virginia. He is a doctoral candidate in American studies from Emory University. Currently, he is adjunct instructor of history and director of the Center for Lesbian, Gay & Bisexual Life at Duke University in Durham, North Carolina. His publications include the introduction to the reprint edition of the

Thomas Hal Phillips novel *The Bitterweed Path,* originally published by Rinehart in 1950 and now available from the University of North Carolina Press.

Elizabeth W. Knowlton was born in Richmond, Virginia, in 1944 and reared in Plainfield, New Jersey. Educated in English literature in New York and North Carolina, she was a part of the 1960s Women's Liberation Movement in Chapel Hill, North Carolina; came out in 1971; and moved to Atlanta, Georgia, in 1974 to join the Atlanta Lesbian Feminist Alliance (1972–1994). She has been an archivist for the state of Georgia for eighteen years. Her interests continue to be feminism, gardening and ecology, family history and records, and contra dancing, all of which inform her writing.

William Armstrong Percy III was born in Memphis, Tennessee, and educated at Middlesex School and Princeton University. He has taught at the University of New Orleans and Louisiana State University. He is currently professor of history at the University of Massachusetts, Boston. His publications include *The Age of Recovery: Europe during the Fifteenth Century* (with Jerah Johnson); *Outing: Shattering the Conspiracy of Silence* (with Warren Johansson); and *Pederasty and Pedagogy in Archaic Greece.*

Meredith Raimondo is a doctoral candidate in Emory University's Institute of Liberal Arts. A transplant to Atlanta from suburban Southern California, she is working on a dissertation about the cultural politics of AIDS in the South.

A native of St. Petersburg, *James A. Schnur* earned master's degrees in history and library science from the University of South Florida (USF). He is an archivist at USF and an adjunct professor of history at Eckerd College in St. Petersburg. Schnur maintains an active membership in many historical organizations throughout the state of Florida. His chapter in this book originally appeared in his 1995 history master's thesis, "Cold Warriors in the Hot Sunshine."

James T. Sears is professor of curriculum and higher education at the University of South Carolina, focusing on sexuality education, curriculum theory, and sexual cultures. In addition to an undergraduate degree in history, he earned a master's degree in political science and a doctorate in education and sociology. Sears was a 1995 Fulbright Southeast Asian Senior Scholar and a 1993 Senior Scholar in Residence at the University of Southern California's Center for Feminist Research. He serves on a variety of boards of editors, including those of the *Journal of Homosexuality* and the *Journal of Sexual Identities*. Teaching courses in research, curriculum, and sexuality, he has written or edited eight books, including *Growing up Gay in the South, Overcoming Heterosexism and Homophobia* (coedited with Walter Williams), and *Generations: An Oral History of Lesbian and Gay Southern Life*.

Donna Jo Smith was born and raised in Pawnee, Alabama. After studying music at Loyola and literature/history at the University of California, Berkeley, she came to the Institute of Liberal Arts at Emory University. Her studies focus on queer history and theory and constructions of southern identities. Her other interests include political activism and playing pool.

Nadiene Van Dyke, a Ph.D. candidate in U.S. women's history at Tulane University, is currently working on her dissertation on the state's role in forming feminine and masculine identities through the use of Cold War era educational films and on the relationship between gender/sexual ideologies and the political culture.

Kathie D. Williams is a native of Louisville, Kentucky. She earned her master's degree at the University of Louisville and is currently a doctoral student in history at the University of Kentucky. Her research focuses on issues of sexuality and the development of women's working-class communities in the 1920s and 1930s.

Index

Abernathy, Ralph, 187
Abraham, Julie, 126 n. 6
ACT UP, 2, 292
Adam, 119, 123
AID Atlanta, 331, 346, 349, 350, 351, 353
AIDS, 9, 319, 331–59; activism, 302, 331, 355; definition of, 360 n. 8; diagnosis of, 335; and employment discrimination, 236; GRID, 340, 362 n. 34; historicizing, 334–37; language of, 360 n. 8; media representations of, 341–54; and racial difference, 353–54; and regionality, 333–34, 339–59, 360 n. 9; theorized origins of, 338–41, 347, 360 n. 9, 361 n. 25; and women, 353
Alabama, 2, 98, 110, 370; Birmingham, 2; Montgomery, 16; Pawnee, 372; Tuscaloosa, 101
Alcoff, Linda, 325 n. 9
Alexander, Jeb, 2–3
Alger, Horatio, 373
Alice, 206, 209, 212, 215
Allen, Frederick, 357
Allen, John S., 142, 144, 145, 148
Alligator, The, 135, 136
All Together Now, 235
Alta, 249
American Family Association, 157
Anderson, Tom, 58
Anne, 254, 261
Ansa, Tina McElroy, 277 n. 32
Ansley Mall Book Store, 263
Anzaldúa, Gloria, 249
Arkansas, 300; West Memphis, 210
Arlington, Josie, 58
Arnold, June, 249, 250, 257
Ashkinaze, Carol, 258
Askew, Reubin, 156

Atkins, Ford, 81, 85, 89
Atlanta, 2, 290; and AIDS, 9, 331–59; Charis Books and More in, 241–72; during the fifties, 7; in nineteenth-century Georgia, 34–35, 43; SNCC conference in, 94
Atlanta Association of Baptist Churches, 115, 116, 117
Atlanta Feminist Women's Chorus, 322
Atlanta Journal and Constitution (AJC), 109, 111, 113, 115, 116, 117, 258, 334, 342, 344–59, 363 n. 55, 364 n. 69, 364 n. 73
Atlanta Lesbian Feminist Alliance (ALFA), 8, 254–72, 287, 289–90, 298, 300–302, 305, 316, 320–22, 324 n. 4, 325 n. 8. *See also* Little Five Points
Atlanta Methodist Ministerial Association, 117
Atlanta Public Library Perversion Case, 8, 109–14, 119
Atlanta Women's Liberation, 253–54
Atthis, 256
Automobile: as site of heteroerotic relations, 114, 117, 121–22

Bailey, Beth, 121
Bailey, Thomas D., 143, 147, 155
Baker, Lewis, 83, 85
Bakerman, Roger, 354
Baldy, Alice, 34–50
Baldy, Eddie, 40–44, 47
Baldy, Marianna Josephine, 42–44
Baldy, Mary Jane, 39–41, 43
Baldy, William H., 38
Barden, Charles, 349
Barker, James D., 141, 154
Barker, Jeff, 2
Barloga, Richia Atkinson, 188